Sustainable Waste Management and Recycling: Used/ Post-Consumer Tyres

Proceedings of the International Conference organised by the
Concrete and Masonry Research Group and held at
Kingston University - London on 14-15 September 2004.

Edited by

Mukesh C. Limbachiya
Reader, School of Engineering
Kingston University

John J. Roberts
Dean, Faculty of Technology
Director, Sustainable Technology Research Centre
Kingston University

 ThomasTelford

Published by Thomas Telford Publishing, Thomas Telford Ltd, 1 Heron Quay, London E14 4JD.
www.thomastelford.com

Distributors for Thomas Telford books are
USA: ASCE Press, 1801 Alexander Bell Drive, Reston, VA 20191-4400, USA
Japan: Maruzen Co. Ltd, Book Department, 3–10 Nihonbashi 2-chome, Chuo-ku, Tokyo 103
Australia: DA Books and Journals, 648 Whitehorse Road, Mitcham 3132, Victoria

First published 2004

The full list of titles from the 2004 International Conference 'Sustainable Waste Management and Recycling' and available from Thomas Telford is as follows

- Glass waste. ISBN: 0 7277 3284 6
- Construction demolition waste. ISBN: 0 7277 3285 4
- Used/post-consumer tyres. ISBN: 0 7277 3286 2

A catalogue record for this book is available from the British Library

ISBN: 0 7277 3286 2.

Printed and bound in Great Britain by MPG Books, Bodmin, Cornwall

PREFACE

With the introduction of waste legislation, in the form of regulations and directives, in many parts of the world a significant move towards sustainable waste management is becoming a legal requirement. Emphasis is now being placed on increasing recycling and promoting more sustainable waste management practices, and greater co-ordination between the public, private and independent sectors, and all concerned with the management of waste and reusable materials.

However, sustainable waste management entails complex technological, environmental, social, culture and economic issues. This together with technological advances in recycling, the waste sector is facing enormous challenges in developing suitable waste management and recycling strategies. It is therefore necessary to share/ explore existing expertise and review, and discuss the challenges and identify opportunities for improving waste management and recycling as widely as possible. Thus promote sustainable resource use.

The Concrete and Masonry Research Group (CMRG) within the School of Engineering at Kingston University organised this International Conference to explore waste minimisation practices and review latest developments in waste management and recycling. It considered regulatory and other pressures which may affect industry's approach, provided a platform to meet and discuss with the leading experts on how the industry can address challenges of sustainable waste management and recycling, and review existing opportunities. This Conference dealt with key waste materials under concurrently proceeded three themes, namely *(i) Construction Demolition Waste, (ii) Used/ Post-Consumer Tyres, and (iii) Glass Waste.* Over 130 papers were presented by authors from 33 countries during this Conference and these are compiled into three theme specific proceedings.

The Opening Addresses were given by Professor Peter Scott- Vice-Chancellor of Kingston University, Professor John Roberts- Dean of Faculty of Technology at Kingston University and Mr Hugh Carr-Harris- Chief Executive of London Remade. All the papers presented under *Used/ Post Consumer Tyres Theme* and two Conference Closing Keynote papers are assembled in this volume. Dr Charles Pierce, University of South Carolina, USA, Mr Paul Roach, Credential Environmental Ltd., UK, and Professor Christian Roy, Université Laval-Québec, Canada, gave Opening Keynote papers. The Conference was closed by Keynote papers from Dr Lindon Sear, United Kingdom Quality Ash Association and Mr John Harrison, TecEco Pty Lt. Australia.

The event was organised with support from four sponsoring organisations: Credential Environmental Ltd., ReMade Kent and Medway, London ReMade and WRAP. All sponsors are gratefully acknowledged for their invaluable support. The work of Conference was an immense undertaking and help from all those involved are gratefully acknowledged, in particular, members of the Organising Committee for managing the event from start to finish; the Authors and the Chair of Technical Sessions for their invaluable contribution. Special thanks to Day Group Ltd., and Used Tyre Working Group- UK for their support.

The Proceedings have been prepared directly from the camera-ready manuscript submitted by the authors and editing has been restricted to minor changes where it was considered absolutely necessary.

Kingston upon Thames
September 2004

Mukesh C Limbachiya
John J Roberts

iii

SPONSORING ORGANISATIONS

Credential Environmental Ltd.

ReMade Kent and Medway

London Remade

WRAP- Waste & Resources Action Programme

ORGANISING COMMITTEE

Concrete and Masonry Research Group-
Kingston University

Dr M C Limbachiya *(Chairman)*

Professor J J Roberts

Professor G Sommerville OBE

Professor N J Bright MBE

Dr A N Fried

Dr K Etebar

Mr A Koulouris

Mr Y Ouchagour

Miss S Fotiadou

Dr A Ahmed

Mr O Reutter

Mr O Kanyeto

Faculty of Technology Research Office

NATIONAL ADVISORY COMMITTEE

Mr John Barritt
Aggregates Technical Advisor, WRAP

Mr Jeff Cooper
Producer Responsibility Policy Manager, Environment Agency

Professor Satish Desai OBE
Visiting Professor- University of Surrey
Chartered Structural Engineer, Butler & Young Ltd.

Mr Hugh Carr- Harris
Chief Executive, London Remade

Mr Paul Hallett
Sustainable Directorate, Department of Trade and Industry

Dr Mukesh Limbachiya (Chairman)
Reader, School of Engineering, Kingston University

Mrs Diana Lock
Programme Manager, Remade Kent and Medway

Professor John Roberts
Dean- Faculty of Technology
Director- Sustainable Technology Research Centre, Kingston University

Professor G Somerville OBE
Independent Consultant
Visiting Professor- Kingston University

CONTENTS

SESSION 4- WAY FORWARD AND DEVELOPING SUSTAINABLE MARKET

KEYNOTE
PAPERS

SCRAP TIRE RUBBER MODIFIED CONCRETE: PAST, PRESENT, AND FUTURE

C E Pierce

R J Williams

University of South Carolina

USA

ABSTRACT. This paper presents recent developments in scrap tire markets in the United States and provides details of specific programs in the state of South Carolina. As of 2001, two of the major markets for scrap tires are tire-derived fuel and civil engineering applications. In many states, legislation is in place to support more civil engineering applications, but the financial incentives are not sufficient. One of the civil engineering markets with potential for growth is scrap tire rubber modified concrete. A synthesis of research on rubber modified concrete is presented. It is shown that concrete workability, mass density, compressive and tensile strength, and modulus of elasticity decrease as rubber content increases. Mass density was found to decrease linearly with rubber content, whereas compressive strength and modulus of elasticity were found to reduce exponentially.

Keywords: Scrap tire, Rubber, Concrete, Workability, Mass density, Compressive strength, Tensile strength, Modulus of elasticity

Dr C E Pierce is an Associate Professor in the Department of Civil and Environmental Engineering at the University of South Carolina in Columbia. His research interests include the recycling and reuse of waste materials in construction, controlled low-strength material properties and applications, and geotechnical instrumentation.

Mr R J Williams is a Graduate Research Assistant in the Department of Civil and Environmental Engineering at the University of South Carolina in Columbia. He is pursuing a MS with a research emphasis on the properties of cement-based materials modified with scrap tire rubber.

INTRODUCTION

Tire disposal remains a problematic issue in industrialized nations around the world. According to the United States Environmental Protection Agency [1], the U.S. generated approximately 281 million scrap tires during 2001.   That output is in addition to the approximately 300 million scrap tires that are already stockpiled. Fortunately, markets for scrap tires consumed 218 million, or 77.6%, of the annual scrap tire output in 2001 [1]. That represents a significant increase from the 17% of scrap tires being recycled or beneficially used in 1990. However, the remaining scrap tires are still being stockpiled or landfilled.

This paper presents statistics on scrap tire market development in the U.S. Details of specific programs in the state of South Carolina are summarized, with an emphasis on the civil engineering applications market for scrap tires.   Finally, a synthesis of scrap tire rubber modified concrete is provided as one example of the civil engineering applications market.

BACKGROUND

Scrap Tire Rubber

According to the Rubber Manufacturers Association [2], scrap tires are generated primarily from passenger vehicles (84%). The remaining scrap tires come from light and heavy trucks (15%) or from aircraft, heavy equipment, and off-road vehicles (1%). Table 1 provides the material composition of scrap tires as a percentage of total weight [2]. The sole difference in composition between passenger tires and heavy truck tires is the ratio of natural rubber to synthetic rubber (1:2 or 2:1, respectively).

Table 1. Typical Composition of Passenger and Truck Tires [2]

MATERIAL CLASSES	COMPOSITION, by Weight (%)	
	Passenger or Light Truck Tire	Heavy Truck Tire
Natural rubber	14	27
Synthetic rubber	27	14
Carbon black	28	28
Steel	14-15	14-15
Other (fabric, filler, accelerators, antiozonants)	16-17	16-17
Average Scrap Tire Weight (lbs)	20-30	100

In a new radial passenger tire, more than 50% of the rubber is used to construct the tread and the sidewall. When scrap tires are processed, the tread and sidewall components are shredded to produce single pass shreds, 2 in. (50 mm) shreds, or 1.5 in. (38 mm) shreds. Steel belts, bead wire and fabric insulation can all be removed to produce useable tire chips. Tire chips can be further processed to finer particle sizes, called crumb rubber, with common gradations of 10, 20, 30, 40 and 80 mesh. Since the specific gravity of tire rubber is 1.15, the bulk mass density of tire chips is relatively low and ranges from 20 pcf (0.32 g/cm^3) when loosely packed to 59 pcf (0.95 g/cm^3) when densely packed [2]. Crumb rubber has a consistent bulk mass density between 25 and 29 pcf (0.40 to 0.46 g/cm^3) [2]. Processed tire rubber is often stored and sold in 1-ton (910 kg) bags.

Scrap Tire Markets

In 2001, scrap tires in the U.S. were consumed by six markets as shown in Figure 1 [1,2]. This figure shows the market distribution for non-landfilled scrap tires. The largest market in 2001 was for tire-derived fuel (TDF), which consumed 115 million scrap tires. The major facilities that use TDF are cement kilns, pulp and paper mills, industrial boilers and utility boilers. This practice is part of a national trend toward greater usage of TDF to reduce fuel costs. Since TDF commands a higher price (US$30/ton in South Carolina) than scrap tire shreds (US$17/ton in South Carolina), this trend is beneficial to scrap tire processors [3].

The second largest market was for civil engineering applications, which consumed 40 million scrap tires. Examples of civil engineering applications include scrap tire chips and/or crumb rubber as sources for natural aggregate replacement in geotechnical fills, concrete, and asphalt pavements. Properties of scrap tire rubber modified concrete will be presented in a subsequent section of this paper.

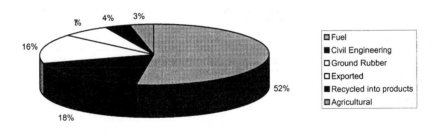

Figure 1: Distribution of Non-Landfilled Scrap Tire Applications in the U.S. in 2001 [1,2]

The national trends are also reflected by scrap tire markets in the state of South Carolina. In 1998, the largest market for scrap tires was the use of tire shreds as drain fields for septic tank systems, as shown in Table 2. During the past five years, however, a dramatic shift in market distribution has TDF as the largest market in South Carolina. The analysis in Table 2 also shows that civil engineering applications for scrap tires have recently developed within the state, starting in 2000-2001. This development coincides with the establishment of Asphalt Rubber Technology Service (ARTS) at Clemson University, which will be discussed further in the next section. Although the civil engineering market share in South Carolina is smaller than the national average, it should be noted that the use of tire shreds in septic drain fields can also be considered as a civil engineering application. The two markets combined exceed the national average for civil engineering applications.

Table 2. Scrap Tire Market Analysis in South Carolina from 1998-2003 [3]

MARKET	MARKET DISTRIBUTION (% of Processed Scrap Tires)				
	1998	1999	2000-2001	2002	2003
Septic drain fields	80	88	52	42	26
Tire-derived fuel (TDF)	13	10	34	35	58
Crumb rubber	1	2	4	14	7
Civil engineering applications	0	0	9	1	5
Landfills	6	0	0	8	4
Tires processed (millions)	3.3	4.0	8.0	6.9	6.5

State Legislation to Manage Scrap Tires

As of 2001, 37 of the 50 states in the U.S. have active bans on the disposal of whole tires in landfills [4]. However, only nine states ban cut or shredded tires from landfill disposal. To better manage scrap tire disposal, 34 states have implemented fees based on tire purchases, vehicle titles, or vehicle registration. The most common fee structure is based on tire purchases, with fees ranging from US$0.25 to US$2.00 per passenger tire. With the collection of fees, 23 of the 34 states have established dedicated scrap tire funds. Such funds are primarily disbursed for two purposes: 1) to provide grants and/or low interest loans to scrap tire processors and recyclers and 2) to subsidize demonstration and development projects and/or innovative technologies that beneficially utilize scrap tires. In several states, funds are still used to support the clean-up of scrap tire stockpiles.

Legislative support for civil engineering applications of scrap tires is fairly high. As of 2001, 39 states approve the use of tire shreds for civil engineering applications [4]. Unfortunately, only 17 of those states encourage the use of tire shreds for civil engineering applications. Such encouragement comes primarily in the form of financial incentives. Not surprisingly, 10 of the 17 states have dedicated scrap tire funds, and four of the seven states that do not have dedicated funds still provide grants or loans for civil engineering projects.

South Carolina manages one of the more successful state programs for scrap tires. The South Carolina Department of Health and Environmental Control (SCDHEC) oversees the Waste Tire Fund that was established in 1991. Monies in this fund accrue by the collection of US$2.00 per passenger tire. Tire dealers collect the fee and are allowed to keep 3% of it for administration costs. As an additional incentive, dealers keep US$1.00 for each scrap tire sent directly to a permitted scrap tire recycling facility. In the early 1990s, the bulk of the funds were consumed to locate and clean up scrap tire stockpiles. As a result, South Carolina has effectively eliminated scrap tire stockpiles in the state. In the mid to late 1990s, the fund redirected its emphasis to support civil engineering projects proposed by city and county governments. In 2000, the Waste Tire Fund awarded US$6M to Clemson University and the City of Clemson to develop and promote rubberized asphalt and other civil engineering applications for scrap tires.

Although other state scrap tire funds support rubberized asphalt, the Asphalt Rubber Technology Service (ARTS) at Clemson University is the only university-based center developed with such state funds. Established in 2000, the ARTS was created with a five-year mission to familiarize paving contractors with rubberized asphalt and to demonstrate its application in parking lots, secondary roads, and ultimately, primary highways. ARTS awards grants to local counties, cities, municipalities and South Carolina Department of Transportation offices interested in using rubberized asphalt in road paving or resurfacing projects. Future directives of the center are expected to emphasize other civil engineering applications, including scrap tire rubber modified concrete.

SCRAP TIRE RUBBER MODIFIED CONCRETE

Published research on scrap tire rubber modified concrete began in the early 1990s. Eldin and Senouci [5] issued one of the first publications that investigated the influence of scrap tire rubber content on mechanical properties of concrete. Subsequent publications [6,7,9-15] provided more data on properties such as concrete workability, mass density, compressive strength, tensile strength, and modulus of elasticity. The following sections synthesize the properties of rubber modified concrete from some published literature. In the following figures, the percent rubber is the percent of either the fine or the coarse aggregate replaced by volume, unless otherwise indicated.

Workability

Workability decreases as the percentage of rubber increases due to the increasing viscosity of the mixture, as illustrated in Figure 2. Six sets of data were used to develop this figure: three sets for coarse aggregate replacement only, two sets for fine aggregate replacement only, and one set for coarse and fine aggregate replacement. Coarse aggregate denoted as Coarse A and Coarse B are referred to as Edgar tire chips and Preston rubber, respectively [5,6]. Edgar tire chips are large angular chips obtained from the mechanical grinding of scrap tires. Preston rubber is a smaller gradation of rounded rubber obtained by cryogenic grinding. Edgar tire chips had a maximum size of 38 mm while Preston rubber had a maximum size of 6 mm [5]. Figure 2 shows that the coarser gradation (Coarse A) reduced slump more dramatically than the finer gradation (Coarse B), especially at lower rubber contents. In all cases, slump is reduced to less than 10 mm when the rubber content reaches 100% replacement.

Slump of rubber modified concrete can be maintained by adjusting the water content and by properly dosing it with admixtures. In experiments reported by Savas, Ahmad and Fedroff [8], slump varied from 25 to 125 mm depending on the amount of air entraining agent and high range water reducer used. Because the mixture proportions were not constant in their investigation, there is no direct correlation between rubber content and slump. Thus the data is not included in Figure 2.

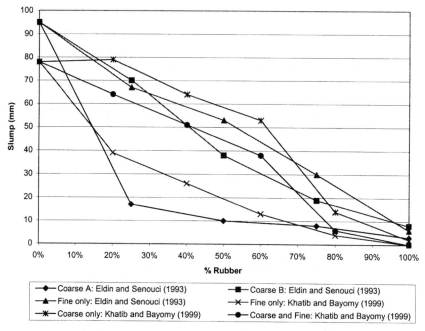

Figure 2: Workability of Fresh, Rubber Modified Concrete

Mass Density

One of the most significant benefits of scrap tire rubber modified concrete is the reduction in mass density. Figure 3 illustrates the linear decrease in concrete mass density as the percent rubber increases. Mass density can be reduced to as low as 1750 kg/m^3 [6,7,9-11]. Figures 4 and 5 show the changes in mass density of rubber modified concrete normalized by the control (0% rubber) concrete mass density. Figure 4 shows a decrease in mass density of up to 20% can be expected when replacing fine aggregate with crumb rubber. Figure 5 shows a decrease of up to 28% can be expected when replacing coarse aggregate with tire chips. Normalized mass density can be estimated by the following linear equations:

$$\frac{\rho_{rc}}{\rho_c} = -X * R_{fa} + 100 \qquad \text{(Eq. 1)}$$

$$\frac{\rho_{rc}}{\rho_c} = -X * R_{ca} + 100 \qquad \text{(Eq. 2)}$$

$$\frac{\rho_{rc}}{\rho_c} = -X * R_a + 100 \qquad \text{(Eq. 3)}$$

where

ρ_{rc} = mass density of rubber modified concrete;

ρ_c = mass density of control concrete;

R_{fa} = percent of fine aggregate replaced by rubber;

R_{ca} = percent of coarse aggregate replaced by rubber;

R_a = percent of aggregate replaced by rubber; and

X = coefficient for fine aggregate (0.15-0.23) in Eq. 1, coefficient for coarse aggregate (0.23-0.28) in Eq. 2, or coefficient for coarse and fine aggregate (0.23) in Eq. 3.

Data from Fedroff, Ahmad and Savas [9] was excluded in determining Eq. 1. Data for coarse and fine aggregate replacement from Khatib and Bayomy [7] was the only set used to determine Eq. 3.

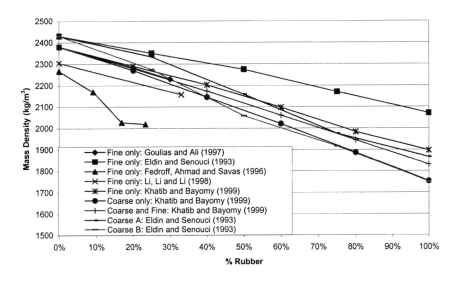

Figure 3: Mass Density of Rubber Modified Concrete

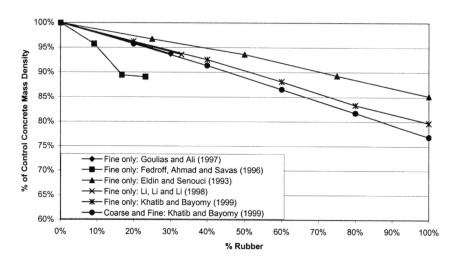

Figure 4: Percentage of Control Concrete's Mass Density with Fine Aggregate Replacement

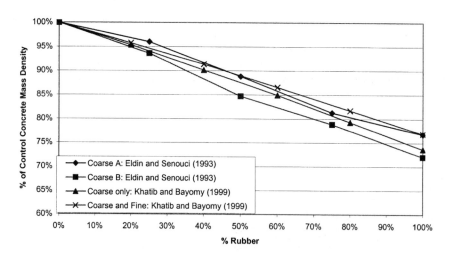

Figure 5: Percentage of Control Concrete's Mass Density with Coarse Aggregate Replacement

Compressive Strength

Figure 6 shows the non-linear decrease in 28-day unconfined compressive strength with increasing rubber content. Figures 7 and 8 separate out the effects of fine and coarse aggregate replacement, respectively. Based on a visual inspection of these figures, coarse aggregate replacement results in less variation of compressive strength than fine aggregate replacement. Compressive strength can be estimated by the following exponential equations:

$$\frac{f_{c\ rc}'}{f_c'} = e^{-X*R_{fa}} \qquad\qquad \text{(Eq. 4)}$$

$$\frac{f_{c\ rc}'}{f_c'} = e^{-X*R_{ca}} \qquad\qquad \text{(Eq. 5)}$$

$$\frac{f_{c\ rc}'}{f_c'} = e^{-X*R_a} \qquad\qquad \text{(Eq. 6)}$$

where
$f_{c\ rc}'$ = unconfined compressive strength of rubber modified concrete at 28 days;
f_c' = unconfined compressive strength of control concrete at 28 days;
R_{fa} = percent of fine aggregate replaced by rubber (decimal form);
R_{ca} = percent of coarse aggregate replaced by rubber (decimal form);
R_a = percent of aggregate replaced by rubber (decimal form); and
X = coefficient for fine aggregate (1.15-2.65) in Eq. 4, coefficient for coarse aggregate (1.50-2.70) in Eq. 5, or coefficient for coarse and fine aggregate (2.65) in Eq. 6.

The range of coefficients in Eq. 5 is smaller than the range in Eq. 4, further suggesting that there is less variation in strength when replacing coarse aggregate with tire chips. Data from Topcu [12] was excluded when determining Eq. 4. The range of coefficients in Eq. 4 would be larger if data from Topcu [12] had been included. Data for coarse and fine aggregate replacement from Khatib and Bayomy [7] was the only set used to determine Eq. 6.

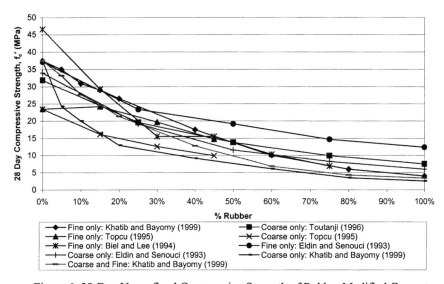

Figure 6: 28-Day Unconfined Compressive Strength of Rubber Modified Concrete

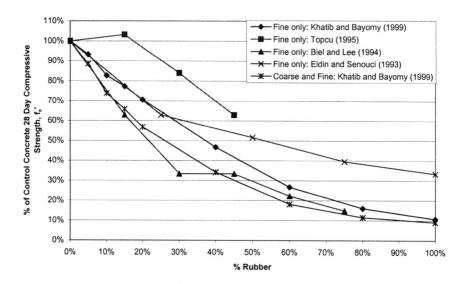

Figure 7: Percentage of Control Concrete's 28-Day Unconfined Compressive Strength with Fine Aggregate Replacement

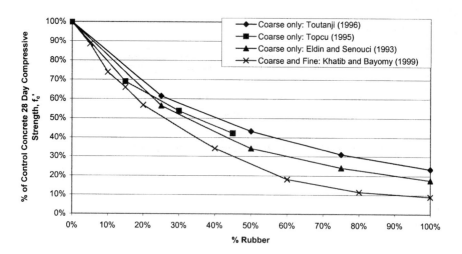

Figure 8: Percentage of Control Concrete's 28-Day Unconfined Compressive Strength with Coarse Aggregate Replacement

Tensile Strength

Most of the published literature on tensile strength has been based on splitting tension of concrete cylinders. Figure 9 shows the effects of rubber content on 28-day split tensile strength of scrap tire rubber modified concrete. Tensile strength clearly decreases as rubber content increases. By normalizing the data in Figure 10, it is shown that decreases of up to 93% can be expected with the replacement of both fine and coarse aggregate. However the tensile strength reduction varies significantly among the published research and thus no correlations were developed to predict split tensile strength.

Flexural strength of scrap tire rubber modified concrete has also been reported. Experiments by Fedroff, Ahmad and Savas [9] showed up to a 42% decrease in the modulus of rupture measured at 100% fine aggregate replacement. Experiments by Toutanji [13] showed up to a 37% decrease in flexural strength in four point bending with 100% coarse aggregate replacement. It should be noted that the strength reductions measured in flexure are less than the strength reductions measured in splitting tension (see Figure 10).

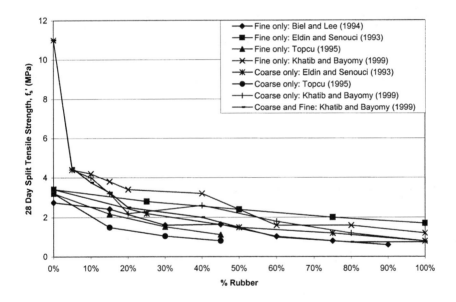

Figure 9: 28-Day Split Tensile Strength of Rubber Modified Concrete

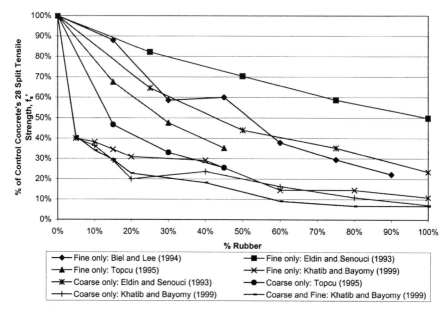

Figure 10: Percentage of Control Concrete's 28-Day Split Tensile Strength

Modulus of Elasticity

Figure 11 shows the change in Young's modulus measured in unconfined compression at 28 days. The addition of scrap tire rubber softens the elastic stress-strain response, yielding Young's moduli as low as 10,000 MPa. Figure 12 shows that decreases of up to 50% can be expected with approximately 50% replacement of coarse or fine aggregate. Based on the data in this figure, Young's modulus can be estimated by the following exponential equation:

$$\frac{E_{rc}}{E_c} = e^{-X * R_a}$$ (Eq. 7)

where

E_{rc} = Young's modulus of rubber modified concrete;

E_c = Young's modulus of control concrete;

R_a = percent of aggregate replaced by rubber (decimal form); and

X = coefficient for either aggregate (coarse or fine) replacement (1.5-3.2).

It should be noted that Eq. 7 was developed with rubber contents limited to 45% ($R_a \leq 0.45$). However Figure 12 suggests that rubber contents greater than 45% will not significantly reduce Young's modulus further.

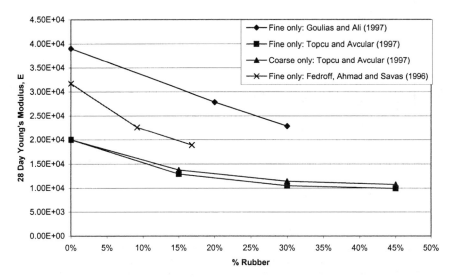

Figure 11: 28-Day Young's Modulus of Rubber Modified Concrete in Unconfined Compression

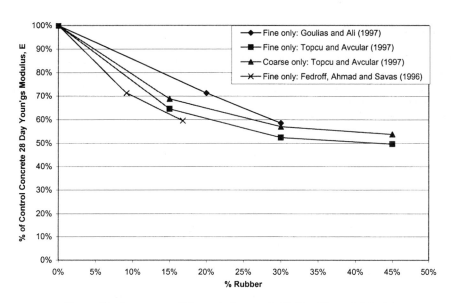

Figure 12: Percentage of Control Concrete's 28-Day Young's Modulus

Current and Future Research

More recent research has concentrated on other physical and mechanical properties of scrap tire rubber modified concrete, such as freeze-thaw resistance [16,17], impact resistance [15,17,18], and thermal insulation [17]. These properties need to be investigated further in the context of potential applications, and trial field applications need to be initiated and monitored for performance. There are promising applications for rubber modified concrete, including its use in barrier walls [19] and culverts [20]. However, one of the concerns that needs to be addressed is durability [21], which can be accomplished through appropriate lab and field-scale research.

SUMMARY AND CONCLUSIONS

In the United States, market demand for scrap tires is on the rise. The two major markets for scrap tires are tire-derived fuel and civil engineering applications. In many states, legislation is in place to support more civil engineering applications, but the financial incentives are not sufficient. The state of South Carolina is one of the more successful states with its scrap tire management program, and its establishment of the university-based Asphalt Rubber Technology Service (ARTS) can serve as a model for other states.

Scrap tire rubber modified concrete is one example of a civil engineering application that has vast potential. This paper synthesized published research data on basic properties of rubber modified concrete. Concrete workability, mass density, compressive and tensile strength, and modulus of elasticity decrease as rubber content increases. Full replacement of either coarse or fine aggregate with rubber can reduce the consistency of fresh concrete to little or no slump. The reduction in mass density with increasing rubber content is linear, and predictive equations (Eqs. 1-3) were developed to estimate the density of a rubber modified concrete. On the other hand, the reduction in compressive strength is non-linear and can be expressed by a series of exponential equations (Eqs. 4-6). The reduction in tensile strength varies much more than compressive strength and thus no equations were developed. Modulus of elasticity also decreases non-linearly with increasing rubber content, and its relationship can be described by an exponential equation (Eq. 7).

ACKNOWLEDGEMENTS

The authors would like to thank the following individuals for their assistance in the preparation of this document: Dr. Dana Humphrey, Professor at the University of Maine; Dr. Serji Amirkhanian and Ms. Mary Corley of the Asphalt Rubber Technology Service at Clemson University; and Ms. Jana White of the South Carolina Department of Health and Environmental Control. The authors would also like to recognize Mr. Ralph Hulseman of Michelin North America Inc. for his support of this research.

REFERENCES

1. United States Environmental Protection Agency. Management of Scrap Tires. http://www.epa.gov/epaoswer/non-hw/muncpl/tires. 2004.

2. Rubber Manufacturers Association. Scrap Tires. http://www.rma.org/scrap_tires. 2004.

3. South Carolina Department of Health and Environmental Control. Tires Market Report. 2004.

4. South Carolina Department of Health and Environmental Control. State Legislation – Scrap Tire Disposal. September 2001.

5. ELDIN NN, SENOUCI AB. Engineering properties of rubberized concrete. Canadian Journal of Civil Engineering 1992; 19(5): 912-923.

6. ELDIN NN, SENOUCI AB. Observations on rubberized concrete behavior. Cement, Concrete and Aggregates 1993; 15(1): 74-84.

7. KHATIB ZK, BAYOMY FM. Rubberized portland cement concrete. Journal of Materials in Civil Engineering 1999; 11(3): 206-213.

8. SAVAS BZ, AHMAD S, FEDROFF D. Freeze-thaw durability of concrete with ground waste tire rubber. Transportation Research Record No. 1574. November 1996. p 80-88.

9. FEDROFF D, AHMAD S, SAVAS BZ. Mechanical properties of concrete with ground waste tire rubber. Transportation Research Record No. 1532. September 1996. p 66-72.

10. GOULIAS DG, ALI AH. Non-destructive evaluation of rubber modified concrete. Proceedings of the Specialty Conference on Infrastructure Condition Assessment: Art Science, Practice 1997. p 111-120.

11. LI Z, LI F, LI JSL. Properties of concrete incorporating rubber tyre particles. Magazine of Concrete Research 1998; 50(4): 297-304.

12. TOPCU IB. Properties of rubberized concretes. Cement and Concrete Research 1995; 25(2): 304-310.

13. TOUTANJI HA. Use of rubber tire particles in concrete to replace mineral aggregates. Cement & Concrete Composites 1996; 18(2): 135-139.

14. BIEL TD, LEE H. Use of recycled tire rubbers in concrete. Proceedings of the Materials Engineering Conference No. 804. October 1994. p 351-358.

15. TOPCU IB, AVCULAR N. Collision behaviours of rubberized concrete. Cement and Concrete Research 1997; 27(12): 1893-1898.

16. PAINE KA, DHIR RK, MORONEY R, KOPASAKIS K. Use of crumb rubber to achieve freeze thaw resisting concrete. Proceedings of the International Conference on Concrete for Extreme Conditions 2002. p 486-498.

17. DHIR R, PAINE K, MORONEY R. Recycling of used tyres in concrete. Concrete (London) 2003; 37(9): 47-48.

18. LEE HS, LEE H, MOON JS, JUNG HW. Development of tire-added latex concrete. ACI Materials Journal 1998; 95(4): 356-364.

19. FORTNER B. Rubber concrete mixes tested for toughness. Civil Engineering (New York) 2003; 73(8): 32-33.

20. YANG SP, KJARTANSON BH, LOHNES RA. Structural performance of scrap tire culverts. Canadian Journal of Civil Engineering 2001; 28(2): 179-189.

21. BLUMENTHAL M. Personal communication. Rubber Manufacturers Association. June 21 2004.

OIL AND CARBON BLACK BY PYROLYSIS OF USED TIRES

C Roy

Université Laval- Québec

Pyrovac International

P Plante

B de Caumia

Université Laval- Québec

Canada

ABSTRACT. A common denominator of modern tire recycling methods is that they are generally subsidized by governments through tipping fees. The paradigm however is that the compounds composing a tire, *i.e.* carbon black, oil and steel, are pricy materials. A technology that could enable the recapture of the above valuable materials may ultimately sustain itself once a market is established for each of these categories of commodity products. This presentation covers R&D activities performed at the Université Laval and Pyrovac International over the last decade during the development of the vacuum pyrolysis process from the laboratory to the industrial scale. The paper focuses on the characterization of the pyrolysis products and various development options that have been investigated for their commercial applications. Process economics for a 36 000 t/y plant is also presented.

Keywords: Scrap Tires, Recycling, Vacuum Pyrolysis, Carbon Black, Oil, End-Uses, Economics

Dr C Roy is a Chartered Engineer and Professor of Chemical Engineer, Faculty of Sciences and Engineering of Université Laval. He is also the president of Pyrovac International. His research interests are in the development of a vacuum pyrolysis process for the recycling and reuse of waste materials such as scrap tires.

Mr P Plante, P. Eng., is a Research Assistant in the Pyrolysis Group, Chemical Engineering Department, Université Laval.

Mr B de Caumia, P. Eng., is a Research Assistant in the Pyrolysis Group, Chemical Engineering Department, Université Laval.

INTRODUCTION

Scrap vehicle tires make a significant contribution to the generation of solid wastes, the rate of scrap tire generation in industrialized countries being approximately one passenger car tire equivalent per capita per year [1]. Furthermore, estimates are that 3 billion tires are stockpiled in Europe, often illegally. In North America scrap tires accumulate as well in unregulated or abandoned sites also for a total of 3 billion tires [2].

Currently in the European Union (EU), as shown in Figure 1, approximately 35% of the scrap tires generated are landfilled, 23% go to energy recovery, 21% to recycling, 11% are retreaded while the remaining 10 % is exported or reused [3].

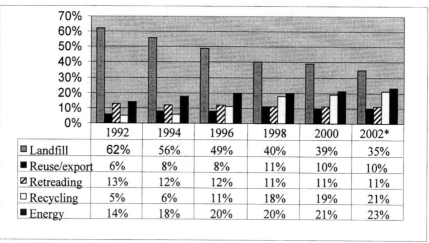

	1992	1994	1996	1998	2000	2002*
Landfill	62%	56%	49%	40%	39%	35%
Reuse/export	6%	8%	8%	11%	10%	10%
Retreading	13%	12%	12%	11%	11%	11%
Recycling	5%	6%	11%	18%	19%	21%
Energy	14%	18%	20%	20%	21%	23%

Reproduced from [3]; *Estimates

Figure 1. Disposal of Scrap Tires in the EU

In the United Stated (US), the market demand for scrap tires in 2001 corresponded to 78% of the annually generated quantities which amounted to 281 millions units [4]. The principal uses of scrap tires in US are in the energy sector (41%), as manufacturing products, mainly ground rubber (15%) and for civil engineering applications (14%). The export and miscellaneous/agriculture routes represent 7%. Landfill is the final destination of about 22 % of the used tires in the USA (Figure 2).

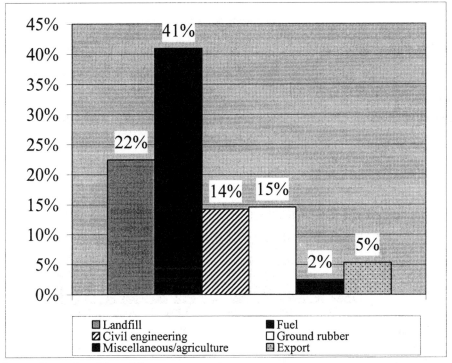

Source: Reproduced from [4]

Figure 2. US Scrap Tire Market

Tire piles can be the source of noxious emissions in the case of a fire and constitute a breeding ground for disease-carrying mosquitoes, such as encephalitis and dengue fever [5]. Throughout the world, from country to country, the efficient management of scrap vehicle tires actually represents a serious logistic, technical and environmental challenge.

Over the last decade, various technologies have been proposed for the management of scrap tires. The technology options pertain to two main process concepts, either the thermal conversion technologies, which mainly include incineration, pyrolysis, gasification and co-combustion, or the mechanical processes involving shredding (a reduction of whole tires to sizes ranging from about 300 mm down to about 25 mm) and granulation (a further reduction of shreds to crumb rubber with size below 10 mm). As well, several legislative measures have been put in place in many countries to address the growing concerns about this solid waste. For instance, the Landfill Directive of the European Union required its member states to stop the landfilling of whole tires by July 2003, while landfilling of crumb or shredded tires will be banned by 2006 [3].

A common denominator for the tire recycling methods is that they are generally subsidized by governments through tipping fees. The paradigm however is that the compounds composing a tire, *i.e.* carbon black, oil and steel, are pricy materials. A technology that could enable the recapture of the above valuable materials may ultimately sustain itself once a market is established for each of these categories of commodity products. Here, pyrolysis appears to be a promising technology to fulfill this goal. Over the last twenty years indeed, various pyrolysis processes have been developed at the pilot and the industrial scale levels [6-12].

This presentation covers R&D activities performed at the Université Laval and Pyrovac International over the last decade at developing the vacuum pyrolysis process from the laboratory to the industrial scale, and focuses on the characterization of the pyrolysis products and various development options that have been investigated for their commercial applications. Process economics for a 36 000 t/y plant is also presented.

SCRAP TIRE VACUUM PYROLYSIS PROCESS

Pyrolysis is a thermal decomposition of organic material in the absence of air. Typically, the process is performed in presence of a flow of inert gas or under vacuum. The main components of tires are elastomers, carbon black filler / reinforcement material and other products such as zinc oxide and steel. Upon heating, the rubber and other organic compounds decompose and are converted into oils and gas. The pyrolysis residue consists of the recovered carbon black filler, inorganic materials and varying proportions of carbonaceous materials formed from the rubber decomposition products. The industrial-scale demonstration vacuum pyrolysis process developed by Pyrovac International jointly with Université Laval is schematized in Figure 3. Photograph of the Pyrovac plant in Saguenay (Quebec, Canada) is shown at the end of the paper.

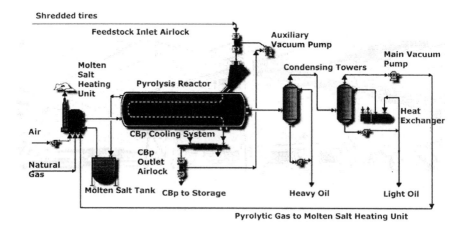

Figure 3. Pyrovac Vacuum Pyrolysis Process

The tire reduced to crumb size (0 – 7 mm) is fed into the pyrolyser by a combination of pneumatic and screw conveying-type devices. The pyrolyser is a 14.6 m-long/ 2.2 m-diameter reactor, in which the tire crumb is conveyed by a raking-mixing system circulating over two fixed heating plates, one on top of the other. Molten salts circulating inside tubes, which constitute the heating plates, serve as the heat carrier medium. Residence time of the pyrolysing tire particles inside the reactor is approximately 12 min. The temperature is maintained at 500°C and the pyrolysis total pressure is 15-20 kPa. The vacuum operation of the process is insured by dual rotary valves at the inlet and the outlet of the reactor, and two liquid-ring vacuum pumps. The main pump maintains the vacuum level set point inside the reactor while the secondary pump c ontrols the vacuum at the reactor inlet and outlet dual rotary valve system. The pyrolytic carbon black (CBp) is cooled down in extracting screw-conveyors prior to be bagged, while the pyrolytic vapours and gaseous products are entrained by the main vacuum pump through a 2-stage (packed tower) condensation system. The heavy oil is condensed in the 1st packed tower while the lighter oil is recovered at the bottom of the second packed tower. The non condensable gas obtained is further cooled past the pump and compressed to 170 kPa prior to be fired in the molten salt furnace. The excess pyrolytic gas is available to generate steam or can be burned in a gas turbine. The molten salt circulates in a closed-loop circuit from a 9 m³-tank, to the furnace, then towards the reactor and back into the tank. More details on the Pyrovac vacuum pyrolysis plant are available in the literature [9, 13]. Yields obtained in oil, CBp and gas at the laboratory, pilot and demonstration scale test runs have been summarized in Table 1.

Table 1. Used Tire Vacuum Pyrolysis Product Yields

	LABORATORY REACTOR	PILOT PLANT	DEMONSTRATION PLANT
Pyrolysis Conditions			
Temperature [°C]	500	450	530
Pressure [kPa]	0.4-0.8	20	15-20
Throughput [kg/h]	0.9	20	540
Pyrolysis Yields			
Pyrolytic oil	57	41.5	<50.7[a]
Pyrolytic carbon black	35.1	38.4	>30.0[b]
Gas	7.9	20.1	19.3
Total	100	100	100

[a] Batch experiment: the tire crumb was heated at a rate of 10°C to a final temperature of temperature of 500°C; the temperature was held constant for 3 hours.

[b] The mass balance closure was not satisfactory. The yield of CBp is probably higher than 30%. The oil yielded is probably overestimated.

PYROLYTIC CARBON BLACK (CBp)

Specific Surface Area and Structure

Many different carbon black grades compose a rubber tire [13, 14]. The surface area and structure of these blacks, the two most important carbon black properties, are in the range of 35-50 m²/g a nd 6 5-125 cm³/100 g, r espectively. T he s tructure o r d egree o f a ggregation i s measured by absorption of di-butyl phthalate (DBP) in the voids in-between the primary particles of the same aggregate. The recovered CBp contains a mixture of all these grades.

One might expect for the CBp surface area and structure values close to that of a mixture of the different grades used in tires. However, during service in the tire and pyrolysis, carbon black aggregates break down, lowering the structure. Ash components and carbonaceous deposits "dilute" as well the recovered carbon black filler in the CBp, leading to lower structure and surface area. Furthermore, carbonaceous deposits fill the voids in-between the primary particles, further reducing the surface area. The surface area and structure of the vacuum CBp from the demonstration plant were indeed close, with respect to its surface area and structure, to the average values of the commercial carbon black (CBc) grades used in tires (Table 2).

Table 2. Surface Area and Structure of CBp and CBc

	CBp	N115	N330	N539	N660
Surface area [m²/g]	77.3	145	82	43	36
Structure, DBP No. [cm³/100g]	95.0	113	102	110	90

The CBp obtained under vacuum conditions is close to commercial blacks of the N300 series, from the material organic feature standpoint. Vacuum pyrolysis is indeed less destructive of the carbon black surface area and structure properties when compared with atmospheric pyrolysis-derived CBp.

Demineralization

CBp contains nearly all of the original inorganic tire additives and, consequently, its ash content is considerably higher as compared to commercial carbon blacks. High ash content can preclude the use of CBp in certain applications. It is certainly an undesirable feature from a market standpoint. To decrease the CBp mineral content, a demineralization treatment was conducted by successive washings with an acid and a base. Treatment of tire sidewall-derived CBp with 1N H_2SO_4 followed by treatment with 1N NaOH reduced the ash content from 14.6 to 6.3 wt. %. With repeated treatments, ash concentrations lower than 1% could even be obtained. As tire sidewalls are made of low-surface area carbon blacks [14], after the one-step acid/base treatment, the surface area was increased from 42 to 53 m²/g and to 65 m²/g after repeated treatments. The effect on the organic CBp portion upon demineralization was studied by surface spectroscopic methods [15]. It was shown that the demineralization treatment affected the organic portion only slightly. The acid or acid/base method represents however an expensive upgrading approach. Gravitational/mechanical methods currently under development [16, 17] may represent an interesting demineralization solution in the future.

CBp Surface Chemistry

The most important commercial application of carbon black is rubber reinforcement [18]. To find out whether CBp can replace some CBc grades as semi-reinforcing filler in rubbers, the surface chemistry of CBp and CBc has been studied by X-ray photoelectron spectroscopy (XPS) and secondary ion mass spectroscopy (SIMS).

The XPS analysis showed that on the surface of commercial rubber-grade carbon blacks, in addition to carbon only oxygen and sulphur are found (hydrogen is not detected by XPS). On CBp, in addition to the elements found on commercial blacks, nitrogen and zinc are also detected [19, 20]. The nitrogen most probably originates from the vulcanization accelerators and the antioxidants used during tire manufacture, whereas zinc oxide is added as a vulcanization catalyst [14]. The carbon XPS spectra of CBc are dominated by an asymmetrical so-called graphite peak for carbon atoms in graphite-like structures. The spectra of the CBp shows, in addition to the peaks related to CBc, a peak assigned to carbon atoms in small aromatic compounds or aliphatic structures (C_1) which are part of the carbonaceous deposits. The amount of carbonaceous deposits decreases with decreasing pyrolysis pressure (100 to 0.3 kPa) and increasing temperature (420 to 700°C). Consequently, in order to preserve as much as possible the integral properties of the virgin carbon black, the pyrolysis should be performed at low pressure and at as high as possible pyrolysis temperature.

Secondary ion mass spectroscopy (SIMS) was used as a second surface spectroscopic analysis method. In the SIMS experiment, the sample surface is bombarded with high energy ions, causing the ejection of charged and neutral fragments from the surface. Charged fragments (ions) are detected in a mass spectrometer. The SIMS spectra of carbon blacks show intense peaks of C_2^- and C_2H^- ions [21, 22]. The concentration of C-H groups at the edges of the small aromatic structures is much higher as compared to a carbon black surface without deposits. Most of the C_2H^- ions originate from the edges of the small aromatic structures. The ratio of the C_2H^-/ C_2^- SIMS peaks is therefore a measure of the concentration of carbonaceous deposits on the CBp surface. The excellent agreement between the two surface spectroscopic techniques confirms that the chemical nature of the surface of CBp from vacuum pyrolysis is much closer to commercial grades as compared to CBp from atmospheric pyrolysis processes.

CBp Applications as Filler in Polymers

Based on the various characterization studies conducted, the surface activity of CBp from vacuum pyrolysis appears high enough to replace low-surface area commercial grades (such as N774) in rubber applications such as conveyer belts and rubber boots [9, 13]. The mechanical properties of CBp-filled PVC were found to be comparable to the compound filled with a low-surface commercial black [23]. An example is the elongation at break which decreases for a laboratory CBp and a low-surface area commercial black in a very similar fashion. The other viscoelastic properties of CBp-filled PVC are in-between PVC filled with low and high surface area commercial blacks [23].

CBp for Reinforcement of Road Bitumen

Extensive testing of pyrolytic carbon black as filler in road bitumen in order to produce a binder with improved properties in comparison to unmodified bitumen concrete, has been performed in the authors' laboratory in collaboration with the Ministère des Transports du Québec (MTQ), Québec City, Canada [24-27]. The U.S. Corps of Engineers Gyratory Testing Machine (GTM) was used to determine the compaction and shear properties of the concrete (method ASTM D 3387). No significant differences between the asphalt samples with and without CBp were observed. The integration of the CBp in the bitumen-aggregate mixtures does not alter the cohesion specifications of the straight binder. As well, in the rutting test (repetitive crossing of a pneumatic wheel exerting a vertical force on a standard parallelepipedic paving sample), the CBp-modified bitumen met all the requirements with an improved performance as a result of the CBp content. The loss of cohesion resulting from the action of water (method ASTM D 1075) was also investigated for CBp-filled bitumen mixtures. Marked improvement in the index of retained strength showed that CBp has, at high temperature, a positive influence on the cohesion and ageing phenomena. Tensile strength testing (method AASHTO TP10-93) revealed also a better resistance to freezing and gradual contraction for CBp-filled bitumen. It has been found that the addition of 5 to 30 wt. % of CBp in road bitumen increased the high service-temperature by reducing the thermal susceptibility of the pure bitumen and increasing the rutting resistance and the cracking resistance. In order to prepare high performance binders without exceeding the processing viscosity, it has been suggested to add CBp in the range of concentrations of 5 to 15 wt. % [26].

Other applications

Another reported potential application of CBp is its use as feedstock for the production of activated carbon [28-30]. Surface areas above 1000 m^2/g were obtained for some CBp-derived activated carbons [29]. CBp was also tested as feedstock material for the production of fluorinated carbon electrodes for lithium batteries. Due to the presence of carbonaceous deposits on its surface, CBp reacts at mild conditions with fluorine. Preliminary tests indicated that CBp is indeed a suitable material for this application [31]. Other industrial uses reported are in the ink industry [32] and in the copper industry as a carbon reducing material [11]. Despite the promising applications discussed above, in reality CBp has found only limited penetration in the user sector. One of the resistances expressed is the CBp suspected heterogeneity, because this recycled material is a blend of various grades of commercial carbon blacks. Until it is produced and made available in bulky volumes through a reliable and steady pyrolysis process, the user sector will be hesitant to afford the right price for this valuable product.

PYROLYTIC OILS (PO)

Physicochemical Properties. Uses of the Whole Oils.

The p hysicochemical p roperties o f P O p roduced d uring a 0 .5 t /h r un a t the d emonstration plant, are presented in Table 3 together with those of the commercial CIMAK-B10 diesel fuel as a reference. The gross calorific value of PO exceeds the heating value of bituminous coal (28 MJ/kg) [33], wood charcoal (30 MJ/kg) [34] and used tires (33 MJ/kg) [35]. Their relatively low values in ash content, sulphur and Conradson carbon residue (CCR) are noticeable. Based on the refractive index, these oils are high in aromatics, which is confirmed by the high density, the low H/C atomic ratio and the high carbon residue.

The vacuum PO represents a valuable raw feedstock material for the production of high quality electrode coke and carbon black (13). As well, their high carbon content makes them suitable for making high value carbon materials that could be used in various industries (*e.g.* production of calcium carbide, steelworks, etc.) (13). The absence of vanadium and the low content in heteroatoms such as sulphur are definite assets for PO.

The chemical composition of PO in terms of unsaturated hydrocarbons is similar to that of oils obtained by coking of various petroleum residues, by thermal cracking of gasoil fractions and by steam cracking of gasoline [36]. Therefore, PO could be blended with these condensates, subject to the usual post-treatment in refineries. The important requirements for heavy fuels used as diesel fuels are their ignition quality, viscosity, water, sediment and sulphur contents. According to their physicochemical properties, tire-derived PO can be blended with fuels such as CIMAK-B10 diesel fuel (Table 3). The addition of PO to a diesel fuel would reduce the viscosity of the resulting blend, thus improving the atomization and ensure a more thorough combustion of the fuel. Hence, PO can be considered a valuable fuel for blending with conventional heating fuels.

Table 3. Properties of PO and CIMAK-B10 Diesel Fuel

PROPERTIES	PYROVAC DEMO PLANT	CIMAK-B10
Gross calorific value, MJ/kg (anhydrous basis)	43.8	-
Density, kg/m^3 25°C	970	975
Viscosity, cSt 50°C	6.1	9.7
Flash point, °C	35	50
Water, wt.%	0.2	0.5
Sulphur, wt.%	1.2	3.5
Ash, wt.%	0.01	0.1
CCR, wt.%	4.5	10
Vanadium (ppm)	Nil	300
Refractive index 25°C	1.5442	-

End-Uses of PO fractions

In addition to its global use as a fuel, the pyrolytic oil can be fractionated into different cuts which could be further blended with the corresponding petroleum fractions. Several schemes of fractionation of the oil can be performed. The following oil fractions have been studied: initial boiling point (ibp) -204°C, >204°C, 240-450°C, >350°C and >400°C.

Noticeably, the light fraction (i.b.p. -204°C) contains 20% by wt. of dl-limonene, a high value chemical which may be used in industrial applications as an environmentally friendly solvent, a component for the production of resins and adhesives and a dispersing agent for pigments [37, 38]. The >204°C and 240-450°C PO fractions were evaluated for their plasticizing properties in rubber formulations by a floor carpet manufacturing company, Mondo Rubber Int'l, Laval, Québec, Canada. The tire-derived PO formulations exhibited lower Mooney viscosity and shorter cure time, compared with the commercial oils Sundex 790 and Dutrex R729. Results showed that the heavy vacuum PO are good plasticizers, exhibiting good mechanical and lubricating properties, quite similar to commercial processing oils.

The pyrolysis residue (>350°C), composing about 55 wt. % of PO, exhibits a high content in asphaltenes, the main precursors of coke [39]. This fraction was subjected to a delayed coking experiment. Low sulphur (0.7 wt. %) and low ash content (0.24 wt. %) characterized the cokes obtained, with zinc (33 ppm) and silicon (15 ppm) being the major metals present [39]. The absence of vanadium, an undesirable contaminant of commercial cokes, is noticeable. The X-Ray diffractogram, characterized by a lower interlayer spacing (d_{002} = 3.498 Å), indicates that this coke is graphitizable.

The coking experiment yielded also a highly aromatic naphtha fraction (i.b.p.-205°C), a light gasoil (205-350°C) rich in aromatic hydrocarbons, a heavy gasoil (>350°C) which can be recycled in the coke manufacturing process and a gas with a high heating value. The pyrolytic bitumen fraction (i.p.b. > 400°C) recovered by vacuum distillation of the pyrolysis residue (>350 °C) constitutes 29 wt. % of PO. Compared with petroleum bitumens, PB has a high penetrability, a low softening point and a low dynamic viscosity. Being rich in carbon and low in hydrogen contents, its sulphur content is rather low while the nitrogen content is similar to that of petroleum bitumens [40].

The carbon/hydrogen ratio (C/H) suggests that PB contains more aromatic hydrocarbons than petroleum bitumens, an advantage for the making of styrene-butadiene-styrene (SBS) blends [41]. For some applications, special aromatic petroleum fractions are added to the bitumens in order to improve their compatibility; the addition of aromatic oils (e.g. furfural extracts) enhances the peptization effect of the SBS-petroleum bitumen blends [42]. The addition of PB to a SBS blend may have the same peptisation effect on the blend components as the addition of petroleum aromatic fractions.

PYROLYSIS GAS

Yield of the pyrolysis gas produced in a 0.5 t/h test at the demo plant accounted for 20 wt. % of the products (Table 1). This gas is rich in hydrogen, methane, propane, butane fractions and exhibits a high gross calorific value, 46 MJ/kg. Being in large excess *vis-à-vis* the pyrolysis heat requirement, it can be burned in a gas turbine to generate electricity or in a boiler to generate steam. In the following technico-economic section with a 36 000 t/y scrap tire vacuum pyrolysis plant scenario, the pyrolysis gas is pre-desulfurized prior to be burned in a boiler to generate steam.

PROCESS ECONOMICS

Technico-economical data have been compiled for a 36 000 t/y scrap tire vacuum pyrolysis plant, using the basic engineering data acquired by Pyrovac International, through extensive R&D activities conducted over the last decade at the laboratory, pilot and demonstration scale. The 36 000 t/y plant scenario has been built with the data and basic assumptions presented in Table 4 below.

A flow diagram of the 36 000 t/y pyrolysis plant process is shown at Figure 4. The large tire chunks feedstock is pulverized to 0-7 mm particle size prior to be fed into the pyrolyser. The steel, fibers and carbon black composing the solid residue at the reactor outlet are separated with a magnetic/filter unit. In the proposed implementation scenario, during the first 2 years of operation the CBp is sold as a powder with ~15 % ash content. A demineralization unit is installed during year 3, to upgrade the CBp so as to lower the ash content to < 5 %. A cyclone at the pyrolyser outlet separates the carbon and fiber particles from the gas/vapour mixture which passes through two cooling packed towers in series where the oils are condensed and recovered. The pyrolysis gas is desulfurized to less than 4-ppm H2S content prior to be burned in the molten salt furnace. The excess gas is burned in a boiler to generate 8.8 t/h of steam.

Table 4. 36 000 t/y Vacuum Pyrolysis Plant Implementation Program

Plant availability	85 % or 7446 h/year		
Scrap tire feedstock	Received pre-shredded in form of large chunks (~100-300 mm x 100-300 mm) 15 % steel and 2 % fiber content		
Pyrolysis products	%	t/y	t/h
Oils	34	12250	1.6
Carbon black	32	11655	1.6
Gas	17	5975	0.8
Steel	15	5400	0.7
Fibers	2	720	0.1
TOTAL	100	36000	4.8
	Year	Installations – Operations	
Progressive capital investments	1-2	Shredding/pyrolysis process and steam boiler installed Oils, steel, steam, as-received CBp are sold	
	3-4	Demineralization equipment installed for upgrading CBp Oils, steel, steam, as-received /upgraded CBp are sold	
	5+	Oils, steel, steam, upgraded CBp are sold	
	Year	% Capacity	
Plant production capacity	1	35	
	2	70	
	3	90	
	4	100	
	5	100	
	6	100	

The projected selling prices for the oils, the steel and the carbon black, either as-received or upgraded, as well as the production ratio for these, the price for steam and a progressive decreasing tipping fee along the 5-year plant development period are presented in Table 5. At the end of the 5-year period, the oils represent 45 % of the incomes, the upgraded CBp 42 %, the steam 12 % and the steel, 1 %.

The initial investments (plant infrastructure / buildings / shredding / pyrolysis / steam boiler / products r ecovery p rocesses) r epresent a c apital o f 1 2.9 M€. The capital invested for the CBp upgrading unit (3rd year) is estimated at 1.6 M€. The total capital investment is 14.5 M€ over the 5-year implementation period.

Using the above assumptions, Figure 5 summarizes the evolution of the operating costs, the sales, the financial aid and the net incomes, per ton of tire processed, during the first 7 years of operation. From year 6, when the financial aid program is abolished, the net income is in the range of 55 €/t of tires.

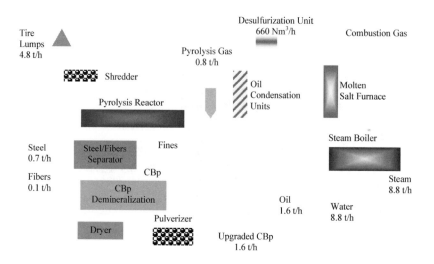

Figure 4. Flow Diagram for a 36 000 t/h Vacuum Pyrolysis Plant

Table 5. Sources of Incomes from a Used Tire Vacuum Pyrolysis Plant

Year	1	2	3	4	5	6
Tipping fee (€/t)	35	30	20	15	10	0
Oils (€/t)	230	230	240	240	250	250
As-received CBp (€/t)	90	90	90	90		
% of production	100%	100%	80%	30%		
Upgraded CBp (€/t)			240	240	240	240
% of production			20%	70%	100%	100%
Steel (€/t)	17	17	17	17	17	17
Steam (€/t)	12	12	12	12	12	12

For a mature scrap tire pyrolysis plant, less development effort will be required to reach full plant capacity. Economic estimates indicate a 21% reduction in the total capital investment, down to 11.5 M€. The investments for the various processing units and the operating costs for the mature plant are presented in Table 6.

The sales of chemical products and steam represent a total revenue of 187 €/t of tire. The operation costs amount to 120 €/t. Hence a net income of 67 €/t of tire is expected for the mature plant or 2.4 M€/y, which does provide for a return on the investment of 21 %.

The process economics indicate that a 36 000 t/y tire vacuum pyrolysis plant has the potential to become a profit centre, with the following assumptions:
- A financial aid decreasing over 5 years with permanent, free delivery of tire lumps.
- A strong R/D program with a focus on CBp to enable the CBp penetration into the market place.

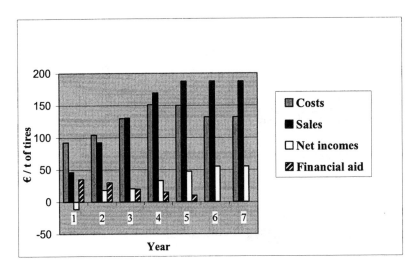

Figure 5. Evolution of the Process Economics during the Program Implementation

Table 6. Capital Investment and Operating Costs for a Mature Vacuum Pyrolysis Plant

CAPITAL INVESTMENT, M€		OPERATING COSTS, €/t (including 10 years of depreciation)	
Pyrolysis process equipment	5.6	Shredding / Pyrolysis	75
Pyrolysis gas desulfurisation	0.5	Steam boiler	10
Steam boiler	1.0	CBp upgrading	35
Tire shredder & product storage facilities	1.6		
CBp crushing / demineralization equipment	1.2		
Buildings	1.6		
Total :	11.5	Total :	120

CONCLUSIONS

The scrap tire vacuum pyrolysis technology has the potential to recapture the valuable compounds composing a tire, *i.e.* carbon black, oil and steel in order to recycle them in various categories of commodity products once a market has been established. Several commercial applications for the different products have been investigated. The CB_P surface chemistry and activity are similar to those of some grades of commercial carbon blacks. Therefore, CB_P has the potential to replace commercial carbon black grades in certain rubber applications. CB_P was successfully tested as filler in road pavement. The pyrolytic oil can be used as a heating fuel. It can also be distilled into different fractions: a light and a middle distillate and a heavy fraction. The light fraction was positively tested as a gasoline additive and contains valuable chemicals such as D,L-limonene. The middle fraction was successfully tested as a plasticizer in rubbers. The heavy fraction represents a good-quality feed for the production of coke and c an also be used in road pavements. The pyrolytic g as has a high calorific value and its volume exceeds the heat requirement for the process. A technico-economic study revealed that a 36 000 t/y scrap tire vacuum pyrolysis plant has the potential to become a profit centre, assuming there is a 5 y-implementation program with the free delivery of tire lumps in the long term. A strong R/D program with a focus on the CBp is also necessary to enable the CBp market penetration.

Photograph 1: Pyrovac Vacuum Pyrolysis Demonstration Plant (Saguenay, Quebec, Canada)

REFERENCES

1. BLUMENTHAL M, Scrap Tire Recycling Markets Update, BioCycle, 43 (2002) 58-62.

2. RESCHNER K., Scrap tire recycling - Market Overview and Outlook, Waste Management World, Vol. 3 No.4, July-August 2003, James & James (Science Publishers) Ltd. http://www.jxj.com/wmw/index.html

3. Anonymous, The Changing Face Of Tire Recycling In Europe, Scrap Tire News, 17, No 1 (2003) 1-14.

4. BLUMENTHAL M, Changes Impacting the Ground Rubber Industry, Scrap Tire News, Vol. 16, No. 11, p. 12-14, November 2002

5.   R. LAMPMAN, S. HANSONAND and R. NOVAK, Seasonal Abundance and Distribution of Mosquitoes at a Rural Waste Tire Site in Illinois, J. Am. Mosquito Control Assoc. 13 (1997) 193-200.

6.   P.T. WILLIAM and A.J. BRINDLE, .Aromatic Chemicals from the Catalytic Pyrolysis of Scrap Tires., Journal of Analytical and Applied Pyrolysis, 67 (2003) 143-164.

7.   P.T. WILLIAMS, Black magic?... High Value Products from Scrap Tires, Chemistry Review, 12 (2002) 17-19.

8.   W. KAMINSKY and C. MENNERICH, .Pyrolysis of Synthetic Tire Rubber in a Fluidised-Bed Reactor to Yield 1,3-Butadiene, Styrene and Carbon Black., Journal of Analytical and Applied Pyrolysis, 58 (2001) 803-811.

9.   C. ROY, A. CHAALA and H. DARMSTADT "The Vacuum Pyrolysis of Used Tires. End-Uses for the Oil and Carbon Black Products", Journal of Analytical and Applied Pyrolysis, 51 (1999) 201-221.

10.   S. KAWAKAMI, K. INOUE, H. TANAKA and T. SAKAI, .Pyrolysis Process for Scrap Tires., in J.L Jones, S.B. Radding (Eds.), Thermal Conversion of Solid Wastes and Biomass, ACS Symposium Series 130, ACS Publishers, Washington, DC, USA, (1980) 557.

11.   H. KONO, ONAHAMA Smelting and Refining Co. Ltd., Iwaki City, Fukushima, Japan, Private Communication (1987).

12.   B. P. FAULKNER and W. WEINECKE, Carbon Black Production from Waste Tires, Minerals and Metallurgical Processing, 18 (2001) 215.

13.   C. ROY, A. CHAALA, H. DARMSTADT, B. de CAUMIA, H. PAKDEL and J. YANG, Conversion of Used Tires to Carbon Black and Oil by Pyrolysis, Chapter in the Book Rubber Recycling (CRC Press). To be published in 2005.

14.   W.H. WADDELL, R.S. BHAKUNI, W.W. BARBIN and P.H. SANDSTROM, Pneumatic Tire Compounds, The Vanderbilt Rubber Handbook, Thirteenth Edition, Edited by R.F. Ohm, R.T. Vanderbilt Company, Norwalk, CT, USA, (1990) 596.

15.   A. CHAALA, H. DARMSTADT and C. ROY, "Acid-Base Method for the Demineralization of Pyrolytic Carbon Black", Fuel Processing Technology, 46 (1996) 1-15.

16.   J.H. FADER, Upgraded Pyrolyzed Carbon Black (CBp) fromWaste Tires and Scrap Rubber as Reinforcing Filler in Rubber Compounds, Paper No. 114, Rubber Division Meeting, American Chemical Society, Cincinnati, Ohio, October 17-20, 2000.

17.   J.H. FADER, Method for Reclaiming Carbonaceous Material from a Waste Material, U.S. Patent No. 5037628, August 6, 1991.

18.   G. KÜHNER and M. VOLL, "Manufacture of Carbon Black" in Carbon Black Science and Technology, Second Edition, Eds. J.-B. Donnet, R.C. Bansal and M.J. Wang, Marcel Dekker, Inc., New York, USA, (1993) 1-65.

19.   H. DARMSTADT, C. ROY and S. KALIAGUINE, "ESCA Characterization of Commercial Carbon Blacks and of Carbon Blacks from Vacuum Pyrolysis of Used Tires", Carbon 32 (1994) 1399-1406.

20.   H. DARMSTADT, C. ROY and S. KALIAGUINE, Characterization of Carbon Blacks from Commercial Tire Pyrolysis Plants, Carbon, 33 (1995) 1449-1455.

21.   H. DARMSTADT, N.-Z. CAO, D. PANTEA, C. ROY, L. SÜMMCHEN, U. ROLAND, J.-B. DONNET, T.K. WANG, C.H. PENG and P.J. DONNELLY, Surface Activity and Chemistry of Thermal Carbon Blacks, Rubber Chemistry and Technology, 73 (2000) 293-309.

22.   H. DARMSTADT, L. SÜMMCHEN, U. ROLAND, C. ROY, S. KALIAGUINE and A. ADNOT, Surface Chemistry of Pyrolytic Carbon Black by SIMS and Raman Spectroscopy, Surface and Interface Analysis, 25 (1997) 245-253.

23.   J.B. DUFEU, C. ROY, A. AJJI and L. CHOPLIN, .PVC Filled with Vacuum Pyrolysis Scrap Tires - Derived Carbon Blacks: An Investigation on Rheological, Mechanical and Electrical Properties., Journal of Applied Polymer Science, 46 (1992) 2159-2167.

24.   A. CHAALA, C. ROY and A. AIT-KADI, "Rheological Properties of Bitumen Modified with Pyrolytic Carbon Black", Fuel, 75 (1996) 1575-1583.

25.   H. DARMSTADT, A. CHAALA, C. ROY and S. KALIAGUINE, "SIMS and ESCA Characterization of Pyrolytic Carbon Black Reinforced Bitumen", Fuel, 75 (1996) 125-132.

26.   S. CHEBIL, A. CHAALA, and C. ROY,Modification of Bitumen with Scrap Tire Pyrolytic Carbon Black, Comparison with Commercial Carbon Black Part I: Mechanical and Rheological Properties, Polymer Recycling, 2 (1996) 257-269.

27.   S. CHEBIL, A. CHAALA, H. DARMSTADT and C. ROY, Modification of Bitumen with Scrap Tire Pyrolytic Carbon Black, Comparison with Commercial Carbon Black, Part II: Microscopic and Surface Spectroscopic Investigation, Polymer Recycling 3 (1997/98) 17-28.

28.   A.M. CUNLIFFE and P.T. WILLIAMS, Influence of Process Conditions on the Rate of Activation of Chars Derived from Pyrolysis of Used Tires, Energy & Fuels, 13 (1999) 166 - 175.

29.   C.M.B. LEHMANN, M ROSTAM-ABADI, M.J. ROOD and J. SUN, Reprocessing and Reuse of Waste Tire Rubber to Solve Air-Quality Related Problems, Energy and Fuels, 12 (1998) 1095-1099.

30.   P. ARIYADEJWANICH, W. TANTHAPANICHAKOON, K. NAKAGAWA, SR MUKAI and H. TAMON, Preparation and Characterization of Mesoporous Activated Carbon from Waste Tires, Carbon, 41, (2003) 157 - 164.

31.   J. M. NEDELEC, Valorisation des noirs de carbone pyrolytiques, Rapport de l'École Nationale Supérieure de Chimie de Clermont-Ferrand, Clermont-Ferrand, France (2002).

32. P. BRIDGES, Conrad Industries inc., Centralia, WA, Private Communication (1987).

33. H. LIN, The Combustion of Anthracites and Low Grade Bituminous Coals, International Conference on Coal Science, Pittsburgh, Pennsylvania (1983).

34. ROY, C., D. BLANCHETTE, B. de CAUMIA, F. DUBE, J. PINAULT, E. BELANGER and P. LAPRISE. Industrial Scale Demonstration of the Pyrocycling^{TM} Process for the Conversion of Biomass to Biofuels and Chemicals. 1st World Conference on Biomass for Energy and Industry. Proceedings of the Conference held in Sevilla, Spain. June 5-9, 2000. S. Kyritsis, A.A.C.M. Beenackers, P. Helm, A. Grassi and D. Chiaramonti, Eds. James & James (Science Publishers) Ltd., London, UK, 2001. Vol II (1032-1035).

35. G. FERRER, The Economics of Tire Remanufacturing, Resources, Conservation and Recycling, 19 (1997) 221 - 255.

36. Petroleum (Refinery process, Survey), Encyclopaedia of Chemical Technology, 3rd edition, 17 (1982) 210 - 218.

37. PAKDEL, H., C. ROY, H. AUBIN, G. JEAN and S. COULOMBE, Formation of dl-Limonene in Used Tire Vacuum Pyrolysis Oils, Env. Sc. Technol., 25 (1991) 1646-1649.

38. PAKDEL, H., D.M. PANTEA and C. ROY. Production of dl-Limonene by Vacuum Pyrolysis of Used Tires. Journal of Analytical and Applied Pyrolysis. 57: 91-107 (2001).

39. A. CHAALA and C. ROY. "Production of Coke from Scrap Tire Vacuum Pyrolysis Oils", Fuel Processing Technology, 46 (1996) 227-239.

40. A. CHAALA, O.G. CIOCHINA, C. ROY and M. BOUSMINA. "Rheological Properties of Bitumen Modified with Used Tire- Derived Pyrolytic Oil Residue" Polymer Recycling, 3 (1997/1998) 1-15

41. G. MANCINI, F. Del MANSO, and L. BOCCHI. Correlation Between Chemical Type of Bitumen Fractions and their Interactions with SBS Copolymers, Paper G-6, Symp. on Chemistry of Bitumens, Roma (1991).

42. P. BREADAEL, P. ANDRIOLO and E. KILLENS. A Structural Study of the Hot Storage Stability of SBS-Modified Bitumens, Paper G-5, Symp. on Chemistry of Bitumens, Roma (1991).

`TYRES- AN OPPORTUNITY, NOT WASTE`

P Roach

Credential Environmental Ltd.

United Kingdom

ABSTRACT. Granulated crumb rubber has been produced for many years and sold to a range o f e nd u se m arkets. T he m arkets h ave t ended t o b e r estricted t o a s mall n umber o f applications such as sports, play and leisure surfaces. Credential Environmental Ltd has been at the forefront in the development of innovative market applications for tyre-derived products. These developments have been extended to include a review of our granulated crumb rubber production in order to engineer products for sale to a much wider market and ultimately to deliver added value return in relation to £ / per tonne payback on the finished product. This paper sets out the production requirements for a graded crumb rubber and explores the marketing and development techniques that we have adopted to reach product acceptance and usability.

Keywords: Granulated crumb rubber, Production techniques and product characterisation, Sustainable crumb rubber application, Market penetration.

Paul Roach has over 25 years experience in both public and private waste management, recycling and end-use material resource management sectors. He has been instrumental in the commercialisation of a major UK integrated waste management project combining a number of technologies for the treatment of household, industrial and commercial wastes and in the last 3 years has concentrated on the end-use market requirement for granulated crumb rubber and other tyre-derived products.

INTRODUCTION

Whilst the EU Landfill Directive has now been incorporated into UK legislation, prohibiting the land filling of whole tyres from July 2003 and shredded tyres from July 2006, the granulation of crumb rubber has been an established technique to transform waste truck and car tyres into saleable product for over 10 years. Two methods of tyre granulation have been via the ambient processing, without pre-treatment and the cryogenic method where the rubber is pre-treated using liquid nitrogen prior to granulation. In the UK, we have seen very little in terms of cryogenic production, with effort been directed in the main toward ambient production.

Crumb rubber production levels in the UK today are at the 40,000 tonne level, with CEL producing over 15,000 tonnes per annum at its Sheffield production facility, thus accounting for 37% of the country's production. Conventional crumb rubber markets have tended to be focused around the following industry sectors:

- Sports and play surfaces – athletic tracks, hockey & football pitches, artificial turf in-fill.
- Leisure industry – equestrian surfaces, golf course, pathways.
- General Flooring – carpet underlay, industrial flooring.

This paper examines our approach to the manufacture and supply of crumb rubber products to an extended market place beyond the more traditional markets as outlined above. It reviews the balance between producing a viable and economical product of a specification that is both suitable and available and sustainable within the given market. The work undertaken is part of an ongoing product development programme within the CEL Group and is aimed at attaining wider market share and acceptability for the crumb rubber products produced.

GRANULATED CRUMB RUBBER

CEL have always produced, along with its competitors, typical granulated crumb rubber that meets the following output specification (Sieve Analysis).

0.5 – 2.0mm Granulated Crumb Rubber

MESH SIZE	%
2.0mm	0.1%
1.6mm	5.6%
1.4mm	16.81%
1.0mm	50.9%
850	12.5%
710	6.5%
500	5.7%
425	1%
355	0.7%
Pan	0.6%

2.0 – 6.0mm Granulated Crumb Rubber

MESH SIZE	%
5.6mm	0%
4.75mm	0.0%
4.00mm	1.5%
3.15mm	16.6%
2.00	60.4%
Pan	21.5%

The Sieve Analysis identifies the particulate size of the crumb as a % of the total sample and is used as a guide for the user to identify product composition against each particular application. For instance, the supply of 0.5 – 2.0mm crumb to comply with Standard DIN 18035-7 for German turf infill market.

PRODUCTION TECHNIQUES

The tyre granulation plant was set up to receive both waste passenger and commercial vehicle tyres, based on primary shredding prior to granulation. In turn, the granulation plant was configured on the basis of two separate lines in order to keep the input feed apart. A key requirement in our investigations into the production of new crumb rubber products is the utilisation of the plant and the output ratio of tonnes / per hour processed. This includes key components such as wearing parts and blade maintenance. The monitoring of the production characteristics of our standard crumb rubber size of 0.5 – 2.0mm with that of the new size of product trialled, 0.8 – 2.5mm, was closely monitored for trends on wearing components and down time impacts.

PRODUCT CHARACTERISATION

For many years, crumb rubber has been manufactured to specifications set by the users, i.e. 0.5 – 2.0mm for artificial turf infill and carpet underlay, 2.0 – 6.0mm for sub-base wearing coarses on sports surfaces and so on. At Credential, we have tackled product manufacture based on the cost effective production of differing crumb rubber sizes and then marketing the range to conventional markets as substitute product (at worse matching the technical requirement of that material previously used, in most cases to a better standard and viability) and to new markets that may require crumb rubber as an additive or composite to a further process or service.

0.8 – 2.5mm Turf Infill from Truck Tyres

Whole waste truck tyre feeds were used to process through to granulation. The plant previously ran on a 50/50 mix of car and truck tyres. The throughput rates increased by over 50% of total product manufactured on a weekly basis and at the bottom end of the range (finer crumb as % of total particulate size) dropped by some 25%. The product was then trialled with one of our major clients who found some significant gains in terms of pitch performance and drainage. Our client also found that this new product flowed freer than the finer material and therefore the contractor gained efficiencies with labour and plant utilisation when laying the surfaces.

The client had to gain acceptability for using the crumb rubber with their specified artificial turf suppliers. Extensive trials therefore took place in the UK and Europe with a carpet manufacturer to determine total surface warranty, durability and performance. Laboratory tests and a full-scale pitch surface installation proved product acceptance and sustainability and the client was able to re-specify their 2004/05 crumb rubber requirement.

MARKET PENETRATION AND ROUTE TO MARKET

Whilst there was a demand to work with this individual client to promote new surface design and installation, we were highly critical of the wider market opportunity with a number of other potential crumb rubber users. Quality and quantity of supply had to be measured against cost economics and operational exigencies, namely:

- Available waste truck tyres.
- Annual production of differing crumb rubber sizes, minimum and maximum available tonnages.
- Residual product sizes and uses.
- Average £ / per tonne selling price versus annual tonnage off-take.
- Current and future market demand for size of product.

At the time of this new work, CEL were embarking on a major shift into the global crumb rubber supply market. Initially concentrating on UK supply only, we found that a wider market opportunity existed and one which would even out the difficult seasonal demand that exists within the UK crumb rubber supply market. This was, therefore, a further consideration into how we evaluated the total market and how we would enter overseas markets.

CASE STUDY

French Sports Surface Market

For m any years t he s ports s urface i ndustry h ave b een u sing a s tandard s ize c rumb r ubber product for turf infill application. Depending on the granulation plant performance, there have been issues over the presence of dust that has caused blockages when applied to artificial grass.

We worked in the UK with a number of contractors and decided to produce a more stable material that the market would accept. We decided to host trials with a French sports surface contractor due to the wider demand for turf infill in Europe and also our company requirement to penetrate a more global market. We had supplied the contractor in the UK previously so there was an awareness of CEL crumb rubber.

As outlined in this paper, we set out to manufacture a 0.8 – 2.5mm crumb rubber at our Sheffield production facility. A number of samples were mailed to France following which the contractors agreed to come to the UK and set up a sectional turf trial at our East Yorkshire Recycling Facility. They laid a sectional piece of turf upon which our product was applied in accordance with their fill rates. The sample was exposed to typical wet climate conditions and a visual inspection of how well the crumb rubber allowed the drainage of surface water through its surface was measured. The sectional piece of turf was configured in such a way to collect the surface water run through so we could analyse the solids content. The crumb samples were manufactured from both car and truck tyres and both products were measured as laid on this trial surface.

The sieve analysis for the larger product confirmed with the trial that there were smaller amounts of fines present within the product and so the client agreed to take two loads for a new surface being planned. Representatives from CEL travelled to France to oversee the installation and all the new product was successfully applied to the artificial grass. The contractor monitored the surface over the coming weeks and reported no problems with dust build up and drainage issues. We were able to negotiate the supply of further product at competitive rates.

CONCLUSIONS

Market acceptability proved to be a major obstacle to supplying the different size crumb rubber product. It was widely accepted that a 0.5 – 2.0mm crumb rubber was the most suitable for turf infill and the sheer presentation of a new material was difficult to introduce to contractors.

The production techniques and monitoring of operational costs allowed us to not only produce a compliant and acceptable material, but also allowed us to take the product to market at a commercial rate that would attract interest. The ability to set up a demonstration site and to track surface performance helped contribute to the success of the product launch. The wider global market, whilst vast, does have its problems as the ability to supply a consistent product can be thwarted by the lack of available truck tyre in-feeds to run at 100%.

SESSION ONE:

REGULATORY FRAMEWORK AND GOVERNMENT POLICY

USED TYRES: BURNING RUBBER-ACCELERATING TOWARDS 2006

P Hallett

Department of Trade and Industry

United Kingdom

ABSTRACT. The paper provides a snapshot of the UK used tyre recovery position. It sets out the general regulatory framework, together with prospects for change. It lists the wider legislative drivers, looks at the various sectors comprising the used tyre recovery infrastructure, and rolls this forward to July 2006, when the tyre landfill disposal ban takes full effect.

Keywords: Tyre recovery, Retreading, Materials recovery, Energy recovery, Tyre collection

Paul Hallett is a member of the Waste Policy and Vehicle Recycling section in the Sustainable Development Directorate of the Department of Trade and Industry, which holds the lead Government interest in used tyre disposal issues. He has been a member of the industry/Government Used Tyre Working Group since 1998.

INTRODUCTION

July 2003 saw the first tightening of the landfill disposal of tyres, with the ban on the disposal of whole tyres to landfill coming into effect. This step had been widely anticipated by those businesses involved in the disposal of used tyres, and was successfully managed. The second phase of the ban, from July 2006, when shredded tyres will also be banned from disposal to landfill is a sterner test. However, the UK appears generally well placed to adapt in time and in good order to this final phase, with increasing numbers of tyres diverted from landfill disposal and a fast growing UK tyre recovery infrastructure.

BACKGROUND

EU Landfill Directive

The EU Landfill Directive, which provides the principal driver to the increased recovery of used tyres by introducing a ban on the landfill disposal of almost all tyres, was published in the Official Journal of the European Communities on 16 July 1999 as Council Directive 1999/31/EC on the landfill of waste. The Directive applies to all tyres save bicycle tyres and tyres with an outside diameter exceeding 1.4 metres. As such it applies not only to car and truck t yres, b ut a lso i ncludes a gricultural, a ircraft, e arthmover, i ndustrial (inc. s olids), a nd motorcycle tyres. The Directive, however, continues to allow the use of whole tyres for landfill engineering purposes.

The Landfill Directive has been implemented [1], and in accordance with the Landfill Regulations, whole used tyres cannot be deposited at landfills for Hazardous waste or at landfills permitted or licensed since July 2001. Under the current transitional arrangements, they can continue to be deposited at other existing landfills, where this is authorised under the existing licence or permit, until the site has received a PPC permit. Because whole or shredded tyres are not inert, they cannot go to Inert landfills. Shredded used tyres may be accepted at landfills until 16 July 2006 where the waste management licence or permit provides that they may be accepted. However, as tyres are not considered to be hazardous waste, a landfill for hazardous waste may not accept shredded used tyres after 16 July 2004.

A landfill ban on tyre disposal had long been mooted and was borne from earlier EC work, where tyres had been considered as a priority waste stream. The justification for the ban was ultimately threefold, but not least that the resources bound in a tyre should not be immediately lost to landfill disposal at the end of their first life. The difficulties that tyres can cause when landfilled were also factors as whole tyres can cause instability in landfills by rising to the surface over time and, due to their high calorific value, represent a significant fire risk when landfilled in large quantities.

End of Life Vehicles Directive

The End of Life Vehicles (ELV) Directive (2000/53/EC) came into force on 21 October 2000. The Directive lays down measures which aim, as a first priority, at the prevention of waste from vehicles and, in addition, at the reuse, recycling and other forms of recovery of end-of-life vehicles and their components so as to reduce the disposal of waste, as well as at the improvement in the environmental performance of all the economic operators involved in the treatment of end-of-life vehicles.

A number of the Directive's provisions were transposed into national law by The End-of-Life Vehicles Regulations 2003 (Statutory Instrument 2003/2635) which came into effect on 3 November 2003, and by equivalent regulations in Scotland and Northern Ireland. The remaining provisions were subject to a February 2004 DTI consultation paper [2], and it is anticipated these will be transposed into national law during the second quarter of 2004.

The Directive applies broadly to cars and vans (up to 3.5 tonnes), and as far as tyres are concerned encourages their increased recovery by requiring their removal prior to the shredding of the vehicle hulk, unless the tyre fraction can be conveniently recovered from the automotive shredder residue, and by introducing re-use, recycling and recovery targets. From 2006, vehicle manufacturers and potentially Authorised Treatment Facilities accepting non-contracted end of life vehicles, will be required to demonstrate that a minimum of 85% by average weight per vehicle has been reused or recovered. It is likely that tyres will help provide a valuable contribution towards meeting this target.

The Definition of Waste

The definition of waste is a complex, but important, area leading to handling and waste management licensing requirements for those holding, transporting and processing waste tyres. When a tyre becomes waste hinges on the point it is "discarded". This is the language used in the Framework Directive on Waste 75/442/EEC and reflected directly in the UK legislation (Regulation 1(3) of the Waste Management Licensing Regulations 1994). Interpretation of the definition of waste has to have regard to judgements made by the courts both at European and national level. There is a growing stock of case law in this respect.

Once a tyre has become waste it remains waste until it has been completely recovered. This test of complete recovery is likely to mean that used tyres are waste for longer than common understanding. As an example, the production of secondary raw material is not considered as complete recovery. This takes place when the secondary raw material is incorporated in the final product or structure. It follows that tyre granulate remains a waste until, say, it is physically incorporated in the sports surface. And for tyre pyrolysis, the oil, carbon char and steel flowing from the process similarly are not completely recovered until a later stage.

Regulatory controls apply as long as a tyre is waste and the longer view of waste has wide-ranging implications for many of those currently involved in the treatment of used tyres, as traditionally they have not been subject to such controls. A working group, facilitated by the Environment Council under the Environment Agency's TyreWatch programme, has been developing a case for exemptions from waste management regulatory requirements on the basis that regulation should be proportionate to the environmental risk posed by that activity. If the work of the group is supportive, the intention is for the working group to press the case with the Department of Environment, Food and Rural Affairs.

UK Waste Disposal Legislation

The disposal of waste tyres is handled under general waste management, rather than tyre specific, legislation. There are many legislative provisions related to waste, but ultimately these aim to provide appropriate controls at all stages, from the point something becomes waste, to its subsequent storage, transport and treatment, whether that be recovery or disposal.

In general terms, those depositing, storing (provided it is not waste they themselves produce), treating o r d isposing o f waste w ill r equire t o b e l icensed o r s ubject t o a n e xemption. T he licensing regime is provided for under The Waste Management Licensing Regulations 1994 (as amended) although certain operators will be covered under different provisions, e.g. some waste disposal and recovery activities require a Pollution Prevention and Control (PPC) permit. Certain low risk waste management activities are exempt from a requirement to hold a waste management license, although there is usually a requirement to register the exempt activity with the regulator e.g. the Environment Agency in England and Wales.

The Controlled Waste (Registration of Carriers and Seizure of Vehicles) Regulations 1991 implements a carriers registration scheme. This requires that those people who transport controlled waste, or brokers who make arrangements on behalf of others to dispose of waste, are registered with the environmental regulators. The Environment Agency holds details in excess of 80,000 registered waste carriers.

The Environment Protection (Duty of Care) Regulations 1991 (as amended) sets down a legal responsibility on businesses to take proper care of waste, and applies to those producing, importing, carrying, keeping, treating or disposing of controlled waste. Broadly, waste should be stored and disposed of responsibly, should only be passed to those that are authorised to deal with it, and a record should be kept of all waste received or transferred through the Waste Transfer Notes system. In essence, this knits together with the other provisions mentioned above. It is worth noting that the Duty of Care follows through until the waste has been finally disposed of or fully r ecovered. This means that a waste producer maintains a responsibility for e nsuring t he p roper d isposal o r r ecovery o f t heir w aste a fter i t h as b een passed to someone else e.g. the Registered Waste Carrier who collected the waste.

DTI Consultation Papers

The Department of Trade & Industry (DTI) has issued two Government consultation papers on used tyre issues [3]. The first, issued in March 2002, looked at a number of issues surrounding the application of a statutory producer model to used tyres. It suggested that producer responsibility focussed on those introducing tyres into the UK for the first time (e.g. principally tyre manufacturers and importers) would be more efficient than spreading responsibility throughout the tyre supply chain (e.g. manufacturer to retailer). The paper examined the prospect of apportioning obligations to recover used tyres by reference to market share of a producers tyre sales, with the potential for a tradable evidence scheme to reconcile obligations with physical used tyre reprocessing activity.

The tyre industry, which submitted a joint industry response comprising tyre manufacturers, importers, retailers and retreaders, accepted the concept of producer responsibility, and agreed with Government that obligations would best be framed in terms of tyre manufacturers and importers. However, the scheme as described in the paper was considered to be overly complex and costly.

In March 2003, DTI issued a second consultation paper inviting industry views on their preferred means of effectively managing the diversion of tyres from landfill disposal. This paper effectively sought views on three options:
- continuation of a voluntary approach, strengthened as necessary
- a statutory reporting system (but without obligations to recover)
- a statutory producer scheme with recovery obligations

The tyre industry again submitted a joint response. This indicated that, in view of fragmented nature of the industry, a voluntary approach could not be expected to deliver a comprehensive, robust solution. Accordingly, the preference was for statutory producer responsibility. Two contrasting compliance mechanisms were set out. A market-based approach building on existing mechanisms and commercial arrangements, and a managed approach, similar to that taken in France, where obligated parties, through a central compliance body, would take an active role in managing the disposal of used tyres from retailer to reprocessor. The proposal for statutory reporting obligations was widely supported, whether as part of a wider producer responsibility approach or, if not, as a standalone measure.

As at May 2004, the Government has not yet announced its decision on the approach to be taken.

Statistics

The Used Tyre Working Group has been collecting statistics on used tyres since 1995. Figure1 shows replacement tyre sales for member companies of the British Rubber Manufacturers' Association and the Imported Tyre Manufacturers Association, coupled with information from the Society of Motor Manufacturers and Traders to include tyres on newly registered vehicles. The information is presented in tonnage terms. Taking 1998 as an example, this translates to some 34.5m passenger car units, 3.5m van and light truck units and 2.5m truck and bus units. These statistics do not include parallel and non-affiliated trade association imports, which industry commentators consider may represent up to 10% of the total market. The linear trend shows year-on-year growth of around 0.65%.

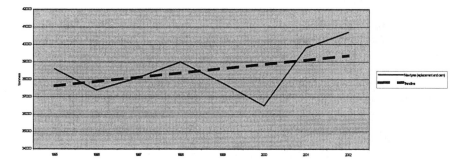

Figure 1 New tyre sales by disposal weight (replacement and original equipment manufacture on newly registered vehicles)

Figure 2 shows used tyre arisings over the period 1995 – 2002 compared to used tyre recovery. Used tyre arisings comprise replacement tyre sales (on the basis of one tyre on one old tyre off), tyres on end-of-life vehicles (in contrast to tyres on newly registered vehicles as in figure 1), and used tyre imports taken from HM Customs and Excise figures. The level of used tyre imports can vary considerably. In 1997, they were reported at almost 50,000 tonnes whereas in 1998 they were reported at under 18,000 tonnes.

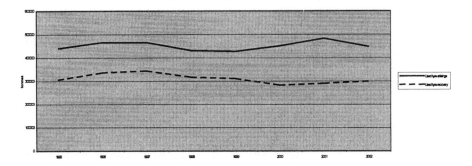

Figure 2 Used Tyre Arisings and Recovery 1995 - 2002

From 1995 through to 1999 used tyre recovery and used tyre arisings broadly maintained a parallel track, with a gap of around 120,000 tonnes between the two. From 1999, arisings and recovery diverged, widening this gap to almost 200,000 tonnes in 2001, but has since improved

REVIEW OF RECOVERY OPERATIONS

Retreading

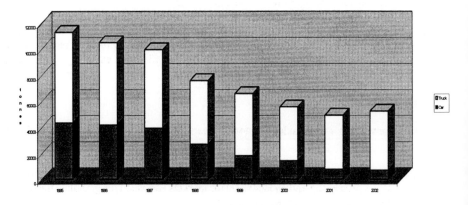

Figure 3 Retread sales (UK and export)

It can be seen that while both the passenger car and truck retread markets have declined over the period, the fall has been significantly worse for car retreads, with the market collapsing from around 6.7m units in 1995 to 1.1m units in 2002. The principal reason for this decline is that the price advantage of retreads has all but disappeared, with worldwide overcapacity and improved production, leading to lower tyre prices, telling factors.
The retread industry is looking to increased, and better promotion, to help regain market

share. T he R etread M anufacturers A ssociation h as l aunched a G reen D ealer S cheme, w ith over 300 tyre retail companies in membership, with the aim of getting closer to the end-consumer, and combating the negative perception of safety and performance that retreads can engender. To this end, ECE Regulations 108 (car) and 109 (truck) are welcomed. The Regulations require retreading facilities to be Tyre Approved and retread tyres to be subject to the same drum tests as new tyres.

Re-use

Tyres are re-used in whole form in a number of ways. One of the foremost options is part-worn tyres where useful tread depth remains, and it is refitted to a vehicle for its originally intended purpose. Sources of part-worn tyres include those taken off end-of-life vehicles and imports. Other whole use tyre applications include silage clamps, barriers around kart tracks, boat fenders and as seats on playground equipment.

A general characteristic of most re-use tyres, as well as retreads, is that the use is temporary and in due course these tyres will re-enter the waste stream for subsequent treatment. For this reason, such activities are counted as both an input to total used tyre arisings and an output to overall r ecovery, m ore or l ess c ancelling e ach o ther o ut. It i s w orth n oting, h owever, t hat temporary tyre uses provide a positive contribution, reducing the numbers of new tyres required, by extending the first life of a tyre (part-worn) or by giving a tyre another life (retreading), and by general resource substitution.

Engineering

The Landfill Directive specifically provides for the use of whole tyres for landfill engineering purposes to continue. The tyres are used to form a leachate drainage layer, typically using around 2,000 tonnes of car tyres for an average cell size.

Applications for tyre bales are also beginning to emerge, where they c an be used to form roadways and for lightweight fill. A bale comprises around 120 car tyres. A recent project for the Environment Agency used 10,000 of these blocks to widen an embankment on the River Witham in Lincolnshire.

Granulation

Figure 4 shows that the granulate sector has performed strongly, particularly so in recent years.

There are around 15 or so companies operating in this sector, of which relatively few account for much of the processing and capacity. Major markets for used tyre granulate include carpet underlay, sports, safety and equestrian surfaces.

The European Centre for Normalization (CEN) published a CEN Workshop Agreement (CWA) in July 2002. PrEN14243 sets down standards that users of tyre derived materials can reference, and it is anticipated that these will become a full EN by the end of 2004.

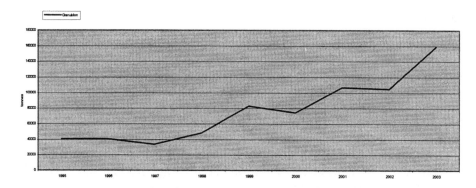

Figure 4 Materials recovery 1995 - 2003

Pyrolysis

Anglo United Environmental (formerly Coalite) have converted one of their smokeless fuel batteries to pyrolyse tyres, with an annual capacity of around 15,000 a year. The process breaks down the constituent parts of the tyre into carbon char, oil, steel and gas, which is used to fuel the process. The company intends to develop further capacity subject to resolving issues related to the Definition of Waste and the Waste Incineration Directive.

Energy recovery

Figure 5 shows the use of tyres as a fuel. The tyre-fuelled electricity generating station at Wolverhampton (Elm Energy/Sita Tyre Recycling), prior to its closure in 2000, accounted for the majority of tyres used for energy recovery. However, the use of tyres as a fuel in cement kilns has been growing steadily, and there are currently six kilns authorised to take them. These kilns provide a reasonable geographic spread. It is anticipated that this sector will account for over 100,000 tonnes in 2004, and capacity is expected to expand further with interest in using tyres at a further four kilns.

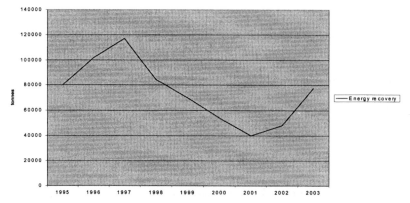

Figure 5 Energy recovery 1995 - 2003

Exports

HM Customs and Excise figures indicate that around 13,000 tonnes of used tyres were exported from the UK in 2003, of which around half went to other EC countries. Most of these tyres will have been for the part-worn market or casings for overseas retreaders.

Tyre collection

Many millions of tyres are disposed of in the UK each year, and UTWG figures estimate that over 40m tyres were disposed of in 2002. This translates to a need to efficiently move many thousands of tyres from thousands of tyre retail premises on a regular basis. Usually, this task is entrusted to a tyre collector, who has the logistical expertise and knowledge of treatment options for used tyres, and provides the linking mechanism between those generating waste tyres and those facilities able to dispose and recover them. Whereas the Environment Agency holds details of some 80,000 registered waste carriers operating in England and Wales, only a very limited number of these specialise in the collection of used tyres. The Used Tyre Working Group lists some 50 companies on its website (http://www.tyredisposal.co.uk), and collectively these account for most activity in this sector.

RESPONSIBLE RECYCLER SCHEME

The Tyre Industry Council's Responsible Recycler Scheme was established in 1999 to cement best practice in the tyre collection sector. A central plank of the scheme is an independent audit, which provides a visible demonstration of the propriety of members operations. The Scheme also now encompasses used tyre reprocessors, and as at May 2004, there are 19 collector and reprocessor members. Further information, including an up to date members list, can be found at http://www.tyresafety.co.uk.

Europe

Table 1, compiled from information in the Winter 2003-4 newsletter of the European Tyre Recycling Association[4], provides a snapshot of the current position in a number of other European countries.

A degree of caution should be exercised in interpreting this information, which should be viewed as indicative, rather than definitive. This is because there is no consistent approach in Member States to reporting arisings or recovery, and other issues, such as the extent to which arrangements put in place in individual Member States provide a partial or full response to the tyre landfill disposal ban.

In volume terms, Germany and France provide the closest comparisons with the UK. The former is pursuing a voluntary, market-led approach, and the latter, along with a growing number of other countries, a legislated, producer responsibility approach.

Forecast

It is extremely difficult to accurately forecast precisely when additional used tyre recovery capacity will be brought forward, and the extent to which this and existing capacity will actually be utilised. The picture is a dynamic and unpredictable one, and previous forecasts have almost inevitably not stood up well to the test of time.

Table 1 Tyre arisings and systems for recovery in various European States.

COUNTRY	ARISINGS (tonnes)	RECOVERY RATE	RESPONSIBILITY	As of	ORG.	FINANCE SYSTEM
Austria	50,000	90%	Last owner			Free market
Belgium	72,000	63%	PR	2003	Rectyre	Fund
Denmark	41,000	81%				Tax system
Finland	42,000	100%	PR	1995	SRO	Fund
France	390,000	53%	PR	2004	Aliapur	Fund
Germany	600,000	96%	Last owner			Free market
Greece	50,000	26%		2004	Ecolastika	
Italy	388,000	59%	Last owner			Free market
Ireland	32,000	45%	Last owner			
Netherlands	67,000	100%	PR	2003		Fund
Portugal	50,000	90%	PR	2002	Valorpneu	Fund
Spain	301,000	25%	Last owner/Env Min talks			
Sweden	64,000	100%	PR	1995	SDAB	Fund
UK	450,000	74%	Last owner			Free market

Nevertheless, it is important to try and look forward to form a view on the UK's ability to meet the certainty that is the 2006 landfill disposal ban, and the sustainability of the infrastructure thereafter.

Figure 6 below takes a central case view on capacity, rather than the tonnage various sectors may physically reprocess from 2004 to 2008, along with UTWG outturn figures for previous years. The statistics specifically exclude those used tyres that are brought back into use, (e.g. retreaded tyres, part-worn tyres, tyres used as barriers on go-kart tracks) as these are effectively retained within the system, and in due course will be disposed of and recovered. The arisings figure has been adjusted accordingly. This does not imply that these re-use activities are less worthy than other recovery options for used tyres, but for the sake of simplicity they can be excluded, whilst recognising, for example, that less retreading would result in the need for greater numbers of new tyres.

The forecast is not a sophisticated one. Exports and engineering uses are deemed to remain flat over the period, although engineering uses are likely to grow. Some commentators consider that the present tonnage attributed to engineering is understated, by up to as much as 50%. Clearly materials and energy recovery will be vital. The materials recovery figure, which includes the Anglo United pyrolysis plant, simply takes what is understood to be presently available processing capacity. While UTWG figures show considerable growth in this sector (the 2003 figure is over 50% higher than 2002), viable end-markets are the cornerstone of a sustainable used tyres materials sector, and these will need to develop further to take-up this available capacity. The energy recovery capacity is based on presently authorised facilities taking tyres at 90% of maximum capacity, with a further two, out of a potential four, facilities which have either run trials or are planning to do so, coming on line by 2006. In practicality, cement kiln use is likely to be somewhat less than these capacities, although it is still expected to grow strongly. Usage in 2004 is anticipated to be in excess of 100,000 tonnes, over 30% higher than in 2003.

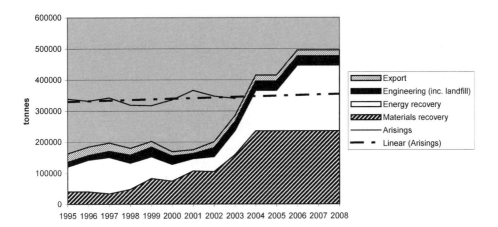

While clearly, uncertainty remains, used tyre reprocessors have reported a tightening in the used tyre supply position, with increased competition for available tyres, which has resulted in downward pressure on reprocessor gate prices. Many of the larger used tyre collectors, who up to a few years ago were landfilling very significant tonnages of tyres, have either already moved away completely from landfill disposal or have made good progress in this direction.

The prospects for meeting the requirements of the landfill disposal ban in good order appear encouraging.

REFERENCES

1   Statutory Instrument 1559/2002 The Landfill (England & Wales) Regulations 2002. Scottish Statutory Instrument 2003 No 235 The Landfill (Scotland) Regulations 2003. Statutory Rule 2003 No 496 The Landfill Regulations (NI) 2003.

2   DTI: Consultation on the Transposition of Articles 5 and 7 of the End-of-Life Vehicles Directive (2000/53/EC) February 2004 pp5-6.

3   DTI Discussion Paper on a Possible Producer Responsibility Model for Used Tyres, March 2002. DTI Follow-up Consultation on Used Tyre Recovery Issues, March 2003.

4   SHULMAN V. ETRA An EU-wide scheme for post consumer tyres? and F. Cinaralp The BLIC Strategy on the management of end of life tyres

PRODUCER RESPONSIBILITY FOR USED TYRES IN THE UK

J Dorken

British Rubber Manufacturers' Association

United Kingdom

ABSTRACT. The question of whether the concept of producer responsibility for the recovery of used tyres should be applied in the United Kingdom has been the subject of debate for some three years and at the time of writing the Government has still not taken a decision. The arguments are finely balanced but with the full ban on landfilling only some two years away time is running out to bring in a producer responsibility regime that has a chance of affecting the position on the ground at the time the ban starts to bite.

Keywords: Tyres, Producer responsibility, Landfill, Sustainability.

John D orken h as b een D irector o f t he B ritish R ubber M anufacturers' Association, w hich represents the interests of the main manufacturers of tyres, general rubber goods and flexible polyurethane foam in the UK, since 1997. He has led for the Association on the question of used tyre disposal over this period.

INTRODUCTION

Producer responsibility is one of the key tools in the locker of environmental policy formulators. It is defined by the OECD 'as an environmental policy approach in which a producer's responsibility, physical and/or financial is extended to the post consumer stage of a product's life cycle. There are two related features of EPR policy: 1) the shifting of responsibility upstream to the producer and away from the municipalities and 2) to provide incentives to producers to incorporate environmental considerations in the design of their products'. It is essentially an instrument to implement the 'polluter pays' principle, which aims to ensure that polluters meet the costs of the environmental impacts that their products generate by focusing costs on them rather than the downstream user or society more generally. In the EU context the work that is being done to follow up the Commission's 'Thematic Strategy on the Prevention and Recycling of Waste' and its strategy on Integrated Product Policy could lead to proposals for further producer responsibility. The notion is one to which many companies with an eye to the principle of corporate social responsibility pay particular heed.

In the UK, within the waste strategy set out in successive policy papers over the last decade, producer responsibility has been highlighted as a key instrument of change. The Government has already applied the principle to packaging waste and is currently implementing it for end of life vehicles and waste electrical and electronic equipment as a result of European Directives in these two areas. It has also been examining extension of the principle to other waste streams such as batteries, junk mail and newspapers as well as tyres.

For all its theoretical virtues producer responsibility does not provide a simple and neat route to constraining waste streams and assuring their effective handling. The key challenge is to accommodate commercial realities without diluting the essential value of the tool. The fact is that the 'producers' are not a few powerful manufacturers, who can be readily identified and brought into line. In reality – in an open economy – they will run into hundreds if not thousands if the policy is implemented on a purely national basis since they will have to cover importers if a level playing field is to be maintained. This means that a voluntary approach is difficult to achieve and, if as a result a statutory regime is applied, that has to be complex if it is to be effective.

Thus the legislators are bound to be cautious in applying the tool. It is also the case that many products that are possible candidates for such treatment are marketed globally and if the manufacturers are to be incentivised to design their products with a view to maintaining stewardship over the whole of their lifecycle the producer responsibility principle has to be applied over a substantial proportion of the markets for the product.

USED TYRES PRODUCER RESPONSIBILITY: EUROPEAN DIMENSION

In contrast to other waste streams addressed at the European level – particularly end of life vehicles and waste electrical and electronic equipment – the concept of producer responsibility has never been formally applied at the European level in the case of the recovery of used tyres. It has long been prayed in aid on a voluntary basis. Indeed it featured in the work done in Europe in the early 1990s when used tyres were identified as a priority waste stream. This work was never however taken to the point of a Directive requiring certain levels of recovery or recycling of used tyres. Instead the focus switched to banning the landfilling of tyres – prescribing what <u>could not</u> be done, rather than what <u>should</u> be done. In short the EU decided as part of the Landfill Directive (1999/31/EC) that as from 16 July 2003 tyres in whole form could not longer be landfilled in the EU and as from 16 July 2006 the ban should extend to tyres in shredded form as well. The only exception are bicycle tyres and tyres with a diameter in excess of 1400 mm though in practice tyres may also be used for engineering purposes at landfill sites.

What is notably missing in the legislation is any reference to producer responsibility, in sharp contrast to say the End of Life Vehicles Directive. This is not to say that the concept has faded into the background. In several European states the legislation implementing this element o f t he Landfill Directive h as n ot b een a s imple m atter o f p rescribing t he b an b ut rather establishing a regime based on the principle of producer responsibility for achieving re-use, recycling and recovery. In others such legislation is being considered. Only in a minority of states, notably Germany, has a regime of statutory producer responsibility been ruled out.

There is no doubt that a uniform set of rules across the Union would make the application of the ban a good deal simpler; thereby a level playing field would be created and the potential distortions to patterns of trade, which comes of having different sets of rules in different countries, would be avoided. However the Commission to date has set its face against proposing such a common set of rules or even putting forward any guidelines, and, though the main manufacturers in the Union are trying to establish such commonality as is possible on the basis of statutory producer responsibility, the aspiration of a common system by the time the ban bites is a mere dream and seems unlikely ever to be fulfilled to the degree that a recognisably level playing field across member states is created.

USED TYRES PRODUCER RESPONSIBILITY IN THE UNITED KINGDOM

The notion that producer responsibility has a place in the development and implementation of policy on used tyres has been accepted in the UK for the last decade or so. All elements in the new tyre supply chain were involved in the debates that went on in the early 1990s on the line to be taken on the EU proposals that were then current and in 1995 the Government/Industry Used Tyre Working Group was established embracing all these parties, and that has been at the centre of policy debate ever since. These parties included the manufacturers despite the fact that they had little commercially or physically to do with the used tyre disposal chain. Their contribution included the financial support of studies into the use of tyres as a barrier against coastal erosion and entering into long term contracts for the supply of tyres to support a technologically innovative tyres-to-electricity plant in the Midlands.

From around 2000 onwards the need to ensure that the landfill ban was introduced without giving rise to undue stockpiling or increasing levels of flytipping added a new dimension to the debate on the appropriate level of industry responsibility for the problem of disposal. The arguments have always been finely balanced.

On the one hand:

- on the whole the UK has had a good record in progressing towards 100% recovery without the need for formal intervention . Over the late 1990s there was steady increase in the rates of recovery so that they reached 73% in 1999. It is true that in

2000 and 2001 they had fallen back sharply in the light of the demise of the tyres-to-electricity plant and the continuing decline in passenger tyre rereading but by 2002 rates of recovery had largely bounced back and it is estimated that they reached around 80% by 2003;

- the UK has a very good infrastructure for collecting tyres which is well able to respond to changes in the marketplace. In addition the reprocessing market is diverse without over-reliance on any particular form of recovery;

- there is a generally good collegiate spirit in the industry, which provides a good basis for voluntary action to be taken as needed. A good example has been the establishment of the 'Responsible Recycler Scheme' whereby tyre collecting companies are audited for strict compliance with waste management requirements in disposing of the product.

On the other hand:

- what has happened in the past is not necessarily a guide to what will happen in the future. It is one thing to move steadily towards 100% recovery when there is always the option of landfilling to act as a safety valve if objectives are not achieved. It is quite another thing to achieve 100% recovery year-in, year-out;

- when the landfilling option, which tends to the cheapest in many cases, is finally removed recovery costs will arguably rise substantially, increasing the incentive to fly tip. A more controlled regime, relying less on compliance with generic duty of care legislation, could be needed to counteract this risk;

- reprocessors of tyres, especially those that can use alternate materials such as cement producers, are not in the business of providing a service for the generators of used tyres and will switch to alternate materials if it suits their commercial interests. The market is not very good at providing the signals in time to enable appropriate action to taken to provide alternate outlets for the volume of tyres at issue. A more managed regime is arguably more likely to provide sustainable long term solutions and thus reduce the risk of shortfall in recovery.

The debate continues. The main manufacturers accept that the concept of producer responsibility should be applied to the manufacturers and other suppliers into the market and would like to see the concept take the form of full statutory producer responsibility: they see this as the only way in the long term to ensure that 100% recovery can be achieved on a sustainable basis and see this as consistent with the way the world will be moving in the future, with manufacturers increasingly being required to exercise stewardship over their products from cradle to grave. Their espousal of this approach is however conditional on there being a robust enforcement regime so that there is an effective level playing field for all suppliers into the market – big or small, importers or domestic manufacturers.

Other players see the merits of such a regime, properly enforced, but are concerned to see that the system goes with the grain of the current market, not one that puts the control firmly in the hands of the suppliers; they tend to the view that, with recovery rates improving as they are, there is a less of a case for full statutory producer responsibility, at least at present. The Government has yet – even almost a year after the closing date for responses to its second consultation document – to reveal its position, but there are signs that it is shying away from imposing full statutory producer responsibility. This is not surprising: to operate a system that captures all the myriad suppliers into the market (reckoned to be upwards of 200) will be demanding on Government resources and expensive both for the Government and industry, with the cost ultimately being paid by the consumer. It is clearly a step only to be taken if the benefits of assuring full recovery make it worthwhile. However the delays in reaching a conclusion has meant that it will be less easy to put in place a regime, statutory or otherwise, that will affect the position on the ground when the full ban comes into effect.

What is clear is that one way or the other if statutory responsibility is not imposed the industry will remain fully involved in making the ban work with as little environmentally adverse effect as possible. Of course the manufacturers – or indeed any supplier into the market - cannot be expected to take on de facto responsibility for ensuring 100% recovery or zero flytipping when it is not given the means to do so. That will always in the end remain the responsibility of Government. Nor can they expected on a voluntarily basis to incur a level of costs in providing support to Government that puts their competitive position vis-a-vis other suppliers into the market under threat when the latter do not make a similar contribution. But they will do whatever they can within these constraints to make the non-statutory regime work, such as developing and participating in data collection and monitoring systems, giving active support for the Responsible Recycler Scheme and monitoring the impact of other EU regimes on trade flows. Through such close involvement they will be best placed to help with taking the action required should full recovery be under threat in the future, taking on more formal responsibilities if this proves necessary.

SESSION TWO:

GENERATION, HANDLING AND CURRENT SITUATION

RECYCLING AND REUSE OF WASTE TYRES IN SOUTH AFRICA

J Bester

D Kruger

A Hinks

R.A.U. University

South Africa

ABSTRACT. There are an estimated ten million waste tyres in South Africa of which only about 10% - 15% are recycled. Following the release of a document called "The Minimum Requirements for Waste Disposal for Landfill", waste minimisation, recycling and treatment were promoted.

Due to the steady increase in landfill operators not accepting waste tyres, many tyres are being illegally scrapped or burnt.

The South African government is in the process of introducing legislation, stating that all new tyres sold in South Africa will be subjected to an environmental levy. The funds obtained will be used to fund the collection of waste tyres, thereafter being recycled.

More light needs to be shed on the current situation of the legislation issued by the government.

Keywords: Waste tyres, Legislation, Tyre collection, Environmental levy, Retreaded tyres, Chipped rubber particles, Rubber chunks, Crumped rubber.

J J Bester is a member of the Institute of Concrete Technologists and is a researcher in the Research Group for Polymers in Concrete at RAU University in Johannesburg, South Africa.

D Kruger is a professional Civil Engineer and head of the Research Group for Polymers in Concrete at RAU University in Johannesburg, South Africa.

A Hinks is a registered student in the Department Civil and Urban Engineering and is in his third year of study at RAU University in Johannesburg, South Africa.

INTRODUCTION

There are an estimated twenty two million waste tyres stockpiled in South Africa, growing at an amount of ten million a year, and only about 10% - 15% of these are recycled.

Traditionally the remaining waste tyres were landfilled, illegally dumped, retreaded or burned. In the mid 1990's the Department of Water Affairs and Forestry (DWAF), after much-wide spread consultation, released a document called "The Minimum Requirements for Waste Disposal for Landfill". This document has had the effect of increased costs for landfilling waste thus promoting waste minimisation, recycling and treatment [1].

Associated problems with landfilling tyres caused many landfills in South Africa to disallow waste tyres onto their premises.

The South African government is in the process of introducing legislation, stating that all new tyres sold in South Africa will be subjected to an environmental levy. The funds obtained from this levy will be used to fund the collection of waste tyres.

RECYCLING TECHNOLOGIES

Scrap tyres can be used for:

- *Fuel in Cement Kilns:* The cement kiln has a high and continuous fuel requirement making it an ideal process for the recovery of energy from waste materials such as tyres.

- *Production of Electricity:* Several studies have concluded that the use of scrap tyres as an a lternative e nergy s ource (34 9 20 k ilojoules (kJ) p er k ilogram, w hich i s g reater than most forms of coal) is the most cost-effective method of utilizing waste tyres [2].

- *Artificial Reefs:* Recent research has shown that an artificial reef can be constructed using w aste t yres. T he r eefs a ct a s a s helter f or m any o rganisms, l ike p out, b rown algae, red algae, crabs and lobsters. There are high zinc levels present in waste tyres which may be detrimental to the reef but the potential damage is not yet known.

- *Recycled Steel Wires as Reinforcement in Concrete:* The main purpose of adding steel fibres to concrete is to control cracking, increase toughness and altar surface characteristics. Wires obtained for the shredding process contain impurities such as rubber and different wire thicknesses, creating a harsh concrete mix.

- *Other Applications include:*
    - In civil engineering works e.g. highway crash barriers
    - As cover material in agricultural application
    - As material to be cut up into mats, floor tiles, dock fenders etc.

CURRENT SITUATION IN SOUTH AFRICA

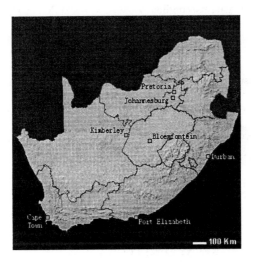

Figure 1: Map Showing Major Cities in South Africa [3]

Large quantities of scrap tyres are illegally dumped in the veldt or burnt to recover the scrap steel. The smoke generated from these fires contributes significantly to air pollution which creates health problems, such as respiratory ailments. Discarded tyres are also a breeding ground for mosquitoes, flies, rodents and certain disease.

Many faulty tyre casing end up as second hand tyres on vehicles contributing to the excessive road accident statistics.

LANDFILLING

The document of DWAF focuses on the forth component of integrated waste management being disposal. Before the introduction of this document, many landfills in South Africa have been badly sited, designed and operated. This document is a vast improvement in the standards of waste disposal causing the increased costs of landfilling. This has had the effect that waste disposal is less attractive which in turn makes waste minimisation, recycling and treatment more economically viable [1].

CURRENT LANDFILLING PRACTICES

As can be seen from Figure 2, tyres are no longer landfilled for the reason that they "migrate" to the surface causing visual and environmental impact. This migration may be attributed to the differential densities between the rubber and the soil it is disposed in. Associated problems with this are fire hazards, which lead to smoke hazards and aesthetical problems.

Figure 2: Landfilled tyres "migrating" to the surface

THE PROPOSED TYRE COLLECTION PROCESS

The tyre industry is assembling a scrap tyre collection process that will make the waste tyres available to private enterprises for recycling purposes. The South African Tyre Recycling Process Company (SATRP Co) will not get involved in the recycling process itself, but will be involved in the management of the process.

All the stakeholders in South Africa have been involved in the planning of the process for the collection of the waste tyres and their delivery to the recyclers. The collection of close to 90 000 tonnes of scrap tyres from every town and major city in South Africa will require a disciplined and well-regulated collection process.

Large and specialised transport vehicles and equipment will be needed. It is proposed that the collection process be contracted to companies specialising in the collection of waste products with an existing infrastructure. The collector will be required to make provision for stockpiling of waste tyres. The proposed process is briefly described in the following sections.

GOVERNANCE

The members of the local tyre manufacturers, importers and retreaders have formed a Section 21 Company (non-profit organisation) to implement and manage the collection process. All stakeholders are being consulted and numerous publications have appeared in the general press throughout the country.

PROVINCIAL COLLECTION AGENCY

The provincial collection agencies will be appointed by the Section 21 Company to arrange for the collection and transportation of the waste tyres from registered dealers and retreaders to the end users. No money will be paid for scrap tyres collected. The dealers and retreaders will b e r equired t o a ssist w ith l oading t he t yres onto t he c ollecting t rucks a nd r etreadable casings will have to be identified and removed before scrap tyres are collected.

ENVIRONMENTAL TYRE LEVY

It is estimated that the collection and transportation process will cost over US $11 million. Therefore an environmental levy will be instituted by the tyre manufacturers and importers to pay for the collection process. The manufacturers and importers will add this environmental levy, which is 1% of the tyre price, as a separate line item on the invoice to the dealer [4]. The tyre dealer will pass the levy onto the consumer at the same rate, without adding a profit margin.

The environmental levy only applies to new tyres. During the first y ear of operation, only passenger, light and heavy commercial tyres will be subjected to the environmental levy and collection. Tyres exported will be exempted from the levy, as they do not contribute to the scrap tyre problem in South Africa.

Value Added Tax (VAT), at 14% is payable on the environmental levy and all suppliers and dealers will charge the same levy. The environmental levy will be instituted before the actual collections start in order to build up a fund for the collection process.

An audit company will be appointed to verify the financials of the stakeholders.

Casings imported for retreading will be subjected to a green fee, payable by the importer. This is because the casings add to the waste stockpile occurring in South Africa. This fee will be absorbed in the cost of retreading the imported casing and in the selling price to the end user.

Discussions are being held with vehicle and equipment manufacturers, government tender board and other bulk tyre consumers that buy directly from the tyre suppliers, to recover an environmental levy and link it into the above processes.

The legislation for the environmental levy should be brought in by April 2004.

BENEFITS

Numerous benefits will be derived with the introduction of this project. Some are as follows:

- *Creating a new industry:* There is a total of 12 plants in South Africa of which one plant is producing rubber crumb, one utilizing rubber crumb and the others are smaller entrepreneurs making mats, sandals, etc.
  New investors are planning an additional five to twenty plants once the tyre collection process is established. Electricity and cement producers should remain a constant consumer of waste tyres once legally converted to accept scrap rubber as part of their fuel source.

- *Exports:* New and small entrepreneurs can export the manufactured product from recycled rubber into new and developing markets worldwide. The South African

Balance of Payments and economy will benefit as well as the unemployment situation. There are approximately 250 products that can be made from recycled rubber, such as rubber mating, shoes, tank linings, rubber mouldings, road tar additives etc.

- *Pollution Reduction:* Four major pollution problems will be eliminated with the collection process:

  ➤ *Water retention:* Tyres form an ideal receptacle for water thus becoming breeding grounds for insects, rodents and diseases. Spraying these tyres to control these hazards is costly and ineffective.

  ➤ *Fire:* A large stockpile of scrap tyres forms a serious fire hazard and once burning, becomes virtually impossible to extinguish.

  ➤ *Smoke:* Burning tyres for the recovery of scrap steel generates acrid smoke which causes respiratory problems and air pollution.

  ➤ *Waste Tyre Stockpiles*: Unsightly stockpiles reduce the value of the surrounding property (4).

ROAD SAFETY

The Department of Transport (DoT) reports that up to 53% of vehicle component failure accidents are caused by tyre failure. The use of second hand tyres is considered the biggest contributor. Owners of tyres discard them as being weathered or damaged. Unscrupulous traders collect, patch or re-groove these tyres which are then sold resulting in them bursting after short use and people are killed in the process.

PERFORMANCE AND SAFETY OF RETREADED TYRES

Around 80% of worn passenger tyres or casing are unsuitable for retreading, the majority of which are rejected only b y virtue of the brand of tyre. Depending of the tread formula or compound used for retreading, a retreaded tyre can have equal mileage to that of a new tyre.

New tyres are subjected to a drum test, which simulates an inflated tyre under load running on the road. In South Africa regulations for retreaded tyres was only introduced towards the end of 2003, as a result the South African Bureau of Standards (SABS) has not set up a testing station to test the quality of retreaded tyres.

WASTE TYRE RECYCLING PLANT

The initial capital cost of a recycling plant could cost anything from US $ 20.5 to US $ 34.5 million. The operating costs are high due to operation of big equipment which consumes large amounts of electricity and requires constant maintenance. After an Environmental Impact Assessment (EIA) the Department of Environmental Affairs will issue the required permit to build the factory while constant monitoring of the surrounding area will be required.

ABILITY OF THE RECYCLERS TO ABSORB THE SCRAP COLLECTED

Provision h as b een m ade t o c ommit 5 0% o f t he c ollections t o r ecyclers a nd 5 0% t o T yre Derived Fuel (TDF) users in the initial stages of the tyre collection process. This allocation will change once the market is established and experience is gained (4).

ALTERNATIVE USES FOR RECYCLED RUBBER

- *Using Chipped Rubber Particles as a Course Aggregate in Concrete:* The use of chipped rubber as a coarse aggregate may be used to produce a concrete for structural use which has a lower unit weight than conventional concrete. The inclusion of rubber tyre particles results in the decrease of the fresh concrete slump and an increase in the air content. The impact resistance is improved using up to 50% of the rubber aggregate. The authors do not know of any projects in South Africa using this application.

- *The Use of Rubber Chunks as a Partial Aggregate in Asphalt:* The production of the material involves the addition of the rubber chunks to hot aggregate prior to mixing with bitumen. The material is then mixed and kept at a high temperature until compaction. The rheological properties of the residual bitumen are affected by the interaction with the rubber chunks leading to an increase in stiffness and a decrease in phase angle (a more elastic response).

- *The Use of Crumb Rubber as a Partial Replacement for Bitumen:* In a normal spray and chip sealing operation between 18 and 22% of the bitumen is replaced with the corresponding percentage crumbed rubber. This product is then mixed heated to a minimum operating temperature of 160°C. It is placed at a temperature of between 180 and 220°C and normal chip operations follow. This product is commonly known as Bitumen-Rubber in South Africa. Figure 3 shows an example of such a blending and heating process.

Figure 3: Rubber Crumb being processed into Rubber Bitumen

CONCLUSIONS

With the implementation of the "Minimum Requirements for Waste Disposal by Landfill", there has been a steady increase in the number of landfill operators that do not accept waste tyres on their premises. This has opened the window for entrepreneurs and other industries to recycle, re-use or recover the energy from the waste tyres.

With an average tyre taking over eighty years to biodegrade, the South African government has had to implement legislation that will induce the recovery of used tyres. If this legislation works, it will create a new industry, with jobs and a cleaner and safer environment.

REFERENCES

1.   Minimum Requirements for Waste Disposal by Landfill, Department of Water Affairs and Forestry, South Africa, 1998.

2.   DHIR R.K, PAINE K.A. LIMBACHIYA M.C. Recycling and reuse of Used Tyres, Cement and Concrete Institute, Britain, 2001, p217.

3.   www.saexplorer.co.za, 16/01/2004.

4.   C. van Gass, Squezing mileage out of Scrap Tyres, Business Day, South Africa, 08/08/2003.

5.   www.rubbersa.com, 17/11/2003 .

SESSION THREE:

MAIN OUTLETS, MATERIAL RECYCLING AND REUSE IN VALUE-ADDED APPLICATIONS

PYROLYSIS; AN ENVIRONMENTALLY ATTRACTIVE RECYCLING ROUTE FOR USED TYRES

P T Williams

The University of Leeds

United Kingdom

ABSTRACT. It is estimated that approximately 250 million used tyres are generated in Europe per year representing a severe economic and environmental disposal problem. The treatment and disposal option for tyres most commonly used throughout the European Union is landfilling, however, European Commission legislation in the form of the European Waste Landfill Directive has the specific proposal to prohibit the landfilling of whole or shredded tyres. In addition, as the costs of disposal inevitably increase illegal dumping is likely to increase. Pyrolysis of used tyres represents a possible attractive recycling route for used tyres, utilising the resource of used tyres. Pyrolysis involves the thermal degradation of the rubber of the tyre to give an oil and gas leaving a residual solid carbon and the steel casing of the tyre. The solid carbon residue left after pyrolysis has potential as a solid fuel or as a low grade carbon black or may be upgraded to activated carbon. The derived oil may be used as a fuel or or upgraded to a chemical feedsoctock. The pyrolysis gases have sufficient energy value that they can be used to provide the energy requirements of the pyrolysis process. The recovered steel may also be recycled back into the steel industry. The current management of used tyres is presented and the potential of pyrolysis to produce useful products is discussed

Keywords: Tyres, Pyrolysis, Recycling, Fuels, Activated Carbon

Professor Paul T. Williams is Professor of Environmental Engineering in the Energy and Resources Research Institute at The University of Leeds and has a research background in both applied chemistry and process engineering. He has published more than 200 academic papers in the area of environmental engineering, including waste incineration and waste and biomass pyrolysis. He is a member of the Editorial Boards of the journals, Environmental Technology and of Fuel.

INTRODUCTION

Approximately 250 million car and truck tyres are scrapped each year in Europe representing about 3 million tonnes by weight of tyre. The worldwide generation of scrap tyres is estimated at 1000 million tyres/year. The generation of waste tyres are linked to the generation of end of life vehicles. The European Union has attempted to control the management of end of life vehicles and tyres through the 2000 End of Life Vehicle Directive (Council Directive 2000/53/EC). The Directive stipulates the separate collection of tyres from vehicle dismantlers and encourages the recycling of tyres. In addition, the 1999 Waste Landfill Directive (Council Directive 1999/31/EC) seeks to ban the landfilling of tyres by 2006. These two Directive's will inevitably impact on the management of tyres throughout the European Union. The main routes for management of waste tyres in Western Europe (2002) are landfill, energy recovery, material recycling, retreading and export [1] (Figure 1).

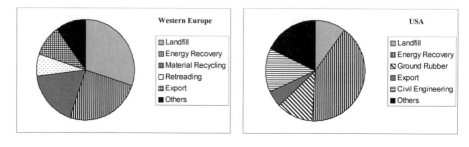

Figure 1. Management of used tyres in Western Europe and the USA

Landfilling of tyres is declining as a disposal option in the EU, to comply with the 1999 EC Waste Landfill Directive. In addition, tyres do not degrade easily in landfills, they are bulky, and can cause instability within the landfill, indeed, many landfill sites refuse to take tyres. In addition, they can be a breeding ground for insects and a home for vermin.

Energy recovery utilises the high calorific value of tyres, about 32 MJ kg^{-1}, and currently accounts for about 25% of the total tyre waste arisings in Western Europe. Waste tyre fuelled incineration plants operate successfully in Germany, Italy and also the USA and Japan [1]. Cement kilns have also been used for the disposal of tyres by combustion to offset the high energy costs associated with cement production. Most of the major cement manufacturers throughout the world use tyres as a fuel source. The tyres are fed directly to the rotary kiln of the process where very high temperatures of the order of 1500 °C ensure complete burnout of the tyre. The metal and ash components of the tyre are incorporated into the cement clinker. Waste tyres are also used in other energy intensive industries such as the pulp and paper industry.

Materials recycling of waste tyres includes the production of rubber crumb which is derived from tyres via shredding and grinding of the rubber part of the tyre to produce a fine grained product for use in such applications as children's playgrounds, sports surfaces, carpet backing and other applications such as absorbents for oils and hazardous and chemical wastes. Rubber reclaim consists of devulcanisation of the rubber by temperature and pressure with various reclaiming chemicals and solvent treatments to produce a rubber which can be used in low grade applications. Such applications include cycle tyres, conveyor belts and footwear.

Retreading of tyres, where a new rubber tread is bonded to the surface of worn tyres accounts for about 10% of annual tyre consumption in Western Europe. The process involves grinding of the tyre surface to produce a clean surface onto which the new rubber is bonded. Car tyres can be retread once only but truck tyres may be retread up to three times. Other routes for the management of scrap tyres includes dumping and stockpiling. This is unsightly and has the potential for accidental fires or arson resulting in high pollution emissions to the atmosphere and water courses.

In the USA in 2001 it was estimated that the production of scrap tyres was 280 million tyres [2]. In addition, it is estimated that there is a stockpile of 500 million tyres awaiting disposal. The main methods of scrap tyre disposal in the USA are energy recovery in cement kilns, pulp and paper works, tyre incinerators and boilers which accounts for 40.9% of the arisings of scrap tyres or some 114 million tyres. About 10% of tyres are landfilled, 14.2% used in civil engineering applications including drainage aggregates, bulk fill aggregates, insulation and landfill engineering. Approximately 1 1.7% of tyres are recycled in g round rubber applications and 5.3% exported [2]. The route for the remaining 17.9% includes miscellaneous methods and a significant proportion (12.5%) where the disposal route is unknown (Figure 1). In the USA, retread tyres are not considered in many scrap tyre data statistics since they are deemed as still to be in use and are only finally scrapped when they cannot be retread further.

TYRE PYROLYSIS

With the increasing emphasis on recovery and recycling of waste throughout the world, there is increasing interest in the development of such technologies for used tyres. One such recovery option is pyrolysis. Pyrolysis of tyres involves the thermal degradation of the rubber o f the t yre t o p roduce a n o il a nd gas p roduct l eaving a r esidual c har a nd t he s teel casing of the tyre [3-5]. The char is very friable and therefore the steel may be easily separated from the char for recycling back into the iron and steel industry. The char may be used as a source of solid fuel or has properties which may be suitable for its use as a low grade activated carbon or carbon black [3] (Table 1). The char has a calorific value of 30 MJ kg^{-1}, and may be regarded as a reasonable solid fuel, it has a high ash and sulphur content. The potential use of the char as a low grade activated carbon should be balanced by the low surface area of 64 m^{2}g^{-1} which compares with commercial activated carbons which typically range in surface area between 500 and 1500 m^{2}g^{-1}. The chars are mainly mesoporous which are defined as pores of radius 2-50 nm.

Depending on process conditions, the oil is produced in high yields of over 55 wt% and is of low viscosity suitable for easy storage and transportation. The conversion of the tyre to an easily storable liquid means that the energy density stored is much greater than that of bulky tyres in a stockpile which have a large void volume within the tyre casing and between the packed tyres. The tyre pyrolysis oil is also easily transportable by pipeline and tanker, a more advantageous situation compared to transporting bulky tyres. The liquid is hydrocarbon in character suitable for use as a fuel (Table 1). The oil has a high calorific value and has been shown to burn efficiently in furnace combustion systems [6]. However, it has a high sulphur and nitrogen content, a low flash point and often contains fine char particles [6]. The combustion of the tyre pyrolysis oil shows that increased sulphur dioxide and nitrogen oxides emissions have been found compared to combustion of gas oil, attributable to the higher sulphur and nitrogen content of the tyre oil. The oil also contains certain chemicals which gives the oil the potential as a chemical feedstock [5,6]. Detailed analyses of the oils has also shown them to contain significant concentrations of polycyclic aromatic hydrocarbons [6]. Amongst the chemical groups, polycyclic aromatic hydrocarbons are known to be of environmental concern, since some compounds are mutagenic and/or carcinogenic. The concentration of such species can reach significant concentrations [6]. The main polycyclic aromatic hydrocarbons in the tyre oil are naphthalene, fluorene and phenanthrene and their alkylated derivatives. In lower concentrations are acenaphthene, acenaphthylene, fluoranthene, pyrene, benzofluorenes, chrysene and benzopyrenes. The environmental impact of significant concentrations of polycyclic aromatic hydrocarbons in tyre pyrolysis oils may limit their substitution for petroleum derived fuels. However, such compounds are also present in petroleum derived fuels such as gas oil and light fuel oil. In addition, combustion of the tyre pyrolysis oils has shown that the combustion emissions contained negligible concentrations of such species [6].

The gas composition from tyre pyrolysis is mainly composed of alkane and alkene gases, carbon monoxide, carbon dioxide and hydrogen and also hydrogen sulphide (Table 1). Butadiene is also a primary product of pyrolysis and is found in high concentration in the gas phase. Carbon monoxide is released early in the pyrolysis process, peaking at between 300 °C and 350 °C. Carbon dioxide is also evolved early in pyrolysis but continues throughout the pyrolysis process. The higher molecular weight hydrocarbons, C_2 to C_4 are evolved mostly in the later stages of tyre pyrolysis. The gross calorific value (GCV) of the gases is between 35 and 58 MJ m^{-3} depending on pyrolysis temperature, reaching a maximum at 500 °C. The increasing GCV up to this temperature is due to the increased production of hydrocarbons, particularly butene and hydrogen. The subsequent decrease is due to methane, ethane and hydrogen becoming more important components of the gas. Because the GCV of fuel gases is calculated on a volumetric basis, these lower molecular weight gases have a much lower GCV than heavier molecular weight and more saturated hydrocarbons. The GCV of the gases was high and the gases represent a very good gaseous fuel and with sufficient energy content to provide the energy requirements to heat the pyrolysis reactor. This demonstrates one of the main advantages of pyrolysis as a treatment technology for scrap tyres, in that the off-gases from pyrolysis can be combusted to provide the heat requirements of the pyrolysis process.

Table 1. Properties of tyre pyrolysis char, gas and oil

CHAR		GAS (wt%)		OIL	
Moisture (wt%)	0.4	CH_4	0.81	Carbon Residue (%)	2.2
Volatiles (wt%)	2.8	C_2H_6	0.30	Viscosity	
Ash (wt%)	11.9	C_3H_8	0.32	60 °C (cs)	2.38
C (wt% daf)	90.6	C_4H_{10}	0.25	40 °C (cs)	6.30
H (wt% daf)	0.9	C_2H_4	1.16	Flash Point (°C)	20
N (wt% daf)	0.7	C_3H_6	0.51	Initial B.Pt. (°C)	100
S (wt% daf)	2.3	C_4H_8	0.32	10% B.Pt. (°C)	140
CV (MJ kg^{-1})	30.5	C_4H_6	1.92	50% B.Pt. (°C)	264
Surface area (m^2 g^{-1})	64	H_2	0.16	90% B.Pt. (°C)	355
Mesopore area (m^2 g^{-1})	33	CO	0.09	Moisture (%Vol.)	4.6
Mesopore radius (Å)	60	CO_2	0.32	S (wt%)	1.5
				N (wt%)	0.5
				CV (MJ kg^{-3})	42.1

Tyres contain vulcanised rubber in addition to the rubberised fabric with reinforcing textile cords, steel or fabric belts and steel-wire reinforcing beads. A number of different natural and synthetic rubbers and rubber formulations are used to produce tyres. Other components in the tyre include; carbon black which is used to strengthen the rubber and aid abrasion resistance; extender oil which is a mixture of aromatic hydrocarbons and serves to soften the rubber and improve workability; sulphur which is used to cross link the polymer chains within the rubber and also to harden and prevent excessive deformation at elevated temperatures; an accelerator, typically an organo-sulphur compound, added as a catalyst for the vulcanisation process; zinc oxide and stearic acid used to control the vulcanisation process and to enhance the physical properties of the rubber [7]. Consequently, it may be expected that different tyres produced from different manufacturers to different specifications may produce a range of product yields and composition. However it has been shown that essentially there is no difference in tyre product yield of char, oil and gas (Table 2) [7]. The yield of char, oil and gas were very similar for a range of tyres and a mixture of the tyres produced a pyrolysis yield consistent with the data obtained from the individual tyres. However, there was significant variation in the gas composition of the individual tyres, with a wide range in the concentration of carbon dioxide, carbon monoxide, hydrogen methane and other hydrocarbon gases found. The oil derived from the pyrolysis of the tyres showed very similar broad compositional properties as measured by infra-red spectrometry [7].

Table 2. Product yield for the pyrolysis of different tyre brands

TYRE BRAND	CHAR (wt%)	OIL (wt%)	GAS (wt%)	TOTAL (wt%)
1. Debica (Poland)	37.5	59.8	2.3	99.6
2. Eurotour (Korea)	37.5	59.7	2.3	99.5
3. Dunlop (Japan)	38.0	56.6	4.1	98.7
4. Goodyear (S.Africa)	37.1	60.1	2.5	99.7
5. Courier (Italy)	38.0	59.6	2.3	99.9
6. Michelin (Italy)	41.7	57.1	1.9	100.7
7. Continental (UK)	38.3	58.7	2.3	99.3
Mean	38.3	58.8	2.5	99.6
Mixture of 7 Tyres	37.9	60.1	2.4	100.4

ENHANCED TYRE PYROLYSIS

Whilst there has been interest in the pyrolysis process since it represents an environmentally attractive route to recycle tyres and produce products which may be recycled as low grade carbon or an oil which may be used as fuel and with the added advantage that the gas produced may be used to provide the energy for the pyrolysis process, there remains resistance to the use of the recovered oil and char. Consequently, research has developed into the enhancement of the pyrolysis process to improve the quality of the derived oil and char.

The use of temperature selective condensation has been used to concentrate the single ring aromatic chemicals known to be present in tyre pyrolysis oils (Figure 2). Such chemicals include benzene, toluene, xylenes (dimethylbenzenes), styrene, limonene and indene.

Benzene and toluene have a wide range of applications as a chemical feedstock and are used for example, in the production of plastics, resins, pesticides, dyestuffs, surfactants and solvents. Styrene is one of the most important building blocks used in the production of plastic materials and is also used to make synthetic rubber and other polymers. Xylenes are regarded as major industrial chemicals and have applications in the plastics industry, toluene is used for example, in the production of pesticides, dyestuffs, surfactants and solvents. Also, indene is used to produce indene/coumarone resins used in the production of adhesives and in paint manufacture and limonene used in the formulation of industrial solvents, resins and adhesives and as a dispersing agent for pigments. Temperature selective condensation enables the concentration of such high value chemicals to be increased, by enabling the heavier molecular mass species to be condensed separately from the lighter, lower molecular, mass aromatic compounds [8]. Condensers held at 100 °C, 150 °C, 200 °C and 250 °C showed that enhanced concentrations of xylenes, toluene and limonene could be obtained (Figure 2).

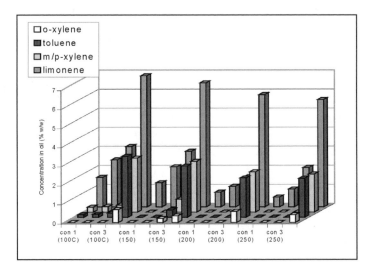

Figure 2. Selective temperature condensation to produce increased concentrations of aromatic compounds in tyre pyrolysis oils.

Single ring higher value aromatic chemicals have also been increased in concentration by the application of low temperature zeolite catalysis to the tyre pyrolysis process. Upgrading the tyre pyrolysis oil has been carried out using on-line zeolite catalysis [9-11]. The oil vapours and gases produced during pyrolysis were passed directly over a heated zeolite type catalyst at 500 °C and the product oils condensed in a condensation system. The aim of the experiments was to use catalyst technology to significantly increase the concentration of valuable aromatic hydrocarbons in the derived oils and thereby increase their potential value. A range of zeolite catalysts with differing pore sizes and surface acidities have been investigated [9-11]. Analysis of the oils derived from the catalytic pyrolysis of tyres for benzene, toluene, m-, p-, and o-xylene, and limonene, in relation to catalyst:tyre ratio for Y-zeolite (CBV-400) catalyst is shown in Figure 3. It can be seen that as the catalyst:tyre ratio was increased there was a dramatic rise in concentration of benzene, toluene and the xylenes.

The maximum concentration of each hydrocarbon, was benzene, 5.2 wt%, toluene 24.3 wt%, m/p-xylene 20.2 wt% and o-xylene 7 wt%, representing a very high concentration of these chemicals. Conversely, there was a complete loss of limonene. Other compounds identified in the catalytic oils were alkylated single ring aromatic hydrocarbons and polycyclic aromatic hydrocarbons mainly of two and three rings and their alkylated derivatives. The higher molecular weight polycyclic aromatic compounds found in the uncatalysed tyre pyrolysis oils were reduced in favour of mainly naphthalene and alklylated naphthalenes [9]

Inevitably, because of the catalytic reactions involved, the oil yield showed a decrease when the catalyst was used and a corresponding increase in the gas yield and formation of carbonaceous coke on the catalyst. For example, at an equivalent catalyst:tyre feed ratio of 1:1.5, there was a reduction in oil yield from 56 wt% for the uncatalysed pyrolysis to 32 wt% and gas yield increase by 14 wt% to 20 wt%. Deposition of carbonaceous coke on the catalyst was 10.1 wt%. Carbonaceous coke has been shown to result from a range of hydrocarbon reactions with zeolite catalysts, involving, in particular alkenes and aromatic hydrocarbons which are known to be present in high concentrations in tyre pyrolysis oils. The increase in gas yield in the presence of the catalyst was attributed to catalytic cracking reactions on zeolite catalysts has been shown to increase the production of C_3-C_6 hydrocarbon gases [9-11].

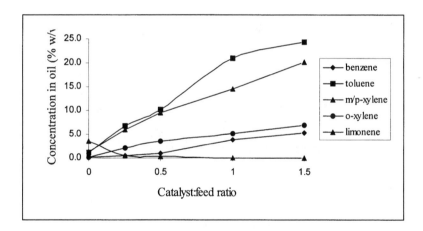

Figure 3. Influence of catalyst:tyre ratio on production of single ring aromatic compounds for the pyrolysis-catalysis of tyres

The char produced from the pyrolysis of used tyres, is regarded as low quality because of the high ash content, typically 10-12wt% and the low surface area of the order of 64 m^2 g^{-1}. This compares with activated carbons produced from traditional sources such as biomass, oil and coal with low ash contents and surface areas up to 1500 m^2 g^{-1}.

The commercial production of activated carbons involves either physical or chemical activation. Physical activation involves pyrolysis of the source material to produce a char followed by steam gasification. The production of activated carbons from scrap tyres has been investigated by physical activation. Tyre pyrolysis char has been activated in steam or CO_2 and also in relation to activation temperature, between 835 and 935 °C [12,13]. Figure 4 shows the influence of the degree of burn-off of the carbon for steam and carbon dioxide in relation to the BET surface area of the derived activated carbons. Burn-off was undertaken at 935 °C. Burn-off may be equated with activation time which ranged from 0.5 to 11.5 hours, and which achieved increasing degrees of burnoff. The degree of carbon loss (burnoff) achieved was calculated from:

$$\text{Burnoff wt \% daf} = \left(\frac{w_1 - w_2}{w_1} \right) x100$$

Where w_1 is the initial mass of carbon on a dry, ash free basis and w_2 is the mass of carbon remaining after activation.

The surface area reached a maximum of 650 $m^2\ g^{-1}$ at approximately 65 wt% burn off and then decreased. At lower degrees of burn off, up to around 15 wt%, there was a relatively slow increase in surface area with increasing degree of burn off, followed by a period of linear increase. The gasification process for tyre char has been described as a two stage process, the first stage attributed to the burn off of carbonised hydrocarbon residue with a less organised structure produced from pyrolysis followed by burn off of the more ordered carbon black [12,13].

It has been shown that disorganised carbon reacts more quickly than better organised carbon exhibiting a more graphitic structure. The burn-off achieved by CO_2 was less than that produced by steam. The reduced reactivity in CO_2 has been attributed to, the lower reactivity of CO_2, to diffusion effects, brought about by the larger size of the molecule or the formation of more stable oxygen groups on the carbon surface, which result in a slower reaction rate. The surface areas produced were very high and comparable to the lower grades of commercial grade activated carbons, representing a significantly enhanced product. Figure 4 shows that at higher degrees of burn-off, the reaction of the carbon with the activating gas results in the destruction of pore walls and reduction of surface area.

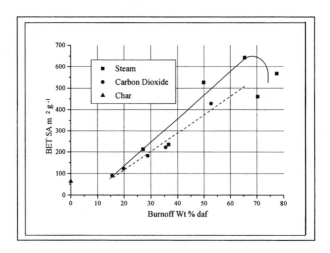

Figure 4. Surface area of tyre derived activated carbon in relation to activating gas (935 °C activating temperature)

Analysis of the activated carbons for the determination of their pore size distributions showed that they were mainly mesoporous [12,13]. The mesopore surface area of the activated carbons increased with the increasing degree of burn-off (Figure 5). This suggests that activation of tyre pyrolysis carbon proceeds by micropore formation, followed by pore enlargement, which is in line with the general carbon activation mechanism.

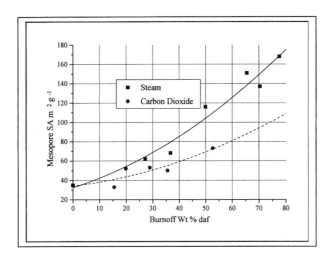

Figure 5. Mesopore surface area of tyre derived activated carbons.

CONCLUSIONS

The thermal degradation of used tyres by pyrolysis produces an oil, char and gas product together with the steel residue. All of the product streams have the potential for recycling. It has been estimated that there are more than 40 processes world wide promoting the pyrolysis of used tyres [1]. These include commercial plants operating in the UK, Taiwan and South Korea. The oil derived from tyre pyrolysis is similar in properties to a gas oil or light fuel oil and has the potential to be used as a fuel. The derived pyrolytic oil has a high calorific value of the order of 42 MJ kg^{-1}, with a sulphur content between 1.3% and 1.5%. The flash point of the pyrolysis oil was low at less than 20 °C. The oils were very aromatic in character containing single ring and polycyclic aromatic hydrocarbons. The oils have been successfully combusted producing higher emissions of sulphur dioxide and nitrogen oxides due to the higher oil content of sulphur and nitrogen compared to gas oil. The emission of polycyclic aromatic hydrocarbons from tyre combustion were negligible.

The application of zeolite catalysis to the tyre pyrolysis process produces an oil suitable for use as a chemical feedstock. For example, maximum concentrations in the oil reached 24 wt% for toluene, 5 wt% for benzene, 20 wt% for m/p-xylenes and 7wt% for o-xylene, representing a very significant potential increase in the value of the derived oils. The char derived from scrap tyre pyrolysis has a low surface area of the order of 64 m^2 g^{-1} and is high in ash content with values between 10 and 12 wt% ash and a calorific value of 30 MJ kg. However, the char may be upgraded in steam or carbon dioxide and acid demineralised to produce a low ash, activated carbon similar in properties to those commercially available.

The maximum surface area generated was 650 m^2 g^{-1} with a mesoporous pore structure. The gas derived from used tyre pyrolysis is mainly composed of alkane and alkene gases, carbon monoxide, carbon dioxide and hydrogen. The gas has a calorific value typically between 35 and 58 MJ m^{-3}, depending on process conditions and is sufficient to provide the energy requirements of the tyre pyrolysis plant. It may be concluded that the pyrolysis of tyres is a viable technological and environmentally attractive process route for scrap tyres, generating liquid, solid and gaseous fuels.

REFERENCES

1. ARCHER E., KLEIN A. AND WHITING K., The scrap tyre dilemma; can technology offer commercial solutions. Waste Management World, January, James & James Science Publishers Ltd., London, 2004.

2. US RUBBER MANUFACTURERS ASSOCIATION, US scrap tyre markets: 2001, Rubber Manufacturers Association, Washington, US, 2002

3. WILLIAMS P.T., Waste Treatment and Disposal, John Wiley & Sons, Chichester, 1998

4. BRESSI G., (Ed.), Recovery of Materials and Energy from Waste Tyres, International Solid Waste Association, Copenhagen, Denmark, 1995

5. BENALLAL, B., PAKDEL, H., CHABOT, S. AND ROY C., Characterisation of pyrolytic light naphtha from vacuum pyrolysis of used tyres; comparison with petroleum naphtha. Fuel, 74, 1995, 1589-1596.

6. WILLIAMS P.T., BOTTRILL R.P. AND CUNLIFFE A.M., Transactions of the Institution of Chemical Engineers, Part B, Process, Safety and Environmental Protection, 76, 1998, 291-301.

7. KYARI M., CUNLIFFE A. AND WILLIAMS P.T., Influence of tyre origin on the yield and composition of products from the pyrolysis of scarp tyres. In, Sustainable Waste Management and Recycling, International Conference, September 14-15, Kingston, London, 2004.

8. WILLIAMS P.T., AND BRINDLE A.J. Temperature selective condensation of tyre pyrolysis oils to maimise the recovery of single ring aromatic compounds, Fuel, 82, 2003, 1023-1031.

9. WILLIAMS P.T. AND BRINDLE A.J. Aromatic chemicals from the catalytic pyrolysis of scrap tyres, Journal of Analytical and Applied Pyrolysis, 67, 2003, 143-164.

10. WILLIAMS P.T., AND BRINDLE A.J. Fluidised bed catalytic pyrolysis of scrap tyres: influence of catalyst:tyre ratio and catalyst temperature, Waste Management & Research, 20, 2002, 546-555.

11. WILLIAMS P.T., AND BRINDLE A.J. Catalytic pyrolysis of tyres: influence of catalyst temperature, Fuel, 81, 2002, 2425-2434.

12. CUNLFFE A.M., AND WILLIAMS P.T., Influence of process conditions on the rate of activation of chars derived from the pyrolysis of used tyres. Energy and Fuels, 13, 1999, 166-175.

13. CUNLIFFE A.M., AND WILLIAMS P.T., Properties of chars and activated carbons derived from the pyrolysis of used tyres. Environment. Technol., 19, 1998, 1177-1190.

RECYCLING TYRE RUBBER IN BUILDING MATERIALS

M C Bignozzi
F Sandrolini
Università di Bologna
Italy

ABSTRACT. Tyre recycling is getting a serious problem to solve in view of the application of the European Community Directive 99/31/CE which forbids the landfill disposal of used tyres. Thanks to the favourable properties (thermal and electrical insulation, vibrations damping, etc.) of the rubber residues, their use in building materials can result particularly attractive. In this paper the main types of rubberised concrete developed in the last ten years and their properties are reviewed; moreover first examples of self compacting mortars containing tyre wastes are reported with the aim to expand profitably the field of utilization of this residue.

Keywords: Tyre rubber, Shred tyres, Waste recycling, Building materials, Rubberised concrete.

Dr M C Bignozzi is tenured researcher of the Faculty of Engineering at the University of Bologna, Italy. She teaches classes for Civil and Mechanical Engineering. Her research interests are mainly focussed on recycling and reuse of wastes for designing new building materials (concrete, composites, etc.).

Professor F Sandrolini is full professor of Materials Science and director of the department of Applied Chemistry and Materials Science in the Faculty of Engineering at the University of Bologna, Italy. He teaches classes for Architecture, Mechanical and Chemical Engineering. His research interests include concrete (mix design and durability), composite materials with tailored properties, rubberised industrial by-products recycling, restoration and recovery of historical building materials.

INTRODUCTION

Waste production is becoming a very serious problem that every country needs to deal with according also to local laws that address towards treatments and recycle of most residues. Even if some wastes such as plastics, rubber, glass and metals are more successfully involved than others in recycling process, a lot of work still needs to be done to achieve satisfactory results. This is the situation for tyres recycling too: over 2.500.000 ton of tyres have been dismissed in the European Union in 2002 and 35 wt% has been disposed to landfill (between 800.000 and 1.000.000 ton per year) [1]. However this amount should decrease in view of the application of the European Community Directive 99/31/CE which forbids the landfill disposal of used tyres from July 2003 and shredded tyres from July 2006. In Italy the D. M. 05/02/1998 (enclosure 1, point 10) deals with tyres waste management in order to recycle them in rubber, bitumen and other industries, but so far not in building materials.

Tyre recycling requires that used tyres be reduced into scraps of different size depending on the final process in which they may be involved. Shredding procedure is usually the first step: in this way the waste volume is compacted, safeguarding the storage sites, and it is also ready for energy production as refuse derived fuel (RDF). In Italy almost 70 wt% of shredded tyres are used as energy source alternative to solid fuels thanks to their high heating value, comparable to that of c oal. Burning tyre wastes seems particularly a ttractive, however the production of gas emissions and the presence of steel fragments, as integral part of the tyre, require high temperature in the combustion process thus limiting their use mostly in cement kilns and paper mills [2-3].

To expand the field of utilisation of recycled tyres, scraps of finer grade are necessary because tyres contains not only rubber, but also steel wires and fiber parts. In fact for many applications in the area of civil engineering, steel and fibers are usually removed. The grain size distribution and the shape of the rubber grains are strongly influenced by milling technology which can lead to crumb rubber with dimension less than 0.5 mm; mechanical grinding at room temperature generally produces rough edged particles with many hair-like attachments, whereas cryogenic process, carried out with liquid nitrogen and in absence of oxygen, leads to a more uniform shape and a narrower size distribution [4].

With the aim to improve temperature resistance and mechanical strength of asphalt cement, the addition of ground rubber coming from used tyres has been under investigation for almost 30 years: these studies have recently undergone a further stimulus as strictly related with the recycling concern [5]. The low cost, the rubber nature, the weather-resistant properties and the easy processing are the main characteristics that make these waste materials so interesting for asphalt cement based materials (waterproof coatings, sealant, binders, etc.) [6]. Scrap tyres have been also involved in highway construction as aggregates replacement, in the construction of non-structural sound barrier, as l ightweight embankment fills, in pavement frost barriers, etc., with the purpose to avoid the utilisation of virgin material coming from non renewable sources [7]. As well as asphalt cement, Portland cement concrete can be conceived as an effective tool for scrap tyres recycling: tyre rubber particles with different shape, dimension and size distribution have been studied since the Nineties as partial replacement of conventional aggregates in order to reduce the fragile fracture behaviour of the concrete and making it somewhat tough. Some of the results obtained in this last decade are reviewed a nd discussed later on; moreover some new formulations of self compacting mortar containing shred tyres (in the range of 10-40 vol% over the total amount of aggregate) will be reported for the first time.

RUBBERISED CONCRETE

In Table 1, three mix proportions, prepared by Eldin et al. [8], Topku [9] and Kathib et al. [10], are reported as typical examples of rubberised concretes: in each case several formulations have been prepared substituting part of the sand and/or coarse aggregates with an equal volume of tyre waste having comparable size distribution. It must be noted that the nature and the origin of tyre wastes used is different: in fact whereas Eldin and Kathib used either scrap tyres obtained by grinding, thus including steel and textile fibers in their composition, and crumb rubber obtained by cryogenic process, Topku employed tyres tread. Other authors have also prepared rubberised concrete with scrap truck tyre rubber [11-13].

Table 1. Examples of mix design for concrete containing tyre waste

	RUBBERISED CONCRETE by		
	Eldin et al. [8]	Topku [9]	Kathib et al. [10]
Coarse aggreg. (kg/m^3) and D_{max} (mm)	1116 (25)	1148 (16)	1024 (25)
Sand (kg/m^3)	629	609	786
CEM I (kg/m^3)	447	358	388
Water (kg/m^3)	214	222	186
Water/cement ratio	0.48	0.60	0.48
Kind and D_{max} of tyre waste (mm)	scrap tyres (38) scrap tyres (25) scrap tyres (19) crumb rubber (6) crumb rubber (2)	tyres tread (4) tyres tread (1)	tyre chips (50) crumb rubber (3)
Vol% of tyre waste on the total aggregate	9-64	15, 30, 45	2-57
Curing time (days)	7, 28	7, 28, 180	7, 28
Sample for compressive strength (mm)	Cylinders, 150x300	Cylinders, 150x300 Cubes, 150	Cylinders, 150x300

The great diversity in the materials choice, mix design, amount of aggregates replaced by tyre wastes makes difficult the comparison between the investigators, however some common results can be highlighted as far as mechanical properties are concerned: compressive strength decreases with the increase of rubber content and average size (falls up to 90% and 65% were respectively detected when about 50 vol% of total aggregates was replaced) [8-10]; from a practical point of view, rubber content should not exceed 20 vol% of the total aggregate to avoid a too severe reduction in strength [10]; no substantial change in compressive strength is detected between 7 and 28 days of curing time for concrete containing tyre amount higher than 20 vol% of the total aggregate [8-10]; rubberised concrete exhibits a gradual failure and the absorbed energy can be calculated [8,9].

Khatib et al. [10] have proposed a characteristic function (1) that is useful to estimate the strength reduction factor (SRF) for any rubberised concrete with respect to rubber content, R, evaluated as volumetric ratio by total aggregate volume.

$$SFR = a + b(1-R)^m \qquad (1)$$

with the condition that

$$a=1-b$$

where a, b and m are function parameters determined by regression analysis. The exponent m reflects the degree of curvature of the function and indicates the sensitivity of the mix to the strength loss with the rubber content. The validity of the SRF function has been proved successfully not only with the data of Khatib [10], but also with data obtained by Eldin [8]. The SFR function can be very useful for mix design purpose in establishing, *a priori*, the target strength.

Recently Hernandez-Olivares et al. investigated the dynamic behaviour and the fire performance respectively of normal strength concrete (NSC) [12] and high strength concrete (HSC) [13] with recycled tyre rubber. Compressive dynamic tests have allowed measuring the dissipated energy, under dynamic load without damage, of samples of rubberised concrete containing low amount of truck tyres (3.5 and 5 vol% on the concrete mix). In the investigated samples high values of the specific energy dissipated (between 23 and 30% with regard to maximum elastic energy stored under load) have been determined, thus underlining the damping properties of these materials. Moreover, the addition of low volume amount of tyre rubber have been helpful in reducing the risk of explosive spalling of HSC at high temperature as vapour can find a way out through the channels left as the polymeric particles get burnt.

SELF COMPACTING MORTARS WITH TYRE WASTES

The self compacting concrete (SCC) is a brand new type of concrete that is lately having a lot of attention from the users and the researchers for its peculiar properties. In fact, thanks to the addition of admixtures, s uch as superplasticizers and modifying viscosity agents, and fine fillers to the traditional concrete mix-design, concrete with high workability and flowability properties can be obtained. SCC does not need to be vibrated when cast in place and exhibits, in the hardened state, better compressive strength, lower porosity and higher durability than ordinary Portland cement concrete of analogous formulation [14-16].

However, although self compacting concrete shows superior strength than ordinary concrete for the presence of a mineral filler (usually calcium carbonate) with average size ranging 10 to 50 μm which allows obtaining an extremely compact microstructure, its failure behaviour is still brittle. For this reason and with the aim to make the SCC a though building material, the possibility to include recycled tyre rubbers in its mix design has been investigated. Accordingly, as first step for the investigation of the feasibility of the formulations, self compacting mortars have been prepared using scrap tyre rubbers with different average size to replace the filler or the sand.

Materials

For mortars formulations the following materials have been used: CEM II/A-L 42.5 R (UNI EN 197/1), normalized siliceous sand (UNI EN 196-1) and, as fine filler, calcium carbonate with an average grain size of about 8 μm. Scrap tyre rubber wastes used were obtained by mechanical grinding and they still contain steel and fabrics fragments. Two different grain size distributions of tyre rubber wastes were chosen: scrap (ST) and crumb (CT) tyres with dimension ranges 0.5-2 mm and 0.05-0.7 mm respectively. As SCC admixtures, an acrylic based superplasticizer (SP, Dynamon SP1, Mapei) and a biopolymer based viscosity modifying agent (VMA, Viscofluid SCC, Mapei) were used.

Sample preparation

For mortars preparation, a normalized Hobart mixer (UNI EN 196-1) was used and the flowability of the mixture was determined measuring the spread mixture obtained using a conical ring (d_{max}=100 mm, d_{min}=70 mm, h=60 mm), in a similar way of the slump flow test for self compacting concrete. Mortars were considered self compacting when a spread mixture with an average diameter greater than 25 cm was obtained [17]. 40x40x160 mm specimens were prepared for each formulation and curing time of 7 and 28 days, at 20°C and with R.U. > 90%, were adopted. In Table 2, the mix design of the formulations prepared is reported: M1 is the reference mix prepared with commercial $CaCO_3$ as fine filler, MCT1-MCT3 are formulated replacing with crumb tyres (CT) respectively 100, 66.6 and 50 vol% of the calcareous filler volume and MCST1-MCST3 are prepared replacing different volume of sand (between 22 and 41 vol%) with both scrap and crumb tyre wastes combined together according to Fuller grain size distribution (55% ST, 45 % CT). The water/cement ratio was kept constant for all the mixes (W/C=0.5), whereas the amount of admixtures was adjusted to obtain self compacting mortar.

Characterization

Compressive (S_{Comp}) and flexural (S_{flex}) strengths were determined with an Amsler-Wolpert machine (200 kN) according to UNI EN 196-1. Water absorption (WA) measurements were performed after 28 days of curing.

Table 2. Mix design for self compacting mortar containing tyre wastes (wt%)

SAMPLE	CEM.	SAND	WATER	CaCO₃	CT	ST	VMA[a]	SP[a]	VOL% of filler replaced
M1	22.2	55.6	11.1	11.1	-	-	0.1	0.6	-
MCT1	23.9	59.8	12.0	-	4.3	-	0.5	3.5	100.0
MCT2	23.3	58.3	11.7	3.9	2.8	-	0.2	1.1	66.7
MCT3	23.0	57.6	11.5	5.8	2.1	-	0.1	0.7	50.0
SAMPLE	CEM.	SAND	WATER	CaCO₃	CT	ST	VMA[a]	SP[a]	VOL% of filler replaced
MCST1	26.0	38.5	13.0	13.0	4.3	5.2	0.1	0.6	40.7
MCST2	25.2	42.0	12.6	12.6	3.4	4.2	0.1	0.6	33.3
MCST3	24.1	46.9	12.1	12.1	2.2	2.7	0.1	0.6	22.2

(a) weight % on the amount of fine components (cement+filler)

RESULTS AND DISCUSSION

All the SCC mixes (detailed in Table 2) exhibited self compacting characteristics except for MCT1 where, although the admixtures were used in large amounts, a spread mixture larger than 25 cm was not achieved. For samples formulated with crumb tyre wastes replacing calcium carbonate (MCT1-MCT3), admixtures quantities are generally higher compared to samples where only $CaCO_3$ is used: this may be due to the greater average size of the rubber particles based filler. In Table 3, compressive and flexural strengths at different curing time are collectively reported.

As general trend, a decrease in the mechanical properties with the increasing amount of tyres waste in the mortar mix, replacing either calcareous filler or sand, occurs. After 28 days of curing, this reduction ranges between 72-90 and 45-67% respectively for flexural and compressive strengths of samples MCT1-MCT3 and between 40-52 and 40-61% respectively for flexural and compressive strengths of samples MCST1-MCST3, thus indicating that it is preferable to use tyre waste to substitute sand instead of fine filler.

Table 3. Mechanical properties of self compacting mortars containing tyre wastes

SAMPLE	S_{flex}– 7 days (N/mm^2)	S_{Comp}– 7 days (N/mm^2)	S_{flex}– 28 days (N/mm^2)	S_{Comp}– 28 days (N/mm^2)
M1	10.5	49.9	12.9	60.3
MCT1	-	-	1.1	21.6
MCT2	2.0	29.0	3.1	28.9
MCT3	4.6	33.5	3.6	32.8
MCST1	1.0	18.3	6.2	23.6
MCST2	1.3	22.4	7.3	27.7
MCST3	2.6	28.8	7.7	35.8

Although lower values of S_{Comp} and S_{flex} have been detected, according to the behaviour of rubberised traditional concrete, visual observations indicate that samples of rubberised mortars had, during flexural test, higher deflections and, during compressive test, larger deformation before failure than the reference mixture. Unfortunately these data were not recorded. Water absorption measurements were carried out to have an estimate of the porosity of the mortars. For all the samples containing tyre wastes, a WA of about 10 wt% has been determined: this value is almost equal that one detected for mix M1, thus involving that the addition of rubber particles does not lead to a more porous microstructure. SEM analysis is now in progress.

CONCLUSIONS

In this last decade the feasibility of rubberised concrete has been assessed, however the mechanical properties obtained do not allow to use this new building material for structural applications yet. Better performances could be achieved if rubber particles were treated (for example, with NaOH solution) to increase the adhesion with cement paste, but of course this procedure could make shred tyres recycle less easy and immediate. Self compacting mortar with tyre rubber particles can be considered as a first step to realize s tructural rubberised concrete: the results, here preliminary shown, are promising and are currently under development.

ACKNOWLEDGEMENTS

MIUR 60 % financial support is gratefully acknowledged.

REFERENCES

1.   FISE ASSOAMBIENTE, L'Italia del recupero, Rapporto sul riciclo dei rifiuti, 2003, www.fise.org.

2.   BARLAZ, M.A., ELEAZER, W.E., WHITTLE, J.: Potential to use waste tires as supplemental fuel in pulp and paper mill boilers, cement kilns and in road pavement, Waste management & research, 11, 1993, 463.

3.   ATAL, A., LEVENDIS, Y.A.: Comparison of the combustion behaviour of pulverized waste tyres and coal, Fuel, 74, 11, 1995, 1570.

4.   OWEN, K.C.: Scrap tires: a pricing strategy for a recycling industry, Corporate Environmental Strategy, 5, 2, 1998, 42.

5.   ZAMAN, A.A., FRICKE, A.L., BEATTY, C.L.: Rhelogical properties of rubber-modified asphalt, Journal of transportation engineering, 121, 6, 1995, 461.

6.   NADKARNI, V.M., SHENOY, A.V., MATHEW, J.: Thermomechanical behaviour of modified asphalt, Industrial and engineering chemistry. Product research and development, 24, 3, 1985, 478.

7.   BOSSCHER, P.J., EDIL, T.B., KURAOKA, S.: Design of highway embankments using tire chips, Journal of geotechnical and geoenvironmental engineering, 123, 4, 1997, 295.

8.   ELDIN, N.N., SENOUCI, A. B.: Rubber-tire particles as concrete aggregate, Journal of materials in civil engineering, 5, 4, 1993, 478.

9.   TOPCU, I.B.: The properties of rubberised concretes, Cement and concrete research, 25, 2, 1995, 304.

10.   KHATIB, Z.K., BAYOMY F.M.: Rubberized Portland cement concrete, Journal of materials in civil engineering, 11, 3, 1999, 206.

11.   FATTUHI, N. I., CLARK, L.A.: Cement based materials containing shredded scrap truck tyre rubber, Construction and building materials, 10, 4, 1996, 229.

12. HERNANDEZ-OLIVARES, F., BARLUENGA, G., BOLLATI, M., WITOSZEK, B.: Static and dynamic behaviour of recycled tyre rubber-filled concrete, Cement and concrete research, 32, 2002, 1587.

13. HERNANDEZ-OLIVARES, F., BARLUENGA, G.: Fire performance of recycled rubber-filled high-strength concrete, Cement and concrete research, 34, 2004, 109.

14. OKAMURA H.: Self-Compacting High-Performance Concrete, Concrete International, 19, 7, 1997, 50.

15. SKARENDAHL, A., PETERSSON, O.: Self-compacting concrete: state of the art, report of RILEM technical committee 174-SCC, RILEM Publications s.a.r.l, Cachan, 2000.

16. PERSSON B.: A comparison between mechanical properties of self-compacting concrete a nd t he c orresponding p roperties o f n ormal c oncrete, C ement a nd C oncrete Research 31, 2001, 193.

17. TAKADA K., PELOVA G. I., WALRAVEN J. C.: Influence of chemical admixtures and mixing on the mix proportion of general purpose self-compacting concrete, Modern Concrete Materials: binders, additions and admixtures, edited by R. K. Dhir and T. D. Dyer, Thomas Telford, London, 1999, 653.

APPLICATION OF GRANULATED RUBBER TO IMPROVE THERMAL EFFICIENCY OF CONCRETE

K A Paine

R C Moroney

R K Dhir

University of Dundee

United Kingdom

ABSTRACT. As part of a much wider study to assess the feasibility of recycling used tyres in concrete, research was carried out to investigate means for exploiting the inherent thermal resistance characteristics of rubber produced from granulated used tyres to improve the thermal efficiency of concrete. Granulated rubber (GR) ranging from 25mm to 0.5mm in size was used in a series of tests in which the GR content was varied from 5% to 100% by volume. It was observed that the use of GR led to values of thermal conductivity that were lower than those of conventional concrete for a given strength and were similar to those of typical thermal insulating building blocks. In the final series, a specimen containing solely GR as aggregate, known as *rubcrete,* was developed which had thermal conductivity values less than 0.3 W/mK and 28-day cube strength greater than 5 N/mm^2. These values compare favourably with most typical brick and block components and are better than that of commercially available foamed concrete. The ability of GR to reduce the thermal conductivity of concrete will help builders meet the requirements for U-value, and aid in the attainment of thermally efficient building materials.

Keywords: Thermal efficiency, Granulated rubber, Post-consumer tyres, Recycled materials, U-value, Thermal conductivity, Concrete

Dr Kevin A Paine is a Lecturer in the Concrete Technology Unit, University of Dundee. His research interests are concerned with the use of recycled materials and industrial by-products as cement constituents, additions and aggregates in concrete.

Mr Robert C Moroney is an Engineer for Scott Wilson Scotland Ltd. He was previously a research student at the University of Dundee where he studied the feasibility of using recycled rubber tyres in concrete.

Professor R avindra K Dhir is Director of the Concrete Technology Unit, University of Dundee. He specialises in binder technology, permeation, durability and protection of concrete. His interests also include the use of construction and industrial wastes in concrete to meet the challenges of sustainable construction.

INTRODUCTION

Post-consumer tyres constitute a significant waste problem in the UK. It is estimated that 40 million tyres are discarded annually [1] and this number is set to increase, in line with the estimated growth in road traffic, by 39% (by 2011) and by 63% (by 2021) [2]. However, from 2006 it will be illegal to landfill post-consumer tyres (either whole or shredded). Therefore, there will be no option other than to recycle. This has led to an urgent need to identify alternative outlets for these tyres, with the emphasis on recycling in line with the UK Governments waste management hierarchy. Fortunately, post-consumer tyres have excellent potential for recycling for use as civil engineering materials since they can form environmentally sound, inexpensive, and lightweight materials that are readily in available in large quantities [3].

Recognising this, the Concrete Technology Unit (CTU) at the University of Dundee has carried out a wide-ranging feasibility study to investigate the recycling of rubber tyres for use in concrete and concrete products [4-5]. This study showed that rubber recycled from post-consumer tyres, in the form of granulated rubber (GR) could be used to improve the performance of concrete in three particular areas: (i) freeze/thaw resistance, (ii) impact resistance and (iii) thermal efficiency.

This paper briefly describes the research carried out to investigate the feasibility of using GR to improve the latter aspect; thermal efficiency of concrete.

MATERIALS

Granulated Rubber

The GR used in this study was obtained from mechanical shredding of lorry tyres, and was supplied in three sizes 0.5-1.5 mm, 2-8 mm and 5-25 mm, referred to, respectively as GR 1, GR 8, and GR 20 throughout this paper. The particle size distribution (psd) of the GR is shown in Figure 1, and compared with the natural aggregate (river sand and gravel) used in the study.

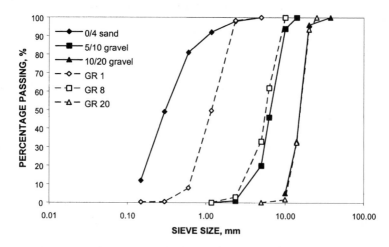

Figure 1 Particle size distribution of GR and natural aggregates

The grading of the two coarsest granulated rubbers (GR 8 and GR 20) had similar particle size distributions to 5/10 and 10/20 natural aggregates, respectively. Furthermore, they both fell within the current limits for single sized aggregate specified in BS EN 12620:2002. The finest GR (GR 1) did not meet the requirements for sand specified in BS EN 12620:2002, falling on the coarse side.

The main physical properties of GR are given in Table 1. As these properties are defined for natural aggregate, they were not necessarily applicable to GR. For example, shape, defined by a visual interpretation, is so irregular with GR that it did not meet one single criterion. It was therefore described as angular/flaky/elongated. Similarly, tests to assess the resistance of aggregate to crushing (aggregate crushing value) and impact (aggregate impact value) failed to cause any damage to GR. Values of 0% were therefore recorded.

Water absorption values were found to be very similar to those of natural aggregate. However, this test and the associated density tests were somewhat difficult to carry out because of the nature of GR, i.e. despite carrying out the tests in non-aerated water, a substantial amount of air bubbles still attach themselves to the GR. Subsequently, the values recorded will be on the low side. Furthermore, the results show that GR has a mean particle density of between 1020 and 1140 kg/m^3, although in all three-size fractions approximately 5% by mass of the GR was found to float. Loose bulk density values were between 460 and 470 kg/m^3. These clearly indicate that GR can be classified as a lightweight aggregate as they fall below the limit of 1200kg/m^3, specified in BS EN 13055-1:2002[7].

Natural Aggregate
The natural aggregates used were 10/20 and 5/10 single-sized river gravels and a 0/4 sand, conforming to BS EN 12620:2002. The main physical properties are given in Table 1.

Cement
The cement used was a CEM I 42.5N cement conforming with BS EN 197-1.

Table 1 Physical properties of GR and natural aggregate calculated
in accordance with British and European standards

PROPERTY	GR			NATURAL AGGREGATE		
	GR 1	GR 8	GR 20	0/4	5/10	10/20
Shape, Visual	Angular/Flaky/Elongated			--	Rounded	
Elongation Index, %	--	44		--	14	
Aggregate Impact Value[‡], %	--	--	0	--	--	24
Aggregate Crushing Value[‡], %	--	--	0	--	--	20
Water Absorption, %	0.6	1.0	0.9	0.5	1.3	1.2
Particle Density (dry), kg/m^3	1020	1110	1120	--	--	--
Particle Density (SSD), kg/m^3	1020	1130	1130	2630	2590	2590
Apparent Particle Density, kg/m^3	1020	1130	1140	--	--	--
Bulk Density (SSD)						
Loose, kg/m^3	--	460	470	1580	1590	1550
Compacted, kg/m^3	--	520	530	1680	1660	1650

-- Not applicable   [‡] *10 to 14 mm sample*

TEST PROGRAMME

The test programme was carried out in three series in which the proportion of GR present within the concrete were gradually increased. In Series 1, concrete with normal engineering and durability properties were investigated in which the level of GR addition was relatively low (5-10% by volume of concrete) and similar to that of adding air. In Series 2, much higher volumes of GR were added (10-100% by volume of aggregate), such that the engineering properties of the concrete were significantly changed. Following this, in Series 3, an attempt was made to optimise the proportions of GR with that of the cement to create a concrete (known as *rubcrete*) with low thermal conductivity and a compressive strength as high as possible.

MIX PROPORTIONS

For **Series 1**, tests were carried out on GR concrete mixes with GR contents of 5% and 10% by volume of concrete. Each of the three sizes of GR were investigated separately. Mix proportions were calculated by adding the GR as volume-for-volume replacement of the appropriate natural aggregate size, i.e. GR 20 for 10/20 natural aggregate, GR 8 for 5/10 aggregate and GR 1 for sand. Mixes were cast at four water/cement (w/c) ratios (0.35, 0.45. 0.55 and 0.65). In all cases the free water content was 180 ℓ/m3.

In **Series 2**, GR contents from 0 to 100% by volume of aggregate were investigated. Both GR1 and GR8 were used. The mix proportions are given in Table 2, and were based on a requirement to obtain adequate compaction at high GR volumes, whilst achieving a degree of strength. The initial mix was based on that which gave adequate performance at 70% GR content. The water and cement contents were then fixed at this level as GR contents were reduced (and increased). Thus, for the plain concrete both the water and cement contents were higher than is typical for a w/c ratio of 0.45.

Table 2 Mix proportions for thermal conductivity tests

MIX PROPORTIONS, kg/m³							
GR CONTENT %	PC	Free Water	Aggregates				W/C
			10mm NA	GR 8	Sand	GR 1	
0	500	225	1030	0	580	0	0.45
10	500	225	925	45	520	25	0.45
20	500	225	825	90	465	50	0.45
30	500	225	720	135	405	75	0.45
40	500	225	620	180	350	100	0.45
50	500	225	515	225	290	125	0.45
60	500	225	410	270	230	150	0.45
70	500	225	310	315	175	175	0.45
80	500	225	205	360	115	200	0.45
90	500	225	105	405	60	225	0.45
100	500	225	0	450	0	250	0.45

The mix proportions used in **Series 3** to produce *rubcrete* are given in Table 3. As mentioned previously, an attempt was made to optimise the proportions of GR with that of the cement to create elements with low thermal conductivity and a compressive strength as high as possible. The mix proportions were based on the BRE mix design approach [6] with adaptions made for the lower density of GR compared with sand. The proportions of fine GR required were large (75% by mass of aggregate) due to the coarse nature of GR 1 compared with concreting sand.

Table 3 Mix proportions for rubcrete

MIX	Free Water	PC	GR	
			GR 1	GR 8
Rubcrete	205	290	685	230

APPROXIMATE MIX PROPORTIONS, kg/m³

TEST METHOD

For each mix, 290mm square and 50mm thick specimens were cast for measurement of thermal c onductivity.   Following 2 8-days se aled c uring t he s pecimens were d ried a t 3 0°C until constant weight, and then placed in an insulated hot-box apparatus (Figure 2). Measurements were initiated 24 hours later when a steady rate of heat transfer had been achieved [7].

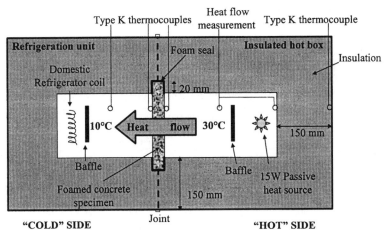

Figure 2 Thermal conductivity measuring apparatus [7]

Indicative thermal conductivity was measured as described in BS 874-3, i.e. the temperature differential on either side of the specimen (20°C) was maintained, while the power required from a heating element was recorded. The indicative thermal conductivity (in W/mK) was calculated as:

Indicative thermal conductivity $\lambda_{ind} = \dfrac{Q\,D}{A\,\Delta T}$

where   Q   = time rate of heat flow (W)
               D   = specimen thickness (m)
               A   = exposed area of specimen (m^2)
               ΔT   = temperature differential between either side of the specimen (°K)

RESULTS

Series 1: Low GR Contents

The results are shown in Figure 2 and show that the use of GR reduces the indicative thermal conductivity. However, it was additionally observed that the effect of GR in reducing thermal conductivity became more pronounced as the w/c ratio increased. For example, for w/c = 0.35 the addition of 10% GR reduced thermal conductivity by approximately 15%. However, for w/c = 0.65 the same volume of GR gave a reduction of about 25%. The reason for this is unclear, and cannot be explained by the general reduction in thermal conductivity as w/c ratio reduced; which is a result of the decreasing density of the concrete.

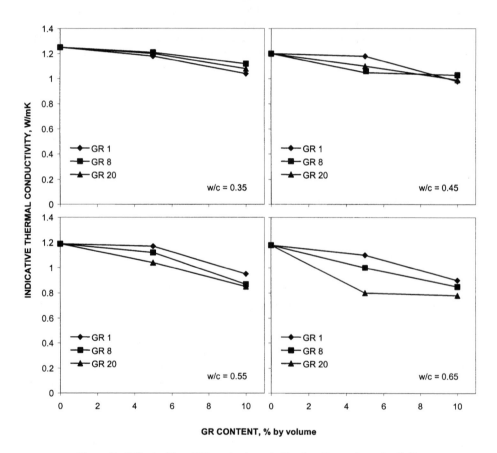

Figure 2. Effect of low GR contents on indicative thermal conductivity

Series 2: High GR Contents

The results of Series 2, are given in Table 4, in addition to measurements of slump, density and 28-day cube strength measured in accordance with BS EN 12350:2000, BS EN 12390-7:2000 and BS EN 12390:2002, respectively. The effect of high GR contents on indicative thermal conductivity is shown in Figure 3. Although it can be clearly deduced that thermal conductivity reduces with an increase in GR content (100% GR giving a thermal conductivity approximately 70% lower than that of plain concrete) and subsequent reduction in concrete density there was some scatter of results.

The dotted line in Figure 3 shows the estimated theoretical thermal conductivity based on the separate thermal conductivity of cement paste, GR, aggregates and air voids, where the air-voids content was approximated using a modified De Larrard particle-packing model [8].

It can be seen that the results resemble this theoretical trend, although the results for 20% and 30% are clear anomalies. This suggests that the lower thermal conductivity of GR concrete can be related to the lower thermal conductivity of GR (0.50 W/mK) compared with that of natural aggregates (2.45 to 5.20 W/mK). The variability in performance may be related to fluctuations in unintentional air entrainment, since air bubbles attached themselves to GR in water. A clear linear relationship between GR content and density was found (Figure 3). The addition of 100% by volume of GR, reduced the density from 2325 kg/m^3 for plain concrete to 1350 kg/m^3 – a reduction of 42%.

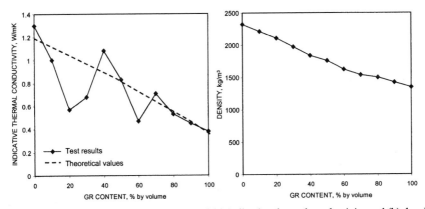

Figure 3. Relationship between GR content and (a) indicative thermal conductivity and (b) density

The effect of GR on cube strength up to 100% addition is shown in Figure 4. The linear reduction in strength, analogous to that of air-entrainment, for low GR contents (5% reduction in strength per 1% of GR by volume) [9] was not found to apply at higher GR contents. Nevertheless, cube strengths recorded at high GR contents (> 60%) were found to be very low (< 5 N/mm^2).

Series 3: Rubcrete

The thermal conductivity value recorded for the rubcrete block was found to be 0.30 W/mK. This compares very favourable with most typical brick and block components (Figure 5) and is lower than most commercially available foamed concretes (0.2 to 0.6 W/mK).

Table 4   Results of tests on indicative thermal conductivity over a range of GR content

GR CONTENT, %	SLUMP, mm	DENSITY, kg/m³	CUBE STRENGTH, N/mm²	INDICATIVE THERMAL CONDUCTIVITY, W/mK
0	110	2325	55.0	1.30
10	95	2215	32.0	0.49
20	80	2110	22.5	0.57
30	60	1975	13.0	0.68
40	50	1840	8.0	1.08
50	45	1760	7.0	0.83
60	40	1625	4.0	0.47
70	35	1540	3.0	0.71
80	30	1500	3.0	0.53
90	30	1425	3.0	0.45
100	20	1350	2.0	0.38

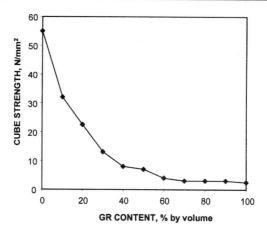

Figure 4. Effect of GR content on cube strength

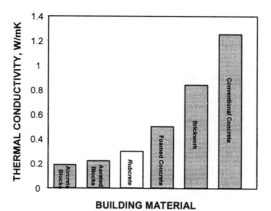

Figure 5. Comparison of thermal conductivity of
rubcrete compared with other common building materials

Furthermore, the density of the *rubcrete* was measured as 1190 kg/m^3, which falls in the mid range of commercially available foamed concretes (600 to 1600 kg/m^3). The cube strength of the *rubcrete* was measured as 5 N/mm^2, which is again in the mid range of typical foamed concretes (1 to 10 N/mm^2), and is of similar magnitude to aircrete blocks which are widely used in housing construction. Note that the *rubcrete* was stronger than the 100% GR concrete in Series 2 because of the lower water content.

THERMAL EFFICIENCY AND APPLICATION OF GR

The maximisation of energy conservation in cold weather and reduction of the environmental impacts associated with heating of buildings are important. Indeed, heating of buildings in the UK accounts for 27% of the total CO_2 emissions [10], and for this reason, in April 2002 the UK Building regulations became more stringent in terms of thermal transmittance (U-value) requirements [11]. For example, the maximum U-value for exposed ground slabs was lowered from 0.45 to 0.25 W/m^{2}K. Most conventional building materials do not meet this requirement.

To show how GR concrete can lead to improvements in thermal efficiency of low-rise dwellings, an example calculation of U-value for a typical dwelling sat on a 600mm wide and 1.5m deep foundation with a 250mm deep ground slab (Figure 6) is given in Table 5. U-values were calculated in accordance with BS EN ISO 13770:2002 using a spreadsheet devised by the CTU [12].

In the first example, the floor slab and foundation have been constructed using normal weight concrete (λ = 1.25 W/mK), and a 25mm thick Styrofoam insulation layer has been laid under the slab to provide additional insulation. The calculated U-value for this construction is 0.42 W/m^{2}K. Whilst this meets the regulations prior to April 2002, clearly this type of construction is no longer permitted. As a comparison, the calculation of U-value for the same construction using *rubcrete* (λ = 0.30 W/mK) is also given. In this instance, the maximum U-value of 0.25 W/m^{2}K is met.

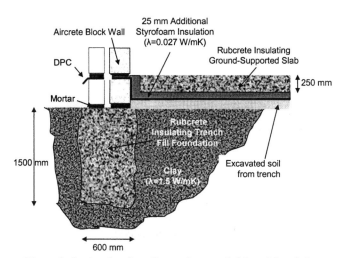

Figure 6. Section drawing of example ground slab and foundation

Table 5. Comparison of U-values for normal weight concrete and
rubcrete used as ground slab and foundation

VALUES	NORMAL WEIGHT CONCRETE	RUBCRETE
Foundation depth D (m)	1.5	1.5
Foundation width dn (m)	0.6	0.6
Thermal conductivity of foundations, λ	**1.25**	**0.30**
Thermal resistance of foundations Rn	0.48 [§]	2
Slab depth df (m)	0.25	0.25
Thermal conductivity of slab, λ	**1.25**	**0.30**
Thickness of slab insulation	0.025	0.025
Thermal conductivity of slab insulation	0.027	0.027
Thermal resistance of slab insulation	0.93	0.93
Thermal resistance of floor Rf	1.13	1.76
Thermal conductivity of soil (W/mk)	1.5	1.5
Wall thickness w (m)	0.3	0.3
Internal surface resistance Rsi	0.15	0.15
External surface resistance Rse	0.04	0.04
Perimeter of dwelling, m	28	28
Area of dwelling, m²	40	40
U-value, (W/m²K)	**0.42**	**0.25**

[§] Note that dense concrete should normally be neglected in calculations of thermal resistance [13].
Based on this approach a U-value of 0.47 would be calculated for conventional concrete. To
achieve a U-value of 0.25 a total of 70mm of additional styrofoam insulation would be required.

CONCLUSIONS

The feasibility study described in this paper has shown that:

1. Use of GR in concrete leads to lower thermal conductivity values than those of conventional normal weight concrete.

2. Concrete containing high proportions of GR will have density and strength properties similar to those of other thermally efficient materials, e.g. foamed concrete and aircrete blocks.

3. GR can be used to produce concrete for use in ground slabs that will conform to the requirements of the UK Building Requirements with less additional insulation than required for normal weight concrete.

ACKNOWLEDGEMENTS

This work was carried out as part of a Partners in Innovation collaborative research project.
The authors are grateful to the Department of Trade and Industry, Aberdeenshire Council,
Castle Cement Ltd., Cemtyre Ltd., Charles Lawrence Group Ltd., DME Tyres Ltd.,
Environment Agency, Highways Agency, Lafarge Aggregates, Marshalls plc and Marshalls
Mono Ltd, Quarry Products Association, Robert Marshall and Associates, and the Used Tyre
Working Group of DTI for funding the project. Dr A McCarthy is thanked for her assistance
with the U-value calculations.

REFERENCES

1. USED TYRE WORKING GROUP. Fifth annual report of the UTWG. July 2001.

2. THE ENVIRONMENT AGENCY. Annual report on tyres in the environment, London, 1998

3. HYLANDS, K.N. and SHULMAN, V. Civil engineering applications of tyres. Viridis Report VR5, TRL Limited, 2003, 92pp

4. DHIR, R.K., PAINE, K.A. and MORONEY, R.C. Recycling of used tyres in concrete. Concrete, Vol. 37, No. 9, 2003, pp 47-48

5. PAINE, K.A, MORONEY, R.C. and DHIR, R.K. Performance of concrete comprising shredded rubber tyres. Recycling and Reuse of Waste Materials, Proceedings of International Symposium, Dundee, Thomas Telford, September 2003, pp 719-729

6. TEYCHENNE, D.C., FRANKLIN, R.E., ERNTROY, H.C. and MARSH, B.K. Design of Normal Concrete mixes; Second Edition, Building Research Establishment, 1997

7. GIANNAKOU, A. and JONES, M.R. Potential of foamed concrete to enhance the thermal performance of low-rise dwellings. Innovations and Developments in Concrete Materials and Construction, Proceedings of International Conference, Dundee, Thomas Telford, September 2002, pp 533-544

8. JONES, M.R., ZHENG, L. and NEWLANDS, M.D. Estimation of the filler content required to minimise voids ratio in concrete. Magazine of Concrete Research, Vol. 55, No 2, April 2003, pp 193-202

9. PAINE, K.A, DHIR, R.K, MORONEY, R.C. and KOPASAKIS, K. Use of crumb rubber to achieve freeze/thaw resisting concrete. Concrete for Extreme Conditions, Proceedings of International Conference, Dundee, Thomas Telford, September 2002, pp 485-498

10. CONCRETE SOCIETY. U-values: understanding heat movement. Environmental Working Party of the Concrete Society's Materials Group. Concrete, Vol. 37, No. 3, 2003, pp 42-43

11. OFFICE OF THE DEPUTY PRIME MINISTER. Building regulations: Conservation of fuel and power. Approved Document L1: Conservation of fuel and power in dwellings. The Stationary office, April 2002.

12. JONES, M.R., DHIR, R.K. and McCARTHY, A. Development of foamed concrete insulating foundations for buildings and final demonstration project, University of Dundee, Report CTU/2604, February 2004

13. ANDERSON, B. The U-value of solid ground floors with edge insulation. BRE Information Paper 7/93, April 1993, 4pp

BIBLIOGRAPHICAL REVIEW OF THE USED TYRE IN CONCRETE

J L Akasaki

A C Marques

M L Marques

A P M Trigo

Universidade Estadual Paulista (Unesp)

Brasil

ABSTRACT. Due to the progressive increase of vehicles, the number of used tires is globally one of the serious environmental problems faced now. Therefore, several researches have being developed for its reuse. The use of tires' rubber in the concrete is a possible form of its application, aiming at the recycling of this material and the improvement of certain properties, as tenacity, impact resistance, thermal and acoustic isolation. This article presents conclusions that several researchers obtained using the rubberized concrete. Thus there were researched several works enclosing the period of 1993 to 2003, presenting then the results of some characteristics of this concrete such as: physical properties in fresh and hardened state, mechanical properties and properties that remit the durability. The bibliographical revision has as objective to subsidize future researches that can contribute to improve the use of this concrete in civil construction.

Keywords: Tire rubber concrete, Civil construction, Mechanical properties.

Dr. J. L. Akasaki is a Professor of Universidade Estadual Paulista (Unesp). His research interests include the use of alternatives materials in civil construction.

Miss A. C. Marques is mastering in Civil Engineering. Her research interests include the use of recycled materials in concrete and mortar.

M. L. Marques is graduating in Civil Engineering. Her research interests the use of tire rubber in mortar.

A P. M. Trigo is graduating in Civil Engineering. Her research interests the use of tire rubber in mortar.

INTRODUCTION

The vulcanization process of natural rubber makes it more durable and resistant. The problem in this material is related to its difficult degradation. In landfills, the rubber, in form of tire, tends to hold backwater, bringing risks to health, because it creates the appropriate environment to the growing of insects and in the granule form it is harmful to the environment.

The Relastomer company affirms that about 300 thousand tons of tires are available in Brazil, but only 10% of these materials are recycled. In Rio de Janeiro, the rubber tires and devices in general correspond 0.5% of the urban garbage. The retreading, that in Brazil reaches 70% of the fleet of transport of load and passengers, is another important way to reduce this type of residue [1]. With the ambient questions comes the increasing technological advance that generates a production of residues from industrial processes that aggravate the damages to the environment causing a great concern with recycling methods or reuse of these materials.

The utilization of this material in concrete is an alternative suggested for many authors. The use of tire rubber is advised when the resistance mechanics is not the main characteristic but the resistance to the impact, low unit weight and higher toughness. In this work are presented bibliographies of authors who had used the tire rubber in concrete, mortar or cement paste. Also it is shown as the gradation of the residue, shape, substitution percentage or treatment of its surface influences in the behavior of the mixture. Thus, the work is divided in the following topics: properties in the fresh state and properties in the hardened state. Fresh property testing includes workability and unitary weight. Whilst, hardened state testing covered compressive strength, tensile strength, flexural strength, toughness, modulus of elasticity, impact resistance, fire resistance, freeze-thaw-resisting process and others.

PROPERTIES IN THE FRESH STATE

Workability

In a general way, workability is an attribute desired in most of the projects, which makes the evaluation of this property very interesting. Studies show that the workability of concrete with rubber is lower than the ordinary one (without rubber) and that the residue shape can influence the result. Mortars containing granular rubber have better workability than mortars with shredded rubber when they are measured with a VeBe test [2]. It was also observed in the same paper that concrete with tire rubber has a better workability than concrete without the residue.

In slump test there is a decrease in the workability when the amount of rubber is raised, 40% of rubber replacing aggregate cause a slump of approximately zero. It was noticed that mixtures with crumb rubber presented better workability than tire chips or a mixture of both [3].

Unit Weight

The use of tire rubber in concrete, mortars or cement paste, cause a decrease in unit weight of the composite [5-8]. It is because of the replacement of a material with higher unit weight for another [5].

This reduction depends on the amount of rubber replaced. A greater replacement of rubber makes the composite lighter. The size of the aggregate influence in the unit weight, smaller aggregate presented a decrease in obtained results [7].

PROPERTIES IN THE HARDENED STATE

Compressive Strength

In a general way, the addition of rubber in cement paste, mortar or concrete, cause a considerable decrease in compressive strength [7-16]. The replacement of sand in mortar by 30% of rubber decreases in 80% the compressive strength [9]. The size and shape of the aggregate have a slightly influence in the resistance because finner aggregate cause less damage to the resistance [7].

In concrete, depending on the replacement of the aggregate by rubber, the decrease in resistance can be up to 75%. The compressive strength of the cement paste, mortar and concrete also vary with the unit weight of the composite. There are two different behavior for this relationship, one for cement paste an mortar and other for concrete. For a similar unit weight, the decrease in the compressive strength of concrete is higher than in mortar and cement paste [5].

Although there is a great decrease in compressive strength, the failure of concrete with tire rubber occurres in a ductile way supporting higher deformations than the ordinary concrete [3,11 - 14]. In order to estimate the reduction in compressive strength, some authors had proposed an equation.

$$SRF = a + b(1 - R)^m \qquad \text{(equation 1)}$$

Where: SRF = Strength Reduction Factor;
R = rubber content (in percentage);
a, b e m = function parameters [3].

Splitting Tensile Test

As in the compressive strength test, there is a reduction in the splitting tensile strength, but this decrease isn't so accentuated as in the first test (compressive strength) [9, 10, 14, 15]. The replacement of 30% of the fine aggregate by rubber causes a decreasing of 70% in the tensile strength [9]. The shape of the rubber aggregate also influences the tests. In a general way the tire rubber used as fibers showed better performance than chips [14].

Flexural Strength

The flexural strength tests, as the tensile tests showed a decrease in resistance when the rubber was added [2, 3, 7, 15]. Comparing this resistance loss it can be noted that it isn't so great as in the compressive strength test [3]. The size of the rubber aggregate influences in the flexural strength, bigger particles caused a greater loss of resistance [7]. Shredded rubber present smaller loss in resistance than the granular one, it shows that the shape also influences in flexural strength [2].

The addition of rubber also raises the toughness of the composite. Specimens with rubber have a ductile behavior comparing with the ordinary mixtures. It happens because of the higher capacity to absorb energy of the composite with rubber [3, 12, 16]. When the cracks reach the rubber particles and because of its elastics properties and low modulus of elasticity, the rubber particles prolonged and underwent part of the load [12].

Modulus of Elasticity

Although the cement paste hadn't been noticed any change in the modulus of elasticity with the addition of rubber [8], its addition in mortar and concrete caused a decrease in it [9, 10, 14, 15]. Studies about dynamic modulus shoewed similar behavior [6]. In order to estimate the modulus of elasticity, some authors proposed an equation:

$$E'_c = k' E_m \frac{1 + 2V_{ar}\left(\dfrac{\alpha-1}{\alpha+2}\right)}{1 - V_{ar}\left(\dfrac{\alpha-1}{\alpha+2}\right)} \qquad \alpha = \frac{E_{ar}}{E_m} \qquad \text{(equation 2)}$$

where : E_c is the modulus of elasticity of the composite;
E_m is the modulus of elasticity of the matrix;
E_{ar} is the modulus of elasticity of the mortar;
V_{ar} is the volume proportion of the mortar;
k is a coefficient.

Experimental results confirm the validity of the equation [17].

Shrinkage

According to the literature, the use of rubber aggregates has improved the performance of materials subjected to shrinkage [2, 9, 18, 19]. The use of rubber also delays the progress of shrinkage, its length and width [2, 9].

Impact Resistance and Abrasion

According with the literature, the use of rubber in concrete can improve the impact resistance comparing the tests with the ordinary concrete, however, the specimens with rubber presented wide cracks [2, 4]. The size and shape of the aggregates also influence in the impact resistance, bigger aggregates showed better response than smaller ones [18]. Abrasion tests, carried out in cement paste and mortar also showed that composites with rubber had better performance than the ordinary [10, 15].

Water Absorption

Sometimes the main attribute in concrete isn't its compressive strength but the water absorption. Thus, it was studied the behavior of this property in cement paste, mortar and concrete. It was observed in cement paste, mortar and concrete, that the water absorption by capillarity decrease with the use of tire rubber as aggregate [8, 15, 20]. It can be justified because of the fact that the tire rubber don't absorb water. [8].

Hydraulic diffusivity and air permeability also were measured and the specimens added by rubber as in the water absorption had lower values than the ordinary composites [20].

Fire Resistance

An interesting attribute to be studied is the fire resistance, because the addition of an organic composite may change the behavior of this property comparing with the ordinary concrete. Tests in high strength concrete indicate that the raise in the content of rubber decrease the depth of damage of the specimens [11]. The Young modulus also varies with the temperature. In higher temperatures (60°C) the dispersion in the results is lesser than in lower temperatures. With 5% of rubber inserted, the Young modulus is higher than the composite with 3,5% of rubber [13]. Another kind of test was the use of blow torches for a period of three minutes to evaluate the reaction of specimens with tire rubber. Although the rubber on the faces was burned, any resulting fire extinguishes itself within 4s to 5s [5]. Showing that the cement and the aggregate lessen the rubber flammability.

Microscopy

Trying to show the feasibility of the use of tire rubber in mortar and concrete, it was analyzed the reaction of residues subjected to an alkaline environment up to 4 months. In this period it was observed that rubber didn't undergo any chemical degradation [2]. The decrease in mechanical strength is many times justified because of the weak adhesion between the cement paste and rubber aggregate. Some authors affirm that the adhesion can be improved by the treatment of the rubber's surface [15]. Some authors, however, affirm that there is a perfect adherence between the cement matrix and rubber. It can be attributed to a high concentration of calcium oxide crystals on the surface of the rubber and the presence of silicon and aluminium oxides. [13].

Other Properties

Besides the previous properties mentioned, there were carried out different ones. One of them is the setting time. It was observed that because of the presence of zinc in the rubber aggregate, it was caused an increasing in the initial and final setting time [21]. The freezing-thaw resistance it was also studied for some researches. And they had the same conclusion, the addition of tire rubber increase the resistance to the freezing-thaw process [18, 21].

CONCLUSIONS

According to the literature it can be conclude the following about the addition of tire rubber in concrete, mortar and cement paste:

- The workability can be influenced by the measured (depend on the test). Using the Ve-Be tests it is concluded that the workability of ordinary concrete is worse than the rubberized concrete. Measuring by the slump test the conclusion is the opposite. The size an shape of the aggregates also influence in the workability.

- The more the addition of tire rubber in concrete, mortar and cement paste, the more the decrease in unit weight.

- Decrease in compressive, tensile and flexural strength when added tire rubber in the composites. Higher contents of rubber c ause higher losses in the composites. Fiber rubber has a better performance than chips.

- The length and progress of fissuration are delayed when it is used the tire rubber aggregate.

- Tests in High strength concrete indicate that raising the content of rubber it happens a decrease in the depth of fire damage of the specimens. It was also observed the decrease in the flammability of the rubber when it is in the composite.

- Some properties were improved like water absorption, impact resistance and abrasion resistance by adding rubber.

- Rubber aggregates don't undergo chemical degradation when subjected to alkaline environments.

It is recommended the use of concrete with tire rubber in places where the mechanical resistance isn't the main attribute of the material. It is also suggested a better evaluation of the microstructure of the composite with rubber because of opposite conclusions found in the literature.

REFERENCES

1. LIMA, I. S.and ROCHA, F. S. Um Estudo da Argamassa de Cimento com Adição de Fibras de Borracha Vulcanizada Para a Construção Civil. Proceedings of CONGRESSO BRASILEIRO DO CONCRETO, 2000. CD-ROM.

2. RAGHAVAN, D., HUYNH, H. and FERRARIS, C. F. Workability, mechanical properties, and chemical stability of a recycled tire rubber-filled cementitious composite, Journal of Materials science, 33, 1998, pp.1745-1752.

3. KHATIB, Z. K. and BAYOMY, F. M. Rubberized Portland Cement Concrete. Journal of Materials in Civil Engineering, 1999, pp.206-213

4. SIDDIQUE, R. and NAIK, T. R. Properties of concrete containing scrap-tire Rubber – an overview, Waste Management , 2004.

5. FATTUHI, N. L. and CLARK, L. A Cement-based materials containing shredded scrap truck tire rubber. Construction and Building Materials, 10, No.4, 1996, pp.229-236.

6. PINTO, C. A., JOSÉ, C. L. V., VIANA, M; M. G. R., KOZIEVITCH, V. F. J., HAMASSAKI, L. T., WIEBECK, H., BÜCHLER, P. M. and VALENZUELA DIAZ, F. R. Study of the mechanical performance of composites of rubber powder and cement. Materials Science Forum, 416-418, 2003, pp.720-724.

7. BENAZZOUK, A., MEZREB, K. DOYEN, G., GOULLIEUX, A., QUÉNEUDEc, M. Effect of rubber aggregates on the physico-mechanical behaviour of cement–rubber

composites-influence of the alveolar texture of rubber aggregates. Cement and Concrete Composites, 25, 2003, pp. 711-720.

8. SEGRE, N., JOEKES, I. Use of tire rubber particles as addition to cement paste. Cement and Concrete Research, 30, 2000, pp.1421-1425.

9. BONNET, S. Effet de l'incorporation des granulats caoutchouc sur la résistance à la fissuration des morties. XXI^{EMES} Rencontres Universitaires de Genie Civil, 2003,pp.59-70.

10. MENEGUINI, E. A. C. Comportamento De Argamassas Com O Emprego De Pó De Borracha. Master of Science's thesis, Universidade Estadual de Campinas, 2003, 85p.

11. HERNÁNDEZ-OLIVARES, F. and BARLUENGA, G. Fire performance of recycled rubber-filled high strength concrete. Cement and Concrete Research, 34, 2004, pp.109-117.

12. TOUTANJI, H. A. The Use of Rubber Tire Particles in Concrete to Replace Mineral Aggregates. Cement and Concrete Composites, 18, 1996, pp.135-139.

13. HERNÁNDEZ-OLIVARES, F., BARLUENGA, G., BOLLATI, M. and WITOSZEK, B. Static and dynamic behavior of recycled tire rubber-filled concrete. Cement and Concrete Research, 32, 2002, pp.1587–1596.

14. LIA, G., GARRICKA, G., EGGERSB, J., ABADIEB, C., STUBBLEFIELDC, M. A. and PANGA, S. Waste tire fiber modified concrete. Composites: Part B, 35, 2004, pp.305–312.

15. BAUER, R. J. F., TOKUDOME, S. and GADRET, A. D. Estudo de Concreto com Pneu Moído. Proceedings of 43° Congresso Brasileiro do Concreto, 2001.

16. TAHA, M. M. R., EL-DIEB, A. S. and ABDEL-WAHAB, M. M. Fracture Toughness of Concrete Incorporating Rubber Tire Particles. Proceedings of ICPCM – A New Era of Building, Cairo, February 2003.

17. TOPÇU, I. B. and AVCULAR, N. Analysis of Rubberized Concrete as a Composite Material. Cement and Concrete Research, 27, No. 8, 1997, pp.1135-1 139.

18. DHIR, R., PAINE, K. and MORONEY, R. Recycling of used tires in concrete. Concrete, London, 37, No.9, 2003, pp.47-48.

19. WANG, Y., WU, H. C. and LI, V. C. Concrete Reinforcement with Recycled Fibers. Journal of Materials in Civil Engineering, 12, No. 4, 2000, pp.314-319.

20. BENAZZOUK, A., DOUZANE, O. and QUÉNEUDEC, M. Transport of fluids in cement–rubber composites. Cement & Concrete Composites, 26, 2004, pp 21–29.

21. AL-AKHRAS, N. M. and SMADI, M. M. Properties of tire rubber ash mortar. Cement & Concrete Composites, 2004.

INFLUENCE OF TYRE ORIGIN ON THE YIELD AND COMPOSITION OF PRODUCTS FROM THE PYROLYSIS OF SCRAP TYRES

M Kyari

A M. Cunliffe

P T Williams

The University of Leeds

United Kingdom

ABSTRACT. There is increasing interest in the application of pyrolysis technology for the treatment of scrap tyres. Pyrolysis involves the thermal degradation of the rubber polymer component of the tyre in the absence of oxygen. There are many different manufacturers, types and formulations of tyre available in the market place. In this paper, seven different brands and types of tyre from different countries have been pyrolysed in a fixed bed reactor and the yield and composition of the products have been determined. In addition, all seven tyres were mixed and pyrolysed together. The product yields of char, oil and gas were very similar for the seven tyres investigated. The main gases produced were H_2, CH_4, CO_2, C_4H_6 and C_2H_6, CO and minor concentrations of other hydrocarbon gases. The gas composition showed significant variation between the tyre types pyrolysed. The oil derived from the pyrolysis of the tyres showed very similar broad compositional properties but differences in their detailed composition. Overall the results suggest that the yield of products from the pyrolysis of tyres are not significantly influenced by the type and origin of the tyre. However, the range of different formulations and rubber types used in the different types and brands of tyre has a significant influence on the composition of the derived oils and gases.

Keywords: Tyres, Pyrolysis, Recycling

Mohammed Kyari is a research student and a Borno State Scholar from, Nigeria. He holds a BSc in Physics and an MSc in Environmental Pollution Control. He is currently investigating the pyrolysis of wastes as part of his PhD research at The University of Leeds.

Dr Adrian Cunliffe is a Research Fellow in the Energy and Resources Research Institute, University of Leeds, with research interests in the thermal processing of waste materials by pyrolysis and incineration. After completing his doctorate at Leeds on the recycling of scrap tyres, he worked as a Research Associate at Cardiff University. He is currently an Incorporated Engineer and an Associate Member of the Energy Institute.

Professor Paul T. Williams is Professor of Environmental Engineering in the Energy and Resources Research Institute at The University of Leeds and has a research background in both applied chemistry and process engineering. He has published more than 200 academic papers in the area of environmental engineering, including waste incineration and waste and biomass pyrolysis. He is a Chartered Engineer and Fellow of the Institute of Energy and is a member of the Editorial Boards of the journals, Environmental Technology and of Fuel.

INTRODUCTION

The current main disposal routes for scrap tyres throughout the world are stockpiling, illegal dumping and landfill [1]. With the increasing emphasis on the re-use, recycling and recovery of all types of waste this is seen as a waste of a resource and potentially harmful to the environment. There has been increasing interest in the development of processes for recycling scrap tyres to recover materials which can be used back in the tyre production process o r to p roduce p roducts w hich can b e u sed i n o ther a pplications. T here a re m any different manufacturers and countless different types and formulations of tyre available in the market place. The composition of the tyre varies depending on the tyre grade and manufacturer.

Tyres are composed of vulcanised rubber in addition to the rubberised fabric with reinforcing textile cords, steel or fabric belts and steel-wire reinforcing beads [2]. The most commonly used rubbers used in tyre manufacture include styrene-butadiene-copolymer, natural rubber, polyisoprene rubber, nitrile rubber, chloroprene rubber and polybutadiene rubber. Other components in the tyre include; carbon black which is used to strengthen the rubber and aid abrasion resistance; extender oil which serves to soften the rubber and improve workability; sulphur which is used to cross link the polymer chains within the rubber and also to harden and prevent excessive deformation at elevated temperatures; an accelerator, added as a catalyst for the vulcanisation process; zinc oxide and stearic acid used to control the vulcanisation process and to enhance the physical properties of the rubber.

There is current interest in the novel application of the technology of pyrolysis to recycle a range of waste materials, including used tyres [3-4]. Pyrolysis is the thermal degradation of the rubber polymer component of the tyre in the absence of oxygen. The polymer breaks down to produce an oil, a gas and a char product in addition to the steel reinforcement. Pyrolysis has the advantage that potentially all of the products from the process can be utilised. The pyrolysis products, in terms of yield and chemical composition may also vary depending on the source of the tyres. For the development of the pyrolysis process, there is a need to understand the influence of the range of tyre compositions on the yield and composition of the derived products. In this paper, seven different brands and types of tyre from different countries have been pyrolysed in a fixed bed reactor and the yield and composition of the products have been determined.

MATERIALS AND METHODS

Seven used tyres were obtained, representing a selection of different types, brands and different countries of origin, i.e., Poland, Korea, Japan, South Africa, Italy and the UK (Table- 1). The tyres were standard saloon car tyres and performance tyres and were all radial tyres. The tyres were cut into 25 mm x 30 mm pieces, from the main tread area of the tyre, including the steel reinforcement. The tyres were characterised using standard proximate analysis.

The tyre pyrolysis results are the mean of at least two pyrolysis experiments. The tyre pieces were pyrolysed in a fixed bed reactor. The reactor was constructed of stainless steel and was a nominal 200 cm^3 in capacity and was heated by an electrical ring furnace. The reactor was continuously purged with nitrogen to reduce the extent of secondary reactions such as thermal cracking, repolymerisation and recondensation. Approximately 45 g of tyre sample was placed on a support in the centre of the hot zone of the reactor and heated at a controlled rate of 10 °C min^{-1} to a final temperature of 500 °C and held at that temperature for 1 h. The oil was condensed in a series of cold traps. Non-condensable gases were sampled at timed intervals throughout the pyrolysis experiments using gas sample syringes and analysed using packed column gas chromatography. The gases were analysed for hydrocarbon and non-hydrocarbon gases. H ydrocarbons f rom C$_1$ t o C$_4$ w ere a nalysed u sing a V arian 3 380 gas chromatograph with flame ionization detector. Nitrogen, hydrogen, oxygen and carbon monoxide were analysed with a Pye Unicam series 204 gas chromatograph with a thermal conductivity detector. Carbon dioxide was analysed using a Gow-Mac Spectra gas chromatograph with a 1.8 m x 6 mm stainless steel column packed with 100-120 mesh silica gel, helium carrier gas and thermal conductivity detector.

Table 1. Proximate analysis of the tyre samples (wt%)

TYRE	MOISTURE	ASH	VOLATILES	FIXED CARBON
1. Debica (Poland)	1.24	2.66	69.35	26.74
2. Eurotour (Korea)	0.37	2.20	68.22	29.20
3. Dunlop (Japan)	0.51	4.81	66.79	27.89
4. Goodyear (S.Africa)	0.57	4.98	67.96	26.49
5. Courier (Italy)	1.31	3.39	65.04	30.26
6. Michelin (Italy)	1.76	2.39	67.13	28.72
7. Continental (UK)	0.47	6.23	67.44	25.86

Functional group, compositional analysis of the oils was carried out using Fourier transform infra-red (FT-ir) spectrometry to determine any broad differences in composition in relation to the origin of the tyre. The system used was a Nicolet Magna 560IR FT-ir spectrometer with spectral library search facility. The spectrometer scanned the sample from 450 cm^{-1} to 4000 cm^{-1} wavelength and spectral peak heights normalised to the major C-H peak. The oils were also analysed in detail using coupled gas chromatography/mass spectrometry for single ring aromatic compounds and polycyclic aromatic compounds [3].

The char product derived from the pyrolysis of the different brands of tyre were characterised in terms of their surface area. Surface area was determined with nitrogen adsorption experiments using a Quantachrome Corp. Quantasorb instrument. Elemental analysis of the chars was performed with a CE Instruments Dynamic Flash EA 112 elemental analyser.

RESULTS AND DISCUSSION

The repeatability of the experimental system was verified by multiple replicate pyrolysis experiments on a single tyre. The results were a char yield between 37.7 and 38.3 with a mean of 38.0 wt% and a standard deviation of 0.3 wt%. The oil yield was between 56.1 wt% and 57.3 wt% with a mean of 56.6 wt% and standard deviation of 0.5 wt%. Gas yield results were between 2.7 wt% and 5.7 wt% with a mean of 4.1 and a standard deviation of 1.2 wt%. The mass closures were in the range 96.5wt% to 100.3wt%, deemed to be acceptable.

Table 2 shows the product yield for the seven tyres under investigation together with the pyrolysis of a mixture of all seven tyres. There were small but significant differences between the yield of char, oil and gas between the seven tyres. For example, the Michelin tyre produced a higher char yield compared to the other six tyres. The standard deviation of the char yield for the replicate experiments was of the order of 0.3 wt%. Suggesting that the difference between the tyre char yield results was small but significant. Similarly, some tyres such as the Goodyear, Debica, Eurotour and Courier tyres produced higher oil yields. However, overall there did not appear to be major differences in the product yield of char, oil and gas between the tyres, ranging from 37.1wt% char to 41.7 wt% char with a mean of 38.3. The oil yield ranged from 56.6 wt% to 60.1 wt% with a mean of 58.8 wt%. There was more variation in the gas yield between the seven tyres, ranging from 1.9 wt% to 4.1 wt% with a mean of 2.5wt%. However, the replicate pyrolysis experiments on a single tyre showed a similar variation in the yield of gas was found for the replicate experiments on the single tyre.

Other researchers have examined the variability of tyre product yield in relation to tyre brand [5]. The system consisted of a pyrolysis unit with a further post-pyrolysis cracking unit which served to decrease the yield of oil and increase the yield of gas. Their char yields were between 41.7 wt% and 45.3 wt% for the six tyres, not too dissimilar to those reported in this work. However, their oil yield data ranged from 37.0wt% to 42.2 wt% and gas yields from 16.2wt% to 19.5wt%, that is, producing reduced oil yield and increased gas yield compared to the work reported here, which was due to the configuration of the experimental reactor with the post-pyrolysis heated cracking unit. Williams and Besler [2] investigated the thermal decomposition of three samples of tyre and the major rubber components of the tyres using thermogravimetric analysis. They reported that the tyre samples showed two distinct areas of weight loss representing a lower and higher temperature of decomposition. Styrene-butadiene rubber decomposed mainly at higher temperatures of pyrolysis, natural rubber at lower temperatures and polybutadiene rubber had both higher and lower areas of decomposition. The thermal decomposition of the three samples of tyre could be related to the known composition of their constituent components.

Table 2. Product yield for the pyrolysis of different tyre brands (wt%)

TYRE BRAND	CHAR	OIL	GAS	TOTAL
1. Debica	37.5	59.8	2.3	99.6
2. Eurotour	37.5	59.7	2.3	99.5
3. Dunlop	38.0	56.6	4.1	98.7
4. Goodyear	37.1	60.1	2.5	99.7
5. Courier	38.0	59.6	2.3	99.9
6. Michelin	41.7	57.1	1.9	100.7
7. Continental	38.3	58.7	2.3	99.3
Mean	38.3	58.8	2.5	99.6
Mixture of 7 tyres	37.9	60.1	2.4	100.4

Table 2 also shows the product yield for the pyrolysis of a mixture of the seven tyres. The results were very similar to the mean of the individual pyrolysis of the seven tyres. These data suggests that a mixture of different tyres produced very similar product yield results to the mean of the individual tyres in the mixture.

Table 3 shows the gas composition for the pyrolysis of the seven tyres. There were significant variations in the composition of the gases derived from the pyrolysis of the seven different tyres. For example, carbon dioxide concentration for the Continental tyre was less than half of that for the Michelin tyre. The Debica tyre from Poland showed high concentrations of carbon monoxide. There were also major differences in hydrogen concentration, the Eurotour and Michelin tyres producing more than 27 vol % of hydrogen in the derived gas. The hydrocarbon gases also showed significant variability in concentration depending on the origin of the tyre. The variation in gas composition was reflected in the calculated gross calorific value of the gases, producing values between 26.3 MJ m^{-1} to 42.1 MJ m^{-1} depending on the brand of the tyre. Cypres and Bettens [5] have also reported significant differences in the gas composition from the pyrolysis of different brands of tyre. For example, for the six different tyres that they investigated there were variations in hydrogen, ethane and ethene concentration of more than 100%. Table 3 showed that the pyrolysis of the mixture of the seven tyres produced gas composition results in most cases similar to those of the mean of the gas composition derived from the pyrolysis of the seven individual tyres.

Table 3. Gas composition from the pyrolysis of different tyre brands (vol%)

TYRE	CO_2	CO	H_2	CH_4	C_2H_6	C_2H_4	C_3H_8	C_3H_6	C_4H_{10}	C_xH_x
1.	24.4	10.5	23.7	18.0	8.3	4.1	4.6	3.8	1.2	1.4
2.	16.9	5.9	27.5	18.5	7.6	9.6	4.0	3.1	1.1	6.0
3.	17.6	4.0	21.5	24.8	11.2	10.4	4.9	4.1	0.9	0.7
4.	15.5	6.3	13.8	27.9	12.6	10.3	6.1	5.6	1.7	0.1
5.	22.6	13.3	16.0	19.1	13.5	4.2	3.1	3.1	1.1	4.2
6.	27.5	7.5	27.6	14.1	5.8	2.8	2.8	2.1	0.8	8.9
7.	12.5	11.6	15.6	25.0	9.3	6.9	4.4	4.3	0.3	10.1
Mean	19.6	8.4	20.8	21.1	9.8	6.9	4.3	3.7	1.0	4.5
Mixture	26.2	5.1	21.5	17.3	8.2	8.7	3.9	3.4	0.7	5.0

The tyre pyrolysis oils were analysed for their broad chemical properties in the form of their functional group chemical composition using Fourier transform infra-red (FT-ir) spectrometry and molecular mass range using size exclusion chromatography. Figure 1 shows the FT-ir spectra for the pyrolysis oil derived from the pyrolysis of the seven tyres, together with the oil derived from the pyrolysis of the mixture of the seven tyres. The =C–H stretching vibrations at 3100 to 3000 cm^{-1} indicate the presence of aromatic groups. The C–H stretching vibrations between 2800 and 3000 cm^{-1} and C–H deformation vibrations between 1350 and 1475 cm^{-1} indicate the presence of alkanes. The C=O stretching vibrations with absorbance between 1650 and 1750 cm^{-1} indicate the presence of ketones or aldehydes. The absorbance peaks between 1575 and 1675 cm^{-1} and 875 and 950 cm^{-1} represent C=C stretching vibrations, and are indicative of alkenes. Aromatic groups are indicated by the absorption peaks at 675-900 cm^{-1} and 1575-1625 cm^{-1}. The presence of alkanes, alkenes and mono, and aromatic compounds together with alkyl derivatives have been identified in the oil derived from the pyrolysis of tyres. There were some significant differences in the functional group compositional analysis of the tyre pyrolysis oils depending on the origin of the seven tyres. For example, the Eurotour and Dunlop tyres produced several peaks in the region 1500 to 1800 cm^{-1}. This region of the infra-red spectrum is characterised by C=O stretching vibrations indicative of oxygenated compounds, C=C stretching vibrations indicative of alkenes and also aromatic groups. The mixture of the seven tyres produced an infra-red spectra which appeared to be an average of the spectra of the seven individual tyre pyrolysis oils.

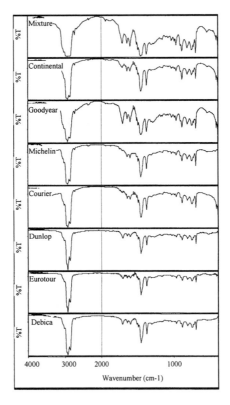

Figure 1. Fourier transform infra-red spectra of the pyrolysis oils derived from the pyrolysis of the seven tyres and a mixture of the tyres.

The tyre pyrolysis oils were also analysed in detail for their concentration of aromatic hydrocarbons. The main single ring aromatic compounds identified in the oils were, benzene, toluene, xylenes, styrene, limonene and indene together with alkylated species. The main polycyclic aromatic hydrocarbons found in the tyre pyrolysis oil consisted largely of alkylated naphthalenes, fluorenes and phenanthrenes. In addition, pyrene, chrysene and other higher molecular weight polycyclic aromatic hydrocarbons were identified. Other workers have also identified such aromatic and polycyclic aromatic hydrocarbons in the oils derived from tyre pyrolysis [3-5,10]. There was significant variation in the concentration of most aromatic compounds found in the pyrolysis oils derived from the different tyre brands. For example, the limonene concentration in the tyre pyrolysis oils was found to range from 2.8wt% to 4.7wt%, naphthalene from 0.09wt% to 0.29 wt%, phenanthrene from 0.03 wt% to 0.08wt% and chrysene from 0.02 wt% to 0.06wt%. Similar variation in the concentration of single r ing a nd p olycyclic a romatic h ydrocarbons i n o ils d erived f rom d ifferent t yre t ypes have been reported [5]

The composition of the derived tyre pyrolysis oil and gases will be dependent on the composition of the rubber formulation used in the specific brands of tyre. The most commonly used rubbers used in tyre manufacture include styrene-butadiene-copolymer, natural rubber, polyisoprene rubber, nitrile rubber, chloroprene rubber and polybutadiene rubber. The thermal degradation of such rubber components have been analysed to determine the products of pyrolysis. For example, Groves et al. [6] analysed the oil derived from the pyrolysis of natural rubber in a pyrolysis-gas chromatograph at 500 °C. They showed that the major products were the monomer, isoprene and the dimer, dipentene with other oligomers up to the hexamer in significant concentrations. Chien and Kiang [7] pyrolysed natural rubber in helium at 384 °C and identified isoprene and dipentene as the main products of pyrolysis. They also identified a wide range of other products including, alkane and alkene gases, toluene, xylene, octene and hydrocarbons up to $C_{16}H_{26}$. Madorsky et al. [8] have examined the pyrolysis of polybutadiene rubber and showed that butadiene, vinylcyclohexene and dipentene were formed in high concentrations. Other compounds formed were, ethene, ethane, propene, propane, butene, butane, cyclopentadienes etc. The pyrolysis of styrene-butadiene-rubber between 240 °C and 450 °C has been investigated by Erdogan et al. [9] using a pyrolysis-mass spectrometer. They identified butadiene and butadiene moities at lower pyrolysis temperatures and styrene and/or benzene at higher temperatures. The range of different formulations and rubber types used in the different types and brands of tyre will consequently have a significant influence on the composition of the derived oils and gases as shown in this work.

The chars were also analysed to determine any variation in their characteristics in relation to tyre origin. The chars were analysed for surface area and elemental composition. The results showed that the surface area ranged from 64.5 and 83.8 m^2 g^{-1} and the mixture of the seven tyres gave a char surface area of 69.5 m^2 g^{-1}, consistent with the surface area expected from the results of the individual tyre char surface areas. The elemental analyses for the tyre derived chars showed similar carbon, hydrogen and nitrogen concentrations, but a small variation in the sulphur content.

CONCLUSIONS

Tyres from different manufacturers and country of origin have been pyrolysed in a fixed bed reactor to determine the influence of tyre source on the yield and composition of the pyrolysis products. The yield of char, oil and gas were very similar for the seven tyres investigated under the process conditions of pyrolysis operating in this work. The mixture of the seven tyres produced a pyrolysis yield consistent with the data obtained from the seven individual tyres. However, there was significant variation in the gas composition of the individual tyres, with a wide range in the concentration of carbon dioxide, carbon monoxide, hydrogen methane and other hydrocarbon gases found. The oil derived from the pyrolysis of the tyres showed very similar broad compositional properties as measured by infra-red spectrometry. However, for some oils there were significant differences in composition. The mixture of the seven tyres produced tyre oil, which showed the average characteristics of the seven individual tyres. The analysis of the tyre derived chars were very similar in terms of their surface area for the individual tyre pyrolysis chars and also the mixture of the tyres. Overall the results suggest that the yield of products from the pyrolysis of tyres are not significantly influenced by the type and origin of the tyre. However, the range of different formulations and rubber types used in the different types and brands of tyre has a significant influence on the composition of the derived oils and gases.

REFERENCES

1. ARCHER E., KLEIN A. AND WHITING K., The scrap tyre dilemma; can technology offer commercial solutions. Waste Management World, January, James & James Science Publishers Ltd., London, 2004.

2. WILLIAMS P.T. AND BESLER S. Pyrolysis thermogravimetric analysis of tyres and tyre components. Fuel, 74, 1995, 74, 1277-1283.

3. CUNLIFFE A .M. A ND W ILLIAMS P .T., C omposition o f o ils d erived f rom t he b atch pyrolysis of tyres. J. Anal Appl. Pyrolysis, 44, 1998, 131-152.

4. BENALLAL, B., PAKDEL, H., CHABOT, S. AND ROY C., Characterisation of pyrolytic light naphtha from vacuum pyrolysis of used tyres; comparison with petroleum naphtha. Fuel, 74, 1995, 1589-1596.

5. CYPRES R. AND BETTENS B. Production of benzoles and active carbon from waste rubber and plastic materials by means of pyrolysis with simultaneous post-cracking. In, Ferrero G.L., Maniatis K., Buekens A. and Bridgwater A.V. (Eds.), Pyrolysis and Gasification, Elsevier

6. GROVES S.A., LEHRLE R.S., BLAZSO M. AND SZEKELY T. J. Natural rubber pyrolysis: study of temperature and thickness dependence indicates dimmer formation mechanism. Anal. Appl. Pyrol., 19, 1991, 301-309.

7. CHIEN J.C.W. AND KIANG J.K.Y., Polymer reactions; thermal pyrolysis of polyisoprene. Eur. Polym. J., 15, 1979, 1059-1065.

8. MADORSKY S.L., STRAUS S., THOMPSON D. AND WILLIAMSON L., Pyrolysis of polyisobutene, polyisoprene, polybutadiene, GR-S and polyethylene in a high vacuum. J. Res. Natl. Bur. Std., 42, 1949, 499-514.

9. ERDOGAN M., YALCIN T., TINCER T. AND SUZER S., Evolved gas analysis of pyrolysis products from some rubbers by mass spectrometry. European. Polymer. J., 27, 1991, 413-433.

10. WILLIAMS P.T. AND TAYLOR, Aromatisation of tyre pyrolysis oil to yield polycyclic aromatic hydrocarbons. Fuel, 72, 1993, 1469-1474.

SOME PROBLEMS OF DESIGNING STRUCTURES USING RECYCLED TYRES FOR CONCRETE COLUMNS, ROAD BASE AND SPOT FOOTINGS

B. P. Pasynkov

S. M. Skorobogatov

Urals State University of Railway Transport

Russia

ABSTRACT. Further improvement of new structure having left a formwork as recycled tyres depends undoubtedly on the formation of the problems in design with the aim of creating the method of their calculation. The paper describes some problems for designing on the most characteristic examples of constructional suggestions. Among them are: a reinforced concrete column element, a spot footing under railway and a floor base.

KEYWORDS: Damper, Modulus of subgrade reaction, Concrete element, Spot footing, Floor base.

Professor B. P. Pasynkov works at the Urals State University of Railway Transport. He took part in inspection, enhancement and rejuvenation of many buildings and bridges. His research interests include dynamics, heatproof walls and design of structures with recycled tyres.

Doctor, Professor S. M. Skorobogatov in 1978 organized a new section of building structures for training civil engineers at the Urals State University of Railway Transport (Russia, Ekaterinburg). Previously he was a professor at the Urals Polytechnical University. He took part in inspection, enhancement and rejuvenation of many buildings including ones damaged in the well-known catastrophe at the railway station Sverdlovsk-Sortirovochny. During the past decade he has been creating the elements of the theory of technical and natural catastrophes.

INTRODUCTION

Repeatedly held international conferences on recycling used tyres are reflecting the great anxiety of the mankind in connection with this challenge and are causing the professional interest of building engineers. Utilization of waste metal-corded tyres in road pavements and in foundation structures under aggressive environment deserves special attention. Among many structural designs devoted to this challenge there is a constructional suggestion of one of the authors of the paper – B. P. Pasynkov (inventor's certificate of the USSR No. EO-2D 5/02, 5/10, EO 4C 3/34). The economic feasibility of cast-in-place concrete made with used tyres is well known.

Further improvement of such structures depends undoubtedly on the formulation of the main problems in the design with the aim of creating the methods of calculation on such specific structures.

PROBLEMS IN DESIGNING

There are some problems in designing these specific structures made from used tyres. Among them are:

1. Closer examination and validity of value of damper characteristics in shell-tyres filled with rigid (concrete) or free-flowing (sand) materials which work under dynamical effect from transport.

2. Elucidation of an optimal possible range of values of the bending and normal rigidity in road pavements.

3. Determination of an optimal possible range of values of modulus of subgrade reaction (by Westergaad) in road pavements.

4. Resistance of used tyres fastened together with connection's details to tensile forces from wheel friction of transport.

5. Determination of minimum values of concrete classes of compression strength and tensile strength under mutual work of concrete and tyres.

6. Justification of the field of operating condition for used tyres and concrete in spot footings under uniaxial loading.

To discuss the principles mentioned above let us take up characteristic examples of our constructional suggestions. We mean a reinforced concrete column element (Figures 1 and 2), a spot footing under railway (Figure 3) and a floor base (Figure 4).

REINFORCED CONCRETE COLUMN ELEMENT

To our opinion, the reinforced concrete column element is still the most characteristic for using recycled tyres as leaving formwork. It consists of a round concrete core 1, goffers of tyres 2 and a cage of reinforcement 3. The cage of reinforcement analogously to round reinforced concrete columns consists of longitudinal steel bars of hoop reinforcement with stirrups. A bar spacing is not more than 400 mm. Minimum number of these longitudinal bars is four as shown in Fig. 1. Independently of calculation minimum diameter must not be less than 10 mm, and reinforcement class – not higher than A 400. The longitudinal bars are joined together with cross lateral stirrups of diameter not less than 6 mm and of class Bp-I. The bar space for stirrups is not more than 400 mm. To use passivation feature of cement past relating to reinforcement there must be a concrete cover 20-30 mm thickness.

To assemble the goffering formwork, the recycled tyres are packed one on each other. Then they are connected together with polymer glue or fasteners, clamps along round on the circumference contact surface. Not to impede the assembling of the internal reinforcement, all the connections over tyres must not lean out of the internal round surface of tyres. One of the most successful technical suggestions of connections is shown in Figure 2.

The reinforced concrete element (Figure 1) can be used as foundation column in construction industry and in frame foundation of engineering industry. From the point of view of statical model, the column element is dedicated to axial and eccentrical compression with small value of the eccentricity $e_o \leq 0.2 \cdot d$, where d – diameter of the cross sectional area of concrete core. In present codes there is no calculation on axial compression, that is why an accidental eccentricity is assumed to be equal to $e_o = d/30$ and not less than 1 cm. Because of hazard of great eccentricity, the tyres of various diameters are inapplicable in column structures except for their lower footings.

The maximum relationship between the length of the column element L and the internal diameter of its tyre d is equal to 12. Minimum class of concrete is C20 (Mpa), and the reinforcement ratio of the longitudinal bars is $p \geq 0.005$. The calculation on fatigue is required for column elements in frame foundation of mechanical engineering. Primitive calculation with a dynamic factor may be neglected. The negative influence of a round tyre as a tension yoke may also be neglected under the calculation on the bearing strength.

The above careful restrictions under a designing process may be lessened or excluded in future as the technical and operational properties of the new structures are investigated. The left formwork made from tyres prevents a loss of free and semi-combined water from cement past. This protective measure reduces or excludes shrinkage phenomenon, shrinkage strain and stress in concrete. Lowering probability of the shrinkage phenomenon increases durability of concrete core. This is the main technical advantage of the new proposed structure.

The main exploitative disadvantage of the proposed structure is impossibility to be observed after long maintenance. Such a necessity arises in a case of a danger from electro-corrosion. That is why, for example, the use of such a structure under the aerial power line should be verified by an experimental approach. To prevent a great internal eccentricity, the assembly of the formwork of tyres is recommended with in a jig. The internal cage of reinforcement is set in its place before concreting. Contact of tyre goffers to reinforcement bars is undesirable. The aggregate grain-size distribution must have two fractions. Maximum value of aggregate grain is equal to 20 mm. The use of a concrete vibration and concreting in lifts is imperative. For purpose of control of filling voids of goffers with concrete, at the top of each goffer there must be two or more holes with diameter 10...15 mm.

The economical advantage of the new structure discussed above lies in the fact that we have no expenditure for steel and wooden formwork. But during the process of concreting a great deal of concrete mix is a waste in voids of goffers. This economical lack is compensated for by ecological consideration.

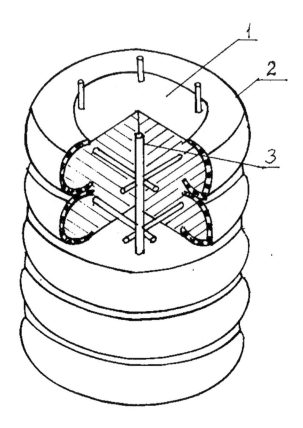

Figure 1. Reinforced concrete column element having left goffering formwork made of recycled tyres: 1 – concrete; 2 – goffers of tyres; 3 – cage of reinforcement.

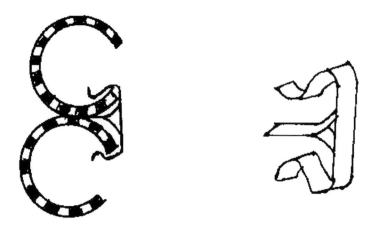

Figure 2. One of the successful suggestions of connection (laid on a clamp).

The column element being unique for the problems discussed above doesn't have structural versatility. It demands a local structural suggestion in each special case of being used in monolitical concrete construction.

ROAD BASE AND FLOOR BASE

The tyres are directly inapplicable in slab structures bearing load. But they can be successfully used in distribution layers as base under these slab structures, that is in road base (Figure 3), in floor base (Figure 4) and pavement base.

Figures 3 and 4 show schemes of using tyres as a spot footing with absorption of vibration and sound. These suggestions are likely the most popular kinds of using tyres in structures. As mentioned above at the beginning of the paper, the damper and other characteristics of distribution layers should be studied. For example, it is also necessary to study the resistance and work of lap plates (fish plates) in Fig. 3 against working shear and tensile forces from wheel friction of transport.

CONCLUSIONS

As a consequence of the above examination of positive and negative properties of these new most characteristic structures having left formwork as recycled tyres, it is possible to predict their social, technical and exploitative advantages in comparison with traditional structures. The prospects of their evolution and realization depend upon solving the problems outlined above at the beginning of the paper.

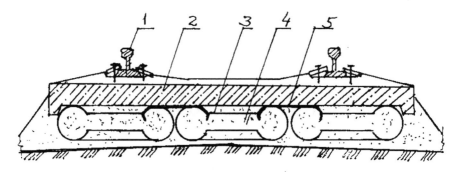

Figure 3. Scheme of road base with absorption of vibration and sound: 1 – rail; 2 – reinforced concrete slab; 3 – aggregate base; 5 – connections (lap plate).

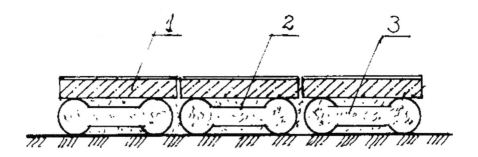

Figure 4. Scheme of floor plate: 1 – reinforced concrete plate; 2 – tyres; 3 – aggregate base.

RECYCLE OF USED TYRES: CRYOGENIC DISINTEGRATION AND REUSE OF THE OBTAINED PRODUCTS

M C Zanetti

G Genon

Polytechnic of Turin- DIGET

Italy

ABSTRACT. In Italy, each year, about 250.000 – 300.000 tons of used tyres are eliminated: about the 15% b.w. is rebuilt, the 30% b.w. is reused for other aims (energy and powder production) and the remaining fraction (about 40% b.w.) is landfilled. Generally the landfilled used tyres necessitate at least of one hundred years for a complete biodegradation. Other technical solutions are reuse and energy recovery. The recycle of used tyres in the next future will be of a great importance in Europe: the target value is the 25% b.w. in the year 2005. Actually the rubber powder production from used tyres for recycle may be achieved by means of mechanical, cryomechanical with liquid nitrogen and cryomechanical with air disintegration. In this paper a new technology concerning the air cryogenic disintegration of used tyres will be examined considering the obtained products (quality and quantity) and a cost – benefit analysis.

Keywords: Used tyres, Recycle, Reuse, Cryomechanical disintegration, Powder rubber, Asphalt pavement, Synthetic court

Professor M.C. Zanetti is a Chartered Engineer in the Polytechnic of Turin, Faculty of Engineering. Her research interests include the recycle and reuse of industrial wastes, the contaminated land remediation and the water and wastewater treatment.

Professor G. Genon is a Chartered Engineer in the Polytechnic of Turin, Faculty of Engineering. His research interests include the recycle and reuse of wastes, the water and wastewater treatment and the study of the dynamics and containment of air pollution.

INTRODUCTION

In Italy, each year, about 250.000 – 300.000 tons of used tyres are eliminated: about the 15 % b.w. is retreaded, the 30 % b.w. is reused for other aims (energy and powder production) and the remaining fraction (about 40 % b.w.) is landfilled. In the last years the fraction of scrap tyres employed for the energy production is increasing: the actually employed technologies are rotating drum and fluidised bed incinerators. About the 15 % b.w. of scrap tyres is sent abroad to other countries like Brazil, Argentina and so on. Actually the most recent Italian law about landfills (D.L. 36, 13/01/2003) established that starting from the 16/07/2003 "no whole scrap tyre may be landfilled any more".

On average a tyre for car has a total weight about equal to 6 kg and it is made of elastomers (50 % b.w.), carbon (20 % b.w.), carbon black, oils, zinc oxides, steel (about 15 % b.w.) and textiles [1]. Elastomers are cross linked thermosetting materials and therefore cannot be softened or remolding by heating again. Chemical additives (mostly in minor quantities) are generally incorporated as stabilizers, flame-retardants, colorants to optimise product properties and performance. Therefore in case of thermosetting materials like rubbers recycling is not easy. The three dimensional network of the thermoset polymer must be broken down either through the cleavage of crosslinks, or through the carbon-carbon linkage of the chain backbone. This is a severe process and the fragmented products thus obtained are entirely different from the starting thermoset [2]. The actual and future perspectives of used tyres in Europe are shown in Table 1.

Table 1: Actual and future perspective of used tyres in Europe.

	Used tyres in EUROPE in 1994 year	Used tyres in EUROPE in 2002 year	U.E. target for used tyres for 2005 year
Reuse and material recovery	13%	14%	25%
Rebuilding	22%	20%	15%
Energy recovery	3%	30%	60%
Landfill	62%	36%	0%

Generally the landfilled used tyres necessitate at least of one hundreds years for a complete biodegradation due to the cross-inked structure of rubbers and presence of stabilizers and other additives. Therefore, landfilling and retreading excepted, the available technical solutions for used tyres are the following:

- Reuse as they are for sound and impact absorption, sea or car racing barriers.
- Energy recovery. This is a potentially good used tyres employment: in fact the calorific power of a scrap tyre is about equal to 8000 kcal/kg. The best users could be the cement industries and/or the electrical energy producers. In fact in Germany and Switzerland the scraps tyres employed for the energy production are more than the 40% b.w.
- Material recovery as a rubber powder.

The material recovery of used tyres therefore in the next future will be of great importance in Europe: the target value in 2005 is the 25 % b.w. Actually the rubber powder production from tyres for recycle may be achieved by means of some physical reclaiming processes. In this paper a new physical process concerning the cryomechanical disintegration with air has been examined considering the obtained products (quality and quantity) and a cost-benefit analysis was undertaken [3].

RECLAIMING OF TYRES BY PHYSICAL PROCESSES

In a physical reclaiming process scrap/waste rubber products are reclaimed with the help of external energy. Thus in physical reclaiming process three-dimensional network of crosslinked rubber breaks down in presence of different energy sources. Due to the breaking of network structure macromolecular rubber chain is transformed into small molecular weight fragments so that it can be easily miscible with the virgin rubber during compounding. So reclaim rubber produced by physical reclaiming may be used as a non-reinforcing filler because, microwave and ultrasonic methods excepted, they don't allow the rubber devulcanization that is compelling to obtain rubber with similar properties to those of original rubber [2].

Mechanical Reclaiming Process

In dry mechanical reclaiming process the crumb rubber is placed in a serrated grinder for preparation of ground rubber of particle size from 10 to 30 mesh. Ambient ground rubber is largely employed in tires and mechanical goods. With higher particle size of ambient ground rubber, smoothness of the product decreases. Although the name of the process is ambient grinding but the grinding in fact generates some heat during processing. In this process drastic molecular weight breakdown takes place due to the mechanical shearing at high temperatures. In this case the plasticity of the reclaimed rubber is very low due to the presence of a high percentage of crosslinked rubber. Wet grinding is a modified ambient grinding process that reduces the particle size of rubber by grinding in a liquid medium. The process involves putting a coarse ground rubber crumbs (10-20 mesh) into a liquid medium, usually water, and grinding between two closely space grinding wheels. Here the particle size is controlled by the time spent in the grinding process. The advantage of the fine particle wet ground rubber is that it allows good processing (particle size of 400-500 mesh could be obtained) producing relatively smooth extrudates.

Cryomechanical Reclaiming Process

In the mid 1960s, the technique of grinding scrap rubber in cryomechanical process was developed. The reclaiming process involves placing small pieces (2"x2") of vulcanised rubber into liquid nitrogen which are transferred to a mill and ground in presence of liquid nitrogen to form a fine powder. The temperature in the process is lower than the glass transition temperature of the polymer in the rubber. The particle size of the cryo-ground rubber varies from 30 to 100 mesh for most products. The particle size is controlled by the immersion time in the liquid nitrogen and by the mesh size of screens used in the grinding chamber of the mill. Generally the cost of the ground rubber increases as the particle size decreases. In the cryogrinding process the obtained product is characterized by a optimum surface smoothness and a limited surface oxidation, thus differentiating itself from ultrafine, high surface area ambient ground filler.

Air Cryomechanical Reclaiming Process

In this work a new process and apparatus for cryogenic tyres disintegration is examined (US Patent No. 5,735,471) [3]. The afore mentioned conventional cryogenic systems foresee a first shredding phase of tyres with the production of 2"x2" pieces at ambient temperatures that then are chemically frozen before being disintegrated in a hammer mill. This operation not only powders the rubber, but also powders the steel and breaks the fibre to a cotton-like fluff that plugs screens and entraps rubber. Besides most cryogenic systems use costly liquid nitrogen or other chemicals that can be dangerous to handle and store. The air cryomechanical reclaiming process (see Figure 1) foresees the following steps:

- tyres shearing and subjecting segments of elastomeric materials to temperature s able to bring said segments into a brittle glass-like state by means of a freezing chamber. Here, air at −170 F is constantly recirculated from a refrigeration unit reducing the temperature of the tyre sections to −90 - -100 F;
- gradual disintegrating of frozen segments by disintegrating means provided to separate segments from wires and fibres. The disintegration is effected by means of a bending force applied to frozen segments causing them to be broken into small particles and wires and fibres remain substantially intact;
- separation of small particles, wire and fibres by separating means: magnetic drum and screen.
- a new grinding phase for the fine rubber powder production (size down – 80 mesh).
- the sidewalls and treads are kept separate in view of the fact that sidewalls contain more natural rubber than treads which makes the powder more valuable.

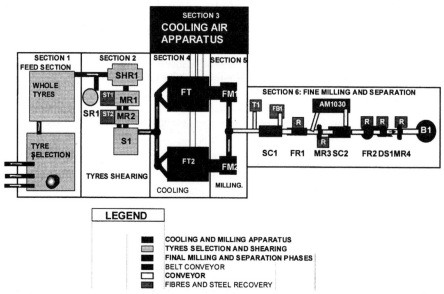

The advantages are essentially a highly efficient cooling process allowing to drastically reduce the cost of the refrigerant, a tyre disintegration system that allows to produce powder rubber of a wide range of particle sizes and the production of clean steel wire, fibre cord and rubber powder uncontaminated by each other.

PRODUCTS FROM TYRES PHYSICAL RECLAIMING PROCESSES

The valuable obtained products are the following: steel and powder rubber. The recovered steel may be reused in steel and cast iron foundries for the production of new steel and/or cast iron.

Powder Rubber

The powder rubber may be divided in different categories according to the particle size (see Table 2) or according to the production processes: normal temperature crushing powder rubber or freezing/crushing powder rubber. The surface of normal temperature crushing powder rubber is rugged, while that of freezing/crushing is smooth. Some potential employment of powder rubber are shown in Table 3. If general powder rubber is blended with rubber directly, in particular if the particle size is big, the tensile behaviour of sulfidized rubber will decline, the abrasion wear and the swelling capacity will increase [4].

Regenerated rubber is obtained from powder rubber by means of physical (microwave or ultrasonic) and chemical methods. Chemical methods are the more frequently employed and generally foresees the use of organic disulfides or mercaptans which are exclusively used during mechanical working at elevated temperature. The regenerated rubber is made through the desulfurization of waste rubber and has physical properties that are very similar to those ones of the virgin rubber. Anyway the regenerated rubber itself is a degraded product and the necessary treatment is expensive.

Activated powder is obtained by means of the surface activation of powder rubber thus obtaining fine compatibility and co-crosslinking with rubber, improving the kinetic fatigue behaviour and tensile strength of the material. There are many approaches in activating powder rubber: mechanochemical reaction, polymer treating, desulfurization, chlorination and so on [4].

Table 2: Classification, manufacture and use of powder rubber

CLASSIFICATION	PARTICLE SIZE		FACILITIES	APPLICATION
	μm	Mesh		
Coarse PR	1400-500	12-30	Grinding mill, rolling mill, rotary crushing mill	Ballast mats, the raw material of degradating regenerated rubber
Tiny PR	500-300	30-47	Rolling mill, rotary crushing mill	The raw material of oiling regenerated rubber
Fine PR	300-75	47-200	Cryogenic mill	Products of molding and extrusion, rubber mats, soft pipes, modified asphalt, used in renew of tyre
Ultrafine PR	Below 75	Below 200	Rotary colloid mill	Used in renew of tyre

Activated powder is obtained by means of the surface activation of powder rubber thus obtaining fine compatibility and co-crosslinking with rubber, improving the kinetic fatigue behaviour and tensile strength of the material. There are many approaches in activating powder rubber: mechanochemical reaction, polymer treating, desulfurization, chlorination and so on.

Table 3: Product of application of powder rubber

PRODUCT NAME	PRODUCT NAME	PRODUCT NAME
Mat	Carpet materials	Detent of car
Mat base for road	Foamed sponge	Car tyre
Animal mat	Indoor decorative floor materials	Solid tyre
Sidewalk surface of golf-course	Wall materials	Arrester rubber
Excising mat for golf-course	Floor rising materials	Bottom rubber
Mat block for road	Blending in concrete	Adhesion band
Elastick brick	Paving materials	Industrial filler
Rubber brick	Blending in asphalt	Transfer band
Rubber floor materials	External pants of car	Cheap soft band
Rubber plate	Foot mat block of car	Half-rubber wood product
Tennis court	Splash board of car	Insulative bakelite modification
Man-made lawn materials	Dust proof of car	Protection block
Inferior shoes bottom	Brake band	Blending rubber materials

The employment as filler in asphalt mix is well developed in US [1]. There are two competing technologies: the rubber modified asphalt concrete (RUMAC) includes about 3% b.w. of ground rubber, replacing some of the aggregate in the original asphalt. The final asphalt is applied by conventional equipment. The actually employed rubber size varies from 0.425 mm (40 mesh) to 5 mm (3 mesh) but the most used dimensions are from 2 mm (10 mesh) to 5 mm (3 mesh). This kind of asphalt attenuates traffic vibrations and has some better mechanical properties. The alternative technology is the asphalt rubber (A-R). In this process, conventional asphalt is blended with up to 25% b.w. of ground rubber, after complete separation of the steel and fibres, at 200 °C. The outcome is a product of higher viscosity requiring a special equipment to apply it on the road surface. Some of the problems is the absence of standardization in application and mixture methods. On the other hand, asphalt rubber presents significant advantages such as better permeability and, apparently, longer life.

A synthetic soccer or tennis court on average contains about 15 kg/m^2 of powder rubber of size equal to 0.5-0.6 mm (30 mesh). In US synthetic courts are very spread out. An interesting fine powder rubber employment (cryogenic, size below 60 mesh) is the recycle with fresh rubber for new tyres production. The cryomechanical reclaiming process is required because of the optimum surface smoothness characteristics. Different mix formulations were tested in laboratory but anyway is not possible to employ more than 10% b.w. of ground rubber. When higher proportion of those types of ground rubber is added with fresh rubber, the product become stiff and those crosslinked ground rubber site become the weak point of the crosslinked vulcanized rubber.

COST-BENEFIT ANALYSIS

A cost-benefit analysis was performed in order to evaluate the economic feasibility in Italy of a air cryomechanical tyres disintegration plant. The examined configuration was a treatment plant for a total capacity equal to 2,000,000 of used tyres per year (the average weight of a tyre is 6 kg). The hypothesized powder rubber size was below 30 mesh (0.6 mm). The total investment costs: 6,893,200 € keep into account the treatment plant, the loft building and the ground. The investment cost was divided in 10 year and the capital rate was hypothesized equal to the 5%. The investment and operative costs per year are shown in Table 4.

Table 4: Investment and operative costs per year of a air cryogenic tyres disintegration plant

INVESTMENT	892,701 €
LABOUR	606,720 €
ELECTRIC ENERGY (TOTAL INSTALLED ELECTRIC POWER: 1713 kW)	799,500 €
MAINTENANCE	175,000 €
TOTAL ANNUAL COST	**2,473,921 €**
POWDER RUBBER PRODUCTION	**13,766,400 kg**
POWDER RUBBER COST	**0,1797 €/kg**

The possible incomes from the reclaiming tyres plant activity are:
o   tyres collection;
o   recovered steel selling;
o   recovered powder rubber selling.

In Italy the tyre collection may be valued around 60 – 80 €/t, corresponding to about 0.36 – 0.48 € for each used tyre. Therefore the total annual income from the tyre collection may be valued around 600.000 – 800.000 €. The steel selling cost is around 0.025 – 0.030 €/kg. Hypothesizing a steel content for each tyre equal to the 15% b.w. the total steel annual income is 45.000 €.

In Italy the powder rubber has a value around 0.25 €/kg and it is employed for pipes, seals, electrical c able, f lush coat, s hoes, b elt, m ixtures. T he p roblem i s t hat actually i n Italy the powder rubber market is very limited and the already existing producers have difficulties in powder rubber selling. A future market expansion may be linked to rubber asphalt production, sy nthetic court a nd r ecycle f or n ew t yres p roduction. T he e nhancement o f t he rubber asphalt production is also related to the Italian laws that actually don't allow the rubber addition in the asphalt process. Anyway for the asphalt production granulated mechanical rubber is enough. Instead the added value of the cryomechanical reclaiming process (good separation of steel, fibres and rubber and optimum surface smoothness characteristics) may be exploited in synthetic soccer court and mostly in the recycle of rubber for the new tyres production. Actually in Italy the employment of synthetic coat is limited to small soccer court waiting for UEFA decisions. The employment of powder rubber for the new tyres production need the execution of several laboratory and industrial tests and besides the strong cooperation of the main tyres producers.

REFERENCES

1. FERRER,G.: The economics of tyre remanufacturing, Resources, Conservation and Recyling, 19, 1997, pp221-255.

2. ADHIKARI, B., DE, D. and MAITI, S.: Reclamation and recycling of waste rubber, Progress in Polymer Science, 25, 2000, pp.908-948.

3. UNITED STATES PATENT by MURO, L. No. 5,735,471, 1998.

4. FANG, Y., ZHAN, M. and WANG, Y.: The status of recycling of waste rubber, Materials and Design, 22, 2001, 123-127.

EFFECT OF TEMPERATURE ON THE PHYSICO-MECHANICAL PROPERTIES OF CEMENT-RUBBER COMPOSITES

F Labbani

A Benazzouk

O Douzane

M Quéneudec

University of Picardie Jules Verne

France

ABSTRACT. This article investigates the effect of temperature variation on the physico-mechanical properties of cement-rubber composites. In this investigation, the volume content ratio of rubber particles has ranged from 0% to 60%. The results obtained show that the incorporation of rubber particles into the cementitious matrix leads to reduced losses in mechanical strength vs. temperature level, which extended from -20°C to 100°C. The study also highlights the importance of rubber elasticity in the reduction of tensile stresses generated within the cement paste matrix due to temperature level variation.

Keywords: Cement-rubber composite, Rubber wastes, Physico-mechanical properties, Temperature

F. Labbani, is a research student at the University of Picardie Jules Verne, Amiens. His research interests is the valorisation of rubber aggregate in concrete.

Dr A. Benazzouk, is a post doctoral research student at the University of Picardie Jules Verne, Amiens. His research interests the valorisation of rubber aggregate in concrete in the aim of developing a highly deformable material.

Dr O. Douzane, Is a lecturer in Civil Engineering, University of Picardie Jules Verne, Amiens. His major center of interest is thermal and mechanical behaviour of building materials.

Professor M. Queneudec, Head of the « Laboratoire des Technologies Innovantes », University of Picardie Jules Verne, Amiens. She is specialised in the design and characterisation of building materials.

INTRODUCTION

The construction industry has expressed the need for new types of materials with special or improved properties, in comparison with conventional materials, particularly when submitted to difficult use conditions. Moreover, for the past several years, products and wastes generated from a variety of industrial sectors have been applied in the field of construction.

Over the last few years, many industrialized countries including France have been faced with the problem of managing large amounts of scrap rubber. Today, the accumulation of rubber waste, and used tyres in particular, constitutes an increasingly-serious environmental problem. In order to protect the environment and in accordance with a European directive mandating further research on waste disposal, several action programs have been implemented for reusing and recycling this type of waste, notably with respect to building materials.

In pursuit of this objective, recent studies conducted in our laboratory have demonstrated the possibility of using rubber aggregates within a cement matrix for the purpose of developing a composite that displays attractive physico-mechanical and hydraulic properties [1-8]. Results from these studies have revealed both the effect of rubber aggregate characteristics on the deformability of cement-rubber composites and the improvement in transport properties of this composite when placed in contact with fluids. Previous research on the durability of cement-rubber composites has shown the effect of rubber aggregate elasticity on the reduction in cement paste drying shrinkage.

These studies however were carried out at ambient temperature. Taking into account the significant difference between the mechanical and thermal characteristics of rubber aggregates and these same characteristics of the cementitious matrix, it was of interest to evaluate the impact of temperatures above the ambient average on the physico-mechanical properties of composites. Variations in temperature can indeed generate, within the matrix, significant stresses capable of leading to cracks and, consequently, to a reduction in durability.

The objective of this study is focused on the effect of temperature on the physico-mechanical behaviour of cement-rubber composites, with rubber dust as the base component, derived from the shredding of rubber waste. This evaluation process consists of determining: the dry unit weight, the dynamic elasticity modulus, and the compressive and flexural strengths. The studied temperature range varies from -20°C (representative of wintertime temperature) to 100°C (representative of exposure to very sunny conditions); this range is considered to represent typical service conditions.

MATERIALS AND EXPERIMENTAL TECHNIQUES

The dust used had been generated from the shredding of rubber waste and then recovered in dust extractors (i.e. exhauster hoods). Such waste comprises rubber particles less than 1 mm in size and approximately 20% textile fibres. The physico-mechanical properties and shape of the aggregates are shown in Table 1 and Figure 1, respectively.

Figure 1. Aspect of rubber dust

Table 1. Properties of rubber dust

PARTICLES SIZE, mm	DRY UNIT WEIGHT, kg/m^3	HARDNESS, Shore	MODULUS OF ELASTICITY, MPa
< 1	180	85	68

The cement used was CPJ CEM II 32.5 [NF P 15-301]. Both the rubber particles and cement were initially dry-mixed. To achieve constant workability (i.e. slump on the order of 90-100 mm), water was added according to the empirical formula for deriving total mixing water, i.e.: $W = 0.3\ Ce + K \cdot Ag$, where Ce and Ag are the respective weights of the cement and rubber particles. The coefficient K, which represents the water content absorbed by rubber particles, was estimated at 0.5. The volume ratio of rubber particles, defined as the ratio of rubber mass to cement mass, varied from 0% to 60%.

Prismatic composite specimens (40x40x160 mm), in which a thermocouple to allow controlling temperature was embedded during casting, were prepared and moist-cured at 20°C and 98% relative humidity, both before and after demoulding. Prior to testing, the specimens were dried in a drying oven at 50°C until reaching constant mass. The material, in its dry state, was then placed in a drying oven until reaching the test measurement temperature.

Composite dry unit weights were determined by means of geometrical measurement and weighing. The dynamic elasticity modulus was then determined by applying longitudinal ultrasonic vibration, as specified in Standard NF P 18-406. The compressive and flexural tests were carried out in accordance with Standard EN 196-1.

RESULTS AND DISCUSSION

Dry Unit Weight

The variation in dry unit weight of the composite (ρ), as a function of rubber particle content (G), is shown in Figure 2; this figure clearly indicates that adding rubber particles reduces dry unit weight in a linear fashion, in accordance with the following proposed empirical relationship: $\rho\ \left(\mathrm{kg/m^3}\right) = 1819.1 - 7.02\ \mathrm{G}\ \left(\%\right)$ (which yields a correlation coefficient of R = 0.98). Values decrease from 1800 kg/m^3 (cement paste) to 1360 kg/m^3 for samples containing 60% rubber particles; these v alues correspond to losses reaching 24%. This level of reduction is higher, especially in building renovation works and lightweight material structures, which serves to facilitate the introduction of materials on building sites.

In addition to a low rubber particle specific gravity, it was observed that the increase in rubber particle content within the cement paste tends to heighten the level of air entrainment during mixing, which then contributes to lightening the material. Table 2 provides a list of these values, as measured using the pressure method. The higher air content of mixtures is probably due to the capability of rubber particles to entrap air at their surface during mixing, given the level of surface roughness.

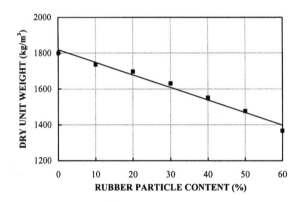

Figure 2. Dry unit weight as a function of rubber particle content

Table 2. Air entrianment as a fuction of rubber particle content

RUBBER PARTICLE CONTENT, %	AIR ENTRAINMENT
0	2.0
10	2.5
20	3.5
30	3.6
40	5.0
50	6.5
60	7.0

Dynamic Modulus of Elasticity

An example of variation in the composite's dynamic elasticity modulus, with respect to rubber volume content at various temperatures, is given in Figure 3a; this figure shows that the addition of rubber particles to the cement matrix reduces the dynamic elasticity modulus, for all temperature levels reached. At ambient temperature (20°C) for example, the value decreases from 2 8 G Pa (cement p aste) t o 1 0 G Pa f or a composite c ontaining 6 0% r ubber particles. This reduction is due to the nature of the rubber, which favours the absorption of ultrasonic waves. The velocity of ultrasonic waves, as determined from measurement values in the rubber both prior to shredding and in the cement matrix, amounts to 175 m/sec and 3,700 m/sec, respectively.

It should be noted that temperature variation does not significantly affect the dynamic elasticity modulus, especially with the addition of rubber particles. Figure 3b shows that this variation is of a linear type at all temperatures. Table 3 indicates that for a temperature variation ranging between -20°C to 100°C, losses in the composite's dynamic modulus of elasticity depend on the rubber volume content; moreover, this trend moves towards a better deformability of the composite, as would have been expected. The loss is about 12% for cement paste and 19.5% for a composite containing 60% rubber; this result can be related to the physico-mechanical evolution of rubber characteristics with respect to temperature. The difference in behaviour between the cement paste and the composite may be tied to the generation of cracks in the cementitious matrix, so that the stresses generated during drying are dampened by the aggregates due to their elasticity characteristic.

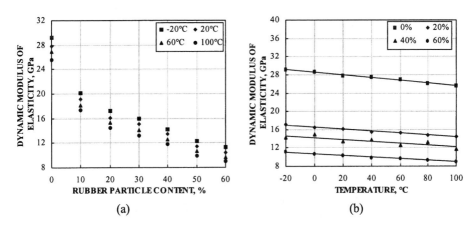

(a)   (b)

Figure 3. Dynamic modulus of elasticity as a function of:
(a) rubber particle content, (b) temperature

Table 3. Losses in the composite's dynamic modulus of elasticity for a variation in
temperature of –20 to 100°C

RUBBER PARTICLE CONTENT, %	LOSSES in the composite's dynamic modulus of elasticity, %
0	12.37
20	15.57
40	16.90
60	19.57

Compressive Strength

The results of compressive strength vs. rubber particle content, at various temperatures, are presented in Figure 4a. The compressive strength considerably decreases with increasing rubber content. Figure 4b shows that the temperature variation does not significantly affect the composite's compressive strength. It should be noted that the compressive strength displays an optimum for temperatures ranging between 0°C and 20°C. At -20°C, the strength values are not heavily affected. The reduction with temperature increase is even less marked when rubber content is high. For a composite containing 60% rubber particles for example, it is obviously necessary to reach 80°C in order to induce a significant loss in compressive strength. It is thus apparent that the presence of rubber counters the drop in cement paste performance with temperature. These results may be correlated with the elastic nature of rubber aggregates, which "absorb" the stresses generated by temperature variations and thus decrease the risk of cracking in the cementitious matrix. This behaviour approximates that observed during the drying-immersion cycles for the same composite. During the transition from a dry state to a water-saturated state, the presence of viscoelastic aggregates in the cementitious matrix has served to reduce the Extreme Dimensional Variation (EDV), in comparison with the cement paste [3]. The behaviour of the composite under alternating climatic conditions (i.e. freeze-thaw) has revealed this same trend [4]; the presence of rubber aggregates has made it possible to improve the durability of the composite.

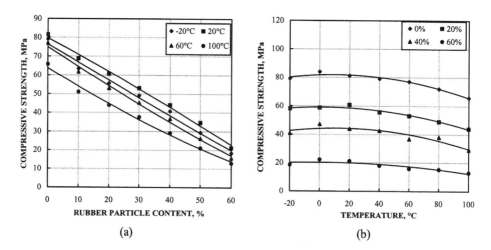

(a)   (b)

Figure 4. Compressive strength as a fuction of:
(a) rubber particle content, (b) temperature

Flexural Strength

Figure 5a shows the variation in 28-day flexural strength as a function of rubber volume ratio for various temperatures. By varying the rubber content, these curves reveal an optimum for the composite, corresponding to an increase in the composite's flexural strength, as opposed to the cement paste. Beyond this optimal rubber content, strength values decrease. This finding is probably due to the elasticity and unbreakable nature of the material as well as to the fibre effect of rubber inclusions, which delays the fracture phase. In contrast, the increase in rubber content serves to decrease the relative quantity of cement in the matrix, thereby inciting a reduction in the level of aggregate/matrix connection and, consequently, in flexural strength. It should also be noted that flexural strength decreases with temperature variation (see Figure 5b), with this reduction being more significant for the cement paste. Figure 5b displays the comparison with a composite containing 60% rubber. Beyond 80°C, it is observed that the cement-rubber composite is more powerful than the cement paste, in spite of a sharply-lower binder proportion. This difference is probably due to the increase in rubber elasticity with temperature, which improves deformation of the composite even further before fracture. This finding has once again shown the benefit of rubber inclusions for the mechanical behaviour of cementitious materials.

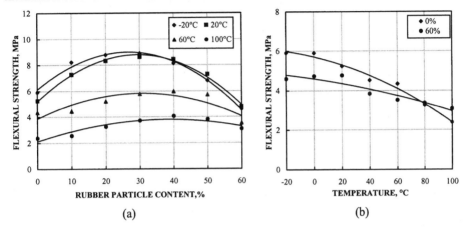

(a) (b)

Figure 5. Flexure strength as a fuction of:
(a) rubber particle content, (b) temperature

CONCLUSIONS

The work presented herein has focused on the impact of temperature variation on the physico-mechanical properties of cement-rubber composites, with respect to rubber volume content. Results have indicated that temperature variation does not significantly affect the composite's mechanical strength, with this relation being more pronounced as rubber content increases. This finding highlights the effect of rubber elasticity in dampening the stresses generated within the matrix during temperature variations. The addition of viscoelastic aggregates to the cementitious matrix provides a glimpse of a potential broad field of application, while lending hope for the improved durability of materials submitted to climatic variations.

REFERENCES

1. BENAZZOUK, A., MEZREB, K., DOYEN, G., GOULLIEUX, A., QUENEUDEC, M.: Effect of rubber aggregates on the physico-mechanical behaviour of cement-rubber composites–influence of the alveolar texture of rubber aggregates, Cement and Concrete Composites, 2003, 25, pp711-720.

2. BENAZZOUK, A., DOUZANE, O., QUENEUDEC, M.: Transport of fluids in cement-rubber composites, Cement and Concrete Composites, 2004, 26, pp21-29.

3. BENAZZOUK, A., DHEILLY, R.M., DOUZANE, O., QUENEUDEC, M.: Dimensional variations of cement-rubber composites–Influence of the physico-mechanical characteristics of rubber aggregates, Cement and Concrete Research, 2004; (submitted paper).

4. BENAZZOUK, A., QUENEUDEC, M.: Durability of cement-rubber composites under freeze thaw cycles, Sustainable Concrete Construction. ISBN 072 77 3177 7, Edited by R.K. Dhir, T.H. Dyer, J.E. Halliday, published by Thomas Telford Publishing-Thomas Telford Ltd, 1 Heron Quay, London E14 4JD, Dundee-Scotland, September 2002, pp355-362.

5. TOPÇU, U.B.: The properties of rubberized concrete, Cement and Concrete Research, 1995; 25,2, pp304-310.

6. FEDROFF, D., AHMED, S., SAVAS, D.Z.: Mechanical properties of concrete with ground waste tire rubber, Transportation Research Record, 1996, 1532, pp66-72.

7. TOUTANJI, A.H.: The use rubber tire particles in concrete to replace mineral aggregates, Cement and Concrete Composites, 1996, 18, pp135-139.

8. BENAZZOUK, A.: Contribution à la valorisation de déchets de caoutchouc : composites cimentaires à base caoutchouc compact et cellulaire, Doctorat thesis, Université de Picardie Jules Verne, Amiens, December 2002.

THE USE OF RECYCLED RUBBER TYRES IN CONCRETE

H Y Kew

R Cairns

M J Kenny

University of Strathclyde

United Kingdom

ABSTRACT. The growing problem of waste tyre disposal in the UK can be alleviated if new recycling routes can be found for the surplus tyres. One of the largest potential routes is in construction, but usage of waste tyres in civil engineering is currently very low. This study investigates the potential of incorporating recycled rubber tyre chips into Ordinary Portland Cement (OPC) concrete. This paper presents the workability and strength properties of concrete incorporating rubber tyre chips as a partial replacement for the coarse aggregate in the concrete. Plain rubber aggregate and rubber aggregate coated with cement paste were used. The results showed that concrete incorporating rubber aggregate has lower workability and unit weight and exhibited a noticeable reduction in compressive strength. However, the rubberised concrete did not exhibit a typical failure mode of plain concrete and a beneficial effect on flexural strength was observed. The potential of rubberised concrete in applications such as lightweight concrete and concrete block is also discussed.

Keywords: Rubberised concrete, Rubber aggregate, Recycled rubber tyres, Recycling, Concrete properties.

Mr H Y Kew is a postgraduate research student in the Department of Civil Engineering at the University of Strathclyde. He is currently carrying out research into the use of recycled rubber from waste tyres in concrete construction with the aim of developing cost effective materials and products for the construction industry.

Mr R Cairns is a Chartered Civil Engineer and a Lecturer in the Department of Civil Engineering at the University of Strathclyde. His research interests include composite construction, and recycling and reuse of waste materials in concrete.

Dr M J Kenny is a Chartered Civil Engineer and a Lecturer in the Department of Civil Engineering at the University of Strathclyde. His research interests include geosynthetics in civil engineering, foundation engineering, and recycling and reuse of waste materials.

INTRODUCTION

The disposal of waste tyres is becoming a major waste disposal problem in the UK. It is estimated that 40 million car and truck tyres are being discarded annually and this figure is expected to increase over the next 20 years, in line with the increase in traffic. At present, it is estimated that 11% of post-consumer tyres are exported, 62% are reused, recycled or sent for energy recovery and 27% are sent to landfill (shredded tyre), stockpiled (whole tyre) or dumped in illegal tyre dumps [1-2].

Landfill has been one of the most common ways of disposing of waste tyres. As rubber tyres are extremely durable and not naturally biodegradable, they will remain in landfill with very little degradation over time, presenting a continuing environmental hazard. However, landfill is no longer a viable option due to the implementation of European Union legislation, which bans the disposal of whole and shredded tyres in landfill sites by the year 2003 and 2006 respectively. There is, therefore, an urgent need to identify alternative solutions, in line with the UK Government's waste management hierarchy. This promotes recycling ahead of disposal and energy recovery. One of the largest potential recycling routes is in construction, but usage of waste tyres in civil engineering is currently very low. This is due to the lack of high volume applications and products involving recycled tyres.

The potential for using recycled rubber tyres in concrete has already been recognised. Since concrete is a low cost, versatile composite material, there is the potential to use rubber tyres in crumb or chip form as a replacement for the natural aggregates in concrete [3-7]. Eldin and Senouci [3] incorporated rubber tyre chips and rubber crumb in ASTM Type 1 Portland Cement Concrete. Their results showed an 85% reduction in compressive strength and a 50% reduction in tensile strength when the coarse aggregate was fully replaced by rubber chips. A smaller reduction in compressive strength (65%) was observed when the sand was fully replaced by fine rubber crumb. Khatib and Bayomy [6] reported a reduction of over 90% in compressive strength when the coarse aggregate volume was fully replaced by rubber and of about 90% when the fine aggregate was fully replaced by rubber. They also reported a similar decrease in the flexural strength of rubberised concrete.

This paper considers the effectiveness and potential of using rubber aggregate chips as a replacement for natural aggregate. Due to the considerable strength reductions reported by previous authors for high rubber contents, smaller rubber contents were used in the present study. In addition, the effect of coating the rubber particles with cement paste was investigated as a possible means of improving the distribution of rubber aggregate particles through the mix. The possible enhancement of concrete in terms of flexural strength was also investigated since the use of large angular rubber chips was anticipated to improve the tensile strength [8]. The potential for using rubber aggregate in various concrete products is also discussed in the light of the results of the experimental programme.

EXPERIMENTAL PROGRAMME

The materials used in this study were BS12 Ordinary Portland Cement, crushed coarse aggregate of 10 mm and 20 mm size and sand as detailed in Table 1. Coarse rubber aggregate of 20 mm maximum size (G_s = 1.14) and angular shape was used to replace the 20 mm mineral aggregate. A control mix with 40 MPa targeted compressive strength and medium workability was designed. This produced a mix with a water/cement ratio of 0.48 and the proportions given in Table 1. For rubberised concrete mixes, the rubber aggregates either coated with cement paste (AC) or plain (AP) were used as a replacement of an equal part of 20 mm coarse aggregate at 10, 25 and 50% by volume. All mix design parameters were kept constant i.e. the cement content, water/cement ratio and the aggregate content. Table 2 gives a summary of rubber contents for rubberised concrete mixes. All mixes were prepared and cured using standard methods.

Table 1. Material properties and mix proportions for the control mix

MATERIALS	SPECIFIC GRAVITY, G_s	MIX PROPORTION (kg/m^3)
Cement	-	438
Water	-	210
Sand	2.8	526
Coarse aggregate (10 mm)	2.69	409
Coarse aggregate (20 mm)	2.69	818

Table 2. Summary of rubber contents

MIXES	SAMPLES	RUBBER CONTENT, %
Control	A	0
AC	AC10	10
	AC25	25
	AC50	50
AP	AP10	10
	AP25	25
	AP50	50

To evaluate the fresh concrete properties, the workability (slump and compacting factor tests) and unit weight were measured. For hardened concrete, all mixes were tested for compressive and flexural strength at 28 days, whereas the splitting tensile strength test was carried out at 14 days. The compressive, splitting tensile and flexural strength tests were carried out using standard cube, cylinder and beam samples in accordance with BS 1881: parts 116 [9], 117 [10] and 118 [11], respectively.

TEST RESULTS

Workability and unit weight

Table 3 shows the workability test results for control and rubberised concrete samples. The results show that increasing the percentage of rubber aggregate to up 50% produced a zero slump value and a lower compacting factor. The reduction in the workability of the concrete can be attributed to a combination of lower unit weight and the higher friction between the rubber aggregate and the mixture. The low specific gravity of the rubber chips produced a decrease in the unit weight of rubberised concrete, as shown in Table 4. A reduction of unit weight up to 10% was observed when 50% by volume of the coarse aggregate was replaced by rubber aggregate.

Table 3. Summary of workability results for control and rubberised concrete

SAMPLES	SLUMP TEST			COMPACTING FACTOR	
	Slump (mm)	Type of slump	Apparent workability	Compacting factor	Apparent workability
A	55	True	Medium	0.95	High
AC10	14	True	Low	0.92	Medium
AC25	3	True	Very low	0.88	Medium
AC50	0	Zero	No slump	0.85	Low
AP10	16	True	Low	0.91	Medium
AP25	6	True	Very low	0.90	Medium
AP50	0	Zero	No slump	0.87	Low

Table 4. Unit weight of control concrete and rubberised concrete

SAMPLES	UNIT WEIGHT (kg/m^3)	% REDUCTION
A	2500	0
AC10	2475	1
AC25	2425	3
AC50	2350	6
AP10	2450	2
AP25	2375	5
AP50	2250	10

Strength

The test results for compressive strength, splitting tensile strength and flexural strength are shown in Figures 1(a), 1(b) and 1(c) respectively. A minimum of ten batches were tested for compressive strength for each sample type. The Relative Strength, S_R, is defined as the ratio of the strength of the rubberised concrete mixture to the strength of the control mix. The results show that the addition of rubber aggregate resulted in a significant reduction in concrete strength. This reduction increased with increasing percentage of rubber aggregate. The compressive strength was reduced by up to 35% for AC samples and 55% for AP samples. The splitting tensile strength was reduced similarly by up to 40% for AC samples and 48% for AP samples. However, as shown in Figure 1(c), an increase in flexural strength for rubber aggregate contents up to 25% was observed.

The reduction in compressive and splitting tensile strength can be expected since the relatively compressible rubber aggregate particles tend to produce weak inclusions in the concrete, thus reducing the strength of the concrete. However, coating the rubber aggregate with cement paste does produce a smaller strength reduction. This is probably due to an enhanced adhesion between the rubber chips and the cement paste. In addition, the cement paste increases the weight of the chips, reducing their tendency to float during mixing and producing a more uniform mix.

Table 5. Summary of the strength of control concrete and rubberised concrete

SAMPLES	COMPRESSIVE STRENGTH (MPa)			SPLITTING TENSILE STRENGTH (Mpa)		FLEXURAL STRENGTH (MPa)	
	Average strength	Standard deviation	Relative strength, S_R	Strength	Relative strength, S_R	Strength	Relative strength, S_R
A	50	4.48	1.00	3.28	1.00	5.20	1.00
AC10	44	3.66	0.86	2.83	0.86	7.36	1.42
AC25	35	3.65	0.68	2.26	0.69	6.24	1.20
AC50	32	2.61	0.63	1.97	0.60	4.45	0.86
AP10	41	4.38	0.80	2.32	0.71	6.16	1.18
AP25	32	2.38	0.63	2.13	0.65	5.85	1.13
AP50	23	3.24	0.45	1.69	0.52	4.36	0.84

It was also observed that rubberised concrete did not exhibit typical compression failure behaviour. The presence of rubber aggregate tends to hold the sample fragments together at failure. Likewise, the rubberised concrete samples did not split into two halves under split tension loading or break into two pieces under flexural loading as for conventional concrete.

DISCUSSION

It is evident from the test results that adding rubber aggregate into Ordinary Portland Cement concrete has a marked effect on the strength properties of the concrete, specifically a significant reduction in the compressive and splitting tensile strength. The Relative Strength, S_R, can be used to quantify these strength changes as shown in Table 5. However these values are specific to the present study. An attempt has been made to compare the results of the present study with those of previous investigations by determining the values of S_R for the relevant test data of other authors. It should be noted that as different studies use a different basis for aggregate replacement and different rubber aggregate sizes, the only valid comparison which can be reasonably made is to determine the rubber content by total concrete volume. The results of the comparison are shown in Figures 2(a) and 2(b) for compressive strength and flexural strength respectively.

It can be seen from Figure 2(a) that for compressive strength, the results of the present study are consistent with those of previous investigations with the exception of Khatib and Bayomy [6], which showed a much greater strength reduction. It should be noted that different initial target strengths were used by the various investigators which may influence the relationship between Relative Strength and rubber content. Coating the rubber aggregate particles with cement paste produced the lowest strength reduction at higher rubber contents. The trend of the data suggests that it may be possible to increase the rubber content further without too great a reduction in compressive strength.

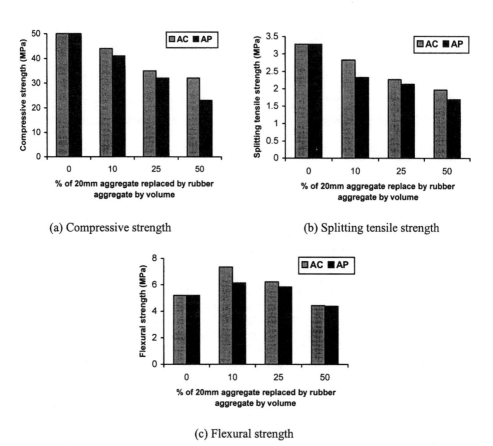

(a) Compressive strength

(b) Splitting tensile strength

(c) Flexural strength

Figure 1. Strength of rubberised concrete

The comparisons for flexural strength in Figure 2(b) show a much greater disparity with previous investigations since these studies produced a reduction in flexural strength, even at low rubber contents. Khatib and Bayomy [6] considered the very low flexural strengths obtained to be due to weak bonding between the cement paste and rubber particles. However in the present study, the use of plain rubber aggregate still produced a flexural strength increase at low rubber contents. The reason for the large variation in flexural strength is unclear and difficult to ascertain on the basis of the published data. Despite this disparity, the test results suggest further investigation of the possibility of increased flexural strength is worthwhile due to the potential benefits in applications such as composite construction.

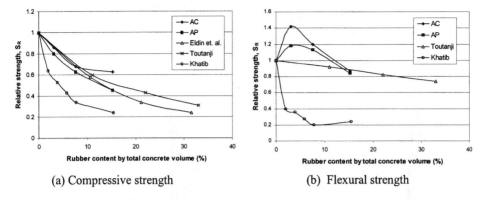

(a) Compressive strength   (b) Flexural strength

Figure 2. Relationship between Relative Strength, S_R, and rubber content by total volume

CONCLUSIONS

In generally, rubberised concrete mixes did not pose any difficulties in term of finishing, casting, or placement and can be finished to the same standard as plain concrete. However, increasing the rubber aggregate content reduces the workability of the mix and more effort is required to smooth the finish surface.

The results of the present investigation and previous investigations show clearly that the use of rubber aggregate in OPC concrete mixes produces a marked reduction in concrete compressive strength. However, if the amount of rubber in the concrete is limited, a normal strength concrete can still be produced with potential uses in non-structural applications. This restriction may limit the volume of tyres which can be recycled in this way. However, there is potential for producing materials and products with enhanced properties, such as improved flexural strength and reduced weight.

The ability to produce cost effective rubberised concrete products for industry depends on overcoming some of the practical production difficulties such as surface finishing and aggregate segregation during mixing. A further difficulty is the current cost of rubber chips, which far exceeds the cost of natural aggregates including the aggregates levy. This is due to the extensive processing carried out during rubber chip production, which required for specific applications such as sports and playground surfacing. This situation should improve after the imposition of the landfill ban in the UK in 2006 as the cost of alternatives to recycling increases.

The development of practicable rubberised concrete products is under ongoing investigation at the University of Strathclyde. In addition to meeting recycling and sustainability objectives, the aim is to produce products with enhanced properties in specific applications. There is potential to produce concrete blocks with enhanced characteristics in terms of reduced weight and improved thermal and acoustic properties. Testing carried out to date has shown that a lighter block can be produced with the required strength characteristics. Ongoing work will investigate the feasibility of producing rubberised concrete block commercially. The abrasion resistance of rubberised concrete is also currently under investigation. Rubberised concrete has the potential to improve the abrasion resistance of concrete floor surfaces. An abrasion test machine has been constructed at the University of Strathclyde and preliminary testing has shown that rubberised concrete exhibits reduced depth of wear under the specific test conditions. However, further work is required to ensure that the results are representative of the modes of abrasion found in practice.

ACKNOWLEDGMENTS

The authors would like to acknowledge the Onyx Environmental Trust for funding this study. The authors also thank Charles Lawrence Recycling for supplying the rubber chips used in the study.

REFERENCES

1.   HIRD, A.B., GRIFFITHS, P.J. AND SMITH, R.A.: Tyre waste and resource management: A mass balance approach, VIRIDIS Report No. 2, UK, TRL Limited, 2002.

2.   USED TYRE WORKING GROUP.: Fifth Annual Report for the UTWG, UK, July 2001.

3.   ELDIN, N.N. AND SENOUCI, A.B.: Rubber-tyre particles as concrete aggregate, Journal of Materials in Civil Engineering, 5, No. 2, 1993, pp478-496.

4.   TOUTANJI, H.A.: The use of rubber tyre particles in concrete to replace mineral aggregate, Cement and Concrete Composites, 18, 1996, pp135-139.

5.   LI, Z., LI, F., AND LI, J.S.L.: Properties of concrete incorporating rubber tyre particles, Magazine of Concrete Research, 50, No. 4, 1998, pp297-304.

6.   KHATIB, Z.K. AND BAYOMY, F.M.: Rubberised Portland Cement Concrete, Journal of Materials in Civil Engineering, 11, No.3, 1999, pp206-213.

7.   FEDROFF, D., AHMAD, S. AND SAVAS, B.Z.: Mechanical properties of concrete with ground waste tyre rubber, Transportation Research Record, No. 1532, 1996, pp66-72.

8.   FOOSE, G.J., BENSON, C.H. AND BOSSCHER, P.J.: Sand reinforced with shredded waste tires, Journal of Geotechnical Engineering, Vol. 122, No. 9, 1996, ASCE, pp760-767.

9.   BRITISH STANDARD INSTITUTION: BS EN 12390, Part 3, Testing hardened concrete: Compressive strength of test specimens, London, 2002.

10.   BRITISH STANDARD INSTITUTION: BS EN 12390, Part 6, Testing hardened concrete: Tensile splitting strength of test specimens, London, 2002.

11.   BRITISH STANDARD INSTITUTION: BS EN 12390, Part 5, Testing hardened concrete: Flexural strength of test specimens, London, 2002.

STRUCTURAL ANALYZES OF THE USE OF RESIDUES OF TIRES IN REINFORCED CONCRETE

J L Akasaki

V H França

M P Barbosa

F M Salles

Universidade Estadual Paulista   University -College of Engineering of Ilha Solteira

Brasil

ABSTRACT. The search for an adequate destination to the tires without use is a problem for many countries. The use of tire rubber in concrete through the partial substitution of the small aggregate has for objective the withdrawal of this material of the environment besides serving as alternative material in places that present sand scarcity. However, to use this type of concrete in civil construction it's necessary to verify its structural behavior. The behavior of the adherence enters the bar of armor and the concrete surrounding it has decisive importance with relation to the load capacity of the structures of reinforced concrete. In this context, this work presents, argues and evaluates the results of the experimental studies for determination of the adherence tension according to pulling up assays "pull-out" normalized for CEB RC6 and also related in the ASTM C-234 in concrete with and without rubber residues. Armors of nominal diameter of 10,0 ; 12,5 and 16 mm had been used and concrete contend 10% of rubber fibres in substitution to the sand in volume.

Keywords: Tire fiber, Adherence steel-concrete, Concrete with tire

INTRODUCTION

In several countries of the world the main means of transportation of loads and passengers are the road, implicating like this a great growth of the fleet of trucks, bus and passenger cars. The production of tires is growing every year and an appropriate destination doesn't exist for the tires without use.

In 1993 0,5% of the Brazilian urban garbage they were of old tires and out of use. Today they are discarded in the country about 17 million tires a year. The used tire is an undesirable residue, that if has become a great problem for society. With respect to health he has been a middle of proliferation of the fly "Aëdes Aegypti", due to the accumulation of water in its internal part. For the environment, the problem caused by the disposition of tires in sanitary embankments and dumping ground is serious, once they possess great resistance to the degradation, could take up to 240 years for if putrefy itself. When she choose for the it burns of those tires the damage caused to the environment happens due to enormous amount of black smoke and oil that penetrate and they contaminate soils and water tables. A form of reducing this impact is to use to advantage again of the tires, process denominated retreading.

In agreement with ANIP (National Association of the Pneumatic Industries) about 70% of the fleet of transport of loads and passengers, in Brazil, they use recapped tires. The retreading process in turn, generates a great amount of residues, that healthy very resistant to the degradation, could also last about 240 years for if putrefy itself, becoming incompatible for the sanitary embankments. Of the retreading process the rubber staple fibers originate that, after bolted (diameter 1,19mm) they were used in this research in substitution the sand, in the production of the concrete. The idea of the use of the eraser fiber in substitution of the sand is being an attempt of lessening the problem of the shortage of the sand that reaches several Brazilian states.

USE OF THE RUBBER OF TIRE IN THE CIVIL CONSTRUCTION

According to Cincotto (1988), the general criteria for evaluation of the residue for use in the civil construction, are:

- The available amount in a place must be enough great so that if it can justify the development of manuscript systems, processing and transport;

- The involved distances of transport must be competitive with the conventional materials;

- The material does not have later to be potentially harmful during the construction or to its incorporation in the structure.

The residue in study takes care of the criteria above, what it allows to conclude that this material can be a good residue for the civil construction, a time that it is found in great amount and that he does not harm the performance of the constructions conceived from its incorporation in the construction materials. Thus, searching one better exploitation of the rubber, studies come being developed so that these can be added to the concrete. One has equipped of the FEIS/UNESP directed for Prof. Dr. Jorge Luis Akasaki comes developing some research with the use of the rubber fiber proceeding from the retreading of tires. The results gotten for concrete with rubber had shown inferior compressive strength of the conventional concrete, but with viable properties its use while material-concrete.

Some properties of the concrete can be improved with the incorporation of these residues, according to Accetti and Pinheiro, (2000) the rubber staple fibres act as obstacles to the development of the fictions.   When intercepting the microcracks that appear during the hardening of the folder, them hinder its progression and prevent the premature appearance of the microcracks. In the hardened mixture, them also they limit the length and the opening of the fictions.

Other research being carried through with intention to use rubber staple fibers in mortars, in order to get an improvement of its characteristics. The results gotten for Lima(2000) carried through in the flexural strength assays (minimum transversal load, modulus of rupture and deflection) had taken care of to the requirements of norm C 208-95, the ASTM Standard Specification will be Cellulosic Fiber Insulating Board, for use as walls and of thermal isolation for covering ends. The plates assayed for it had presented good characteristics of thermal isolation, with inferior values of thermal conductivity to the maximum value allowed by the norm previously mentioned.

Currently, however, the recycled rubber has been more regularly added to the concrete in the construction of roads and highways. The material is proceeding from old tires that, triturated and mixed the cement and the coarse aggregate, the floor of the streets becomes most adherent and facilitates the lockwire of the vehicles, besides contributing for the to diminish the pollution of the nature. In Brazil they are extracted about 220 million tons of added per year to be used in concrete and mortars. With the necessity of if using new materials that come to substitute these aggregates, some researchers had had the idea to use the rubber residue, proceeding from the retreading, thus promoting the withdrawal of this aggressive material of the environment and saving our natural deposits. To make possible the use in armed concrete it is necessary the study of the behavior of the bond steel-concrete, that is the objective of this work.

THE STUDY OF THE BOND

The bond is the existing connection between the steel and the concrete making that the materials if deformed consequently in set and transfers efforts from one to the other. This connection between the armor and the concrete is the main factor of the good performance of the a rmed concrete. T he o riginary t ensions o f t he o perating requests i n t he f aying s urface steel-concrete a re c alled b ond t ensions, w hich c an b e e steem f rom c alculation e xpressions proposals for norms proceeding from executed assays or mathematical models. Some reports exist that determine the values of the bond tension enter the steel armor and concrete .If to detach:
      Test of Direct Pulling up: Pull-out TEST (POT)
      Test of Pulling up with Circumferential Ring - Ring Pull-Out-Test
      Test of Flexão - Beam Test (Bt)
      Test of Extremity of Beam - Beam End Test
      Assay of Bond of the Type Push-Out Test Assays of the Four Bars
      Test of Symmetrical Traction In this work was opted to the accomplishment of the assays of direct pulling pull-out-test, which we describe to follow.

TEST OF DIRECT PULLING UP - PULL-OUT-TEST

This is the most traditional of the tack assays, consists of extracting a bar of steel located in the center of a body of test of concrete placed on plates of support of an assay machine. The two extremities of the bar are projected for are of the test body, measuring it snatch force applied to one of the extremities and the slippings in the other extremity. The advantages of this assay are that beyond the low cost and simplicity the assay gives a clear idea of the anchorage concept, that is, the length that is absorbed in the concrete is what it defines the proper length of anchorage.

It has as disadvantage that the gotten results serves only for comparative research or qualitative studies, therefore the form to request the test body does not reproduce the real conditions of request of the when projected bars of steel to the use purposes. This test of direct pulling up is normalized by the RILEM, doc 7.II.128 (1973) and also is related in the ASTM C234 (1991) with all necessary detailing its execution as laboratory assays.

EXPERIMENTAL PROGRAM

We present the used procedures for evaluation and comparison of the tack between steel-concrete, using two types of concrete: conventional and with tire rubber staple fiber incorporation, and three diameters of bars of steel of the ribbing type.

Bars of Steel

The bars used in this work had been of the type ribbing with circular section of equal nominal diameter the 10,0; 12,5 and 16,0 mm of the Ca-50 classroom, manufactured for Siderurgical Belgo-Mineira located in Piracicaba-SP Brazil. In table 1 we present the characteristics of the armors.

Table 1 Characterization of the bars of steel.

DIAMETER mm	INCLINATION Ribbing (°)	LIM. DRAINING (Kgf/mm^2)	LIM. STRENGHT (Kgf/mm^2)	ALLONGE (%)
10,0	51	619,0	778,3	14,00
12,5	46	609,7	776,3	14,67
16,0	47	630,7	795,0	16,07

Concrete

The materials used for confection of the concrete ones had been proceeding from the region of Ilha Solteira-SP-Brazil I, as it follows below described:
Small aggregates: average sand proceeding from the riverbed Paraná, sand port Nossa Senhora Aparecida of the city of Ilha Solteira -SP;
Added Graúdo: brita 1, limy, proceeding from the city of Monções-SP Mineradora Great Lakes;

Cement: Portland cement of high initial resistance (Cpv-ari); Rubber staple fibres: proceeding from the process of retreading of tires, passers-by in the bolter n° 16 opening 1,19 mm.

As mentioned two types of concrete had been confectioned, the conventional and the concrete with addition of 10% of rubber staple fibres, whose compositions meet in table 2 to follow:

Table 2 – Concrete mix proportions used

MATERIALS	CONVENTIONAL CONCRETE Kg/m³	CONCRETE WITH ADDITION STAPLE FIBRES kg/m³
Cement	295,57	325,80
Water	195,03	215,03
Sand	931,53	768,35
Coarse aggregate	1.000,57	1.000,57
Rubber fiber		36,06

The evaluations mechanical properties of the concrete ones (fc, ft and Ec) had been gotten through the carried through assays according to Brazilian norms. Table 5 presents the gotten results, for Compressive strength, Tensile strenght and Module of Deformation in the ages of 7, 28 and 90 days.

Table 5 – Values obtained from the assays of characterization of the concrete.

	AGE (days)	CONVENTIONAL CONCRETE	CONCRETE WITH ADDITION STAPLE FIBRES
Compressive strength	7	24,18	17,24
(Kgf/mm²)	28	27,97	19,29
	7	2,84	1,88
Tensile strenght (Kgf/mm²)	28	3,57	2,34
Module of Deformation	7	25,09	23,50
(GPa)	28	35,05	32,50

RESULTS AND ANALYSES

As we can observe the compressive strength of the concrete with rubber suffered a decrease in relation to the conventional concrete, this age waited, and confirmed for literature, where all the researchers are unanimous in this point of view. It was also observed a decrease in the module of deformation in relation to the conventional concrete, where we detach a lesser imbalance in comparison the compressive strength. This fact can have occurred due the presence of the rubber fiber that promotes to the concrete a bigger deformation and with this a rupture less brusque than the conventional concrete. Already for tensile strength we can observe a fall very next with the one to the compressive strength this occurs, therefore the tensile strength it is correlated related with the compressive strength.

To evaluate the tack steel-concrete was opted to the accomplishment of the pulling up assay pull-out that the conventional was carried through for the two types of concrete and it I contend staple fibers of erase.

The procedure of assay determined in the related norm was followed. With the accomplishment of the assay of pull-out it was possible to get the value of the mean stress of tack, using itself the corresponding values to the landslides 0,01(small), 0,1(work) and 1,0 (rupture), illustrated in Table 6, these assays had occurred in the age of 28 days. Salient that τ average it corresponds the average of the tensions of tack for the landslides of 0,01; 0,1 and 1,0 mm.

The form of predominant rupture in the conventional concrete was for fail to concrete of the specimen already for the concrete with staple fibers the predominant rupture was the landslide of the bar.

Table 6 – Tensions of tack to the long one of the anchorage length

TYPE OF CONCRETE	Ø (mm)	$\tilde{\tau}_1$ (Kgf/mm²)	$\tilde{\tau}_1$ (Kgf/mm²)	$\tilde{\tau}_1$ (Kgf/mm²)	τaverage (Kgf/mm²)
Conventional Concrete	10,0	1,08	2,06	3,87	2,34
	12,5	1,46	2,56	6,39	3,47
	16,0	1,63	3,93	11,75	5,77
Concrete with addition staple fibres	10,0	0,89	1,19	2,74	1,61
	12,5	0,71	0,94	2,76	1,47
	16,0	1,18	1,59	4,65	2,47

With the applied forces and the respective occurred landslides force for the diameter of 10,0 12,5 and 16,00mm was possible to trace the curve landslide x that they are illustrated respectively in Figures 4, 5 and 6.

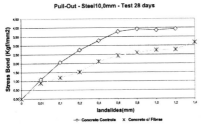

Figure 4 – Test Pull-Out Ø 10,0mm

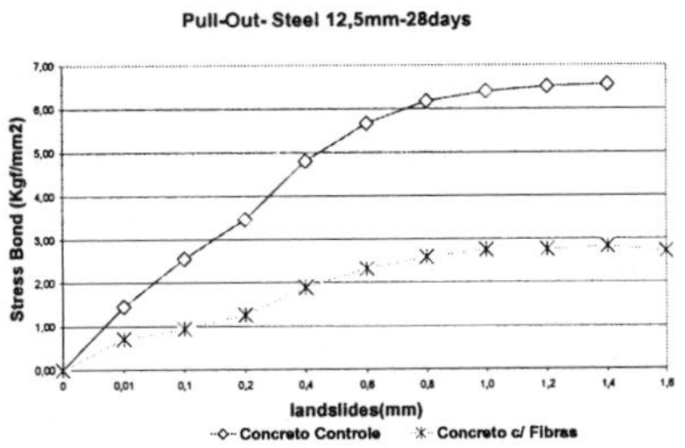

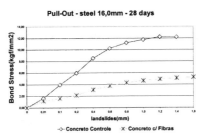

Figure 5 – Test Pull-Out Ø 12,5mm

Figure 6 – Test Pull-Out Ø 16,0mm

CONCLUSIONS

The use of the rubber in the concrete is an attempt to attenuate the impact that the tires provoke to the environment and also to classify them as new alternative materials for civil construction, saving the natural and added sand deposits. This justifies the necessity of advances in this line of research.

With the gotten results, and observed others in literature, it is given credit the possibility of use of the concrete with rubber staple fibres, since that destined to the use in constructions where great operating efforts are not had. Although to present decrease in the compressive strength, in relation to the conventional concrete, this concrete presented acceptable characteristics and performance for these uses.

For situations where if it has significant solicitant efforts, it is necessary an improvement in the matrix of the concrete, that consequently results in additions in the mechanical indices and in the tack steel-concrete. Therefore, it can be concluded that the use of the concrete in the composition established with substitution of 10% of the small aggregate for the pneumatic rubber is viable.

BIBLIOGRAPHY

1. ACCETTI, K. M., PINHEIRO, L.M. Tipos de fibras e propriedades do concreto cm fibras. In: CONGRESSO BRASILEIRO DO CONCRETO, 42, 2000, Fortaleza. Anais... Fortaleza: Arte Interativa, 2000. CD-ROM.

2. AKASAKI, J. L., NIRSCHL, G.C.,Influência da granulometria das fibras de borracha vulcanizada em dosagens de concreto. *In*: CONGRESSO BRASILEIRO DO CONCRETO 2002

3. CINCOTTO, M. A. Utilização de Subprodutos e Resíduos na Indústria da Construção Civil. Tecnologia das Edificações. São Paulo: Editora Pini Ltda, 1998, p.23-26.

4. LIMA, I. S., ROCHA, F. S. Um estudo da argamassa de cimento com adição de fibras de borracha vulcanizada para a construção civil. In: CONGRESSO BRASILEIRO DO CONCRETO, 42, 2000, Fortaleza. Anais Fortaleza: Arte Interativa, 2000. CD-ROM.

5. RILEM, FIP, CEB, 1973, "Essai portant sur l'adhérence des armatures du béton. 1. Essai par flexion (7-II-28D). 2. Essai par tration (7-II-128), Recomamdations Provisoires. Matériaux et Constructions, (mars – avr), v. 6, n. 32, pp. 96–105.

LABORATORY INVESTIGATION TO ASSESS MOISTURE SENSITIVITY OF DRY PROCESS CRM ASPHALT MIXTURES

M M.Rahman

Babtie Group

G D Airey

A C Collop

University of Nottingham

United Kingdom

ABSTRACT. Crumb rubber manufactured from scrap tyres has been used in asphalt mixtures as a binder modifier (known as the wet process) or as an aggregate (known as the dry process) since the late sixties. Compared to the wet process, the dry process has been a far less popular method due to inconsistent field performance in terms of cracking and fretting. However, mixtures produced using the dry process do consume larger quantities of recycled crumb rubber and the dry process is logistically easier than the wet process and therefore potentially available to a larger market. Limited fundamental studies have been performed to understand the mechanical properties including durability of CRM mixtures. This paper investigates the effect of moisture conditioning on the mechanical properties of dry process crumb rubber modified (CRM) bituminous mixture containing different quantities of crumb rubber using Nottingham Asphalt Tester (NAT). The stiffness modulus, fatigue and permanent deformation resistance have been determined for dense graded asphalt mixtures containing 3% and 5% crumb rubber by the total aggregate mass and compared with mixtures tested in their unaged state. The results show that CRM mixtures are more susceptible to moisture damage compared to conventional asphalt mixtures with approximately 30% and 75% reduction of stiffness for mixtures containing 3% and 5% crumb rubber respectively. In addition, fatigue life and resistance to permanent deformation are also adversely effected and showed a general reduction in performance compared to similar mixtures tested in their unaged state.

Key words: Crumb rubber, Moisture sensitivity, Stiffness, Fatigue and permanent deformation

Mujib Rahman is an engineer working at Babtie, a leading Engineering and Management consultant in the UK and overseas. Mujib is presently in the process of completing his PhD study at the University of Nottingham.

Dr Gordon Airey is a Senior Lecturer within the Nottingham Centre for Pavement Engineering, School of Civil Engineering at the University of Nottingham. He has been involved in pavement engineering research both in South Africa and the UK since 1990. His research interests include fundamental rheological testing of bitumen and asphalt mixtures; the durability of asphalt materials; the use of secondary materials in pavement applications; and constitutive modelling of asphalt mixture behaviour.

Professor Andrew Collop is Deputy Director of the Nottingham Centre for Pavement Engineering at the University of Nottingham and Director of Research for the School of Civil Engineering. His research interests include vehicle-pavement interaction, mechanical behaviour of asphalt mixtures; specialist pavements, highway structures and non-destructive evaluation; and rail track engineering. He is currently a Director of the International Society for Asphalt Pavements.

INTRODUCTION

Scrap tyres form a major part of the world's solid waste management problem. Each year the UK alone p roduces a round 3 0 m illion w aste t yres w ith 1 b illion b eing produced globally. Almost half of them are landfilled or stockpiled with the rest being recycled. In the Europe, governments are attempting to find alternative uses of scrap tyres as new European Union Landfill Directives will prohibit land filling by 2006 [1]. Within the expanding recycling market, only two, to date, have shown the potential to use a significant number of scrap tyres, (i) fuel for combustion and (ii) crumb rubber modified (CRM) material for asphalt paving. Although combustion can consume millions of tyres, it is not an ideal environmental solution. The only remaining potential market for using crumb rubber is CRM m aterial for asphalt paving. In the last two decades, utilisation of scrap tyres as a road construction material has become a popular means to minimise this environmental pressure. Considerable work has been done in various countries in terms of the utilisation of scrap tyres and there is a long list of published literature dealing with different aspects of this challenging material.

CRM asphalt is a general type of modified asphalt that contains scrap tyre rubber. Modified asphalt paving products can be made with crumb rubber by several techniques, including a wet process and a dry process. In the wet process CRM binders are produced when finely ground crumb rubber (.075 mm to1.2 mm) is mixed with bitumen at elevated temperatures prior mixing with the aggregate. Binder modification of this type is due to physical and compositional changes in an interaction process where the rubber particles swell in the bitumen by absorbing a percentage of the lighter fraction of the bitumen, to form a viscous gel with an increase in the overall viscosity of the "modified" binder [2-4]. In the dry process, granulated or ground rubber and/or crumb rubber (0.4 to 10 mm) is used as a substitute for a small portion of the fine aggregate (typically 3-4 percent by mass of the total aggregate in the mixture). The rubber particles are blended with the aggregate prior to the addition of the bitumen [2].

Materials produced using both the wet and the dry processes have the potential to demonstrate improved properties compared to conventional asphalt materials. These improved benefits include increased fatigue life or fatigue resistance, reduced reflective cracking and low temperature cracking, improved tensile strength, ductility, toughness, adhesion, resilience, tenacity, durability, skid resistance and finally resistance to rutting [14-19]. C ompared t o t he w et p rocess, t he d ry p rocess h as b een a f ar l ess popular m ethod o f CRM asphalt production. The reasons for this include the increased costs of having to use specially graded aggregate to incorporate the reclaimed tyre crumb, construction difficulties and most importantly poor reproducibility and premature failure of dry process CRM asphalt road surfacing [20-22]. However, the dry process has the potential to consume larger quantities of recycled crumb rubber compared to the wet process resulting in greater environmental benefits. In addition, the production of the CRM asphalt mixture by means of the d ry p rocess i s l ogistically e asier t han t he w et p rocess a nd t herefore t he d ry p rocess i s potentially available to a much larger market. An assumption that is generally made with the use of the dry process is that the rubber crumb is solely part of the aggregate and that the reaction between bitumen and crumb rubber is negligible. This is usually achieved by limiting the time at which the bitumen and crumb rubber are maintained at high mixing (reaction) temperatures and specifying a coarse granulated crumb rubber with a low surface area and smooth (less reactive) sheared surfaces. However, recent research has shown that during the mixing period as well as during transportation and laying, rubber crumb does swell and react with bitumen changing the properties of the residual bitumen, the shape and rigidity of the rubber and consequently the performance of the asphalt mixture [5-6].

Durability of bituminous mixtures is defined as their ability to resist damage caused by environmental factors, including water, temperature and fuel in the context of a given amount of traffic for a long period of time without any significant deterioration. Water damage mechanisms result in a reduction of the structural integrity of the mixture and can lead to early failure and are normally manifested in the loss of adhesion between the aggregate and the bitumen commonly referred to as stripping and/or loss of strength or stiffness of the mixture [11-13]. Numerous test methods have been developed to determine if a bituminous mixture is prone to moisture induced damage but laboratory fabricated specimens often overestimate the effect of moisture on the real pavement structure [11]. Therefore, any results obtained from a laboratory investigation should be treated as indicative and further verification would require with field data.

This paper describes a laboratory investigation of the influence of moisture on mechanical properties of different CRM mixtures using the NAT, principally on the stiffness, fatigue and resistance to permanent deformation. In addition, results obtained from moisture conditioning tests are also compared with similar mixtures tested in their unaged state.

EXPERIMENTAL PROGRAMME

Materials

A c ontinuously graded, 20 m m m aximum a ggregate s ize d ense b itumen m acadam (DBM) asphalt mixture, as specified in BS 4987-1:2001, Table 15, was used to manufacture a range of control and dry process CRM asphalt mixtures. Figure 1 shows the grading envelopes of the DBM mixture and the design grading that were used in the study. All the mixtures were produced with a Middle East 100/150 penetration grade bitumen, as specified in BS EN 12591, with a binder content of 5.25% by mass of total mixture.

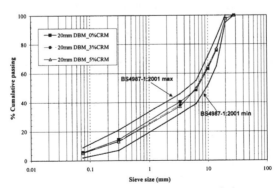

Figure 1: 20 mm DBM aggregate gradation

The CRM asphalt mixtures were produced by replacing a portion of the aggregate fraction with granulated crumb rubber between 2 and 8 mm in size. The procedure that was used consisting of sieving the crumb rubber to obtain two single size fractions; passing 6.3 mm and retained on 3.35 mm, and passing 3.35 mm and retained on 0.3 mm and then substituting these two fractions into the design DBM gradation. As the majority of the granulated crumb rubber was less than 3.35 mm, the two fractions were not placed in equal amounts but consisting of 20% < 6.3 mm & > 3.35 mm and 80% < 3.35mm & > 0.3 mm.

A total of three control and CRM asphalt mixture combinations were therefore produced in the laboratory with the following variables:

- Crumb rubber content by mass of total aggregate: 0, 3 and 5%,
- Target air void content: 4 %

The CRM asphalt mixtures were batched gravimetrically by replacing either 3% or 5% of the aggregate function with granulated crumb rubber. The gravimetric gradings were then converted to volumetric gradings to check that they were still within the grading envelopes of the 20 mm DBM asphalt mixture. Twenty-four specimens were produced for each of the six asphalt mixture combinations by means of gyratory compaction with the following compaction parameters:

- Axial pressure: 0.6 MPa
- Gyratory angle: 1.25°
- Speed of gyration: 30 gyrations per minute
- Compaction temperature: 140°C
- Specimen diameter: 100 mm
- Compacted specimen height: 90 mm, and
- Trimmed (final) specimen height: 60 mm.

All the specimens (control and CRM) were compacted to a design density (target air voids content) or 600 (maximum number) gyrations whichever occurred first. Photographs of 0%, 3% and 5% crumb rubber mixtures are presented in Figure 2. It was observed that rubber particles formed cluster and tend to pluck out from the surface during trimming. For simplicity, the different materials were coded as follows; crumb rubber content as R0, R3 and R5 and "M" for moisture and "U" for unaged mixtures. For example, UR3 refers to the unaged CRM asphalt mixture with 3% rubber content by mass.

Mechanical properties

The mechanical properties of the primary and secondary aggregate asphalt mixtures were measured using the NAT [7]. The three main parameters that were measured were the stiffness modulus (load bearing capacity) of the asphalt mixtures and the two main pavement distress mechanisms of permanent deformation and fatigue cracking.

The stiffness moduli of the primary and secondary asphalt mixtures were measured using the Indirect Tensile Stiffness Modulus (ITSM) test on 100 mm diameter specimens with an average height of 60 mm. During the test a load pulse is applied along the vertical diameter of a cylindrical specimen and the resultant peak transient deformation measured along the horizontal diameter. The stiffness modulus is then a function of load, deformation, specimen dimensions and an assumed Poisson's ratio of 0.35.

Cluster of rubber particles tend to fall out during trimming

Figure 2: Specimens with 0%, 3% and 5% rubber contents

The ITSM test was performed in accordance with the British Standard DD213 using the following test parameters [8]:

- Test temperature: 20°C,
- Loading rise-time: 124 milliseconds, and
- Peak transient horizontal deformation: 5 μm.

The permanent deformation resistance of the different asphalt mixtures was determined by means of the Confined Repeated Load Axial Test (CRLAT) using a direct uniaxial compression configuration on specimens with a diameter of 100 mm and a height of 60 mm. In addition, the tests were conducted at 60^0C to simulate extreme high temperature pavement conditions. The CRLA tests were performed in accordance with the British Standards DD185 using the following test parameters [9]:

- Test temperature: 60°C,
- Test duration: 7200 seconds (3600 cycles) with a load pattern 1 second loading on (load application period) followed by one second off (rest period),
- Axial stress: 100 kPa,
- Confining pressure: 50 kPa, and
- Conditioning stress: 10 kPa for 600 seconds.

The fatigue resistance of the asphalt mixtures was determined by means of the Indirect Tensile Fatigue Test (ITFT) with an experimental arrangement similar to that used for the ITSM but under repeated loading and with slight modifications to the testing modulus crosshead [10]. The ITFT tests were performed using the following test parameters:

- Test temperature: 20°C,
- Loading condition: Controlled-stress,
- Loading rise-time: 120 milliseconds, and
- Failure indication: 9 mm vertical deformation.

Moisture Sensitivity Test Protocol

The procedure of moisture sensitivity testing using the Link Bitutest testing protocol [11-12] for asphalt mixtures was followed in this investigation, where the ratio of conditioned to unaged indirect stiffness modulus is used to predict the moisture sensitivity of a particular asphalt mixture. The testing procedures of this method are as follows:

- Saturation of specimen under a partial vacuum of 510mm Hg at 20^0C for 30 minutes.

- Percentage saturation is calculated using the following formula;

$$S = \frac{M_w - M_d}{\frac{M_d}{G_{mb}} - \frac{M_d}{G_{mm}}} X100 \tag{1}$$

Where; S is percent saturation (%), M_d is mass of dry specimen in g, M_w is mass of wet specimen in g, G_{mb} is bulk specific gravity and G_{mm} is maximum specific gravity.

- The specimens are then transferred to a preheated water bath at 60°C at atmospheric pressure for 6 hours and then saturated at atmospheric pressure at 5°C for further 16 hours. The specimens are finally conditioned under water at 20°C (atmospheric pressure) for 2 hours prior to stiffness testing.

- Determine stiffness ratio= $\frac{ITSM_{Ci}}{ITSM_U}; i = 1,2,3.... \tag{2}$

- Above steps are repeated for subsequent cycles.

After each conditioning cycle, the specimens were allowed to dry for further 2 hours at 20°C in a conditioning chamber prior to ITSM testing and the same procedure was followed for the subsequent cycles. The number of moisture conditioning cycles was limited to three for control mixtures and due to significant stiffness reduction, two for the CRM mixtures. It is important to note that after ITSM testing, half the specimens from each mixture were tested using the Indirect Tensile Fatigue (ITFT) test for fatigue and the other half was subjected to the Confined Repeated Load Axial (CRLAT) test to evaluate the resistance to permanent deformation. In addition, similar mixtures were also tested in their unaged state and the results compared with corresponding moisture conditioned mixtures.

RESULTS AND DISCUSSION

Saturation
The percentage saturation versus voids contents for control and CRM mixtures is presented in Figure 3. In general, the percentage saturation increases with increasing rubber content in the mixture due to the higher void content of the CRM mixtures. In addition, It was observed that rubber particles generally plucked out from the surface of the specimen which formed paths for water to enter in the mixture matrix, consequently increasing the percentage of saturation during partial vacuum water conditioning.

Stiffness Modulus

The average stiffness modulus for control and CRM mixtures subjected to different degree of moisture conditioning are presented in Figure 4. In the unaged state (0 cycle), the replacement of aggregate sizes between 2 and 8 mm with crumb rubber leads to a reduction in the bearing capacity (stiffness) of the asphalt mixture. This reduction can be high as 20% for the 3% CRM mixtures and as high as 44% for the 5% CRM mixtures. In their moisture conditioned state, the CRM mixtures undergo a significant reduction in stiffness within the first conditioning cycle. The stiffness reduction was on average 25% for R3 mixture and 66% for R5 mixture. The stiffness modulus ratio was also calculated using Equation 2 and plotted against conditioning cycles in Figure 5.

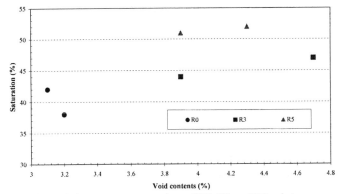

Figure 3: Percentage saturation of R0, R3 and R5 mixtures

It can be seen that the stiffness modulus ratio for the control mixture increases with no noticeable moisture damage. On the other hand, both the CRM mixtures show a reduction of stiffness with the 3%CRM mixture being significantly lower than the 5%CRM mixtures.

This is partly the consequence of increased saturation in the 5%CRM mixture, which allows more water to penetrate into the mixture matrix, and weakens the structure. This increased saturation combined with rubber rebounding effect during six hours conditioning at 60^{0}C when bitumen is not capable of halting any rebound results in the overall reduction of mixture's load bearing capacity. In addition, as the CRM mixtures were produced with an extra compaction effort to achieve target density, the rebound effect of rubber particles is greater in 5%CRM mixtures due to the extra rubber content in the mixtures.

Permanent Deformation

The permanent deformation results for the control and CRM DBM asphalt mixtures tested in their unaged and moisture conditioned states are presented as measures of total strain (%) after 3600 cycles and average strain rate (microstrain/cycle) between 1500 and 3000 cycles in Table 1. In addition, average permanent strain versus loading cycles for the control and CRM mixtures are presented in Figure 6.

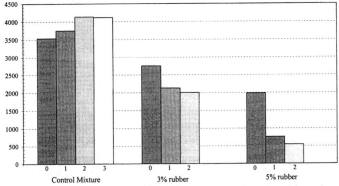

Figure 4: Mean ITSM values for R0, R3 and R5 mixtures subjected to moisture conditioning cycles

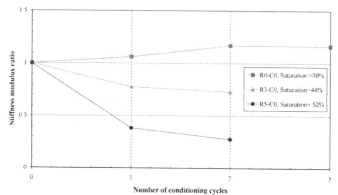

Figure 5: Stiffness modulus ratio of the control and CRM mixtures

Table 1: Permanent deformation parameters for control and CRM asphalt mixtures

MIXTURE	UNAGED				MOISTURE CONDITIONED			
	Strain rate (µε/cycle)		Total strain (%)		Strain rate (µε/cycle)		Total strain (%)	
	Avg	Std dev	Avg	Std dev	Avg	Std dev	Avg	Std dev
R0	0.6	0.3	0.8	0.3	1.1	0.5	1.5	0.7
R3	2.1	0.8	4.7	0.7	4.8	1.0	4.4	0.1
R5	1.3	0.2	4.6	1.1	8.6	3.7	12.1	1.2

The differences in material ranking by means of the two permanent deformation test parameters can be attributed to the sensitivity of the total strain parameter to any initial slack in the test apparatus due to rough top surface of the CRM mixtures (Figure 2) as well as the fundamental differences in what each parameter is measuring. For total strain, any delayed elastic response that cannot be recovered during the one second recovery period will be added to the final strain measurement, while the strain rate parameter is a more direct measurement of the viscous response (permanent strain) of the material. For the highly elastic (rubberised), lower stiffness modulus CRM mixtures, the proportion and actual strain magnitude of the delayed elastic component will inevitably be relatively high resulting in an increase in total strain. For this reason the strain rate parameter can be considered to be a more reliable and accurate means of assessing the permanent deformation performance of the dry process CRM asphalt mixtures.

Compared to the unaged state, the resistance to permanent deformation for the continuously graded DBM control mixtures decreases due to the reduction of mixture's cohesion after moisture ageing. Relative to the control mixtures, the replacement of part of the aggregate fractions with crumb rubber results in an increase in permanent strain in both the unaged and moisture conditioned states. In terms of strain rate, relative to control mixture, the resistance to permanent deformation is significantly decreased in CRM mixtures due to moisture conditioning. The increase in strain rate is significantly higher for the R5 mixture than the R3 mixture indicating that the mixture with 5% crumb rubber content is more susceptible to moisture induced damage, therefore, potentially less durable in service.

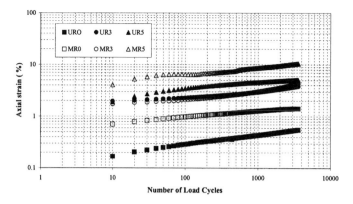

Figure 6: Permanent strain versus loading cycles for control and CRM asphalt mixtures tested in unaged and moisture condition state

Fatigue

The regression lines for strain and fatigue life with co-efficient of correlation for each mixture tested in their unaged and moisture conditioned states are presented in Table 2. With the exception of mixture UR5, the fatigue and strain equations have all been established with a fairly good degree of confidence. Using equations presented in Table 2, predicted fatigue life for $100\mu\varepsilon$ and predicted strain for million load cycles were calculated to study the effect of rubber content and moisture conditioning.

Table 2: Fatigue line equations for control and CRM mixtures

MIXTU-RE	FATIGUE EQUATION	STRAIN EQUATION	FIT (R^2)	STRAIN @ 10^6 cycles ($\mu\varepsilon$)	CYCLES @ 100 $\mu\varepsilon$ (in thousand)
UR0	$N_f = 1.6*10^{11} \varepsilon^{-3.45}$	$\varepsilon = 1534 N_f^{-0.27}$	0.94	36	20
UR3	$N_f = 4.8*10^{16} \varepsilon^{-5.42}$	$\varepsilon = 887 N_f^{-0.15}$	0.81	111	706
UR5	$N_f = 1.0*10^{15} \varepsilon^{-4.70}$	$\varepsilon = 858 N_f^{-0.13}$	0.63	134	416
MR0	$N_f = 2.0 \times 10^{11} \varepsilon^{-3.70}$	$\varepsilon = 918 \times N_f^{-0.25}$	0.91	31	8
MR3	$N_f = 1.0 \times 10^{9} \varepsilon^{-2.24}$	$\varepsilon = 2033 \times N_f^{-0.26}$	0.99	56	91
MR5	$N_f = 2.0 \times 10^{14} \varepsilon^{-4.36}$	$\varepsilon = 7353 \times N_f^{-0.38}$	0.86	37	33

It can be observed that although in unaged state, the partial replacement of aggregate with crumb rubber results in a significant increase in fatigue performance, the performance is reduced following the adverse effect of moisture conditioning. However, in terms of predicted life, despite the fact that CRM mixtures are adversely affected by moisture conditioning, their relative fatigue performance is still superior to similarly conditioned control mixtures.

The relative fatigue performance of the unaged and moisture conditioned control and CRM mixtures are presented in Figure 7. The graphs demonstrate that the superior fatigue performances of the CRM mixtures in their unaged state deteriorate after moisture conditioning of the mixtures.

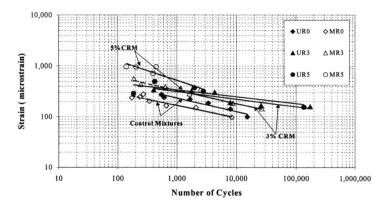

Figure 7: Fatigue equation for control and CRM mixtures tested in unaged and moisture condition state

CONCLUSIONS

The NAT has been used to conduct a study on the mechanical performance of unaged and moisture conditioned dry processes CRM continuously graded asphalt mixtures. The results are compared to the performance of conventional, primary aggregate mixtures produced in similar conditioned and compaction regimes. The mechanical properties that were investigated consisted of stiffness modulus, resistance to permanent deformation and resistance to fatigue cracking.

In terms of the bearing capacity, CRM mixtures are found to be more susceptible to moisture induced damage compared to traditional DBM mixtures. The reduction of stiffness was approximately 30% for the mixture with 3% crumb rubber and 70% for the 5%CRM mixture indicating less durable service life. The permanent deformation resistance of the unaged and moisture conditioned CRM mixtures was found to be inferior to that of the control mixture. On the other hand, the fatigue performance in unaged state was found to be superior for both the 3% and 5% CRM asphalt mixtures compared to that of the control mixtures, although performance deteriorated after moisture conditioning. The reduction of overall fatigue performance of the CRM mixtures after moisture conditioning was predominantly due to considerable reduction of stiffness. Therefore, although in their unaged state the CRM mixtures demonstrate overall better mechanical properties relative to a control DBM mixture, their long-term durability needs to be investigated for future application.

REFERENCE

1. Hird, A.B., Griffiths, P.J., Smith, R.A., " Tyre waste and resource management: A mass balance approach", Viridis Report VR2, Transport Research Laboratory (TRL), Crowthorne, UK, 2002

2. Heitzman, M. "Design and Construction of Asphalt Paving Materials with Crumb Rubber Modifier", Transportation Research Record 1339, TRB, Washington, D.C., pp. 1-8, 1992.

3. Bahia, H.U. and Davis, R. "Effect of Crumb Rubber Modifiers (CRM) on Performance Related Properties of Asphalt Binders", Journal of the Association of Asphalt Paving Technologists, Vol. 63, pp. 414-449, 1994.

4. Kim, S., Loh, S.W., Zhai, H., Bahia, H. "Advanced Characterization of Crumb Rubber-Modified Asphalts, Using Protocols Developed for Complex Binder", Transport Research Record 1767, TRB, Washington, D.C., pp. 15-24, 2001.

5. Singleton, T.M., Airey, G.D. and Collop, A.C. "Effect of Rubber-Bitumen Interaction on the Mechanical Durability of Impact Absorbing Asphalt", Proceedings of the 2nd Eurasphalt and Eurobitume Congress, Vol. 4, Barcelona, pp. 1053-1060, 2000.

6. Airey, G.D., Mujibur, M.M. and Collop, A.C. "Absorption of Bitumen into Crumb Rubber Using the Basket Drainage Method", International Journal of Pavement Engineering, 2003

7. Cooper, K.E. and Brown, S.F. "Developments of a Simple Apparatus for the Measurement of the Mechanical Properties of Asphalt Mixes." Proceedings of the Eurobitume Symposium, Madrid, pp. 494-498, 1989

8. British Standards Institution. "Method for Determination of the Indirect Tensile Stiffness Modulus of Bituminous Mixtures." DD 213, BSI, London, 1993.

9. British Standards Institution. "Method for Assessment of Resistance to Permanent Deformation of Bitumen Aggregate Mixtures Subject to Unconfined Uniaxial Loading." DD 185, BSI, London, 1994.

10. British Standard Draft for Development DD ABF: 2002, "Method for the Determination of the Fatigue Characteristics of Bituminous Mixtures Using Indirect Tensile Fatigue Test."

11. Scholz, T.V., "Durability of Paving Mixtures", PhD Thesis, School of Civil Engineering, The University of Nottingham, October 1995.

12. Brown, S.F. and Scholz, T.V, " Development of Laboratory Protocols for the Ageing of Asphalt Mixtures", Proceedings of the 2nd Euroasphalt & Eurobitume Congress, Session 1: Performance Testing and Specification for Binders and Mixtures, pp. 83-90, Barcelona, September 2000

13. Mostafa, A., Halim, A.A. and Hassan, Y. (2003), "Laboratory Testing of Moisture Susceptibility of Asphalt Concrete," 3rd International Symposium on Maintenance and Rehabilitation of Pavements and Technological Control, The University of Minho, Guimaraes, Portugal, July 7-10.

14. Airey, G.D., Collop, A.C. and Mujibur, M.M. "Mechanical Properties of Crumb Rubber Modified Asphalt Mixtures", 3rd Eurasphalt & Eurobitume Congress, Vienna, 2004

15. Takallou, H.B., Hicks, R.G. and Esch, D.C. "Effect of Mix Ingredients on the Behaviour of Rubber-Modified Asphalt Mixtures", Transport Research Record 1096, TRB, Washington, D.C., pp. 68-80, 1986

16. Epps, J.A. "Uses of Recycled Rubber Tires in Highways", NCHRP Synthesis of Highway Practice 198, Transportation Research Board, National Research Council, Washington D.C., 1994.

17. McQuillen, J.L., Takallou, H.B., Hicks, R.G. and Esch, D.C. "Economic Analysis of Rubber-Modified Asphalt Mixes", Journal of Transportation Engineering, Vol. 114, pp. 259-277, 1988.

18. Way. G.B. "OGFC meets CRM: Where the Rubber Meets the Rubber." Proceedings of the Asphalt Rubber 2000 Conference, pp 15-32, Vilamoura, Portugal, 2000.

19. Oliver, J.W.H. "Rutting and Fatigue Properties of Crumb Rubber Hot Mix Asphalts." Proceedings of the Asphalt Rubber 2000 Conference, pp 221-240, Vilamoura, Portugal, 2000.

20. Amirkhanian, S.N. "Utilization of Crumb Rubber in Asphaltic Concrete Mixtures-South Carolina Experience", South Carolina Department of Transportation, South Carolina, USA, 2001.

21. Fager, G.A. "Asphalt Rubber: A Summary of the Use of Crumb Rubber in the Hot Mixes: Kansas Experience 1990-2000", Kansas Department of Transportation, Kansas, 2001.

22. Hunt, E.A. "Crumb Rubber Modified Asphalt Concrete in Oregon", Oregon Department of Transportation, 2002.

MODIFIED BITUMINOUS CONCRETE USING A RUBBER POWDER

R Kettab

A Bali

Ecole Nationale Polytechnique (E.N.P)

Alger

ABSTRACT. The paper examines the behaviour of a modified bituminous concrete using a rubber powder. In our tests ground rubber has not been added to the binder but to the granular skeleton. The optimum proportion which gives the best performances (stability, creep, compression strength at a dry and saturated state) has been determined. The tests have been carried out for two types of aggregate of different mineralogical nature (carbonated sedimentary rocks and basalt rocks) and two types of bitumen (35/50 and 70/100 classes). This additive has improved significantly the behaviour of the coated granular towards water. The stiffness module has been determined for different rubber powder proportions. This allows us to understand in which direction the layer thickness varies.

Keywords: Asphalt, Polymers, Rubber, Pavement, Bitumen, Concrete.

R. Mitiche spouse Kettab : is a doctor lecturer in Civil Engineering at Ecole Nationale Polytechnique of Algiers. Researcher teacher in local materials and their valorization.

A. Bali is professor in the Civil Engineering department, head of materials laboratory at Ecole Nationale Polytechnique of Algiers.

INTRODUCTION

A particular interest has been given to the modified binders for several years. The Binder is improved by the addition of polymers and rubber in order to make it work in more severe conditions and fulfill requirements to which the pure ordinary binder which is a thermoplastic material while presenting inconveniences in either very low temperatures or in very high temperatures is not able to give satisfaction. In practice, this technique is difficult to exploit because of the feasibility an industrial scale (manufacture, storage, transport.....)

In the present work, additives are inserted directly in the granular skeleton of an ordinary bituminous concrete destinated to the rolling layer of the pavement. The additive comes from the recuperation of waste of rubber and polymers (used tires of vehicles, carpet of cars, soles of shoes....etc) ground to powder. The latter has been added to the mixture it different percentages. The mechanical performance evolution has been examined in order to obtain the optimal powder content that could guarantee an improvement of the stability and a reduction of the layer thickness.

In this work, the type of aggregates (chalky and basaltic) has been varied as well as the bitumen class (35/50).The behaviour of the mixture has been evaluated using the classic tests (Duriez and Marshall) and the static creep test .

FORMULATION OF THE BITUMINOUS CONCRETE:

Introduction

The formulation of a bituminous concrete consists of determining the best mix between aggregates of different diameters and a binder (asphalt) in order to get a material of some mechanical properties: roughness, impermeability, fatigue resistance, orniérage, creep....

Criteria of Formulation

The main qualities bituminous concrete must have are: the stability, flexibility and the callousness to water. The main factors are: the type of the structure, the thickness of the layer, the climatic conditions and the site.

Methodology for the Survey of a Formulation

The determination of a formulation of bituminous concrete for a rolling layer is based on three essential stages: aggregates composition, the binder content and the concrete caracteristics.

USE OF ADDITIVES IN COAT THEM BITUMINOUS

The objective of the use of additives

The researches of improvement of properties of the bituminous concrete either by modification of the structure of binding or by addition of additives are ancient [1]. So for example, BENCOVITZ and BOES published in 1938 in the magazine of the ASTM, a paper on the addition of sulfur to the bituminous mixture.

When it's grading well chosen, the asphalt in mort cases, will garanter the properties of adhesion and satisfaction mechanical properties in different traffic and climate conditions. However, conditions of traffic become more and more aggressive, linted to economy imperatives that require an important investment and thinner layers, brought the pure asphalts to some limits of use;

- Pure asphalt does not allow anymore the traditional concrete (bituminous concrete 0/10 or 0/14) to assure in all cases a resistance to the satisfactory orniérage under very heavy traffic and for elevated temperatures;

- A harder asphalt, if it brings to concrete a better behavior to the orniérage (advantage at high temperatures) increases the thermal cracking risk on the contrary at low temperatures;

- Some miscellanies coated of open granularity won't have the mechanical resistance wished of the fact of the cohesiveness and the tackiness gotten with a pure bitumen, nor same a good durability of the fact of a wealth while weak binder.

Use of Additives in Bituminous Concrete

The effect of the additive is appreciated directly on the bituminous mixture. Different nature additives can be used in order to modify the characteristics of bituminous of mixes, bituminous concrete or superficial smears. They are distributed in the following families: polymers added in power station, the recycled plastics, of rubber aggregates, mineral, synthetic or metallic fibers, bitumen and natural asphalts [2].

Effects of the additive addition

The addition of an additive in bituminous concrete can lead to three effects according to its chemical nature, its size and its physical caracteristics (point of fusion, tenacity, etc.) [2].

1. An effect on the binder due to the increase of the viscosity of the asphalt by true dissolution of some matters or scattering it the melted state.

2. An effect of blocking due to grains weakened provisionally during the placing, of short size and that are going to be thermoformed when compacting to fill the voids of the granular skeleton.

3. An effect of reinforcement causes by thongs or the still sufficiently rigid and sufficiently long fibers to create bridges inside the granular skeleton.

The above three effects, alone or accumulated, can lead to a hydrocarbon material less sensitive to temperature and therefore less sensitive to creep strain.

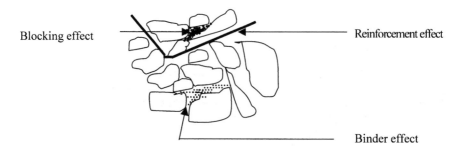

Blocking effect   Reinforcement effect

Binder effect

Figure 1. Effects of the additive addition to the bituminous concrete

IDENTIFICATION OF MATERIALS

Introduction
A formulation of bituminous concrete consists of: [3, 4];

- Choosing the granulometrie of the skeleton more or less tight (continues).
- Searching the quantity of binder necessary to coat granulates without excess of binding that will lead to a too viscous coated.

Presentation of Material Used

Asphalts
Two classes of bitumen have been used: the asphalt 35/50 and the asphalt 70/100

The results of identification tests bitumen used for the different formulations are given in Table 1.

Table1. Tests characterization tests of the used bitumen

TEST	BITUMEN 35/50	BITUMEN 70/100
Penetrability to the needle (1/10 mm)	42	85
Temperature of softening (°C)	58	58
Point of lightning (°C)	268	260
Point of flame (°C)	314	333

The granular materials
Two types of aggregates have been used

- Granulometrical Analysis:
The resulting of granulometrique analysis as well as spindles of specification are given in the following Figures 2 and 3.

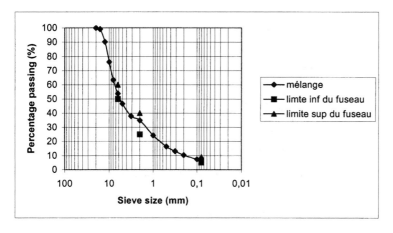

Figure 2. Curve of aggregate mixture of Cap Djinet

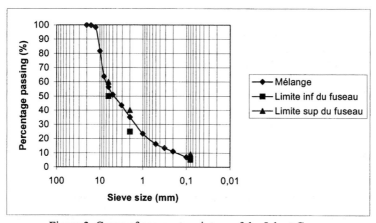

Figure 3. Curve of aggregate mixture of the Jobert Career

The Additive (powder of rubber)

The additive is a powder of rubber (waste) which comes from the grinding of pieces of rubber used in the manufacture of car carpet; these wastes are ground to a powder of 2 mm of maximum size whose density is 0.8.

RESULTS AND DISCUSSION

Results of the Marshall [5] test:

The main results of test are given in the following figures [6]:

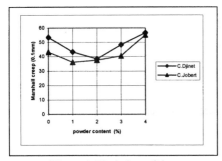

Figure 4. Variation of the
Marshall creep (bitumen 35/50)

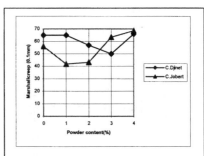

Figure 5. Variation of the
Marshall creep (bitumen 70/100)

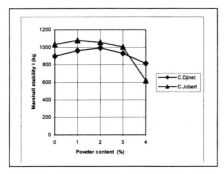

Figure 6. Variation of the Marshall
stability (bitumen 35/50)

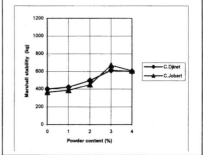

Figure 7. Variation of the Marshall
stability (bitumen 70/100)

Results of the Duriez [7] test:

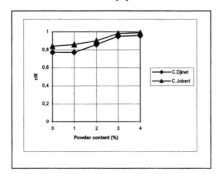

Figure 8. Variation of the (r/R) ratio
(bitumen 35/50)

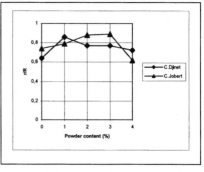

Figure 9. variation of the(r/R) ratio
(bitumen 70/100)

R: Dry strength
r: Strength after immersion

Results of static creep test:

bi: bituminous concrete with i % of addition.

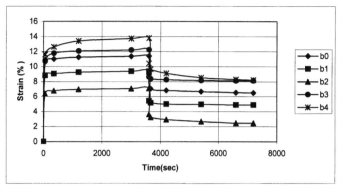

Figure10. Variation of the strain with time

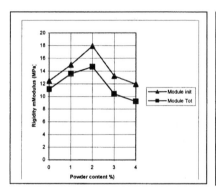

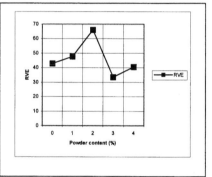

Figure 11. Variation of rigidity modulus
(initial and final)

Figure 12. Variation of viscoplastic
recovery (RVE)

CONCLUSION

The work undertaken is a part of a large programme of research activities planned in the Construction and Environment Laboratory (LCE). It consists of a theoretical and experimental survey about the effect of rubber powder on the behaviour of the modified bituminous concrete. This modification cannot be taken into account only on the basis of technical criteria but must include the environmental aspect.

The improvement of bituminous concrete with regard to the actual characteristics of an ordinary concrete allows to increase both the level and durability of the performances of the mixture. If the modification of the bituminous concrete using the well chosen additives more after allows to improve the properties of mixture and if this improvement increases generally with the modification level, the excess may sometimes lead to the contrary giving in fact a bad bituminous concrete.

A global analysis of the results obtained from the experimental work allow to draw the following conclusions:

- The addition of the rubber powder in the formulation of the bituminous mixes gives an improvement of the overall properties of the elaborated material.

- Began an optimal percentage of the rubber powder in the mix a decrease of the material characteristics is noticed. The excess of powder content may lead to the contrary of the slacked goal

- It is confirmed that rubber powder behaves as a fine (filler) within the granular skeleton filling the existing voids. This rubber powder contributes to the improvement of the compactness and mechanical strength.

- The rubber powder can as well be considered as a binder by fusion with bitumen. This way be explained by the difference recorded in the optima when different bitumen classes have been used.

- When manufacturing (confectioning) the test specimens it has been noticed that the workability has decreased with the increase in the powder percentage with the formation of the binder-polymer phases.

REFERENCES

1. BULLETIN DE LIAISON DES LABORATOIRES ROUTIERS DES PONTS ET CHAUSSEES. Spécial D journées d'études des bitumes caoutchouc Paris, 1964

2. REVUE GENERALE DES ROUTES ET AERODROMES. Utilisation du caoutchouc recyclé dans les revêtements routiers. Paris N° 763, 1998

3. KETTAB, R., BALI, A. : Béton bitumineux modifié à la poudrette de caoutchouc, Proceedings, IIIéme congrès algérien de la route, Algérie, 2001.

4. KETTAB, R., FLEUREAU, J.M., BALI, A : Improvement of properties of the bituminous concrete, Proceedings of International Conference on Performance of Construction Materials in the new millennium, Egypt, 2003.

5. BRARA, A., KETTAB, R., : Amélioration des propriétés d'un enrobé bitumineux par la poudrette de caoutchouc, Thèse de magister, Alger ENP, 2004.

6. NORME FRANÇAISE NFP 98-251-1, Essais statiques sur mélanges hydrocarbonés, partie1 : Essais Duriez sur mélanges hydrocarbonés à chaud, Paris, 1991.

7. NORME FRANÇAISE NFP 98-251-2, Essais statiques sur mélanges hydrocarbonés, partie2 : Essai Marshall, Paris, 1991.

REUSE OF RUBBER WASTE IN CEMENTITIOUS COMPOSITES: HYGROTHERMAL BEHAVIOUR

B Laidoudi

L Marmoret

M Quéneudec

Laboratoire des Technologies innovantes- UPJV

France

ABSTRACT. This w ork l ies w ithin t he g eneral o bjective o f c haracterizing c ement-rubber composites. Its specific aim is to study the thermal behavior of such composites in a dry state and with respect to moisture conditions. In this study, rubber aggregates of the compact type have been used with a rubber volume content ratio varying from 10% to 50% in a cementing matrix. Thermal conductivity measurements were performed using the Transient Plane Source (TPS) method. In order to demonstrate the influence of moisture on the thermal conductivity of this type of material, the present study has been narrowed to composites manufactured with a 30% rubber content. Experimental results indicate an improvement in heat insulation as aggregate size increases and enable deriving evolution laws for conductivity with respect to water content.

Keywords : Composite, Rubber aggregates, Thermal conductivity, TPS, Water content.

B Laidoudi, is a resarch student at the University of Picardie Jules Verne, Amiens. His research interests thermal transfer in industrial wastes.

Dr L Marmoret, Is a lecturer in Civil Engineering, University of Picardie Jules Verne, Amiens. His major center of interest is heat and mass transfer in building materials.

Professor M Quéneudec, Head of the « Laboratoire des Technologies Innovantes », University of Picardie Jules Verne, Amiens. She is specialised in the design and characterisation of building materials.

INTRODUCTION

Research efforts [1-9] have been undertaken in the area of reusing scrap rubber in the field of civil engineering; these efforts have led to developing a broad range of applications, including soil reinforcement, construction of lightweight embankments and road-building. The substitution of mineral aggregates in concrete by aggregates stemming from the crushing of worn tires has already been studied by several authors [1-5]. The work completed on associating rubber aggregates with a cementing matrix has revealed that the addition of rubber aggregate considerably improves both concrete ductility and durability throughout consecutive freezing/thawing cycles [6,7]. A recent study showed that substituting mineral aggregates by rubber aggregates enhances the thermal behavior of this type of material [8]. Similarly, a systematic study focusing on the rubber volume content in a cement paste has allowed quantifying the resultant effect on the thermal behavior of cement-rubber composites [9].

In the field of construction, materials placed into service can be exposed to moisture to varying degrees; these materials are generally porous and capable of affixing such moisture, which not only can cause disorder but can also considerably modify the material's thermal performance. The purpose of the present work is to study the influence of saturation rate on the thermal conductivity of cement-rubber composites manufactured using different-sized aggregates.

MATERIALS AND EXPERIMENTAL TECHNIQUES

Materials

The material studied herein is a composite with two solid phases (cement and rubber) as well as a gaseous phase (air). The rubber aggregates introduced have been supplied from crushed and filtered vehicle scrap, with particle sizes lying in the ranges of 1-4, 4-8 and 8-12 mm. The aggregates used all have smooth surfaces and a unit weight of approximately 1286 kg/m^3 [7]. The cement employed is a CPJ CEM II 32.5 [NF P15-301].

Sample Preparation

The production of prismatic specimens with dimensions 10*10*10 cm^3 was carried out in accordance with the standard [IN 196-1]. The total water quantity is a function of aggregate type and diameter, as well as of rubber volume percentage. These factors were addressed in a study conducted by A. Benazzouk [6,7] and have been adjusted in order to achieve constant workability regardless of the composition.

The composites were stored in a wet room at $20 \pm 1°C$ and 98% relative humidity for 28 days. Upon completion of this storage period, the samples were placed in a drying oven at 60°C until reaching constant mass. They were then individually packed in plastic film in order to maintain a dry-state environment.

To study the evolution in thermal characteristics with respect to saturation rate, the protocol previously adapted from autoclaved concretes by J.P. Laurent [10] and A. Bouguerra [11] to the study of wood concretes, was selected herein.

The samples were saturated by immersion under ordinary atmosphere until reaching total saturation. Although saturation can never be 100% [11], it is considered that total saturation has been reached once the mass no longer varies. Samples were then weighed and packed in a heat-retractable plastic film, thereby making it possible to preserve the sample's water content throughout the thermal conductivity measurement campaign.

Once the initial measurement has been completed, water is gradually removed from the samples by means of a microwave drying oven. According to the numerous studies conducted on the drying of materials by microwave [11], this technique serves to obtain as homogeneous a distribution as possible within the material.

It is to be recognized that at testing temperature ($\approx 20°C$), heat transfer through the solid, liquid and gaseous phases is primarily performed by pure conduction inasmuch as evaporation-condensation mechanisms generally appear at temperatures of higher than $20°C$. It should also be noted that for 6 very short minutes of measurement time, the rise in temperature does not exceed the degree and limits the appearance of these phenomena.

Experimental Set-up and Procedure

The thermal conductivity of a material is not influenced solely by the physical characteristics of the components and their relative contents, but also by the configuration of the porous network.

The thermal conductivity measurements of samples have been performed using the Transient Plane Source (TPS) method developed by Gustafsson [12], which has also been the topic of considerable research [11,12,13]. The advantage of such techniques lies in limiting the total transient recording time. The TPS sensor consists of a hot disc, made of a bifilar spiral 30 mm in diameter and 0.01 mm thick, enclosed between two insulating layers composed of "Kapton" 40 mm in diameter and 0.025 mm thick.

A disc-shaped TPS sensor was placed in between two samples. Once isothermal conditions in the samples had been attained, a constant current pulse was passed through the heating element and the change in temperature, which leads to a variation in element resistance, was recorded. This element resistance depends on the properties of the material being tested.

The theoretical bases of the TPS technique were established by Gustafsson [12] and other authors [14,15]; they consist of solving the expression of heat conduction, which describes the conductive transfer taking place within an infinite, homogeneous and isotropic solid.

The diagrammatic sketch of the experimental set-up for the TPS method is shown in Figure 3 and includes: the TPS element, a voltage-stabilized power supply, a "Whestone" bridge, a data acquisition system (of the Fluke Hydra type), and a computer for data processing and analysis.

In order both to obtain a distributed heat flow over an area more representative of the sample and to protect the TPS element from damage, two 50 mm x 50 mm x 1 mm copper plates were introduced between the TPS element and the samples. Sample thickness was selected to satisfy the depth of the heat-produced "probing depth" [12].

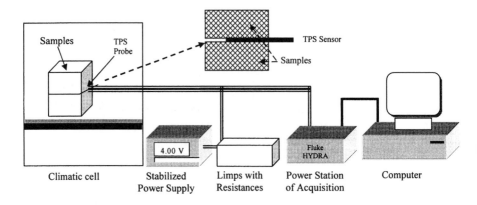

Figure 1. Shematic of the experimental TPS set-up

In the aim of reducing the effect of resistance on the contact, sample surfaces were polished beforehand. A chucking device was used to ensure good contact between the TPS element and the samples. Each sample was then placed into the drying oven in order to control the experimental temperature. To measure the pretest temperature, two thermocouples were welded onto the copper plates.

Validation of the method as a measurement technique for thermal conductivity was carried out on materials such as polystyrene, wood and glass wool. Results obtained are comparable with those found in the literature. The various research investigations completed using this technique allow estimating that such a technique yields an approximation of about ±5% and moreover the standard deviation observed tends to be rather small [11].

For each water content level, three measurements were carried out in order to obtain an average value.

RESULTS AND DISCUSSION

Before analyzing the influence of moisture on thermal conductivity, it is necessary to recall the results obtained at the dry state and under ambient temperature (20°C). The full set of results recorded for compact aggregates have been presented once again in Figure 2; they generally show a reduction in thermal conductivity with both an increase in aggregate size and an increase in rubber volume content. For aggregates 1-4 mm in size for example, thermal conductivity varies from 1.1 W/(m.K) to 0.76 W/(m.K) as the percentage of rubber volume varies between 0% and 50%, hence a reduction of approximately 40%. For a 30% content, thermal conductivity is equal to 0.78 W/(m.K) with aggregate sizes of 1-4 mm and 0.6 W/(m.K) for 8-12 mm aggregates.

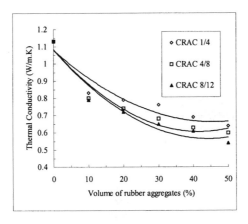

Figure 2. Evolution of the thermal conductivity according to the volume content of rubber

This reduction in observed thermal conductivity with respect to the rubber particle size distribution is due to the fact that aggregate size exerts a direct impact on the progression of the thermal signal. The porosity induced by the quantity of water is significant at least to the mixing, in order to ensure constant workability, and evolves in the opposite direction since the quantity of additional water varies indirectly with aggregate size. This variation cannot therefore explain the variation in thermal conductivity.

It should also be pointed out that difference in particle size distribution increase as the proportion of aggregate increases. This finding can be explained by the significant level of macroporosity present in the material. The entrained air bubbles constitute additional thermal barriers, which also increase as aggregate size increases [7].

Thermal conductivity results vs. moisture for composites manufactured with a 30% rubber content have been shown in Figure 3. It can be considered that thermal conductivity increases almost linearly with the saturation rate up to a level of 80%.

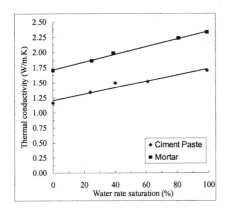 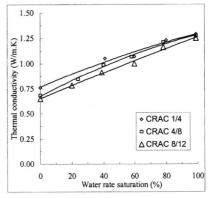

Figure 3. Evolution of the thermal conductivity according to the water rate saturation

It should also be noted that the evolution in conductivities of various samples is similar, especially at low or average saturation rates. In contrast, for higher saturation rates, differences according to aggregate size become less apparent. This feature may be explained by the evolution in transfer phenomena with increasing water content [16]:

❖ In the dry state and at low water contents, heat transfer primarily relies upon the level of contact between the aggregates and the matrix forming the material, which generates small increases in thermal conductivity;

❖ An increase in water content entails the formation of cold bridges or heat conduction bridges within the material, which generates an increase in the material's thermal conductivity;

❖ When water content reaches a maximum value corresponding to either the state of saturation or the state of continuity, the thermal conductivity tends to be stabilized. This phenomenon has been observed beginning at saturation rates of 80%.

As an example, thermal conductivity at saturation is on the order of 1.32 W/(m.K) for aggregates 1-4 mm size, 1.28 and 1.26 W/(m.K) for aggregates with diameters of 4-8 and 8-12 mm, respectively, whereas for saturation rates in the vicinity of 20%, the thermal conductivity varies from 0.94 to 0.78 W/(m.K) for 1-4 mm and 8-12 mm aggregates, respectively.

A comparison of thermal conductivity values for the cement-rubber composites, as well as those for the normal mortar and cement paste, shows that the relationship between the two extreme values (saturation /dry) is more distinct in the latter case. This finding can be explained by the type of porosity existing at the level of each material. In the cement-rubber composites, the porosity inaccessible to water is in fact highly significant, which induces weak moisture fixation. Table 1 lists the equations and coefficients of correlation between thermal conductivity and saturation rate for composites with saturation rates of less than 80%. The type of relationship existing between these two properties proves to be linear with correlation coefficients varying from 0.93 to 0.98. The relationships derived are of the following type:

Table 1: Summary table of correlations between conductivity and water content

Rubber aggregates type	Rubber particles size (mm)	Relationship between thermal conductivity and water rate saturation	Correlation coefficients
Mortar		$\lambda = 0.0064 * S_r + 1.71$	0.99
Ciment Paste		$\lambda = 0.0053 * S_r + 1.2$	0.95
CRAC	1/4	$\lambda = 0.0056 * S_r + 0.77$	0.96
	4/8	$\lambda = 0.0059 * S_r + 0.70$	0.97
	8/12	$\lambda = 0.0062 * S_r + 0.65$	0.93

$$\lambda = a * S_r + \lambda_0$$

(1)

With : λ thermal conductivity,

λ_0 thermal conductivity in a dry state, S_r rate of saturation.

This result is in conformity with those obtained by other authors working on composite materials of the same type as cement-rubber composites [10,11].

CONCLUSIONS

Studying the influence of moisture on the thermal conductivity of cement-rubber composites has made it possible to highlight the linearity of the thermal conductivity vs. saturation rate variation law (for S_r < 80%), as well as the influence of the size of rubber inclusions, which appears all the more distinct at lower saturation rates. This study has also enabled highlighting the benefit of cement-rubber composites through the evolution in thermal conductivity with respect to saturation rate. In the case of a normal mortar, a more significant difference ($\lambda_{sat}-\lambda_{dry}$) m ay b e o bserved t han i n t he c ase of c ement-rubber composites: t his difference amounts to 0.65 for a normal mortar and 0.53 for aggregates 1-4 mm in size.

The addition of rubber aggregate is thus of dual interest: it improves the thermal behavior of a cementing material while reducing sensitivity to moisture, thereby preserving strong thermal performance within a wet medium.

REFERENCES

1. Y. Fang, M. Zhan, Y. Wang, The Status of recyling of waste rubber, Materials and Design, Vol 22, 2001, pp.123-127.

2. R. Siddique, T. R. Naik, Properties of concrete containing scrap-tires rubber – an overview, Waste Management, (Article in press).

3. N. N. Eldin , A. B. Senouci, Rubber tires particals as concrete aggregate, Journal of materials in civil engineering, Vol. 5, N°4, 1993, November, pp.478-496.

4. U. B. Topçu, The properties of rubberized concrete, Cement and concrete Resarch, Vol. 25, N°2, pp.304-310.

5. A. S. El-Dieb, M. M. Abdel-wahab, M. E. Abdel-Hameed. Concrete using rubber tyre particales as aggregate. Recycling and Reuse of Used Tyres, Edited by R. K. Dhir, M. C. Limbachyia, K. A. Paine, Published by Thomas Telford, March 2001, pp.252-260.

6. A. Benazzouk, G. Doyen, M. Queneudec, Physico-mechanical properties of cement-rubber composites, Recycling and Reuse of Used Tyres, Edited by R.K. Dhir, M.C. Limbachiya, K.A. Paine, Published by Thomas Telford, March 2001, pp. 237-249.

7. A. Benazzouk, Contribution à la valorisation des déchets de caoutchouc : Composites cimentaires à base de caoutchouc compact et cellulaire, Thèse de doctorat, Université de Picardie Jules Verne, 150p, 2002.

8.   K. A. Paine, R. C. Moroney, R. K. Dhir, Performance of concrete comprising shredded rubber tyres. Recycling and Reuse of Waste Materials, Edited by R.K. Dhir, M.D. Newlands, J. E. Halliday, Published by Thomas Telford, September 2003, pp. 719-729.

9.   B. Laidoudi, A. Benazzouk, L. Marmoret, T. Langlet, M. Queneudec, Recycling of automotive industry rubber waste : Thermal performance of cement-rubber composites, Recycling and Reuse of Waste Materials, Edited by R.K. Dhir, M.D. Newlands ,J. E. Halliday, Published by Thomas Telford, September 2003, pp. 355-364.

10.   J. P. Laurent, C. Guerre-Chaley, Influence de la teneur en eau et de la température sur la conductivité thermique du béton cellulaire autoclavé. Materials and Structures, Vol. 28, pp. 464-472.

11.   A. Bouguerra, Contribution à l'étude d'un procédé de valorisation de déchets argileux: Comportement hygrothermique des matériaux élaborés, Thèse de doctorat, INSA de Lyon, 212p, 1997.

12.   S. E. Gustafsson, Transient plane source techniques for thermal diffusivity measurements of solid materials, Review Scientific Instruments, Vol.62, N° 3, 1991, pp. 777-804.

13.   N. S. Saxena, P. Pradeep, G. Mathew, S. Thomas, M. Gustafsson, S.E. Gustafsson, Thermal conductivity of styrene butadiene rubber compounds with naturel rubber prophylactics waste as filler, European Polymer Journal 35, 1999, pp. 1687-1693.

14.   S. Saxena, P. Pradeep, G. Mathew, S. Thomas, M. Gustafsson, S.E. Gustafsson, Thermal conductivity of styrene butadiene rubber compounds with naturel rubber prophylactics waste as filler, European Polymer Journal 35, 1999, pp. 1687-1693.

15.   G. kalaprasad, P. Pradeep, G. Mathew, C. Pavithran, S. Thomas, Thermal conductivity and thermal diffusivity analyses of low-density polyethylene composites reinforced with sisal, glass and intimately mixed siasl/glass fibres, Composites Sciences and Technology 60, 2000, pp. 12967-2977.

16.   H. Ezbakche, S. Boussaid, A. El bakkouri, T. Ajoul, Méthode générale d'identification thermophysiques du matériau terre utilisé dans la construction dans le nord du Maroc, 9èmes JITH, Liège, Belgique 15-18 septembre 1999, pp. 91-98.

MORTAR ADDED BY TYRE RUBBER RESIDUES: CHARACTERISATION IN FRESH AND HARDENED STATE

J L Akasaki

A C. Marques

M L Marques

A P M Trigo

Universidade Estadual Paulista

Brasil

ABSTRACT. Due to the progressive increase of vehicles, the number of used tires is globally one of the serious environmental problems faced now. Therefore, several researches have being developed for its reuse. The use of tires' rubber in the concrete is a possible form of its application, aiming at the recycling of this material and the improvement of certain properties, as tenacity, impact resistance, thermal and acoustic isolation. This article presents conclusions that several researchers obtained using the rubberized concrete. Thus there were researched several works enclosing the period of 1993 to 2003, presenting then the results of some characteristics of this concrete such as: physical properties in fresh and hardened state, mechanical properties and properties that remit the durability. The bibliographical revision has as objective to subsidize future researches that can contribute to improve the use of this concrete in civil construction.

Keywords: Tire rubber concrete, Civil construction, Mechanical properties.

Dr. J L Akasaki is a Professor of Universidade Estadual Paulista (Unesp). His research interests include the use of alternatives materials in civil construction.

Miss A C. Marques is mastering in Civil Engineering. Her research interests include the use of recycled materials in concrete and mortar.

M L Marques is graduating in Civil Engineering. Her research interests the use of tire rubber in mortar.

A P M Trigo is graduating in Civil Engineering. Her research interests the use of tire rubber in mortar.

INTRODUCTION

The vulcanization process of natural rubber makes it more durable and resistant. The problem in this material is related to its difficult degradation. In landfills, the rubber, in form of tire, tends to hold back water, bringing risks to health, because it creates the appropriate environment to the growing of insects and in the granule form it is harmful to the environment. The Relastomer company affirms that about 300 thousand tons of tires are available in Brazil, but only 10% of these materials are recycled. In Rio de Janeiro, the rubber tires and devices in general correspond 0.5% of the urban garbage.

The retreading, that in Brazil reaches 70% of the fleet of transport of load and passengers, is another important way to reduce this type of residue [1]. With the ambient questions comes the increasing technological advance that generates a production of residues from industrial processes that aggravate the damages to the environment causing a great concern with recycling methods or reuse of these materials.

The utilization of this material in concrete is an alternative suggested for many authors. The use of tire rubber is advised when the resistance mechanics is not the main characteristic but the resistance to the impact, low unit weight and higher toughness. In this work are presented bibliographies of authors who had used the tire rubber in concrete, mortar or cement paste. Also it is shown as the gradation of the residue, shape, substitution percentage or treatment of its surface influences in the behavior of the mixture. Thus, the work is divided in the following topics: properties in the fresh state and properties in the hardened state.

Inside the topic of properties in the fresh state there are references about the workability and unitary weight. In the properties in the hardened state there are related the tests of compressive strength, tensile strength, flexural strength, toughness, modulus of elasticity, impact resistance, fire resistance, freeze-thaw-resisting process and others.

PROPERTIES IN THE FRESH STATE

Workability

In a general way, workability is an attribute desired in most of the projects, which makes the evaluation of this property very interesting. Studies show that the workability of concrete with rubber is lower than the ordinary one (without rubber) and that the residue shape can influence the result. Mortars containing granular rubber have better workability than mortars with shredded rubber when they are measured with a VeBe test [2]. It was also observed in the same paper that concrete with tire rubber has a better workability than concrete without the residue.

In slump test there is a decrease in the workability when the amount of rubber is raised, 40% of rubber replacing aggregate cause a slump of approximately zero. It was noticed that mixtures with crumb rubber presented better workability than tire chips or a mixture of both [3].

Unit Weight

The use of tire rubber in concrete, mortar or cement paste, cause a decrease in unit weight of the composite [5-8]. It is because of the replacement of a material with higher unit weight for another [5]. This reduction depends on the amount of rubber replaced. A greater replacement of rubber makes the composite lighter. The size of the aggregate influence in the unit weight, smaller aggregate presented a decrease in the results [7].

PROPERTIES IN THE HARDENED STATE

Compressive Strenght

In a general way, the addition of rubber in cement paste, mortar or concrete, cause a considerable decrease in compressive strength [7-16]. The replacement of sand in mortar by 30% of rubber decreases in 80% the compressive strength [9]. The size and shape of the aggregate have a slightly influence in the resistance because finner aggregate cause less damage to the resistance [7].

In concrete, depending on the replacement of the aggregate by rubber, the decrease in resistance can be up to 75%. The compressive strength of the cement paste, mortar and concrete also vary with the unit weight of the composite. There are two different behavior for this relationship, one for cement paste an mortar and other for concrete. For a similar unit weight, the decrease in the compressive strength of concrete is higher than in mortar and cement paste [5]. Although there is a great decrease in compressive strength, the failure of concrete with tire rubber occurs in a ductile way supporting higher deformations than the ordinary concrete [3,11 - 14].

In order to estimate the reduction in compressive strength, some authors had proposed an equation.
$$SRF = a + b(1 - R)^m \qquad \text{(equation 1)}$$

Where: SRF = Strength Reduction Factor; R = rubber content (in percentage); a, b e m = function parameters [3].

Splitting Tensile Test

As in the compressive strength test, there is a reduction in the splitting tensile strength, but this decrease isn't so accentuated as in the first test (compressive strength) [9, 10, 14, 15]. The replacement of 30% of the fine aggregate by rubber causes a decreasing of 70% in the tensile strength [9]. The shape of the rubber aggregate also influences the tests. In a general way the tire rubber used as fibers showed better performance than chips [14].

Flexural Strength

The flexural strength tests, as the tensile tests showed a decrease in resistance when the rubber was added [2, 3, 7, 15]. Comparing this resistance loss it can be noted that it isn't so great as in the compressive strength test [3]. The size of the rubber aggregate influences in the flexural strength, bigger particles caused a greater loss of resistance [7]. Shredded rubber present smaller loss in resistance than the granular one, it shows that the shape also influences in flexural strength [2]. The addition of rubber also raises the toughness of the composite. Specimens with rubber have a ductile behavior comparing with the ordinary mixtures. It happens because of the higher capacity to absorb energy of the composite with rubber [3, 12, 16]. When the cracks reach the rubber particles and because of its elastics properties and low modulus of elasticity, the rubber particles prolonged and underwent part of the load [12].

Modulus of Elasticity

Although the cement paste hadn't been noticed any change in the modulus of elasticity with the addition of rubber [8], its addition in mortar and concrete caused a decrease in it [9, 10, 14, 15]. Studies about dynamic modulus shoewed similar behavior [6].

In order to estimate the modulus of elasticity, some authors proposed an equation:

$$E_c^{'} = k^{'} E_m \frac{1 + 2V_{ar}\left(\dfrac{\alpha - 1}{\alpha + 2}\right)}{1 - V_{ar}\left(\dfrac{\alpha - 1}{\alpha + 2}\right)} \qquad \alpha = \frac{E_{ar}}{E_m} \qquad \text{(equation 2)}$$

where : E_c is the modulus of elasticity of the composite; E_m is the modulus of elasticity of the matrix; E_{ar} is the modulus of elasticity of the mortar; V_{ar} is the volume proportion of the mortar; k is a coefficient. Experimental results confirm the validity of the equation [17].

Shrinkage

According to the literature, the use of rubber aggregates has improved the performance of materials subjected to shrinkage [2, 9, 18, 19]. The use of rubber also delays the progress of shrinkage, its length and width [2, 9].

Impact Resistance and Abrasion

According with the literature, the use of rubber in concrete can improve the impact resistance comparing the tests with the ordinary concrete, however, the specimens with rubber presented wide cracks [2, 4]. The size and shape of the aggregates also influence in the impact resistance, bigger aggregates showed better response than smaller ones [18].

Abrasion tests, carried out in cement paste and mortar also showed that composites with rubber had better performance than the ordinary [10, 15].

Water Absorption

Sometimes the main attribute in concrete isn't its compressive strength but the water absorption. Thus, it was studied the behavior of this property in cement paste, mortar and concrete. It was observed in cement paste, mortar and concrete, that the water absorption by capillarity decrease with the use of tire rubber as aggregate [8, 15, 20]. It can be justified because of the fact that the tire rubber don't absorb water. [8]. Hydraulic diffusivity and air permeability also were measured and the specimens added by rubber as in the water absorption had lower values than the ordinary composites [20].

Fire Resistance

An interesting attribute to be studied is the fire resistance, because the addition of an organic composite may change the behavior of this property comparing with the ordinary concrete. Tests in high strength concrete indicate that the raise in the content of rubber decrease the depth of damage of the specimens [11].

The Young modulus also varies with the temperature. In higher temperatures (60°C) the dispersion in the results is lesser than in lower temperatures. With 5% of rubber inserted, the Young modulus is higher than the composite with 3,5% of rubber [13]. Another kind of test was the use of blow torches for a period of three minutes to evaluate the reaction of specimens with tire rubber. Although the rubber on the faces was burned, any resulting fire extinguishes itself within 4s to 5s [5]. Showing that the cement and the aggregate lessen the rubber flammability.

Microscopy

Trying to show the feasibility of the use of tire rubber in mortar and concrete, it was analyzed the reaction of residues subjected to an alkaline environment up to 4 months. In this period it was observed that rubber didn't undergo any chemical degradation [2]. The decrease in mechanical strength is many times justified because of the weak adhesion between the cement paste and rubber aggregate. Some authors affirm that the adhesion can be improved by the treatment of the rubber's surface [15]. Some authors, however, affirm that there is a perfect adherence between the cement matrix and rubber. It can be attributed to a high concentration of calcium oxide crystals on the surface of the rubber and the presence of silicon and aluminium oxides. [13].

Other Properties

Besides the previous properties mentioned, there were carried out different ones. One of them is the setting time. It was observed that because of the presence of zinc in the rubber aggregate, it was caused an increasing in the initial and final setting time [21]. The freezing-thaw resistance it was also studied for some researches. And they had the same conclusion, the addition of tire rubber increase the resistance to the freezing-thaw process [18, 21].

CONCLUSIONS

According to the literature it can be conclude the following about the addition of tire rubber in concrete, mortar and cement paste:

- The workability can be influenced by the measured (depend on the test). Using the Ve-Be tests it is concluded that the workability of ordinary concrete is worse than the rubberized concrete. Measuring by the slump test the conclusion is the opposite. The size an shape of the aggregates also influence in the workability.

- The more the addition of tire rubber in concrete, mortar and cement paste, the more the decrease in unit weight.

- Decrease in compressive, tensile and flexural strength when added tire rubber in the composites. Higher contents of rubber cause higher losses in the composites. Fiber rubber has a better performance than chips.

- The length and progress of fissuration are delayed when it is used the tire rubber aggregate.

- Tests in High strength concrete indicate that raising the content of rubber it happens a decrease in the depth of fire damage of the specimens. It was also observed the decrease in the flammability of the rubber when it is in the composite.

- Some properties were improved like water absorption, impact resistance and abrasion resistance by adding rubber.

- Rubber aggregates don't undergo chemical degradation when subjected to alkaline environments.

It is recommended the use of concrete with tire rubber in places where the mechanical resistance isn't the main attribute of the material. It is also suggested a better evaluation of the microstructure of the composite with rubber because of opposite conclusions found in the literature.

REFERENCES

1. LIMA, I. S.and ROCHA, F. S. Um Estudo da Argamassa de Cimento com Adição de Fibras de Borracha Vulcanizada Para a Construção Civil. Proceedings of CONGRESSO BRASILEIRO DO CONCRETO, 2000. CD-ROM.

2. RAGHAVAN, D., HUYNH, H. and FERRARIS, C. F. Workability, mechanical properties, and chemical stability of a recycled tire rubber-filled cementitious composite, Journal of Materials science, 33, 1998, pp.1745-1752.

3. KHATIB, Z. K. and BAYOMY, F. M. Rubberized Portland Cement Concrete. Journal of Materials in Civil Engineering, 1999, pp.206-213

4. SIDDIQUE, R. and NAIK, T. R. Properties of concrete containing scrap-tire Rubber – an overview, Waste Management , 2004.

5. FATTUHI, N. L. and CLARK, L. A Cement-based materials containing shredded scrap truck tire rubber. Construction and Building Materials, 10, No.4, 1996, pp.229-236.

6. PINTO, C. A., JOSÉ, C. L. V., VIANA, M; M. G. R., KOZIEVITCH, V. F. J., HAMASSAKI, L. T., WIEBECK, H., BÜCHLER, P. M. and VALENZUELA DIAZ, F. R. Study of the mechanical performance of composites of rubber powder and cement. Materials Science Forum, 416-418, 2003, pp.720-724.

7. BENAZZOUK, A., MEZREB, K. DOYEN, G., GOULLIEUX, A., QUÉNEUDEc, M. Effect of rubber aggregates on the physico-mechanical behaviour of cement–rubber composites-influence of the alveolar texture of rubber aggregates. Cement and Concrete Composites, 25, 2003, pp. 711-720.

8. SEGRE, N., JOEKES, I. Use of tire rubber particles as addition to cement paste. Cement and Concrete Research, 30, 2000, pp.1421-1425.

9. BONNET, S. Effet de l'incorporation des granulats caoutchouc sur la résistance à la fissuration des morties. XXI^{EMES} Rencontres Universitaires de Genie Civil, 2003,pp.59-70.

10. MENEGUINI, E. A. C. Comportamento De Argamassas Com O Emprego De Pó De Borracha. Master of Science's thesis, Universidade Estadual de Campinas, 2003, 85p.

11. HERNÁNDEZ-OLIVARES, F. and BARLUENGA, G. Fire performance of recycled rubber-filled high strength concrete. Cement and Concrete Research, 34, 2004, pp.109-117.

12. TOUTANJI, H. A. The Use of Rubber Tire Particles in Concrete to Replace Mineral Aggregates. Cement and Concrete Composites, 18, 1996, pp.135-139.

13. HERNÁNDEZ-OLIVARES, F., BARLUENGA, G., BOLLATI, M. and WITOSZEK, B. Static and dynamic behavior of recycled tire rubber-filled concrete. Cement and Concrete Research, 32, 2002, pp.1587–1596.

14. LIA, G., GARRICKA, G., EGGERSB, J., ABADIEB, C., STUBBLEFIELDC, M. A. and PANGA, S. Waste tire fiber modified concrete. Composites: Part B, 35, 2004, pp.305–312.

15. BAUER, R. J. F., TOKUDOME, S. and GADRET, A. D. Estudo de Concreto com Pneu Moído. Proceedings of 43° Congresso Brasileiro do Concreto, 2001.

16. TAHA, M. M. R., EL-DIEB, A. S. and ABDEL-WAHAB, M. M. Fracture Toughness of Concrete Incorporating Rubber Tire Particles. Proceedings of ICPCM – A New Era of Building, Cairo, February 2003.

17. TOPÇU, I. B. and AVCULAR, N. Analysis of Rubberized Concrete as a Composite Material. Cement and Concrete Research, 27, No. 8, 1997, pp.1135-1139.

18. DHIR, R., PAINE, K. and MORONEY, R. Recycling of used tires in concrete. Concrete, London, 37, No.9, 2003, pp.47-48.

19. WANG, Y., WU, H. C. and LI, V. C. Concrete Reinforcement with Recycled Fibers. Journal of Materials in Civil Engineering, 12, No. 4, 2000, pp.314-319.

20. BENAZZOUK, A., DOUZANE, O. and QUÉNEUDEC, M. Transport of fluids in cement–rubber composites. Cement & Concrete Composites, 26, 2004, pp 21–29.

21. AL-AKHRAS, N. M. and SMADI, M. M. Properties of tire rubber ash mortar. Cement & Concrete Composites, 2004.

TESTING OF WHOLE AND SHREDDED SCRAP TYRES FOR USE AS LANDFILL ENGINEERING DRAINAGE MATERIAL

A P Hudson

R P Beaven

W Powrie

University of Southampton

United Kingdom

ABSTRACT. Leachate drainage layers are necessary in most waste landfill sites to minimise the accumulation of leachate within the site and thereby reduce the risk of contamination of surrounding ground and groundwater. Large quantities of aggregates are usually used in the construction of drainage layers but a cheaper and environmentally preferable option may be the use of scrap vehicle tyres. Normally layers of whole or shredded tyres exhibit excellent drainage properties but if tyres are used as the main drainage layer at the base of a landfill they may compress under the overburden stress from the weight of the waste above and cease to act as an effective drainage layer. In response to the limited published information on the bulk compressibility and hydraulic conductivity of used tyres, the University of Southampton conducted a series of tests on shredded vehicle tyres and compared the data with results from previous work on whole tyres. Samples were subjected to a range of stresses typical of those acting at the base of a waste landfill. Compressibility and changes in hydrogeological properties were measured. The results are presented in this paper and the use of tyres in landfill drainage systems is discussed.

Keywords: Used tyres, Landfill drainage, Overburden stress, Hydraulic conductivity, Compressibility

Mr A P Hudson is a Research Assistant at the University of Southampton. He is responsible for the running of the large scale Pitsea compression cell, principally concerned with evaluation of the hydrogeological properties of landfill waste

Dr R P Beaven worked as a hydrogeologist in the waste management industry for 12 years before joining the University of Southampton as a Senior Research Fellow. He also runs an independent Hydrogeological Consultancy. His primary research areas are landfill processes and modelling, including work on liquid and gas flows, tracers, waste degradation and emission potentials.

Professor W Powrie is Professor of Geotechnical Engineering and Head of the School of Civil Engineering and the Environment at the University of Southampton. His areas of research include groundwater flow and control, mechanics of particulate materials and hydrogeomechanical properties of wastes.

INTRODUCTION

In the UK over 400,000 tonnes of used vehicle tyres are produced each year [1]. The problem of disposing of used tyres has been made worse by the EU Landfill Directive which prohibited the disposal of whole used vehicle tyres to new landfills from 16 July 2003. The disposal of shredded tyres to landfill will be banned on 16 July 2006. There is, therefore, a need to establish alternative methods of re-use, materials/energy recovery and disposal of tyres.

The Landfill Directive permits used tyres to be utilised as engineering material in landfills and many operators incorporate them into the construction of leachate drainage or recirculation trenches. It is estimated that 16, 000 tonnes per annum of scrap tyres are used for this purpose in the UK. However, most landfill drainage systems are constructed using aggregates. Suitable aggregate material is not always readily available and it can be argued that this is not an appropriate use of a finite resource if recycled alternatives are available.

In most countries the requirement is for landfill drainage layers to have a minimum hydraulic conductivity of 1×10^{-3} to 1×10^{-4} m/s [2]. Uncompacted drainage layers constructed from whole or shredded tyres exhibit excellent drainage properties and will easily comply with this requirement. However drainage layers at the base of landfills will be subjected to high stresses exerted from the waste above. If the density of saturated waste is assumed to be about 1 tonne/m^3 [3], the stress will be approximately 10 kPa per metre landfill depth. For landfills of depths of several tens of metres, the drainage layer will be subjected to stresses of several hundred kPa. There is little published research indicating i) the extent to which tyre drainage layers will compress under such stresses, ii) the reduction in hydraulic conductivity due to compression and iii) the effect of tyre shred size on the compressibility and hydraulic conductivity of tyre layers.

The research described in this paper was undertaken by the University of Southampton in a large scale compression cell in order to investigate the above.

DESCRIPTION OF SAMPLES TESTED

Three samples were tested:

- WT 1: Whole used car / light van tyres. Sample weight approximately 2.5 tonnes
- ST1: Coarse shredded car / light van tyres passed through a 200 mm square screen. Sample weight 2.555 tonnes. The particle size classification of a 39.5 kg sub-sample is shown in Table 1.
- ST2: Fine shredded car / light van tyres (designated ST2) passed through a 50 mm square screen. Sample weight 2.885 tonnes. The particle size classification of a 7.8 kg sub-sample is shown in Table 2.

Samples ST1 and ST2 were supplied by Credential Environmental Ltd. The specification for the shredding process required that the tyres were free of contaminants such as grease, oil and hydrocarbons. Steel wire was not removed from the tyres but the shredding process worked to a specification of a maximum wire projection of 15 mm and 30 mm for 75% and 100% of the sample respectively.

Table 1. Size distribution of sample ST1

SHRED SIZE – maximum dimension (mm)	NUMBER OF PIECES	MASS (kg)
< 100	135	1.4
100 – 150	124	9.7
150 – 200	60	9.8
200 – 300	35	13.0
> 300	15	5.6

Table 2. Size distribution of sample ST2

SHRED SIZE – maximum dimension (mm)	NUMBER OF PIECES	MASS (kg)
< 25	135	1.4
25 – 50	124	9.7
50 – 100	60	9.8
100 – 170	35	13.0

EXPERIMENTAL APPARATUS AND PROCEDURES

There a re g uidelines i n s oil m echanics t hat t he m inimum s ample d iameter u sed i n l aboratory equipment to determine the hydraulic conductivity of a soil should be at least 6 times the maximum particle size of the sample [4]. It will be noted from Table 1 that s ome p articles exceeded 300 mm. Consequently, to comply with the above recommendations, a minimum sample size measuring 1.8 m would be required. This far exceeds the size of typical laboratory soil testing equipment. The equipment used for the tests was the University of Southampton compression cell facility based at Pitsea in Essex (Figure 1). This accommodates 2 m diameter

Figure 1. The Pitsea compression cell

samples and has previously been used extensively for the measurement of the hydrogeological properties of mixed domestic wastes under typical landfill stresses [3,5]. The tyre samples were loaded into the cylinder which measures 2 metres diameter × 3 metres high and has a water-tight base. High permeability gravel layers were installed above and below the sample during loading to distribute water evenly across the sample during hydraulic conductivity testing. Samples were then subjected to vertical compressive stresses by means of hydraulic rams acting on a plate on the top of the sample. The applied stress was increased in several stages up to a maximum of 600 kPa, simulating overburden pressures at landfill depths up to approximately 60 m. At each compression stage, the settlement was recorded and the drainable porosity and hydraulic conductivity measured.

RESULTS

Compression

Sample compression in response to applied stress is shown in Figure 2. Both shredded samples exhibited similar compression (the coarse shred ST1 compressed slightly more than the finer shred ST2 sample). The sample comprising whole tyres (WT1) compressed much more, particularly at low applied stress (72% compression at 40 kPa applied stress, compared to about 21% of the shredded samples at the same stress). These differences are considered to reflect different packing geometries of hoop structures (representing whole tyres) and discs or elongated particles (shredded tyres). The initial packing geometry of the whole tyres created large voids within the sample that collapsed rapidly in response to applied loads. A more compact initial packing structure of the tyre shreds meant that there were no large voids that would collapse in the same way.

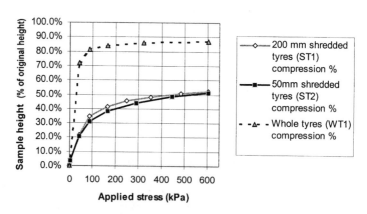

Figure 2. Compression vs. applied stress for shredded and whole tyres

Drainable Porosity

Drainable porosity is defined as the volume of water released from a unit volume of fully saturated material, when the material is allowed to drain freely under the influence of gravity. The drainable porosity of the sample was measured after each compression stage as follows. The sample was first allowed to drain to completely remove any water that could be released under gravity. Measured volumes of water were then admitted into the sample in stages until it was fully saturated. The water level after each stage was obtained from piezometer standpipes. The data was checked by draining the sample in stages and measuring the water level and volume drained for each stage. The drainable porosity was calculated from the gradient of a graph of water level plotted against volume of water added.

The drainable porosity of the tyre samples measured at different applied stress is shown in Figure 3. Also shown are typical drainable porosity values for a household waste. The uncompacted drainable porosity of both shredded tyre samples was about 60 %, reducing to approximately 12% at an applied stress of 600 kPa. The fine shred (ST2) sample maintained a slightly higher drainable porosity than the coarse shred (ST1) sample at applied stresses above 100 kPa. The initial drainable porosity of the whole tyre sample was much higher (81%), but this reduced significantly with increasing applied stress (again assumed to be due to the collapse of large voids). At applied stresses above 40 kPa the whole tyre samples exhibited a *lower* drainable porosity than the shredded samples. It will be noted in Figure 3 that the corresponding drainable porosity for a household waste is significantly lower than all the tyre samples.

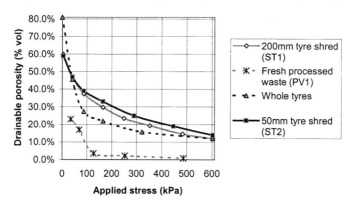

Figure 3. Drainable porosity vs. applied stress for shredded and whole tyres

Hydraulic Conductivity

The hydraulic conductivity of the samples was assessed at each compression stage by inducing a constant upward flow of water. Flow rates were measured using flow meters. Hydraulic gradients were calculated from pressure head measurements from standpipes connected to open-ended piezometers tubes at the top, bottom and intermediate levels of the sample. Hydraulic conductivity w as c alculated u sing D arcy's l aw. N o h ydraulic c onductivity d ata a re s hown for sample ST1 or WT1 for the 40 kPa and 87 kPa compression stages as the hydraulic gradient was too small to be measured (indicative of a hydraulic conductivity $> 1 \times 10^{-1}$ m/s).

From the available data shown in Figure 4 it can be seen that the hydraulic conductivity of all the samples were similar at stresses below 300 kPa. The hydraulic conductivity of the shredded tyre samples reduced by approximately 2 orders of magnitude over the applied stress range tested. The reduction in hydraulic conductivity of the whole tyre sample was slightly less and at an applied stress of 603 kPa exhibited a hydraulic conductivity about 2 ½ times greater than the shredded tyre samples. The typical household waste values in Figure 4 show that at a given applied stress the waste hydraulic conductivity is about four to five orders of magnitude lower than that for the shredded tyre samples.

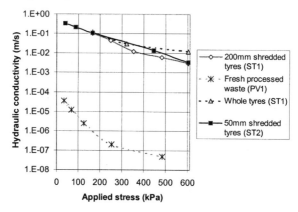

Figure 4. Hydraulic conductivity vs. applied stress for shredded and whole tyres

DISCUSSION

The data presented in this paper demonstrate that tyre layers will compress under stress and this will result in a reduction of the drainable porosity and hydraulic conductivity of the tyres. The construction of any leachate drainage layer using whole or shredded tyres within a landfill would need to take into account the compressive behaviour of the material under load. For example, Figures 2 shows that for the shredded tyre samples, there was a 50% reduction in initial thickness under an applied stress of approximately 450 kPa. This equates to a landfill depth of 45 metres (assuming a bulk waste density of 1 tonne/m^3), and implies that to achieve a final drainage layer depth of 300 mm, a minimum 600 mm thickness of tyre shreds would need to placed in a drainage layer at the base of a site of this depth. Figure 2 also indicates that the compressive behaviour of tyres is probably related to the degree of processing or shred size, and this factor would need to be taken into account in any drainage design.

Countries that have specified a minimum hydraulic conductivity for landfill drainage layers generally give values of between 1 x 10^{-3} and 1 x 10^{-4} m/s. Austria has more stringent requirements of 1 x 10^{-2} m/s for certain sites, whilst some countries accept a minimum of 1 x 10^{-5} m/s in certain situations [2]. Figure 4 indicates that shredded tyres would easily comply with requirements as low as 1 x 10^{-3} m/s at stresses up to 600 kPa, but would only meet the most stringent requirements at stresses below 400 kPa.

There are a number of other factors that may affect the hydraulic conductivity of tyre shreds used in landfill situations and these are discussed below.
Differences in vertical hydraulic conductivity (K_v) and horizontal hydraulic conductivity (K_h) values: In the above tests hydraulic conductivity for the samples was determined using a vertical flow of water (*i.e.* flow was in the same plane as applied stress). In field conditions, fluid flow through drainage layers is predominantly horizontal (perpendicular to the stress plane). Higher

horizontal (K_h) than vertical (K_v) hydraulic conductivities have been measured in landfill wastes [6,7] and soils [8] consisting of elongated or plate-like particles. As tyre shreds tend to be elongated, it is also probable that the structure of a tyre layer will be anisotropic and exhibit a higher horizontal than vertical hydraulic conductivity. This may be particularly pronounced when the tyres are compressed.

Physical clogging: Ingression of particulates into void spaces in the tyre matrix is likely to reduce porosity and hydraulic conductivity. Hydraulic conductivity tests on tyre shreds and granular soil (e.g., sand, gravel) mixtures have shown that the hydraulic conductivity decreases significantly as the soil content in the mix increases. The hydraulic conductivity of mixtures with soil contents of 30% to 50% by weight approach those of the soil itself [9]. Consequently, the use of tyres in leachate drainage systems would need to be combined with measures to restrict the ingress of particulate matter if this was considered likely to be a problem.

Biological clogging: Anaerobic conditions in landfill drainage media lead to the accumulation of biofilms and bacterial colonies. The clogging rate has been shown to be governed by the leachate strength and the number of leachate bed volumes that have passed through the granular material, and thus not strictly a time dependent feature [2]. Biological clogging may reduce porosity and hydraulic conductivity. For example up to a 12% reduction of drainable porosity has been recorded in aggregates due to clogging [10,11]. For aggregate material a D_{10} size of at least 10mm has been recommended to guard against biological clogging [11]. As tyre shreds maintain a high drainable porosity and void ratio at even quite high effective stresses, it is possible that the associated large pore sizes would mitigate against the adverse effects of any biological clogging.

Gas accumulation in void spaces: Gas accumulation in (free venting) household waste causes significant reductions in drainable porosity and hydraulic conductivity [5]. Reductions in the drainable porosity of drainage aggregate due to the formation of gas bubbles has also been recorded in aggregates [10]. It is probable that the drainable porosity and hydraulic conductivity data shown in the above tests (which were conducted in nominally gas purged conditions) will be reduced by accumulated gas in landfill drainage layers especially if confined by overlying relatively impermeable waste. However, considering the high drainable porosity and relatively large pore structure of tyre shreds it is thought that the effect of gas accumulation is unlikely to be too significant. Furthermore, any effect is likely to be of a similar scale to that which would occur in an aggregate based drainage layer.

CONCLUSIONS

The data presented in this paper demonstrate that the hydrogeological properties of whole and shredded tyres change according to the applied stress. In general the data indicates that shredded tyres are suitable for use as a drainage medium in landfill applications but consideration needs to be given to the effect of stress, shred size, anisotropy, clogging and gas accumulation. Further research is required in some of these areas.

ACKNOWLEDGEMENTS

The work described in this paper was carried out as part of a programme of research funded by the Engineering and Physical Sciences Research Council (GR/L16149), and Cleanaway Ltd under the UK Government's landfill tax credit scheme. However, the views expressed are solely those of the authors.

REFERENCES

1. HIRD, R.B., GRIFFITHS, P.J. and SMITH, R.A.: Tyre waste and resource management: A mass balance approach, Viridis Report VR2, TRL Limited 2002

2. JONES, D.R.V. AND HALL, D.H.: Landfill Engineering: Leachate drainage, collection and extraction systems, R&D Technical Report P1-397. Environment Agency 2002

3. POWRIE, W. AND BEAVEN, R. P.: Hydraulic properties of household waste and implications for liquid flow in landfills. Proceedings of the Institution of Civil Engineers, Geotechnical Engineering, 1999, **137**, October, pp235-247

4. DANIEL, D. E.: State-of-the- Art: Laboratory Hydraulic Conductivity Tests for Saturated Soils, in Hydraulic Conductivity and Waste Contaminant Transport in Soil ASTM STP 1142, 1994

5. HUDSON, A.P., BEAVEN, R.P. and POWRIE, W.: Interaction of water and gas in saturated household waste in a large scale compression cell. Proceedings of the 8th International Sardinia Landfill Conference, S.Margherita Dipula, Cagliari, Italy. 2001 Vol III pp585 – 594

6. BUCHANAN, D., and CLARK, C.: The impact of waste processing on the hydraulic behaviour of landfilled wastes. Designing and Managing Sustainable Landfill, IBC 1997

7. HUDSON, A.P., BEAVEN, R.P. and POWRIE, W.: Measurement of the horizontal hydraulic conductivity of household waste in a large scale compression cell. In Proceedings of the 7th International Sardinia Landfill Conference, S.Margherita Dipula, Cagliari, Italy. Vol III, 1999 pp461-468.

8. PRICE, M.: Introducing Groundwater, George Allen & Unwin 1985

9. GEOSYNTEC CONSULTANTS: Guidance manual – tire shreds as leachate drainage material at municipal solid waste landfills, prepared for the California Integrated Waste Management Board, 15 December 1998

10. NIKOLOVA, R., POWRIE, W., HUMPHREYS, P. and SMALLMAN, D.J.: Performance of leachate drainage systems. Proceedings of the 8th International Sardinia Landfill Conference, S.Margherita Dipula, Cagliari, Italy. Vol III pp103 – 112

11. PAKSY, A., POWRIE, W., ROBINSON, J.P. and PEELING. L.: A laboratory investigation of anaerobic microbial clogging in granular landfill drainage media. Geotechnique 48, no 3, pp389-401

THE USE OF POST-CONSUMER TYRES IN CIVIL ENGINEERING

J M Reid

Viridis

M G Winter

TRL

United Kingdom

ABSTRACT. The implementation of the Landfill Directive will result in the progressive banning of the disposal of tyres in landfills by 2006. However, recycled tyres are suitable for a wide range of applications in civil engineering. Their low density makes them suitable as lightweight fill in areas of soft ground and as backfill to retaining structures. They can be used in a variety of forms, including tyre bales, whole tyres, shred, chips and granulate, and in a variety of applications including lightweight fill, soil reinforcement, drainage, erosion control, landfill engineering, artificial reefs and use in asphalt and concrete. Many of these applications are common in various parts of the world, and they are being increasingly used in the UK, particularly in the form of tyre bales. Examples of the use of tyre bales in the UK are given and a new project to develop specifications for tyre bales is described.

Keywords: Tyres, Tyre bales, Recycling, Specifications, Road construction, Flood defence embankments

Dr J M Reid is a Chartered Geologist and Technical Manager in Viridis, the sustainability and waste management arm of the Transport Research Foundation. He has 24 years experience in geotechnical and geoenvironmental engineering and specialises in the use of alternative materials in construction.

Dr M G Winter is both a Chartered Engineer and Chartered Geologist and Technical Manager at TRL's office in Scotland. Mike has 19 year experience in geotechnical and geoenvironmental engineering and specialises in the use of a wide range of materials in construction from natural fill, through waste construction materials to industrial wastes and by-products.

INTRODUCTION

Post-consumer tyres are those which have been permanently removed from vehicles without the possibility of being remounted for further road use. Approximately 480,000 tonnes of post-consumer tyres arise each year in the UK [1]. Of these, it is estimated that about 60% were recovered, of which 25% were reused or retreaded, 22% were recycled, mostly as granulate, 8% sent for energy recovery and 3% used for landfill engineering. A total of 145,000 tonnes was disposed of to landfill, of which 57,000 tonnes were from shredding of end-of-life vehicles [1].

The Landfill (England & Wales) Regulations 2002 introduce new operating requirements for landfill sites, including a ban on the disposal of both whole and shredded tyres. From July 2003, in accordance with the Landfill Regulations, whole used tyres cannot be deposited at landfills for hazardous waste or at landfills permitted or licensed since July 2001. Because whole or shredded tyres are not inert, they cannot go to inert landfills. Shredded used tyres may be accepted at landfills until 16 July 2006 where the waste management licence or permit provides that they may be accepted. However, as tyres are not considered to be hazardous waste, a landfill for hazardous waste may not accept shredded used tyres after 16 July 2004.

In the light of these developments, there is a need to find alternative uses for post-consumer tyres. One area that is at present little used is in civil engineering. However, this is an area where a number of uses are possible, and examples are available from the UK and many other parts of the world. A guidance document has recently been produced to describe these applications and encourage their use [2]. This paper describes the engineering properties of tyres and gives an overview of their potential applications, with case studies from the UK, and describes a current project to produce specifications for the use of tyre bales. The emphasis is on unbound applications for shred, chips, whole tyres and tyre bales rather than the use of granulate in asphalt, concrete or other products.

MATERIALS

Post-consumer tyres have a number of properties that make them attractive for use in civil engineering. These include being lightweight, durable, inert and having good thermal insulation properties. Tyres can also be used in a number of forms, as whole tyres, tyre bales, or processed into shred, chips or granulate. An industry standard has been developed to provide a European system of reference for materials produced from post-consumer tyres based upon their physical properties [3]. The terminology used for the different size fractions is shown in Table 1.

The engineering properties depend to some extent on the fraction that is being used. Typical values for material from chips to bales are shown in Table 2. The main properties that are of interest for civil engineering are described below:

Lightweight: The compacted dry density of shredded tyres is about one third that of a typical soil [4]. This makes them attractive for use as a lightweight fill for embankment construction where the foundation soils are weak or compressible. Because of their low density, tyre shreds produce lower horizontal stress than normal soils. If used as backfill to retaining walls and abutments this reduces the earth pressure on the back of the structure, enabling the walls to be thinner.

Table 1 Terminology for different size fractions for post-consumer tyres

NAME FOR FRACTION	MINIMUM SIZE (mm)	MAXIMUM SIZE (mm)
Powder	0	1
Granulate	1	10
Buffings	0	40
Chips	10	50
Shreds (small)	40	75
Shreds (large	75	300
Cut	300	Half tyre
Whole tyre	-	-
Tyre bales	-	-

Hydraulic conductivity: Whole and shredded tyres have high hydraulic conductivity. This makes them suitable for drainage applications or where free-draining fill is required.

Durability: Tyres are inert materials. They are non-toxic, non-biodegradable and resistant to a wide variety of chemicals and climatic conditions.

Thermal resistivity: Thermal resistivity is around seven to eight times higher than for a typical granular soil [4]. Tyres are thus a suitable alternative for use as an insulating layer.

Table 2 Typical values of engineering properties of post-consumer tyres

PROPERTY	TYPICAL VALUES
Compacted density	$600 - 700$ kg/m^3
Angle of friction	$19 - 26$ degrees
Cohesion	$1 - 5$ kN/m^2
Compressibility	$20 - 50$ % (at $21 - 147$ kN/m^2)
Hydraulic conductivity	$1 \times 10^{-2} - 1 \times 10^{-3}$ m/s
Poisson's ratio	$0.2 - 0.35$
Resilient modulus	$1 - 2$ N/mm^2
Specific gravity	$1.1 - 1.27$ kg/m^3
Thermal conductivity	$0.15 - 0.23$ W/mK

WASTE MANAGEMENT LICENSING REGULATIONS

Although post-consumer tyres are suitable for a wide range of civil engineering applications, they are still regarded as waste under the UK Waste Management Licensing Regulations [5].

This means that a waste management license is required for all operations to transport, process and store tyres until they have been completely recovered. The point at which this occurs is subject to debate, but the view currently taken by the Environment Agency in England and Wales is that this does not occur until the material is incorporated into the final product: for granulate, this might be incorporation in asphalt in a road surface layer; for shred, whole tyres or tyre bales this might be until they are placed in their final position in a road, embankment or other structure.

Regulatory controls apply as long as a tyre is waste and the longer view of waste has wide-ranging implications for many of those currently involved in the treatment of used tyres, as traditionally they have not been subject to such controls. A working group, facilitated by the Environment Council under the Environment Agency's TyreWatch programme, has developed a case for exemptions from waste management regulatory requirements on the basis that regulation should be proportionate to the environmental risk posed by that activity[6].

APPLICATIONS

Tyres can be used in a number of ways in civil engineering including:

- Lightweight fill
- Backfill to structures
- Drainage for roads
- Landfill engineering
- Fluvial and coastal erosion control
- Artificial reefs
- Noise absorption bunds
- Insulating layers
- Absorption layers for hydrocarbons in ground remediation
- As a constituent in asphalt and concrete
- As a constituent in sport and safety surfaces
- As a constituent of building products

Examples and design guidance are given in [2]. Although the use of tyres has been demonstrated in civil engineering applications, such as repairs to slope failures on highways [7], for many years, most of these applications have only been used on a small scale in the UK to date. This may partly be because tyres are not included in most civil engineering specifications, such as the UK Specification for Highway Works [8]. Each application therefore has to be decided on a case-by-case basis, which causes delay and expense and acts as a disincentive.

However, in North America a standard has been developed for the use of tyres in civil engineering by ASTM [9]. The standard provides guidance for the testing of physical properties and data for the assessment of leachate generation potential of processed tyres. The document covers the use of whole and shredded tyres in: lightweight fill applications; reinforced retaining walls; drainage applications; and thermal insulation. The draft standard prEN 14243 [3] provides a means of standardising and testing tyres for civil engineering applications. A TRL project is currently underway to develop specifications for tyre bales; this project is described in more detail later in the paper.

Although applications are available for all the forms of post-consumer tyre listed in Table 1, tyre bales are a particularly attractive option for a number of reasons. They involve much less processing than the fractions where size reduction is required, such as shred and chips, and are hence much cheaper to produce. The plant used in their production is mobile, which reduces transport costs. Tyre bales are prepared from whole passenger car, utility or truck tyres, with about 125 passenger car/utility tyres compressed mechanically into bales approximately 0.75m x 1.50m x 1.25m. Each bale weighs approximately 1 tonne. The bales are each bound with five bands of galvanised steel. The lack of exposed steel, as in shred or chips, reduces the possibility of leaching of metals. Bales are adaptable to numerous applications, as a type of lightweight gabion, as shown by the following case studies.

Pevensey Beach Recharge

Pevensey Beach is a 9 km shingle embankment that protects 50 km^2 of the low-lying Pevensey Levels, 35 km^2 of which is a Site of Special Scientific Interest (SSSI). Major beach replenishment took place during the summer of 2002. However, littoral drift through Pevensey bay results in a net loss to the frontage of 20,000 m^3 per year. This amount has to be added annually by way of maintenance recharge to preserve the improved defences. This would normally require the import of large amounts of natural shingle to build up the beach to the required level. If some of the shingle could be replaced by other materials this would preserve scarce resources of this valuable natural material. If materials that would otherwise be waste, such as used tyres, can be used to replace the shingle this gives additional environmental benefits.

A trial was carried out in which 350 tyre bales were buried in the landward side of the beach in November 2002, generating shingle that could be used elsewhere on the beach. The performance of the tyres bales has been monitored over a year since construction. The trial was carried out as an awareness raising exercise of the potential uses of tyre bales in construction. It is partly funded by the Partners in Innovation programme run by the Department of Trade and Industry.

Tyres are generally inert and durable materials. However there are concerns that they could release contaminants adhering to them as a result of use on roads, and metals from the reinforcing cords within the tyres. To assess leaching, five groundwater sampling wells have been placed in and around the tyres bales. Zinc is used as the main indicator of tyre leaching. Monitoring will be continued for a year after construction and the results will be given in the final project report, due in 2005.

Unsurfaced Road, East Sussex

A 180 metre long section of an unsurfaced road through an area of soft ground in woodland near the Sussex Downs had developed deep ruts as a result of use by four-wheel drive vehicles and motorcycles. Normally this would have been repaired by excavating the rutted area and replacing the soil with free draining granular aggregate. As an alternative, the excavated soil was replaced by tyre bales, with a 150 mm layer of crushed natural stone to form the road surface. This resulted in savings of about 75% in the cost of materials and a significant reduction in the overall cost of the repair as well as avoiding the use of natural aggregate.

The use of tyre bales avoided the use of natural aggregates and required less construction traffic, as the equivalent volume of stone would have weighed a great deal more and required more lorries to bring it to site. The site is in an Area of Outstanding Natural Beauty (AONB) and limiting the amount of construction traffic was an important consideration in the choice of repair method. The lightweight nature of the tyre bales is a considerable advantage for placing in soft ground, as it imposes much less load on the underlying soil than natural aggregate would. The density of the tyre bales is approximately 0.7 tonnes/m^3, about one third that of natural aggregate.

Landfill Site Haul Road, Fochabers

The Nether Dallachy landfill site at Fochabers is located at a former sand and gravel quarry near the Moray Firth. The site is subject to flooding in the winter due to seasonal variation in the ground water level. An extension to the existing haul road was required to service a new landfill cell.

The majority of the new road utilises cobbles from the sand and gravel quarry for general fill and unbound sub-base. The project aimed to investigate how other materials could be utilised for these applications. The replacement material had to provide a robust alternative. Tyre bales were chosen as a test material due to the ban of whole tyres from landfill and availability from a local source. The use tyre bales also had the advantage of giving an overall cost saving to the project.

The total length of the road construction was 200 m. Two trial sections 16 and 18 m in length were constructed using tyre blocks. The rest of the road was constructed using cobbles. The road is used by 30 to 40 vehicles/day, with gross weights ranging from 10 to 40 tonnes. The access road will be in use for 1.5 years, the trial areas will then be deconstructed to allow construction of the next landfill phase.

The tyre blocks have proved fit for use in this situation as they are free draining and can therefore cope with the frequent flooding that the landfill site experiences. The road has now been in place for over one year and has been monitored for signs of potholing, cracking and settlement. No evidence of failure has been observed and the areas of road constructed with tyre bales are performing equally with those constructed using cobbles.

The road has been constructed so that the edges of the tyre blocks project from the shoulder to allow observation of the blocks as vehicles pass, and a shallow bund has been constructed to collect water running off from the tyres. This area is being observed for visual signs of pollution. If any are seen the water can be sampled for pollution. To date no visual signs of pollution have been observed.

Road Embankment over Peat, Sutherland

The B871 road in Central Sutherland between Kinbrace on the A897 and Syre at the junction with the B873 is typical of the types of lightly trafficked road found in much of the Highlands. Despite its low traffic levels it provides a vital link for isolated communities and is constructed across an area of soft peat. In 2002 settlement had become evident along its length. At Loch Rosail the pavement surface had settled to the extent that it was located below the ground water table and was frequently covered with water to a depth of 0.2 m. The Forestry Commission planted two large conifer forests near the B871 in the 1950s, due to mature in the late 1990s. However, given the condition of the B871 road it was deemed unlikely that it would be economic to get the timber to market. However strenuous efforts by the Highland Council and the Forestry Commission led to an agreement that the timber would be transported along the B871 to Kinbrace. Detailed studies of the B871 also identified that the Loch Rosail road required urgent treatment before being exposed to the substantial increase in heavy traffic due to timber extraction vehicles. A 100 m section was selected for reconstruction with the central 55 m section being constructed using tyre bales.

Construction of the tyre bale embankment took place during a two week period in December 2002. The construction sequence was important to the successful installation of the tyre bales and involved excavation to 1500 mm below existing road level, then placing the geosynthetic and the first layer of bales. At this stage the gaps between the bales and the accessible voids in the bales were filled with lightweight fill. The second layer of bales and lightweight fill was then placed before the geosynthetic was wrapped around the entire assembly and a 250 mm layer of fine rockfill was placed to create a working platform. A nominal layer of welded reinforcing mesh (8 mm bars at 200 mm centre-to-centre spacings) was included in this layer to provide additional stiffness, following common practice in Finland. These operations were carried out in 5 m long bays, such that each complete bay created a secure working platform from which the next could be constructed.

A 100 mm layer of primary Type 1 sub-base was compacted on top of the fine rockfill layer to provide a running surface to the road that was then opened to traffic. After three months some loosening of the Type 1 sub-base surface was observed and a 50 mm layer of fine sand and gravel was added using a paving machine to provide better interlock at the surface. This enabled the timber extraction traffic to commence in that month. To further bind and waterproof the surface, two layers of surface dressing were applied in July 2003, comprising 10 mm chippings and 2 litres/m^2 of bitumen spray on each layer.

Monitoring indicated that maximum settlements were 200 mm and 450 mm either side of the road during the first ten months of opening. However, most (in excess of 75%) of this settlement occurred in the first four months after opening to traffic. The rates of settlement are now such that cumulative settlements over the next year are anticipated to be a maximum of 150 mm. In reality these are likely to be considerably less due to further decreases in the rate of settlement. Of the gross settlements between 0 and 10 mm is attributed to compression of the lower tyre bale layer.

SPECIFICATIONS FOR TYRE BALES

The baling of tyres to form blocks for use in construction represents not so much a means of disposal as a means of c reating a valuable c ommodity. H owever, at present tyre bales are generally being used in informal civil engineering applications (e.g., small erosion protection projects) and also in landfill construction where innovation is less constrained than in other sectors of the construction industry. The project on the B871 and described above is something of an exception to this rule.

Applications in other sectors of the civil engineering industry require a greater degree of design and specification, and a greater consideration of the design life of the completed construction. Experience strongly suggests that without formal design procedures and specifications, consultants and other designers will not use tyre bales in more critical, higher value applications.

Thus, further information in a simple and easily usable format is required to allow the application of tyre bales to higher value applications. A project is currently underway to develop specifications and design methods for tyre bale applications in civil engineering. The work is funded by Onyx Environmental Trust, Inverness & Nairn Enterprise and the Scottish Executive.

CONCLUSIONS

The case studies illustrate some of the uses to which tyre bales can be put. As shown by their properties and the range of fractions in which post-consumer tyres are available, there is a wide range of options for their use in construction. Developing specifications for these uses and resolving the waste/product issue will be important in unlocking this potential. Recent guidance documents and standards are helpful steps in this direction and should encourage greater use of tyres in civil engineering.

REFERENCES

1.   USED TYRE WORKING GROUP: 2001 statistics, www.tyredisposal.co.uk.

2.   HYLANDS, K N AND SHULMAN, V: Civil engineering applications of tyres. Viridis Report VR5. Crowthorne, TRL Limited, 2003. Available at www.viridis.co.uk.

3.   COMITÉ EUROPÉEN DE NORMALISATION (CEN): prEN 14243 Tyre Recycling. 2002.

4.   HUMPHREY, D N, WHETTEN, N, WEAVER, J AND RECKER, K: Tire shreds for highway construction. TR News, Issue 207, pp 8-10, Mar/Apr 2000.

5.   THE STATIONERY OFFICE: The Waste Management Licensing Regulations 1994, SI No 1056. London, The Stationery Office.

6.   USED TYRE WORKING GROUP: Sixth Report of the Used Tyre Working Group, covering the period August 2001 to July 2003. www.tyredisposal.co.uk.

7.   JOHNSON, P E: Maintenance and repair of highway embankments: Studies of seven methods of treatment. Research Report RR30. Crowthorne, TRL Limited, 1985.

8.   HIGHWAYS AGENCY, SCOTTISH EXECUTIVE, NATIONAL ASSEMBLY FOR WALES AND NORTHERN IRELAND DEPARTMENT FOR REGIONAL DEVELOPMENT: Specification for Highway Works. London, HMSO.

9.   AMERCIAN SOCIETY OF TEST METHODS (ASTM): Standard practice for the use of scrap tires in civil engineering applications. ASTM D-6270-98. 1998.

USED TYRE PROCESSING - ENERGY RECOVERY IN CEMENT PRODUCTION
Way Forward and Developing Sustainable Markets

M Hislop

Lafarge Cement UK

J Randall

Sapphire Energy Recovery Ltd

United Kingdom

ABSTRACT. Sapphire Energy Recovery Ltd., a Joint Venture Company formed By Lafarge Cement and Michelin Tyre Energy Recovery in Cement Production – Used Tyre Supply Chain Management. The Paper encompasses the following broad aspects:

- The use of used tyres and their benefits for energy recovery in cement manufacture and the wider benefits for the environment.

- The need for focused supply chain management from tyre producer to end of life disposal, leading to the creation of Sapphire Energy Recovery Ltd.

Keywords: Cement Manufacture, Recovery of Energy from Waste, Sustainable Solution

Murray Hislop is Technical Director of Lafarge Cement UK. He is responsible for all the technical aspects of L CUK Operations as well a s its Environmental Performance. He has been employed with the company in various technical roles for over 30 years. He is also a Director of Sapphire Energy Recovery.

Jamie Randall is Managing Director of Sapphire Energy Recovery Ltd. He is responsible for the Operation and Development of the Sapphire business to source and process waste tyres for energy recovery in cement.

LAFARGE AND CORPORATE RESPONSIBILITY

Lafarge Cement is the largest cement manufacturer in the world, with operations in North and South America, Europe, the Middle East, Africa and the Far East including China. Lafarge Cement UK's overall manufacturing capacity is in excess of 6.0 million tonnes per annum of cement accounting for over 40% of the domestic market.

The Cement industry has long been noted for its environmental impacts and its energy intensity and it is towards improving its image and its cost base that the industry has focussed heavily on its wider environmental management aspects. Lafarge Cement has a global commitment towards sustainable development not only with its social responsibility to its employees and to its stakeholders but also with its internal energy and wastes minimisation programmes. In addition to its internal wastes programme, Lafarge are committed to a global, wastes reuse programme, which combines the recovery of alternative raw materials for use in the cement process as well as energy recovery in its alternative fuels programmes.

In March 2000 Lafarge and WWF, the conservation organisation, signed a world-wide partnership agreement. Lafarge is a founding member of the WWF conservation partnership programme. The UK has two greenhouse g as reduction programmes aimed at meeting the government's Kyoto commitment and Lafarge Cement UK (LCUK) participates in both schemes. One scheme the Climate Change Agreement (CCA), covers energy consumption, fuels and electricity while the second the UK Emissions Trading Scheme (UK-ETS) with its voluntary cap covers process CO2 generated from prime raw materials.

At the current time LCUK has met its bi-annual and annual targets for the two schemes respectively and its alternative fuels programme offers, not only energy replacement and CO2 reduction, but also, in many cases, additional environmental benefits together with production cost savings. The EU emissions Trading Scheme (EU- ETS) scheduled to be operational in 2005 effectively combines both UK schemes and Lafarge look forward to active engagement in this new scheme

In 2003 Lafarge Cement UK consumed over 588,000 tonnes of coal sourced domestically and internationally along with some 140,000 tonnes of petroleum coke and some 98,000 tonnes of materials sourced and classified as alternative fuels, mostly in the form of scrap tyres. The company continues to seek out alternative and sustainable sources of renewable fuel for our cement kilns and has now added PSP to its catalogue of authorised alternative fuels, which includes, whole and chipped tyres as well as recycled organic liquids.

The use of scrap tyres as a partial replacement for traditional fuels in cement manufacture represents a well proven and established technology throughout the world. For this reason, scrap tyres along with other 'mature' alternative fuels such as RLF (recycled liquid fuel) form the mainstay of Lafarge Cement UK's strategy, increasing the utilisation from less than 3% on an energy basis in 1999 to in excess of 20% by 2006. The usage of scrap tyres was less than 18,000 tonnes in 1999 and is forecast to increase to some 160,000 tonnes by 2005.

SCRAP TYRES AS A FUEL FOR CEMENT WORKS

Benefiting the Environment

The use of tyres as a fuel in cement manufacture has a number of global benefits to the environment:

- Elevation of waste streams up the waste hierarchy, recovering energy from materials instead of disposal.
- Conserving virgin fossil fuels
- Reducing global carbon dioxide emissions
- Conserving landfill void space

Lafarge Cement UK considers the use of tyres as a fuel in cement kilns to be Best Practicable Environmental Option for the disposal of scrap tyres. In addition, the use of scrap tyres as a fuel leads to an overall reduction in the environmental impact of the cement manufacturing process, principally through the reduction in the emission of oxides of nitrogen (NOx), from the process. NOx emission in cement works is essentially thermal NOx generated in the coal flame by nitrogen burning in Oxygen at temperatures of 2000°C. This is illustrated in Figure1, where the use of whole tyres at Westbury Works saw a 42% reduction in NOx. Similarly it is normal to find that volatile organic carbon (VOC) emissions are similarly reduced as these appear to be generated from coal burning, see Figure 2.

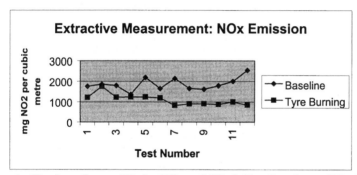

Figure 1 - Westbury Cement Works, Effect of Whole Tyre Burning on NOx Emission

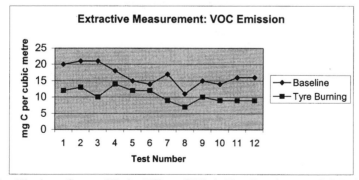

Figure 2 - Westbury Cement Works, Effect of Whole Tyre Burning on VOC Emission.

Cement Manufacturing Process

Cement manufacture involves the heat treatment, calcining and sintering of a blend of argillaceous and calcareous raw materials to form an intermediate product known as cement clinker. The typical raw materials being shale and limestone or clay and chalk. These raw materials are ground and blended prior to being fed into the part of the process known as clinker burning. Clinker burning takes place at material temperatures in excess of 1500°C in rotary kilns. These rotary kilns are large rotating steel cylinders lined with refractory bricks. The clinker once produced is cooled before being finely ground with the addition of a small amount of gypsum to produce cement.

The rotary kiln acts as a counter current heat exchanger with heat for the process being supplied by burning a fuel in preheated air to produce flame temperatures of 2000°C. The heat exchange taking place between the combustion gases travelling upwards through the process and the raw materials travelling downwards through the process. The cement manufacturing process has a number of attributes that make it ideal for the use of fuels such as tyres that would otherwise be disposed of via landfill or incineration.

High Temperature

Temperatures in excess of 1500°C are required in order to form cement clinker from the constituent raw materials fed to the kiln. In order to heat the raw materials to these temperatures within the kiln, the traditional fuels - coal and petroleum coke - are burnt at temperatures of around 2000°C. These temperatures are much higher than those found within commercial incinerators which typically operate at 1100°C.

Long Residence Times

The hot gases from the kiln flame, which burns at 2000°C, remain at high temperature for a period of 4 to 5 seconds compared to typically 1 to 2 seconds in a commercial incinerator.

High Thermal Inertia

There are typically several hundreds of tonnes of process material at these elevated temperatures, resulting in a very high thermal inertia. This inertia makes temperatures within the system relatively unaffected by short-term fluctuations in fuel supply. Indeed the kiln system and its contents remain at high temperatures for several hours after the fuel supply has been stopped.

Alkaline Environment

The raw materials within the kiln system are essentially alkaline as one of the principal reactions within the system is to produce lime (calcium oxide) from the chalk raw material (calcium carbonate). This alkaline environment effectively scrubs any acid gases from the kiln gas stream in the same way as a lime scrubber on incinerator or power station exhausts.

Oxidising Atmosphere

It is a requirement of the cement manufacturing process that it is carried out in an oxidising atmosphere, hence excess oxygen is available to ensure complete combustion of fuels.

Ash Residue

Ash from the combustion of the fuels is combined within the clinker produced by the kiln. The cement clinker, is a vitreous, glassy material and the ash is chemically combined within the glass matrix, effectively binding constituents such as heavy metals and removing them from the environment.

CONCLUSIONS

The combination of the above process characteristics result in organic constituents of the fuels being effectively destroyed by the combination of high temperatures, long residence time and oxidising atmosphere. Acidic gases, formed by the combustion of the fuels are scrubbed by the alkaline environment into the cement clinker. Inorganic constituents leave the process as part of the cement clinker and heavy metals are effectively removed from the environment by being locked into the chemical matrix of the clinker. Any remaining inorganic constituents are effectively caught within the dusty environment of the kiln gas stream and are removed in the electrostatic precipitators or bag filters and recycled to the process.

The cement kiln has a high and continuous fuel requirement making it an ideal process for the recovery of energy from materials such as tyres that would otherwise be waste materials, and solves a major environmental problem whilst reducing the environmental impact of the cement manufacturing process.

AUTHORISATION PROCESS

The Substitute Fuels Protocol

The Environment Agency guidance document, known as the Substitute Fuels Protocol is used to regulate the use and application of substitute fuels. In order to use any alternative fuel an operator must undertake rigorous trials for evaluation and assessment of environmental impact. This is to demonstrate to the public that thorough and scientific consideration of the issues pertaining to the use of the substitute fuel is undertaken and that public is extensively consulted, Applying only to cement manufacture, the protocol has been blamed for dramatically slowing down the authorisation process and hence the environmental benefits associated with the application. Within the last 3 years the Agency has introduced a variant called the Tyres Protocol, this potentially eases the determination process by including success criteria as a predicted trial outcome, and offers a one application process and a methodology for authorisation of an incremental increase in firing rate. Provisional upon verification of meeting the predefined and agreed success criteria the hither-to-fore mandatory stop after trialling may now be removed if the new consultation SFP document is formally approved.

Future Implications of Changing Legislation (WID)

In December 2005 the Waste Incineration Directive becomes Law for existing plant, this directive treats incineration and co-incineration (the cement alternative fuelling process) plants the same way. The directive applies to all cement works using wastes as a fuel and it includes s pecific o perational a nd e mission l imits f or c ement k ilns a nd i mposes m andatory emission limits The directive covers reception and storage of wastes prior to use and operators must prevent negative environmental effects during waste delivery and reception e.g. odours, noise, pollution of air land and water.

There are strict conditions for the incineration or co-incineration process e.g. must combust waste at 850°C for 2 secs. under the most unfavorable conditions, this is increased to 1100°C if Waste contains more than 1% halogen. There is a requirement for continuous monitors for NOx, SO2, Dust, CO, TOC, HCl, (HF) and for the continuous operational measurements of combustion gas temperature and pressure, exhaust gas O_2 and H_2O. Apart from two exceptions W.I.D. sets identical Emission Limit Values (ELV's) for kilns as for Incinerators. The Exceptions are dust and NOx, (Incinerators dust 10 mg, NOx 200/400 mg.) If more than 40% hazardous waste is used then the incinerator limits. Standard conditions are referenced and these are referred to standard temperature pressure and Oxygen content (273°K,101.3 kPa, 10% O2, dry gas.)

POTENTIAL CAPACITY OF CEMENT WORKS TO USE TYRES

Cement Industry as Long Term Route

In the UK the cement industry will over the next 2 years supply a major disposal route for scrap tyre arisings. In the face of the removal of the landfill disposal option, the tyre industry needs a large volume viable alternative. The UK cement industry can provide such a route but there are challenges such as seasonality leading to stockpiling and adding cost by double handling. The UK cement industry has almost completed the authorisation process to use tyres as a fuel, and optimisation of combustion and fine tuning is required to secure this sustainable route. Commercial pressures and e nvironmental regulation a re never static and the balance of these forces will ultimately determine how sustainable this future is.

Global and European Perspectives

Globally, Lafarge Cement and the cement industry in general is active in pursuing a strategy of seeking and implementing alternative fuels as a substitute for fossil fuels. The necessary precursors or building blocks for implementing a substitution programme are generally the following:

- A free market economy
- Competing alternative disposal routes allowing effective competition
- The existence of the necessary building blocks for a collection infrastructure
- An Environmental "conscience"
- An active environmental enforcement infrastructure.

Within Europe the major alternative fuels used in the industry are organic liquids and tallow, Meat and Bone Meal (MBM) and refuse derived fuel (RDF) or packaging wastes. The competing materials are commercially driven and emphasis is generally both technically and politically motivated. The introduction of the EU ETS will, along with commercial drivers reshapes this over the next decade.

Financial Considerations

Capital for alternative fuels reception and firing systems has in the past been a major difficulty, with justification in a given time period almost impossible to guarantee. The trial process commits capital up front of the project to provide for the reception storage, preparation and firing of the fuel without the certain knowledge at the outset, that the project will be progressing to its full authorisation. There are risks that the trial will not be successful and the Environment Agency will reject the application. Environmental action groups have significantly slowed the permitting process at all points in the trials procedure. At Westbury the four-month process from successful trial to authorisation to burn continuously took over 12months to complete. The ability of businesses to sustain this level of zero capital payback is increasingly more difficult. The trialling process itself is costly and in the case of LCUK, excluding any capital, costs are £550,000. In addition to the above LCUK has to date incurred Capital costs of £12m for tyre processing and firing equipment alone. Gate fees are essential to the justification and longevity of all alternative fuels projects.

Cement Kiln Firing

The use of tyres as a fuel in UK cement kilns has risen gradually since 1995, reaching 98,000t in 2003 and is forecast to exceed 160,000t in 2005. The introduction of EU-ETS in 2005 which has a definition of carbon neutrality that excludes tyres suggests that only the commercial attractiveness of tyres as a substitute for coal will guarantee its continued use as a cement kiln fuel. The use of tyres provides a win-win-win situation, preserving fossil fuels, reducing the environmental emissions from the process and providing the industry with a competitive advantage. Lafarge Cement UK predicts it will be in a position to dispose of 200,000 tonnes per annum by 2006. The timeframe however will be significantly influenced by the regulatory regime. Currently the Substitute Fuels Protocol constrains the timeframe to a minimum of 15 months, however in practice a time-scale of two years would be the norm.

The UK government recognises that use of scrap tyres as a cement kiln fuel represents the most sustainable disposal route for the majority of scrap tyres. However the process of permitting is difficult due to the current regulatory framework.

SAPPHIRE ENERGY RECOVERY LTD

Background

In 1998, Lafarge Cement UK (then Blue Circle Cement) embarked on an extensive performance improvement programme. At the core of this activity was the potential to reduce costs through more effective procurement activity. At a very early stage in the process it became apparent that the creation of an effective supply chain for alternative fuels required specific focus. It was recognised that the acquisition of waste derived fuels and their subsequent processing would take the business into new areas of both technical knowledge and a new regulatory regime requiring practices and procedures necessary to protect the interests of the business both legally and commercially.

At the core of the alternative fuels strategy was the use of used tyres. At this time only one Works was authorised to use tyres as a fuel and it was sourcing its requirements from the general market. The Works' authorisation to use tyres was based on the use of a tyre chip produced on a Columbus McKinnon tyre chipping machine acquired by Blue Circle but operated under a contract by a separate entity which also had the responsibility for supplying whole tyres sufficient to meet the needs of the works. Blue Circle itself had very little knowledge of the used tyre market and effectively distanced itself from the volatile activities taking place in that market. Blue Circle Cement UK had plans to adopt the use of used tyres at four other works in the UK and it became apparent that other cement companies had plans for the use of used tyres as a fuel.

In industry the concept of autonomy of operations is generally sound. Businesses which have a number of sites across different regions or countries are difficult to manage entirely from the centre. Finding the right balance between centre led control and autonomy is an area which has and continues to be problematic. In the procurement field though it is often found that autonomy can conflict strongly with the benefits that can be brought to companies through professional, co-ordinated and focussed supply management. These conflicts arise frequently when common commodities are involved.

In the specific area of wastes and in particular used tyre disposal Blue Circle realised that the potential for conflict between different cement works chasing the same common resource was very high. This needed to be avoided. Thus it was realised that there was a need to protect the commercial interests of the business by defining and adopting a co-ordinated approach. Additionally, and of equal importance, is the need to protect the interests of the business in the Licence to Operate areas. Within Lafarge Cement, great focus is placed upon both health and safety and environmental compliance. The entry in to the area of waste management and a different regulatory regime necessitated dedicated focus.

It was against this backdrop that a strategy for the long-term sourcing of used tyre was developed. It was realised at the outset that any strategy needed to recognise that the issue is as much about the tyre industry as the cement industry. This realisation led to Blue Circle and Michelin, the respective world leaders in their industries, agreeing to create a business dedicated to used tyre recovery, initially as use as a fuel in cement production, but with the freedom to work as a provider of used tyres for any legally authorised process operating in the market. Called Sapphire Energy Recovery, its goal was to become a full service provider to the tyre industry, meeting complimentary needs and demonstrating a commitment by them both to make a significant long-term contribution to used tyre disposal. Sapphire is owned 75% by LCUK and 25% by Michelin. It has grown dramatically since it commenced business in 2001.

The objective of creating a long term sustainable and environmentally sound solution for significant volumes of used tyres had been established. The logic to create a separate business followed recognition that no acceptable alternative option was available in the UK.

At this stage of Sapphire's development the focus remains on the use of used tyres as a fuel in cement but the commercial, operational and logistical platform has been effectively laid for entry in to other markets. This will inevitably take place should customers wish to take advantage of Sapphire's services. From the outset Sapphire was planned to be a used tyre recovery business of a wider nature.

Supply Chain and Processing Locations
It is Sapphire's responsibility to manage the used tyre supply chain from the point of used tyre arising through to use as a fuel in cement production or other acceptable and legally

authorised option. This involves providing a service to a used tyre market the structure of which is relatively complex and fast moving. From the point of removal of the tyre at the tyre depot a used tyre can be collected and processed on occasions within a day or two depending upon the volumes arising. From the point it is removed from the vehicle a car or van tyre becomes a waste and is subject to the relevant regulatory regime. All of those holding, collecting and processing this waste are subject to waste management regulations. The tyre depot has a duty of care responsibility to ensure that their used tyres are collected by an authorised collector and disposed of in a legal manner.

Sapphire and the cement industry has invested in creating a nation-wide infrastructure capable of providing an efficient, flexible and competitive service to the tyre industry. This includes major investments in processing capacity placed in London and Birmingham which are compatible with the proximity principle and positioned to provide high levels of service currently unmatched in the UK.

This processing network can provide an uninterrupted service with tyres being processed on a just in time manner and moved out speedily for final use. Sapphire seeks to minimise stocks of both whole tyres and processed product but recognises the need to have a storage capability for finished product in order to be able to absorb supply chain fluctuations. The ability exists to move finished product from any chipping plant to any cement work. The shortest route to final processing though, is both environmentally and economically sound. The establishment of a nation-wide and flexible capability has provided the collection industry with the opportunity to avoid the long distance movement of whole tyres which effectively creates a lower cost base. The tyre industry has yet to fully recognise this potential.

All of Sapphire's operations comply with, or are set to comply with environmental standard ISO14001. This accreditation reflects standards not yet achieved to the same extent elsewhere in the industry and enables those truly aware of their environmental responsibilities to be assured that their legal obligations will be securely met. Of equal importance to Sapphire is the knowledge that all of its employees, customers, suppliers and contractors are working safely on its sites. Sapphire applies the same attention to the area of health and safety as it does to environmental performance. Both of these aspects reflect the ethos of its respective parent companies.

Sapphire Processing Capacity

Sapphire has adopted the use of tyre chipping machines produced by Columbus McKinnon of the USA. Four machines are now placed across the UK. These machines produce a cut tyre chip product designed and specified for use as a fuel primarily in cement production. Other uses for tyre chip of this type are being developed and through its Lafarge parentage Sapphire is placed to play a part in these developing markets. Such a capability will enable a continuous service for used tyres in the event that consumption problems arise at any cement works or to meet increasing customer demand. Additionally the ability to achieve optimum use of assets is also achieved.

Sapphire has processing capacity available in excess of 200,000 tonnes per annum. This can be used entirely to meet the growing demands of cement or can provide a processed material for use in alternative options. This flexibility has been created deliberately with the key objective to be able to provide a continuous service to the tyre industry.

Regulatory Regimes

Sapphire's processing operations are based either on a cement works or within a conurbation close to the sources of tyre arisings. When operating within the cement works boundaries Sapphire has to comply with the environmental regulations governing that activity. This placed difficult constraints as the approach is not always helpful to a business effectively engaged in waste management. The pace at which the authorisation process for a cement works to use tyres has been very slow and based on complete uncertainty that authorisation will be achieved. This has worked against Sapphire selling its services and sadly has also worked against the timely achievement of the solution to used tyre disposal that the cement option will bring. Sapphire is in the process of seeking to operate within the realm of waste management and indeed this is the already the case at those locations placed in Birmingham and London.

Used Tyre Market

The statistical data available for used tyres in the UK has yet to achieve total credibility. The complexity of the markets structure has made it extremely difficult for the DTI to collect accurate data. Whilst it is hoped that this situation will be addressed in the near future the industry has a record of unwise investment, occasionally resulting in the demise of businesses. Government and the industry now have a clear responsibility to ensure that accurate data is established if more "tears" are to be avoided in the future.

The tyre distribution chain is convoluted and there appears to be little loyalty between commercial entities encompassed in the chain. There appears to be a minimal amount of loyalty between many retailers and collectors and collectors to processors. Secure contracts cannot be meaningfully established in this scenario. Perhaps this is historical. In the past the wide availability of the landfill option meant that there was no problem in disposing of a used tyre and many retailers were happy to leave the responsibility for disposal to a collector assuming that they would act responsibly and legally. Sadly the number of illegal tyre dumps created in the past is evidence that this approach was not always a success.

Naturally, against this backdrop the tyre retailer has not always focused on the issue of disposal. In the past they also benefited from a healthy remoulding market using the value left in a used tyre to subsidise or carry completely the cost of collection and disposal. The reduction in scale of the remoulding industry has significantly reduced the opportunity to reduce costs although the sorting of casings continues at a reduced level and the value used as a means to provide a competitive collection price.

In order to meet their legal responsibilities those seeking to dispose of used tyres will need to continue to pay for the service of collection and final processing. Effectively the industry is in many cases already making a charge to the consumer for this service which is in line with government policy that "the polluter pays." It is apparent though that in many cases this charge does not in whole pass through to the collector and processor.

The tyre industry needs to recognise that for an acceptable and legal environmental solution to be sustained sufficient liquidity will be required. Liquidity equals sustainability. It is apparent that tighter regulation by the Environment Agency and the industry itself may well be required to achieve full compliance with the laws.

EU Landfill Directive/End of Life Vehicle Directive

Sapphire has determined its own view on the volumes of used tyres arising in the UK. Used tyre volumes are what they are and neither that volume nor the locations where they arise will change significantly in the coming years. As a consequence of the full implementation of the Landfill Directive by July 2006 all of these arisings will have to find an alternative authorised end of life solution. It is this Directive which is the key driver to environmental improvement for the tyre industry and for the creation of alternative processing activities including their use as a fuel in cement. Whilst it is likely that there may be delays in achieving full implementation of the Directive as a consequence of the Environment Agency being unable to complete IPPC authorisation for some landfill sites it is Sapphire's view that the use of this option will be very limited beyond 2006.

A second piece of legislation will also have an impact on the availability of used tyres arisings for end of life processing. The End of Life Vehicle Directive is likely to create additional tyres as it will place an obligation on the vehicle dismantling industry to remove tyres on end of life vehicles and to direct these to an authorised processing option. These tyres are currently often shredded and disposed of to landfill alongside other automotive wastes. The implementation of this legislation is currently under discussion but moves are already being made by various parties which will be effected by it to prepare themselves for its impact.

Possible Producer Responsibility Legislation -Tyre Producers

Whilst this issue continues to be discussed it now appears increasingly unlikely that government will place a Statutory obligation on tyre producers to ensure recovery of their products. It is estimated that the current recovery rate for used tyres in the UK, which excludes landfill, is at the 80% level. This is a high recovery level compared to many other countries and it is viewed that with a great deal of planned additional processing capacity yet to commence that the UK is likely to meet its obligations under the Landfill Directive. As a result the driver for legislation is greatly reduced.

Government has indicated its preference for a voluntary free market solution and whilst other approaches proposing a managed solution have been made, this approach seems unlikely to be adopted. The managed option is viewed in many quarters as likely to be heavily bureaucratic, cumbersome and expensive. It might also be seen as anti-competitive.

I am sure that the BRMA (British Rubber Manufacturers Association) will reach a conclusion in due course which will be acceptable to government, their membership and all of those committed to solving the used tyre problem.

Additional Processing Capacity - Barriers to Entry

Earlier in this paper the matter of reliable statistics was touched on. As a first step, the creation of a process which places a requirement on relevant parties to provide numerical information in an accurate and timely manner is essential. If investment disasters are to be avoided in the future this information is a key element. Clearly vested interests will be present and confidentiality of key information will be an important issue. However if the industry is to raise its reputation then it must improve its professionalism in many respects. This is part of that need.

The creation of the Responsible Recycler Scheme represents an important initial step towards greater professionalism in the tyre recovery industry. Comprised of businesses from both processors and collectors the objective is to raise operating standards in the industry. Part of the qualification for admission to the scheme is an agreement that each member will be subject to an independent audit to determine that they are not only complying with the rules of the scheme, but are also operating legally. An important part of the audit is the verification of the numbers of tyres handled. This may therefore be a way forward to gaining statistical data that has greater integrity. It may well be wise for potential new investors to await for better information before committing themselves to investment.

The nature of supply relationships is again critical to any future investors. Capital cannot be committed to in an environment where supply arrangements cannot be reliably contracted. What use to an investor is a supply of used tyres today which can be taken away tomorrow?

Current indications are that the UK is recovering around 80% of used tyre arisings and that significant additional capacity is likely to come on stream. The 80% level now being recovered is currently going to an existing processor. The entry of new processors logically implies that to obtain their supplies they will have to take volumes from existing uses. When combined with the proximity principle any new investments will need to be extremely efficient and logistically well placed to succeed. Investors entering this unreliable supply chain do so at their own peril.

CONCLUSIONS

The major players in the industry need to demonstrate their leadership by long term commitments to secure processing solutions.

The market will inevitably stabilise but it may not be surprising to see further unwise investments being made or indeed existing players leave the market.

Whilst new technology will undoubtedly bring new solutions and change to the industry any new process will need to possess the strong environmental benefits presented by energy recovery in cement.

Sapphire is well placed to continue to provide a service to the tyre and cement industries and any new options that may develop.

SESSION FOUR:

WAY FORWARD AND DEVELOPING SUSTAINABLE MARKET

CHEMICAL RECYCLING OF POST-CONSUMER TYRES

I de Marco

B.M. Caballero   **A. Torres**

Basque Country University   **M.J. Chomón**

M.F. Laresgoiti

Engineering School of Bilbao

Spain

ABSTRACT Chemical recycling include those processes in which tyres are transformed in a completely different matter (gas, liquids, energy), Three type of processes meet this definition. Incineration, either stand-alone incineration or co-combustion in existing installations such as cement kilns; this is the process at present most used. Gasification converts tyres by heating at high temperatures with oxygen and steam, in a synthetic gas (mainly $CO + H_2$) which is usually used as fuel. Pyrolysis involves heating tyres to moderate temperatures without oxygen; as a result liquids and gases which can be used as fuels or petrochemical feedstock are obtained; the steel and carbon black can be recovered as value added products. In this paper the possibilities and limits of chemical processes for recycling tyres are discussed.

Keywords: Pyrolysis, Gasification, Incineration, Co-combustion, Recycling, Tyre

Dr. I. de Marco: is chemical engineer and lecturer at the Engineering School of Bilbao (Spain). She lectures in Chemical Engineering, more specifically, in polymers science and technology, and in safety in the chemical industry Her research interests include chemical recycling of polymeric wastes, as well as coal liquefaction processes.

Dr. B.M. Caballero: is a Chemistry Graduate and lecturer in the Mine and Civil Engineering School at the Basque Country University. She lectures in Chemical and Environmental Engineering and researches on coal liquefaction and chemical recycling of polymeric wastes.

Dr. A. Torres: is a Chemistry Graduate. She lectures in Chemical Engineering at the Engineering School of Bilbao. Her research activities are mainly focused on chemical recycling of polymeric wastes.

Dr. M.J. Chomón: is a Chemistry Graduate and lecturer at the Engineering School of Bilbao, specifically in Chemical Engineering. Her research works are coal liquefaction processes and chemical recycling of polymeric wastes.

M.F. Laresgoiti: is a Chemistry Graduate. She is a Laboratory Technician at the Engineering School of Bilbao (Spain). Her labours include student's practical lessons preparation and chemical analysis in the Chemical and Environmental Engineering Department

INTRODUCTION

The disposal of used tyres is a major environmental problem in nowadays. It is estimated [1,2] that more than 2.5×10^6 tons/year are generated in the European Union, 2.5×10^6 in North America, 1×10^6 in Japan and $0,3 \times 10^6$ in Spain. The complex nature of tyres makes it difficult to recycle them. At present there are four types of markets for post-consumer tyres: reuse, retreading, material recycling and chemical recycling. The two former involve that the physical condition of the tyre is still sound, and therefore they can be resold for continued road use, either directly, after regrooving or after reconditioning it by retreading. *Material recycling* includes the preparation and use of tyre materials for a broad array of consumer, industrial and construction products and applications, such as artificial reefs, dock bumpers, playground surfaces, sport surfaces, rubber modified asphalt, additive to other polymers (rubbers or plastics), drainage mediums, leaching fields and many more. *Chemical recycling* involves that tyre itself as a material disappears and is converted into a completely different matter: energy, chemicals, gas, carbon products, etc. There are three main chemical recycling processes for discarded tyres: Incineration, gasification and pyrolysis. Incineration implies the use of tyres as fuel in cement or other kilns, and in energy generating facilities; it is the chemical recycling process most used today.

Table 1 provides a summary of post-consumer tyre treatments in the last years, in the European Union [1] and in Spain [2]. Landfill has been the alternative most widely used for many years, though it has been continually decreasing (from 62% in 1992 to 40% in 1998 in the EU [1]). The Landfill Directives bans land-filling whole tyres since 2003, and shredded tyres from 2006, so this disposal alternative will disappear soon. On the contrary energy recovery has been growing in the last years up to 20% at present in EU. The Incineration of Waste Directive demands lower emissions to air from 2008 in any combustion installation, and therefore it will not be possible to treat tyres in some facilities which are at present incinerating them, such as some cement kilns. This stricter environmental legislation will probably bring about an expansion of existing markets and the commercial development of emerging technologies such as pyrolysis and gasification. In this paper a discussion of the three tyre recycling chemical processes, incineration, gasification and pyrolysis, is presented.

Table 1. Post-consumer tyres treatments (weight %)

	LANDFILL	RESOLD	RETREAD	MATERIAL RECYCLING	ENERGY RECOVERY
European Union [1]	39	11	12	18	20
Spain [2]	63	4,5	14	7,8	10

CHEMICAL NATURE OF TYRES

Tyres are very complex products, which are composed of several very different ingredients. *Rubbers* are the major component of tyres (44-55 wt%); those most used for tyre manufacture are natural rubber (*cis* 1,4-polyisoprene) and styrene-butadiene rubber (SBR). These products are high molecular weight polymeric chains, which in the vulcanisation process are cross-linked with sulphur (Figure 1). As a consequence the polymeric chains are not free, and cannot flow ones with respect to others; consequently rubbers are not fusible and therefore cannot be remoulded into other shapes without serious degradation. *Carbon black* is another major ingredient of tyre (~25-30 wt%). It is a high carbon content pulverized material (almost 100% carbon), which is added to tyre in order to increase its tensile strength, and abrasion and wear resistance. *Steel cords and filaments* are another important ingredient of tyres (~8-10 wt%); they provide the necessary mechanical structural strength. Other ingredients of tyres are: sulphur (1-2 wt%), ZnO (1-2 wt%), and some others such as accelerators, synthetic fibres, extender oils, stearic acid, etc., which amount up to 10-12 wt%.

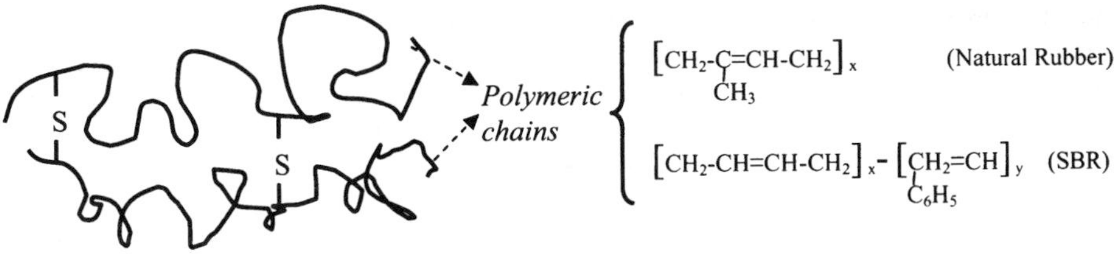

$$\left[CH_2\text{-}\underset{\underset{CH_3}{|}}{C}=CH\text{-}CH_2\right]_x \qquad \text{(Natural Rubber)}$$

$$\left[CH_2\text{-}CH=CH\text{-}CH_2\right]_x\text{-}\left[\underset{\underset{C_6H_5}{|}}{CH_2}=CH\right]_y \quad \text{(SBR)}$$

Figure 1.- Chemical structure of rubbers

In chemical recycling processes, the rubbers decompose and/or react, yielding low molecular weight products which are either gases such as CO, CO_2, CH_4, etc. or a wide variety of liquids including aromatics, aliphatics, etc. Carbon black which is a rather stable product, does not decompose when heated in inert atmosphere (pyrolysis), but do react with oxygen in the incineration and gasification processes. Steel is not significantly modified in chemical recycling, therefore it could be one of the products to be recovered from these processes. The other ingredients of tyres may be altered or not in chemical recycling processes depending on their organic or inorganic nature.

INCINERATION

In incineration processes tyres are burned with an excess of oxygen in order to maximize the conversion of the organic matter of tyres and the carbon black into CO_2 and H_2O. The major aim of tyre incineration is energy recover. Two different types of incineration processes should be considered, stand-alone incineration and co-combustion or co-incineration.

Stand-alone Incineration

This term applies to the process specifically devoted to get rid of tyres by incinerating them and recovering energy from the process. Tyres either whole or shredded, are fed to the incinerator where the combustion with oxygen takes place. A residue (ash) containing the steel and other inorganics of tyres is obtained. Tyre steels could theoretically be recycled, however steel recovered from some plants have turned to be carbonized and unsuitable for recycling, so this residue frequently requires land-filling.

The heat from the gases leaving the incinerator is recovered, steam produced and electricity generated by means of a steam turbine. Before the gases are emitted to the atmosphere a series of gas clean up operations are carried out in order to eliminate NO_x soot, PAH, and other contaminants, which are frequently generated in the incineration of carbonaceous materials.

Technologies for waste incineration are continuously evolving The main goals in this evolution are the increase in the combustion and energy production efficiency, and the improvement of the efficiency of the emissions control. Three are the types of furnaces most widely used in waste incineration [4]. 1) Grate furnace incinerators, in which the waste burns over a grate; air for combustion is supplied by fans or blowers under and over the grate. They usually operate in a gas temperature range of 750 to 1000 °C. It is the most common technology used for waste incineration. 2) Rotary kiln incinerators, in which the waste rotates in a cylindrical furnace and so mixing is optimised and uniform burn is provided. It usually operates in a gas temperature range of 800 to 1000 °C, possibly with a post combustion chamber reaching temperatures of 850 to 1200 °C. 3) Fluidised bed furnaces which consist of a bed of fine solids kept in motion buy hot air flowing upwards through it. They typically operate in a temperature range of 750 °C to 1000 °C. They have high combustion efficiency, but they require shredding the feedstock to a suitable size.

Stand-alone incineration has achieved for the moment very limited success for tyre disposal. There have been several tyre incineration plants (in UK, Germany, California,…) which have been forced to close due to two main problems, poor burn-out of the organic carbon content, and inefficient control of the gaseous emissions. On the contrary there are some tyre incineration plants (one in Connecticut, one in Italy and several fluidised bed plants in Japan) that have been operating successfully [3].

The main drawbacks for the development of tyre incineration processes in a commercial scale are the following. a) It faces a strong public opposition. b) There is a poor burn-out of tyre, due to the greater stability of tyres in comparison to other fuels. c) It is necessary to use higher temperatures, longer reaction times and greater excesses of O_2 to promote complete breakdown of the tyre components (polymeric rubbers and carbon black) into carbon dioxide and water, this implies energy loss in the stack and the need of larger boiler volumes. d) There may be inefficiency in the control of gas emissions. e) Tyre steels recovered are frequently unsuitable for recycling, so they have to be land-filled at a considerable cost. f) It requires high capital investments and operating costs due to the increasingly stringent emission limit requirements.

The key factors for increasing commercial tyre incineration processes are the following. a) Use of improved fluidised bed incinerators with higher efficiencies and improved environmental performance. b) Operation at higher temperatures and/or with longer residence times in order to guarantee complete burn-out of tyres. c) Improvement in the control of gas emissions.

Co-combustion

The term co-combustion or co-incineration applies to processes in which tyres are burned in existing industrial installations in replacement of fossil fuels. The main difference with incineration is that co-combustion does not take place in a dedicated installation but in industrial facilities devoted to the manufacture of other products. Tyres may be used in co-combustion just as received or once the metallic components have been separated; in this case the co-fuel is commonly known as tyre derived fuel (TDF). Currently the main industrial sector that makes use of tyre co-combustion is cement production followed by power plants. It has been reported that in the countries in which co-combustion is practised in cement kilns, 15-40% scrap tyres are recovered by this route [3]. Co-incineration in power plants only aims to recover the energy content of tyre under the form of electricity, while co-combustion in cement kilns recovers both the energy from the carbonaceous matter of tyres, and the minerals which remain after combustion as raw material in the clinker, so that there is little or no residue at all to dispose of.

Co-combustion of tyres in cement kilns requires minimum capital investment. Shredded tyres are fed into the rotary cement kiln where the clinker is produced at temperatures of about 1500 °C. The energy of the tyres is utilized in situ as heat, and the incombustible parts are incorporated to the clinker. Around 12 % of the energy used in the European Union for cement production comes from waste [4]. Tyres are the type of waste at present most used in co.combustion, but other wastes, such as packaging wastes, which have higher calorific values and are environmentally less hazardous, might also be used, restricting the growth of co-combustion of tyres in cement kilns.

Co-combustion of tyres is not exclusive to cement kilns. Tyres are also used in the pulp and paper industry, in limes kilns and some other sectors. When tyres are co-fed in boilers TDF is the suitable fed material. There are a series of problems associated with the use of TDF in boilers. a) The high sulphur content may cause boiler corrosion problems. b) Tar in the gas phase can cause fouling of the boiler tubes. c) The high calorific value of TDF can cause refractory damage since many boilers have been designed to handle other lower calorific value fuels. d) The need to shred and separate the metallic components, as well as the need of expensive system for control of emissions, implies considerable capital investments and operating costs. All these difficulties limit the use of tyres in co-combustion in other industries than cement production.

On the contrary co-combustion of tyres in cement rotary kilns has a series of beneficial conditions. a) It does not need TDF as feed material, but can use roughly shredded tyres. b) It takes place at very high temperatures and with long reaction times, so that all the combustible matter is burned. c) The inorganic matter is retained as raw material in the cement clinker. d) Acid gases are absorbed by the alkaline environment within the kiln. For these reasons cement kilns are more appropriate for tyre co-combustion than any other installation, even stand-alone incinerators. However there are also several minor limitations for widespread of tyre co-combustion in cement kilns. a) It has many opponents which argue its environmental impact. b) The recent Waste Incineration Directive regulates cement-kiln emissions as strictly as those of stand-alone incinerators; as a consequence some cement installations will have to stop burning tyres. c) There are other alternative co-fuels such as packing wastes, which have higher calorific values and are environmentally safer than tyres. In spite of these difficulties, co-combustion of tyres in cement-kilns is expected to increase in the next years.

GASIFICATION

Gasification is a process that converts carbonaceous matter into an energy-rich gas ("syngas"), which can be used as a fuel or as a petrochemical feedstock. The process involves partial oxidation of the feedstock in a reducing atmosphere, normally in the presence of steam, at high temperatures.

Gasification is not new, it has been in commercial use for many years as a process technology for the refining, chemical and power industries. Coal has been the feedstock mainly used along the years for gasification processes. Historically coal gasification has been used for town gas generation and also for the production of chemicals. Sasol plants in South Africa have been commercially producing transportation fuels and chemicals from coal for many years. According to the 1999 World Gasification Survey of the Gasification Technologies Council [5], Sasol plants accounted for over 31 % of total world gasification capacity at the end of 1999.

In the last years two tendencies are taking place in the development of gasification processes. On the one hand petroleum based materials such as residual oil, coke, tars, etc, are being used more and more as feedstock for gasification, nevertheless there is also some progress towards commercialising gasification of municipal solid waste (MSW) and of biomass, and attempts are being made to develop processes for other wastes such as tyres, automotive shredder residue (ASR), etc. On the other hand the last gasification processes developed are devoted to a greater extent to power generation than to the production of chemicals. In 1989 chemical production accounted for almost one-half of syngas use worldwide; from the 1990s most of the new gasification facilities are being devoted to power generation; it is expected a 3:1 power-to-chemicals syngas volume ratio starting from 2000 [5].

Gasification Process

It consists typically of three fundamental sections: the gasifier, the gas cleanup system and the energy and/or product recovery section. Tyres are fed into the reactor (gasifier) along with the gasification agent (a controlled and limited amount of oxygen, and steam in most of the cases). Typically gasifiers operate in a high temperature range (1200-2000 °C) [6,7], though there are also systems that work at lower temperatures. In the gasifier a thermal chemical conversion of the feedstock into a synthesis gas is produced. The main reactions that take place in the presence of steam in an oxygen starved atmosphere are presented below; carbon (C) comes from the rubbers and carbon black of tyres.

$$C + 1/2O_2 \rightarrow CO \qquad \text{(exothermic)}$$
$$C + O_2 \rightarrow CO_2 \qquad \text{(exothermic)}$$
$$H + O_2 \rightarrow H_2O \qquad \text{(exothermic)}$$
$$C + H_2O \rightarrow CO + H_2 \qquad \text{(endothermic)}$$
$$C + CO_2 \rightarrow 2CO \qquad \text{(endothermic)}$$
$$CO + H_2O \rightarrow CO_2 + H_2 \qquad \text{(exothermic)}$$
$$C + 2H_2 \rightarrow CH_4 \qquad \text{(exothermic)}$$
$$CO + 3H_2 \rightarrow CH_4 + H_2O \qquad \text{(exothermic)}$$
$$CO_2 + 4H_2 \rightarrow CH_4 + 2H_2O \qquad \text{(exothermic)}$$

The reducing atmosphere within the gasifier prevents the formation of oxidized species such as SO_x and NO_x. Instead sulphur and nitrogen in the feedstock are primarily converted to H_2S and NH_3. Depending on the feedstock, gasification agent and operating conditions used, the final gas composition varies, but as a general rule CO and H_2 are the major components which are accompanied by variable amounts of CO_2, H_2O, CH_4, H_2S, etc.

The types of gasifiers most widely used along the years for coal and petroleum residues have been fixed bed (or moving bed) gasifiers, fluidised bed gasifiers and entrained bed gasifiers. In fixed-bed systems the feedstock is loaded at the top of the gasifier and moves down through the bed counter-currently to the rising oxygen and steam which enter at the bottom, where the solid residue is also withdrawn. In fluidised bed gasifiers a bed of fine solids, typically silica sand, is maintained in a liquid-like state by the upward flowing gasification agent; the feedstock is introduced at the top and the O_2 + steam at the bottom, operating in counter-current mode. In entrained bed gasifiers the feedstock and the gasification agent enter the reactor in concurrent flow arrangement. In the last years many other novel and innovative gasification technologies are growing into demonstration an even commercialisation scales, specially for the gasification of municipal solid wastes (MSW) and of biomass. There are very interesting reviews of novel gasification and pyrolysis technologies for waste disposal such as that carried by Juniper [8] and that made by Malkow [6].

Two types of primary products leave a tyre gasifier. The solids, mainly composed of steel, which if possible should be recovered for sale, and the raw synthesis gas which is subjected to a series of cleanup operations in order to remove particulates, sulphur compounds, etc. If the objective of the process is energy recover, the clean syngas can be fed to either a combustion turbine (in a IGCC process), to a conventional steam turbine, or to appropriate engines. The integrated gasification combined cycle (IGCC) is the most efficient environmentally effective process. The combined cycle has two basic components: a high efficiency gas turbine, widely used in power generation today, which burns the clean syngas to produce electricity. Exhaust heat from the gas turbine is recovered to produce steam to power traditional high efficiency steam turbines. The net electrical efficiency of a single gasification steam turbine cycle and of a gasification/engine configuration are about 20-25%, while for an IGCC process can be as high as 40% [9]. The main limitation of IGCC is that the gas turbine requires extremely low levels of contaminants in the gas. Alternatively if the objective of the process is feedstock recycling the syngas can be processed using commercially available technologies to produce a wide range of products: fuels, chemicals, industrial gases, etc.

Possibilities and Limits of Tyre Gasification

At present there are few dedicated gasification processes being developed for treating scrap tyres. Gasification is more often used in conjunction with pyrolysis and or incineration. It is worth mentioning the Krupp Polysius Technology, which operates on a semi-commercial basis in Switzerland. Consuming 24000 tonnes of tyres each year [3]. It is not a stand-alone gasification system, but it is incorporated in a cement making process; it gasifies tyres, the syngas is burnt in the calcining section of the cement kiln and the solid is fed into the cement kiln where it is fused with the clinker.

The following barriers for the development of tyre gasification processes on a commercial scale can be mentioned. a) Since tyres are composed of stable heavy organic molecules, it is perceived that its conversion in a relatively clean syngas is very difficult. b) It could have high capital and operating costs. c) There is no proven commercially operating facility processing tyres at this time, so this technology is perceived as a risky enterprise.

On the other side, the main drivers for tyre gasification development are the following. a) Desire to avoid incineration. b) Ban to tyre landfilling. c) Desire to use green solutions. d) It is a more publicly acceptable alternative than incineration. e) Gasification is giving good results with coal and with petroleum residues. In view of these facts gasification can be considered as a potentially thermal treatment alternative for tyres.

A report presented in the Gasification Technologies Conference (San Francisco, 2003) [10] about the progress towards commercialising waste gasification worldwide indicated that the use of gasification processes for treating wastes (MSW, biomass, ASR) is at present very active in Japan, where there are various plants operating in a commercial scale (in the range of 10^5 ton/year); Nippon Steel technology is the most widely used. On the contrary progress towards commercialising gasification has slowed down outside Japan, although there are a few commercial scale plants in Europe, such as Thermoselect in Germany. The report also points out that in order to achieve a big market for waste gasification, Japanese processes must be adapted to be cost-effective and/or other local technology suppliers should demonstrate the feasibility of their technologies at scale. If progress is made in commercialising gasification of MSW or other wastes, a progress in tyre gasification may also be expected.

PYROLYSIS

Pyrolysis (also termed thermolysis) is a process in which carbonaceous matter is heated to moderate temperatures (450-700 °C) in the absence of oxygen. Consequently only thermal degradation of the organic matter takes place and, unlike gasification, no oxidation reactions occur. The high molecular weight polymeric rubbers are decomposed yielding a wide range of lower molecular weight products, which include both liquids, usually termed oils, and gaseous products. The stable carbon black likewise the steel cords, do not decompose or react during pyrolysis, so that they can be recovered almost unaltered.

Pyrolysis Process

The pyrolysis process is not new; it has been applied in the past to carbonaceous materials such as coal or wood, in order to obtain coke and charcoal respectively. In pyrolysis processes tyres are fed to the pyrolysis reactor, where an inert atmosphere is maintained. There are many different types of pyrolysis reactors including fixed bed reactors, fluidised bed reactors, vacuum units, rotary kilns, etc., and also non conventional techniques such as microwave systems, molten salt bath process (Pyrovac), etc. and ranging from pilot to laboratory scale plants.

Three type of products, solids, liquids and gases are obtained in pyrolysis processes, the ratios of which depend on the specific feedstock and operating conditions used (time, temperature, pressure, heating rate, etc.). The solids are mainly composed of the tyre steel cords and carbon black; the latter is usually termed char or pyrolytic carbon black. Steel and char can be easily separated by vibrating and sieving operations. Possible markets for pyrolytic char are carbon black, activated carbon, pigments, component for asphalt fabric, etc. Liquids, which are fuel like complex mixtures of organic products, can be used as chemical feedstock to recover valuable pure products or valuable fuels (petrol, diesel oil, etc.). Gases are mainly composed of hydrocarbons together with small quantities of CO, CO_2, SH_2, etc. It has a gross calorific value and can be used to recover heat or electricity for operation and/or for sport. Pyrolysis is claimed to be a very attractive process for tyre recycling since all the components of tyre may be recovered as theoretically marketable added value products, and therefore minimum residues requiring disposal are generated.

An Example of the Characteristics of Tyre Pyrolysis Products

There is a lot of published information about tyre pyrolysis products. In this section a summary of the characteristics of the products obtained in laboratory scale experiences carried out by the authors, is presented. The experiments were carried out in a 3.5 dm^3 fixed bed autoclave, under nitrogen, at temperatures from 300 to 700 °C, for 30 minutes, with cross-section samples (2-3 cm wide) of a whole car tyre. No influence of temperature in the characteristics of tyre products was observed over 500 °C. *Tyre derived liquids* were a complex mixture of C_6-C_{24} organic compounds, with a lot of aromatics (53.4-74.8%), some nitrogenated (2.47-3.5%) and some oxygenated compounds (2.29-4.85%). Their GCV (42 MJ Kg^{-1}) was even higher than those specified for commercial heating oils, but sulphur contents (1-1.4%) were near or slightly over the law limit value. Significant quantities of valuable light hydrocarbons such as benzene, toluene, xylene, limonene, etc. were obtained, and also an important proportion of polycyclic aromatics such as naphthalenes, phenanthrenes, fluorenes, diphenlys, etc. Distillation data of the 500 ºC oils showed that ≈20% have the boiling range of light naphtha (<160 ºC), ≈10% of heavy naphtha (160-204 ºC) and ≈35% of middle distillate (204-350 ºC). As far as distillation data are concerned, the tyre oil fractions with the same boiling range as commercial automotive diesel oils and heating diesel oils fulfil the present specifications of such commercial products. *Pyrolysis gases* were composed of hydrocarbons of which C_1-C_5 were the predominant (~75 vol.%), together with some CO, CO_2 and SH_2; they had very high gross calorific values (68-84 MJ m^3). *Tyre pyrolysis solids* had equal dimensions as the original tyre portion, and were easily disintegrable into black powder and steel cords. The black powder had surface areas comparable to those of commercial carbon blacks, but it had a great proportion of ash and impurities (~12 wt.%), which came from the inorganic fillers contained in the original tyre rubber; it may have a potential use as semi-reinforcing or non-reinforcing carbon black. A more detailed description of tyre pyrolysis products has been presented elsewhere [11,12].

Possibilities and Limits of Tyre Pyrolysis

At present there is a great promotion of pyrolysis processes for recycling scrap tyres. A detailed research carried out by Juniper [3] identified more than 40 companies worldwide that offer technologies for tyre pyrolysis. More than the half have been specifically designed for this purpose, while others have been designed for other waste streams, but are promoted of being capable of treating also tyres. However currently there is only one dedicated tyre pyrolysis plant in Europe operating on a semi-commercial basis [3]. It is located in the UK, owned by Anglo United Environmental (AUE) and handles 1500 tonnes/year. There have been other semi-commercial plants that have operated in UK, Germany, South Corea, Taiwan, etc., with limited success for longer or shorter periods, but most of them have ceased operation, reportedly due to financial issues.

The main barriers for the development of tyre pyrolysis processes on a commercial scale are the following. a) Markets for pyrolytic char are at present not sound; its application as virgin carbon black is very much restricted since it contains a lot of impurities (≈10%) and therefore can only be used as low quality grade carbon black. Similarly the use of char as activated carbon requires upgrading techniques to increase the specific area, and this results uneconomic. b) Tyre pyrolysis oils can theoretically be used as a chemical feedstock to recover valuable chemicals. However tyre oils are such a complex mixture of organics that the separation of compounds as pure products is not easy. In fact today most projects assume the oil will be combusted to produce energy [13], either in the plant or in other facilities to which it is sold. c) Scrap steel recovered from tyre pyrolysis is usually tangled, which make it costly to handle and transport, and is often contaminated with carbon and thus it is undesirable for many metal re-processors. So to summarize at present there are no secure markets for char, steel and oils at attractive prices and this is essential for the economic feasibility of the process.

The main advantages of tyre pyrolysis as compared with gasification are the following. a) Pyrolysis is carried at lower temperatures than gasification. b) If one of the objectives of the process is petrochemical feedstock, tyre pyrolysis is a more direct route to obtain chemicals from tyres than gasification + further synthesis. c) Theoretically marketable value added products are obtained in tyre pyrolysis, although at present gasification products can be more easily handled and used. In comparison with incineration the main drivers fur the commercial development of tyre pyrolysis are equivalent to those previously mentioned for tyre gasification, such as negative image of incineration, perception of new processes as greener solutions, bans on landfilling tyres, etc. Consequently it can be expected that pyrolysis likewise gasification will play an increasingly important role in tyre disposal as an alternative to co-combustion and incineration.

CONCLUSIONS

Chemical recycling processes are at present a potential alternative for treating scrap tyres. Co-combustion of tyres in cement kilns is today the process most used and the one which is expected to grow more in the near future. Stand-alone incineration has achieved for the moment less success with tyres than with other wastes; it faces a strong public opposition and requires improved technologies with higher efficiencies and improved environmental performance. Gasification and pyrolysis are the more innovative chemical recycling processes. They are at present being proved on a commercial scale for other wastes (MSW, biomass). There are many different technologies available at present in the market for tyre pyrolysis and gasification, specially for pyrolysis, and the suppliers claim they are promising. However their technical and economical feasibility on a commercial scale has not yet been fully demonstrated. If more stringent regulatory measures are implemented and sound markets are found for pyrolysis/gasification tyre products, progress towards commercialising these technologies may be expected. However the key factor is the successful extended operation of reference actually operating waste treating facilities over the next few years.

REFERENCES

1. SHULMAN, V.L. The recycling in the EU member states. In: Club Español de los Residuos (Ed.), Gestión europea de residuos especiales: vehículos fuera de uso, aceites usados y neumáticos. 2000

2. GOIKOETXEA, G. Reciclaje de neumáticos: la visión de los fabricantes. RECCON´03 Int. Conf. on Recycling Information Exchange and Industrial Practices. Bilbao-Spain. Nov. 2003

3. ARCHER, E., KLEIN, A. WHITING, K. The scrap tyre dilemma. Can technology offer commercial solutions? Waste Management World Magazine. Jan.-Febr. 2004

4. BONTOUX, L. The incineration of waste in Europe. Report prepared by the Institute for Prospective Technological Studies for the European Commission. March 1999

5. Gasification a growing worldwide industry. http://www.gasification.org/worldwide/worldwid.html. 2004

6. MALKOW, T. Novel and innovative pyrolysis and gasification technologies for energy efficient and environmentally sound MSW disposal. Waste Management, 2004, 24, 53-79

7. ORR D., MAXWELL, D. A comparison of gasification and incineration of hazardous wastes. U.S.Department of Energy Report. 2000

8. JUNIPER. Pyrolysis & gasification of waste. Worldwide technology & business review. Juniper Consultancy Services Ltd. 2000

9. BELGIORNO, V., DE FEO, G., DELLA ROCCA, C., NAPOLI, R.M.A.. Energy from gasification of solid wastes. Waste Manegement 2003, 23, 1-15

10. SCHWAGER, J., WHITING, K. Progress towards commercialising waste gasification. Gasification Technologies Conference. San Francisco. October, 2003.

11. DE MARCO, et al. Pyrolysis of scrap tyres . Fuel Processing Technology, 2001, 72, 9-22

12. LARESGOITI et al. Characterization of the liquid products obtained in tyre pyrolysis. Journal of Analytical and Applied Pyrolysis, 2004, 71/2, 17-934.

13. SCRAP TIRE NEWS ON-LINE. Is pyrolysis of scrap tires poised for widespread acceptance?. http://scraptirenews.com.

TYRES IN COASTAL AND FLOOD DEFENCE ENGINEERING – ENVIRONMENTAL MONITORING

K J Collins

D Howell

N Fisher

University of Southampton

United Kingdom

ABSTRACT. Recycled tyre products can offer a number of positive engineering advantages such as stability or lightness, which are discussed for coastal and flood defence engineering applications. There is concern that the mass use of tyres in construction projects may lead to environmental impacts arising from compounds leaching from the tyres. Provided that the tyres are in a stable environment (buried underground or below seawater), away form the degrading effects of sunlight (ultraviolet radiation) they are unlikely to degrade over many decades. Leaching by seawater or fresh water from tyres appears to be from the outer surface only, which declines with exposure.

Detailed monitoring of the Pevensey beach tyre bale trial has demonstrated that levels of zinc leachates in beach interstitial water are below EQS levels and are declining with time. It has proved possible to model the levels of zinc observed within the tyre bales. No evidence of cadmium contamination has been found even within the tyre bales.

A road runoff equivalent to an engineering project utilising tyres is proposed to help visualize the magnitude of likely environmental impacts. There needs to be an element of environmental monitoring built into tyre-based construction projects to build a database and models of actual impacts to help inform decision makers.

Keywords: Tyres, Coastal engineering, Environmental impact, Leaching, Zinc, Cadmium, Modeling, Road run-off

Dr K.J. Collins is a senior research fellow in the School of Ocean and Earth Science, University of Southampton. His research interests include the environmental impact evaluation of re-using waste materials for marine construction projects such as artificial reefs for fishery enhancement or coastal protection.

D. Howell has recently completed his Oceanography MSc studies in the School of Ocean and Earth Science, University of Southampton.

N. Fisher is completing his Oceanography BSc studies in the School of Ocean and Earth Science, University of Southampton.

INTRODUCTION

The European supply of waste tyres and legislative drivers requiring increased recycling of tyres, are dealt with elsewhere in this publication and have summarized by many authors [1], [2], [3]. The disposal (or gate) fee paid to recyclers is a strong economic incentive to find applications. The use of tyres as construction material simply because of low cost is not sufficient justification. There needs to be selection of appropriate material with specific advantages. Applications considered at the 2004 ETRA (European Tyre Recycling Association) conference [2] include:

- Impact and vibration absorbance - sports surfaces, roads, noise barriers
- Lightweight - embankments, landfill, backfill
- Insulation - foundations in cold climates
- Durability and shape - artificial reefs

These have been detailed in a set of standards, CWA14243, for a wide range of recycled tyre products [4]. Civil engineering applications of tyres have been recently reviewed by Viridis (www.viridis.co.uk) [3]. A current UK project "Sustainable re-use of tyres in port, coastal and river e ngineering" (www.tyresinwater.net) i s s pecifically examining a pplications t o c oastal construction, protection and flood defence [5].

Figure. 1 Lorry tyre unit for beach protection, prior to deployment off Odessa, Ukraine, courtesy of Prof. B. Alexandrov.

The durability and complex open shape of tyres is a distinct advantage in constructing artificial reefs for fishery enhancement [6], [7] and has been exploited in structures for attenuating wave energy deployed parallel to the coast, as illustrated in Figure 1. The large void space can be a disadvantage in sub-surface applications, but compression to form bales has produced a useful and easily handled product. One US company, Encore (www.tyrebaler.com) has exported plant to the UK, in which typically 100 car tyres are compressed to form a rectangular block 1.5 x 1.25 x 0.75m. Three hundred of these bales were deployed in November 2002 as a pilot project at Pevensey, East Sussex [5], on a shingle beach managed by Pevensey Coastal Defence PPP [8]. These were buried within the beach

(Figures 2 and 3) as a material replacement releasing shingle for strengthening beach, which would otherwise have come from offshore dredging.

Figure 2. Tyre bale block during installation at Pevensey, East Sussex. Note the vertical pipes which mark the wells for sampling interstitial beach water.

A more extensive project (completed May 2004) using these bales has extended the width of a 1500m stretch of river embankment on the River Witham (www.river-witham.co.uk/site23.html). The relatively light weight of the bales is an advantage on soft, peat ground plus the block shape enabled a steeper slope than with clay giving a smaller footprint [5].

ENVIRONMENTAL IMPACT

The EU 6th Environmental Action Plan Article 8(2)iii requires "environmentally sound recycling". DEFRA Guidance on the role of flood and coastal defence in nature conservation in England (1999) High Level Target 9A states that "Flood and coastal defence work should avoid environmental damage and ensure that there is no net detriment to Biodiversity Action Plan habitat". Tyre applications in close proximity to salt or fresh water require special consideration of the likely leachates from tyres, mainly zinc and to a lesser extent organic compounds such as benzothiazoles [6], [7]. In 1998 a small experimental tyre artificial reef was deployed in Poole Bay, Dorset specifically to study the colonization by marine organisms and look for evidence of uptake of tyre compounds by the plants and animals growing on the tyres. When compared to organisms growing on concrete control units and natural substrata No significant differences in growth or bioaccumulation were detected [9]. This was not surprising as these studies have demonstrated that leaching in seawater is limited to the outer 10μm, so that whilst a car tyre may contain up to 200g of zinc, only some 10-20mg is likely to be lost

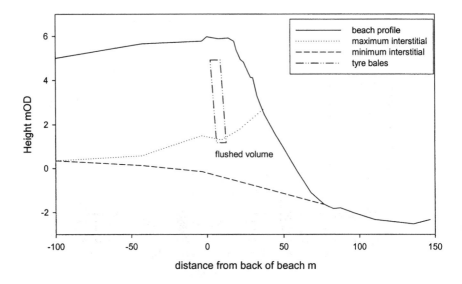

Figure 3. High and low water levels within the Pevensey beach 9.3.04

Pevensey Monitoring

A grid of wells were sunk within the beach at Pevensey, within the tyre bales, 10m seaward and 10m landward of the bales to allow sampling of interstitial beach water. Similarly a line of reference wells were sunk 50m to the west for comparative data. The base of the bale block is at the level of neap high water, but given the distance from the sea and low permeability of the mixed beach material only the highest spring tides each month raise the water table sufficiently to wet the lower tyres. Sampling has been undertaken on the highest tide each month since December 2002, measuring the height of water within the wells, salinity and retaining sub-samples acidified with concentrated nitric acid for heavy metal analysis. Levels of zinc, cadmium and copper were determined using flame AAS, details are given in previous papers [10], [7].

Cadmium and copper were not found in significant EQS levels at any point within the beach, even within the tyre bales. The maxiumum EQS level (500µg l^{-1} = 0.5ppm) [11] for zinc is exceeded within the tyre bales only on the highest spring tides but never attained some 10m from the tyre bales within the beach. This is diluted further before reaching the sea the earliest point at which living organisms can come into contact with the leachate. There is a general trend in falling levels of leachate winter to summer and from year to year.

The volume of water entering and leaving a 1m wide section of the beach during tidal cycle (9.3.04, Fig.3) was approximately 35m3, assuming a void volume of 15%. At the height of this tide the tyre bales were submerged to a depth of 10cm representing a leachate volume of 0.3 m3 within the tyre bales (50% void space). Thus the tyre leachates are diluted 120 times before entering the sea.

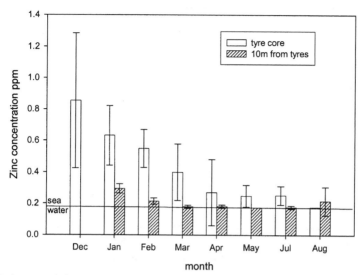

Figure 4. Average (+/- one standard deviation) zinc concentrations, (corrected for salinity) in tyre core wells and wells 10m seaward and landward of the tyre block (December 2002 – August 2003).

A laboratory study was made to examine leaching rates from 1cm diameter tyre plugs undergoing constant and periodic immersion in seawater and rainwater. Zinc leaching rates were comparable with other studies. Cadmium was not detected within the sensitivity of the analyses.

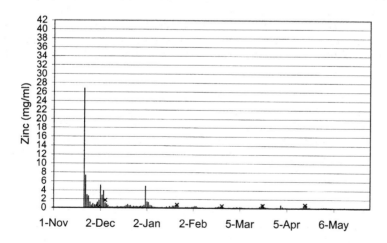

Figure 5. Modelled peak zinc concentrations within the tyre bales showing monthly spring tide peaks and decline with time.

To fully understand the processes occurring within the tyre bale block and beach, a model was constructed [12] to predict the apparent volume of water passing through the tyre bale installation at 15 minute intervals. By knowing the effective void volume (of the tyre bales one can then calculate the actual volume of water flushing the beach and the volume of tyres in contact with water. A relationship was found between the NTFSL tidal data and the data from tyre core block, seaward and landward wells, by constructing an Microsoft Excel model that related time, National Tidal Facility for Sea Level (NTFSL) tidal height and well height.

The rate of leaching per m^2 of tyre surface was calculated from laboratory data, and the area in contact with seawater was modelled at 15 minute intervals. The initial model model was rewritten so that every $100m^2$ of tyres had their own leaching rate ($100m^2$ equates to 91 tyres or 0.01m depth of the tyre bale block).

The model (average and standard deviation) gave closed agreement to observed peak zinc levels (ppm):

	MODELLED	OBSERVED
5 December	1.17 ($^+$.0.48)	1.71
22 January	0.65 ($^+$.0.23)	0.75
21 February	0.31 ($^+$.0.11)	0.5
20 March	1.12 ($^+$.0.41)	0.62
17 April	0.78 ($^+$.0.34)	0.75

Fenner and Clark [13] acknowledge that whilst zinc is the major heavy metal present in tyres and tyre leachates, the lower levels of cadmium present may determine if tyres are acceptable in an aqueous environment. The Environment Agency's maximum environmental quality standards (EQSs) for water are much lower for cadmium ($5\mu g\ l^{-1}$) than zinc ($500\mu g\ l^{-1}$). No evidence of cadmium contamination of interstitial water samples from Pevensey (Dec.02-Aug.03) using the direct AAS method with a detection limit of $1.5\mu g\ l^{-1}$. A more sensitive analytical procedure was employed in Autumn 2003, using a chelating resin and solvent extraction to concentrate the metals in the beach samples reducing the detection limit by an order of magnitude. No evidence of cadmium contamination was found, even in the samples from within the tyre bales.

Comparison with Road Run-off

During the road use of a tyre it abrades leaving a trail of fine rubber dust (<100um, [14]) which exposes a large surface area and is likely to leach all its soluble components when washed away by rainfall into local water courses, groundwater and ultimately the sea. Tyre compounds derived from road run-off have been detected in coastal sediments off California ([15]; [16]) and northern Wales [7]. Road runoff is not simply the product of tyre wear, there are breakdown products from brakes, lubricants and fuel combustion ([17]; [18]; [19]; [20]; [14]).

Estimates above have shown that a whole tyre, when immersed, will leach in the order of 10-20mg zinc. During the courses of use an average car tyre will loose some 1.5kg through tread wear as dust which will potentially leach 2% of its mass as zinc, i.e. 30g zinc, thus in use the environmental impact is 300 times greater than post use as a whole in a construction project. Thus it would be possible to estimate the environmental impact of a tyre construction project in terms of an equivalent road length.

The Environment Agency's report [21, Appendix 5] on tyres in the environment, calculates the average road loss of tyre rubber from cars alone to be 144g/m/yr (= 3g zinc/m/yr). At Pevensey some 35,000 bales have been used which are likely to produce 700g zinc leachate (20mg/tyre), equivalent to a typical small boat sacrificial zinc anode, which is replaced annually. Tyres buried away from the degrading effects of sunlight and abrasion are likely to be very stable and unlikely to breakdown, so a conservative estimate of this release would be over 20 years, i.e. 35g zinc/yr, equivalent to 12m of average road car tyre wear. This is an overestimate because the road impact does not include lorries or the effects of other pollutants.

CONCLUSIONS

Recycled tyre products can offer a number of positive engineering advantages such as stability or lightness. There is concern that the mass use of tyres in construction projects may lead to environmental impacts arising from compounds leaching from the tyres. Provided that the tyres are in a stable environment (buried underground or below seawater), away form the degrading effects of sunlight (ultraviolet radiation) they are unlikely to degrade over many decades. Leaching by seawater or fresh water from tyres appears to be from the outer surface only, which declines with exposure. Detailed monitoring of the Pevensey beach tyre bale trial has demonstrated that levels of zinc leachates in beach interstitial water are below EQS levels and are declining with time. It has proved possible to model the levels of zinc observed within the tyre bales. No evidence of cadmium contamination has been found even within the tyre bales.

The r oad-run o ff equivalent t o a n e ngineering p roject u tilising t yres h as b een p roposed t o help visualize the magnitude of likely environmental impacts. There needs to be an element of environmental monitoring built into tyre-based construction projects to build a database and models of actual impacts to help inform decision makers.

ACKNOWLEDGEMENTS

This work was supported in part by the Department of the Environment Transport and the Regions Partners in Innovation Contract reference CI 39/3/714 cc2428 "Sustainable re-use of tyres in port coastal and river engineering" with considerable practical support from Pevensey Coastal Defence Ltd.

REFERENCES

1.   Schulman, V., The status of post consumer tyres in the European Union. 2003, Viridis, TRL Ltd, Crowthorne. p. 35.

2.   ETRA. 11th ETRA European Conference. in Tyre Recycling - a European industry. 2004. Brussels: European Tyre Recycling Association.

3.   Hylands, K.N. and V. Schulman, Civil engineering applications of tyres. 2003, Viridis, TRL Ltd, Crowthorne. p. 85.

4.   CEN, CWA (14243-2002) Inovative material, products and applications from post-consumer tyres. 2002, European Centre for Standardisation.

5.   Simm, J.D., et al., Sustainable re-use of materials in coastal and river engineering. Engineering Sustainability, Proceedings of the Institute of Civil Engineers, 2004(Sept. 04): in press.

6.   Collins, K.J., A.C. Jensen, and S. Albert, A review of waste tyre utilisation in the marine environment. Chem. Ecol., 1995. 10(3-4): p. 205-216.

7.   Collins, K.J., et al., Scrap tyres for marine construction: environmental impact., in Recycling and Reuse of Used Tyres Symposium, R.K. Dhir, M.C. Limbachiya, and K.A. Paine, Editors. 2001, Thomas Telford: Dundee, Scotland. p. 149-162.

8.   Hardacre, G. and F. Chester. Pevesey Bay sea defences P.P.P. - the contractors perspective. in 36th DEFRA Conference of River and Coastal Engineering. 2001. Keele University: DEFRA.

9.   Collins, K.J., et al., Environmental impact assessment of a scrap tyre artificial reef. ICES Journal of Marine Science, 2002. 59: p. S243-S249.

10.   Collins, K.J. and A.C. Jensen, Stabilized coal ash artificial reef studies. Chemistry and Ecology, 1995. 10(3/4): p. 193-203.

11.   EA, Environmental Quality Standards (EQS) for hardness related List 2 dangerous substances, EC Dangerous Substances Directive (76/464/EEC). 2002.

12.   Howell, D.J., Environmental impact assessment of tyres in coastal defence., in School of Ocean and Earth Science. 2003, University of Southampton. p. 58.

13.   Fenner, R.A. and K. Clark, Environmental and structural implications for the re-use of tyres in fluvial and marine construction projects. Water and Environmental Management Journal, 2003. 17(2): p. 99-105.

14.   Drapper, D., R. Tomlinson, and P. Williams, Pollutant concentrations in road runoff : Southeast Queensland case study. Journal of environmental engineering, 2000. 126(4): p. 313-320.

15.   Spies, R.B., B.D. Andresen, and D.W. Rice, Benzothiazoles in estuarine sediments as indicators of street runoff. Nature, 1987. 327(6124): p. 697-699.

16.   Schiff, K. and S. Bay, Impacts of stormwater discharges on the nearshore benthic environment of Santa Monica Bay. Marine Environmental Research, 2003. 56: p. 225-243.

17.   Robotham, P.W.J., R.A. Gill, and K.M. Evans, Source, composition and flux of polycyclic aromatic hydrocarbons in sediments of the River Derwent, Derbyshire, U.K. Water, Air and Soil Pollution, 1990. 51(1): p. 1-12.

18.   Boxall, A.B.A. and L. Maltby, Characterization and toxicity of sediment contaminated with road runoff. Water Res, 1995. 29(9): p. 2043-2050.

19.   Maltby, L., et al., The Effects of Motorway Runoff on Fresh-Water Ecosystems .1. Field-Study. Environmental Toxicology and Chemistry, 1995. 14(6): p. 1079-1092.

20.   Osterkamp, S., U. Lorenz, and M. Schirmer, Constructed wetlands for treatment of polluted road runoff. Limnologica, 1999. 29(1): p. 93-102.

21.   EA, Tyres in the Environment. 1998, Environment Agency: Bristol.

ENERGY RECOVERY FROM USED TYRES
IN
THE EUROPEAN CEMENT INDUSTRY

C Loréa

W van Lo

CEMBUREAU- The European Cement Association

Belgium

ABSTRACT. Used tyres, classified as non-hazardous material, are used as an alternative fuel in cement kilns. More than 550 kt of whole and shredded tyres save, each year in the European countries, the same amount of fossil fuels equivalent to high quality coal. The potential impacts from the open-air burning and landfilling from residual ashes or landfilling of whole tyres are thereby avoided. Tyres are introduced at different points of the process depending on the type of kiln. The iron content of tyres are dealt with by modifying the raw meal composition and the substitution rate. In this process, high calorific value of tyres, provided by natural and synthetic rubbers, is recovered without any significant impact on air emissions. The chemical elements in the ash are incorporated in the mineral structures and have no negative impact on clinker quality.

Keywords: Cement production, Raw materials and fuels, Used tyre substitution, Process, Environment, Health and safety

C. Loréa is Technical Consultant in CEMBUREAU since January 2003. Before that she had a position in the Environmental Department of the Belgian cement company CBR, member of the HeidelbergCement Group. Her background is chemical engineering with specialisation in environmental issues.

Dr. W. van Loo is Technical Director of CEMBUREAU since September 2002. His professional background is solid state chemistry and physics. He has had almost 30 years of experience in the cement industry in various positions in ENCI, member of the HeidelbergCement Group.

INTRODUCTION

Cement is a finely ground mineral powder, which when mixed with water forms a paste that sets and hardens. After hardening, it retains its strength and stability, even under water. This hydraulic hardening is primarily due to the formation of calcium silicate hydrates, which is the result of the reaction between water and the constituents of cement.

Cement production inherently consumes large amounts of raw materials and energy. For example, a dry process cement plant needs roughly 1 600 000 t raw materials and 150 000 t fuels (equivalent high quality coal) to produce 1Mt of Portland cement clinker per year. For example, In the EU 25, and Switzerland, Norway and Candidate countries (Bulgaria, Romania and Turkey), 375 Mt of raw materials and 30 Mt fuels are consumed for 267 Mt of cement production in 2002.

The European Cement Industry has been increasingly replacing, for many years, these non-renewable resources with alternative raw materials and fuels. Different type of alternative raw materials and fuels can be introduced at various stages in the process, and recovered in clinker and in cement production processes. These are important levers for the cement industry in saving natural resources, and in reducing the environmental impact of quarrying and process emissions.

Tyres are also introduced as alternative fuel in the clinker production to recover its thermal energy. This is recognised as an environmentally sound and neutral solution compared to landfill option (1,2). Landfill, being the less attractive option mainly due to the long-term leaching of metals resulting in a relatively high ecotoxicity score (2), is suggested only when other solutions like material recycling or energy recovery cannot be applied (1). In addition, open-air uncontrolled (sometimes incomplete) burning can release potentially hazardous levels of carbon monoxide, mono- and polycyclic aromatic hydrocarbons in the smoke plume, causing damages to flora and fauna (1). For that reason, the European Union adopted within the frame of Directive (1999/31/EC) a general ban of the landfill of whole tyres from 2003 and shredded tyres by 2006.

This paper, describes briefly the cement production and the different aspects of the use of tyres as alternative fuels on the basis of experiences in the European Cement Industry.

CEMENT PRODUCTION

Manufacturing Process

Cement clinker is produced in rotary kilns mainly with dry process, which consumes considerably less thermal energy than wet processes. During the production process, which can be divided in a number of sub-processes, the natural mineral resources are mineralogically transformed into clinker by using energy from fossil fuels and than into different cements. These sub-processes are: Extraction of Raw Materials (Blasting or excavation, loading and transport), Preparation of Raw Materials (Crushing, storage, blending and grinding), Mineralogical Transformation or Kiln Operations (Fuel storage and preparation & Clinker burning, cooling and storage, and Preparation of Cement (Blending, grinding and storage & Packing and dispatch)

The mineralogical transformation or clinker production process in the rotary kilns, which consumes the main portion of energy used, begins with the thermal decomposition of calcium carbonate ($CaCO_3$) at about 900°C and liberates carbon dioxide (CO_2). In the clinkering phase at high temperature (typically 1400-1500°C), the calcium oxide reacts with silica, alumina, and iron oxide to form calcium silicates, aluminates and ferrites being the clinker minerals. The clinker is then ground together with calcium sulphate and other additives to produce different cement types.

Natural Raw Materials and Fossil Fuels

Ordinary Portland cement clinker is produced from a mixture of natural minerals like limestone/chalk and clay/shale, which supply the main chemical components of clinker minerals (calcium, silicon, aluminium and iron oxides).

Clinker production is located close to, or even integrated with, the mineral extraction site. In order to reduce the environmental impact of transport in a cost-effective way, cement plants are frequently situated close to carbonate rock, which makes up more than 80% of raw materials used in the raw mix. Large deposits of these industrial minerals are commonly found in Europe. Their access and extraction are becoming more and more difficult because of environmental constraints, which result from the lack of land management balancing the sustainable industrial and urban developments in the past.

Various fossil fuels can be used to provide the thermal energy required in the manufacturing process. The main fossil fuels used in cement kiln firing are pulverised coal (black coal and lignite), petcoke, fuel oil and natural gas. Cost normally precludes the use of natural gas or oil, but the selection of fuels depends entirely on the local situation (3).

Alternative Raw Materials and Fuels

Different type of alternative raw materials can be in introduced in various ways and recycled in the clinker and cement production sub-processes. For example in 2001, ~12 % of alternative materials have been used essentially in cement production, and 35 Mt of natural mineral resources saved.

Fly ash, slag and various mineral wastes, which contain the cement main constituents (CaO, Al_2O_3, SiO_2, Fe_2O_3, SO_3), can be recycled in the clinker production. Organic free mineral wastes can be added in the raw meal preparation (used catalysts, pyrites, bauxites...). Mineral wastes, contaminated with organics, are introduced through the solid fuel handling, directly to the burning and/or the calcining zone (contaminated soils, sewage sludge's dredging sludge's, filtration earths, diatomee earths, paper and deinking sludge's, filter cakes.)

Cementitious natural materials and industrial by-products (limestone, pozzolana, fly ash, blast-furnace slag, silica fume, burnt shale) can be ground with clinker to produce different cements according to the European Standard EN-197, which is implemented in the Member States as of April 2002. In the mineralogical transformation or clinker production processes, a part of the fossil fuel can be substituted with alternative fuels, recovered from different selected waste streams. Alternative fuels are frequently prepared and blended outside the cement plant by specialised companies in facilities specially designed for this purpose. Cement plants provide the storage and feeding systems.

The conditions in the kiln system, like high temperatures (>1200°C), long residence times, high thermal inertia and alkaline environment, create considerable potential for destruction of organic substances, and makes a wide variety of less expensive fuel options possible. Used tyres, refused oil, solvents, plastics, paper and sewage sludge, animal meal and impregnated saw dust are the main alternative fuels presently used by the European Cement Industry. In 2001, 12% alternative fuels replaced the traditional fossil fuels, which is equivalent to 3.3 Mt of coal.

This substitution, regulated within the framework the Waste Incineration Directive (2000/76/EC), is also an important lever for sustainable waste management. In addition to the thermal energy, material content of alternative fuels is also recovered in this process. For example, in the case of used tyres, the rubber is completely consumed as fuel, and the remaining chemical elements from steel reinforcement like iron and zinc are incorporated in the structure of clinker minerals.

TYRES AS ALTERNATIVE FUELS

Every year in Europe, about 200 million units or 2,6 Mt or of used tyres are generated, and 2Mt end-of-life tyres have to be managed for recycling and recovery (4). A portion of whole or shredded tyres is used as alternative fuels substituting traditional fossil fuels in cement kilns.

According to available statistical data from the EU, the amount of tyres used in cement kilns for energy recovery was 410 kt in 1997 or ~16% of the total used tyres. As a result of a continuos increase, since 2001, more than 550 kt whole and shredded tyres (~23%) replace each year equal amount of high quality coal. Further increase would occur by 2006 with the full implementation of the directives regulating the landfill (1999/31/EC) and the end-of-life vehicles (2000/53/EC).

This application, experienced by the European Cement Industry for many years, saves the non-renewable fossil fuels and contributes to the sustainable waste management by consuming all the components of the tyre. In general, the decision to use whole or shredded tyres depends of several factors, including the type of kiln, process constraints, market issues, pricing, storage area available in the plant etc.

The general properties of used tyres, and the technical, environmental, health and safety aspects of their usage as alternative fuel, compiled from the experiences of the Cement Industry, are given below.

General Properties of Tyres

Automotive tyres are manufactured using following raw materials (5,6): Rubber (45-48%), carbon black (22%), Iron (15-25%), textiles (0-5%), additives facilitating compounding and vulcanisation (5-8%), zinc oxide (1-2%) and sulphur (1%).

The tyres have, worldwide, the same inherent characteristics like chemical and physical resistances, non-biodegradability, non-toxicity, weight, shape, elasticity etc. Many of themes, which are beneficial during their service life, can create problems in their post-consumer life management such as collection, storage and disposal (6).

Tyre is classified as non-hazardous waste by the Basel Convention, and is not present in any list of dangerous materials under the EU legislation. Its net calorific value is the same as coal (Table 1) and approximately equivalent to 0.7 tons of fuel oil. The variations in the calorific value and ash content are usually associated to the percentage of steel in the tyres. Moisture may also vary depending on storage conditions.

Table 1. Some characteristics of tyre derived fuel and coal (data taken from 6)

PARAMETERS	USED TYRE	COAL
Energy content (MJ/t)	25–30	25-30
Moisture (%)	3-5	5-20
Ash (%)	15 – 20	10-15
Carbon (%)	60-70	
Sulphur (%)	1 – 2	0.3-2
Nitrogen %	0.3-0.5	
Chlorine (%)	0.2	
Bulk density (kg/m3)	300-600	300-500

Process Aspect

Used tyres can be delivered from the collection centres by trailer trucks, and be partly stored in the cement plants. Baling the whole tires is an efficient solution for transport costs and storage area reduction but requires the supplier to get equipped with a baling press. The storage of large quantities of whole tyres can be a problem due to the high need of space, whereas tyre chips have a higher bulk density, hence require smaller storage place.

Whole or shredded tyres are handled by semi-manual or fully automated systems. The plants, equipped several kiln lines can have a common handling system to discharge, store and extract the tyres from the storage place. Nevertheless, the weighting and feeding systems need to be independent for each kiln. In order to avoid the risk of plugging caused by the iron wires the size reducing and special feeding devices like flap valves may be needed.

As the chemical composition of tyres is relatively homogeneous, quality controls are performed mainly on the basis of size. The whole tyres are controlled to avoid non-conformities, which can damage the handling systems or stick to the flap when entering into the kiln. The size of chipped tyres is controlled to minimise risks of agglomeration and to assure a good combustion. The chips can be as small as 4 centimetres or much bigger up to a 1/16 of whole tyres.

Depending on the type of kiln system, tyres can be introduced in various ways: Into the mid-kiln in long kilns, onto the Lepol grate in case of semi-dry or semi-wet process, at the back-end or riser duct of the pre-heater or into the pre-calciner or as chips via the main burner (see 7 for details). The introduction point should assure the complete burning of tyres. In some cases blasters must be installed to get rid of build-ups generated by sulphur and chlorine volatilisation.

From the process point of view, their homogeneity, high calorific value and relatively low sulphur and chloride contents make tyres good alternative fuels for clinker production. Depending on the type o f kiln system, they may s ubstitute fossil fuels up to 25% without major problems related to clinker burning process and quality (8). In general, a good control of oxydising conditions and fuel feed rate regularity are the main operational parameters assuring the efficient combustion of tyres and the prevention of build-ups at kiln inlet. However, the following points should be taken into account in processing used tyres (7,8).

> When injecting chipped tyres at the front end of the kilns reducing conditions, that may have negative impacts on clinker quality, must be avoided.

> Due to their big size, the complete burning of whole tyres requires a relatively long residence time. This may produce local reducing conditions with a decrease in clinker quality and an increase of coating requiring a high frequency periodical cleanings.

> The whole tire burning can be a limiting factor for plants with high pyritic sulphur in the raw mix because of build-up problems, process fan limitation and trips in the electrostatic precipitator.

> At high substitution rates, the iron content of tyres can affect the Al/Fe ratio or clinker mineralogy. Consequently a correction of the raw mix chemistry is required.

> Due to its potential impacts on setting time requirements, the high zinc content in tyres can limit the substitution rate depending on the zinc content in raw mix.

> At high substitution rates (>20%), a net production loss may occur in preheater kilns.

Environmental Aspect

Potential environmental issues related to clinker production are emissions of CO2 CO, NOx, SOx, dust, volatile organic compounds and metals. These are related to decarbonation of limestone and/or fuel combustion. The emission ranges from cement kilns depend largely on the nature of raw materials, fuels, age and design of the plant, and also on the requirements laid down by the permitting authority. The details of this issue could be found in the referred documents (3).

Experience demonstrates that used tyres could substitute fossil fuels like coal or petcoke without any significant increase in emissions (Table 2), and that the good combustion practices and proper operation of effective emission control systems were essential to maintain the stack emissions in the same range compared to the use of fossil fuels. The main conclusions of these substitution experiences are can be summarised as following (7,8,9,10):

> No significant changes o ccur in the e missions of carbon dioxide, dust and   heavy metals.

> As a result of low nitrogen content of tyres and staged combustion effects as well, sizeable reduction in NOx emissions can be achieved in many cases.

> Special care is needed to maintain the complete burning condition required to avoid potential increases in volatile organic carbon and carbon monoxide emissions (associated with electrostatic trips).

Table 2. Emissions measured during tyre burning trial from a cement kiln in the UK (data taken from Ref [9])

POLLUTANT	FOSSIL FUELS (caol and coke)	FOSSIL FUELS and 15% TYRES
Particulates mg/m3	60	60
NOx mg/m3	1180	800
SOx mg/m3	500	500
CO mg/m3	985	948
Chlorine and fluorine mg/m3	1.13	1.0
VOC mg/m3	129	68
Dioxins ng/m3	0.12	0.03

Health and Safety Aspect

Although the tyres do not self-ignite special precautions should be taken when storing and handling tyres. They should be stored far enough from one another to prevent a potential fire from spreading and the heap size should be kept below safe regulated dimensions. Free flames, sparks and hot spots should be avoided in the storage area. The handling systems must be designed to enable fire control (temperature/fire detectors; cameras, automatic fire extinguishers and emergency procedure, etc). Due to the difficulty to extinguish tyres fires, a pile of sand should be added to the standard water-fire station.

Personal protective equipment such as helmet, safety shoes and spectacles is mandatory and leather gloves should be used when handle tyres and tyre chips handled manually.

In certain climatic conditions, particularly in tropical and subtropical regions, used tyre dumps and stockpiles can become the breeding ground for insects, such as mosquitoes, which are capable of transmitting diseases to humans (1). In order to avoid this health risks, the tyres should be stored in a closed place, for a short time, protected from rainfall or baled, so that little space is available for water to be trapped in the tyres.

CONCLUSIONS

Used tyres are good alternative fuels for cement kilns, and create benefits in saving fossil fuels, in providing environmentally sound solutions for waste tyre management, and in reducing the overall environmental impact of cement manufacturing.

When used at appropriate rates and conditions, used tyres do not raise any special problems in maintaining a stable clinker process. As the greater flexibility in the feeding systems may be deployed in different kilns, they are used without major influences on pollutant emissions and cement quality.

This application of waste tyres could increase in the EU25 in the coming years with the implementation of Directives regulating the used tyre management and end-of-life vehicles.

This will require a regional collection and transportation infrastructure to secure a consistent quantity of feedstock, and investment in cement plants in storage, handling and feeding systems. Measures to avoid uncontrolled burning (open-air or in systems without emission control), and development of analytical standards for natural and synthetic rubbers would also be needed.

REFERENCES

1. UNEP: Technical Guidelines on the identification and management of used tyres. Basel Convention Series No. 00/03,1999.

2. SPRIENSMA, R. et all. Life cycle analysis of an average European car tyre. PRé Consultant B.V., The Netherlands, 2001.

3. CALLEJA I. et al. Promoting environmental technologies: Sectoral analyses, barriers and measures. IPTS, The European Commission DG JRC, 2004, 311p.

4. BLIC. End-off-life tyres. 2004, http://www.blic.be/public/activitieseofltelts.htm

5. IVM. Tyre recycling in Europe: Open borders in the waste hierarchy. EPCEM report 1998.

6. SCHULMAN, V.L. Tyre recycling after 2000: Status and options. ETRA Publications, 2000.

7. ROSENHOJ, J. A. The cement kiln: the optimal solution for waste tyre burning. International Cement Review, May 1993, pp30-36.

8. SMITH, I. Co-utilisation of coal and other fuels in cement kilns. IEA Clean Coal Centre, United Kingdom, 2003, 63 p.

9. WOLFENDEN, L. Tyres in the environment. Report of the Environment Agency, the United Kingdom, 1998.

10. DAMES & MOORE. Analysis of emissions test results and residual by-products from facilities using tyres as a fuel supplement. California Integrated Waste Management Board, Report no IWM-C5064, 1997.

USE OF WASTE FROM RUBBER SHREDDING OPERATIONS FOR IMPROVING THE HYDRIC PERFORMANCES OF AERATED CLAYEY CONCRETE

N. Madjoudj

R M Dheilly

M. Quéneudec

Laboratoire des Technologies innovantes- UPJV

France

ABSTRACT. The manufacturing of rubber aggregates by means of shredding produces a dust, collected by aspiration, that constitutes a waste difficult to handle due to its smoothness and one that has no current reuse. In the present work, the central idea has been to introduce such dusts into a building material in order to improve technical performance as a result of the non-sorptive characteristic of the rubber particles. The studied case deals with an aerated concrete m ixed w ith c lay and cement a nd o btained b y p roteinic foaming, which h as b een exposed to a wet environment and in contact with liquid water. Results show an improvement in material performances for the lower rubber mass proportions.

Keywords: Aerated clayey concrete, Proteinic foaming agent, Dust from rubber shredding, Hydric performances.

N. Madjoudj is a research student in Civil Engineering, University of Picardie Jules Verne Amiens. Her main research interest concerns transfers in building materials.

Dr R.M. Dheilly is a lecturer in Process Engineering. University of Amiens. Her major centre of interest is the relationship between microstructure and reactivity.

Professor M.Queneudec is the head of the "Laboratoire des Technologies Innovantes", University of Picardie Jules Verne, Amiens. She is specialised in the designed and characterisation of building materials.

INTRODUCTION

In the aim of better managing our natural resources, the reuse of clayey co-products resulting from the extraction of fossil sands has been undertaken in the laboratory. One of the preferred means is making aerated clayey materials through use of a proteinic foaming agent. The presence of moisture however and its transfer can influence material durability and performance considerably, especially in the presence of clay. It is therefore important to evaluate such materials' interactions with water, whether in the liquid or vapor state.

Previous research [1] has shown the positive influence of rubber inclusions on the hydric behavior of cementing materials. Yet the manufacturing of rubber aggregates by means of shredding serves to produce a dust that gets collected by aspiration. This dust then constitutes an awkward waste due to its smoothness; moreover, no reuses are currently being developed for this material. The idea herein has thus been to introduce it into the study material in order to improve hydric performance owing to the non-sorptive characteristic of this dust. In this work, the impact of this addition on the behavior of an aerated clay-cement composite will be evaluated during exposure to a humid atmosphere and upon contact with liquid water.

MATERIAL AND EXPERIMENTAL TECHNIQUES

Raw Materials

The material used for purposes of this experiment has been prepared beginning with a mixture of clay, a CPA CEM 52.5 cement (EN196-1), hemoglobin and water in the proportions determined by *Mr. Ruzicka* [2] at the time of his study on optimizing the proteinic foaming process for clay-cement paste, i.e.: $W/Cl = 0.7$; $C/Cl = 0.35$; $H/Cl = 0.021$ (with W = water, Cl = clay, C = cement and H = hemoglobin).

Rubber inclusions were then added in proportions ranging from 0% to 10%. The clay used was an industrial aggregate waste composed almost exclusively of kaolinite [3]. Hemoglobin (see Figure 1a) is a reused waste from the food industry, marketed under the brand name "Vepro95 BHF".

The mixing water used was treated by NaOH soda in the aim of both enhancing the formation of foam and increasing material workability [2]. Rubber fines result from the manufacturing of aggregates, whereby the process relies upon automobile industry scraps. These fines are obtained by aspiration during shredding and exhibit particle sizes of less than 1 mm. Image analysis conducted on this powder has revealed the existence of a majority of fine rubber particles ranging between 300 μm and 600 μm, some of which are quite elongated, along with a small percentage of other fibers (see Figure 1b); these fibers are of a residual synthetic textile nature.

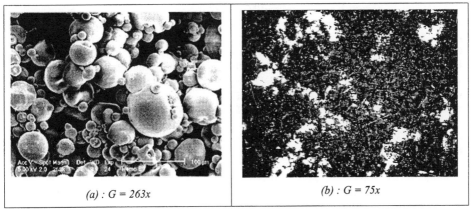

(a) : G = 263x   *(b) : G = 75x*

Figure 1. (a) Scanning electron micrograph of haemoglobin powder and (b) aspect of the rubber fillers in optical microscopy.

Material Elaboration

According to the experimental procedure, the clayey material recovered in the mud tanks is dried, crushed and filtered. Chemical treatment is then applied to the mixture by means of mixing water with a concentration of 0.0385 (mol/l) in NaOH soda, in accordance with recommendations set forth by *Mr. Ruzicka* [2]. Mixing is first performed in the dry state in order to homogenize the mixture to a considerable extent; this takes place during 1 minute at a speed of 60 revolutions per minute. The water quantity is then added while continuing mixing at the same speed for another minute.

Once the walls have been scraped, hemoglobin powder is added with precaution so as not to lose matter and mixing is then resumed at a high speed of 120 revolutions per minute for 2 more minutes. The fresh material is then poured into moulds and into molds, and placed in a climate-controlled room (R.H. = 98%, T° = 20°C) for 24 hours. Following demolding, specimen conservation takes place either in a suitable storage room at R.H. = 98% or within a controlled atmosphere, depending on the specific test to be carried out.

EXPERIMENTAL TECHNIQUES

Affixing humidity within the vapor phase

This test consists of placing, within a sealed enclosure, a representative test specimen of the dry product (sorption) in hydric equilibrium with an atmosphere of a given relative humidity. Preliminary drying proceeds under non-extreme conditions in order to avoid any product deterioration: the test specimen is maintained in a drying oven at 50°C until its mass has stabilized.

Affixing humidity within the liquid phase

The objective here is to determine the coefficient of sorptivity representative of an intrinsic macroscopic characteristic of the porous material. This coefficient reflects the capacity held by a material to absorb water by means of capillarity; it is derived from monitoring the evolution in volume of water absorbed by the sample (as a ratio of the contact surface area (40 × 40 mm)) versus. the square root of time. Test specimens are initially dried in a drying oven at a temperature of 50°C. They are then sealed with a heat-retractable plastic film, which serves to both block any lateral exchange and accommodate an ascending one-dimensional flow. Liquid water is supplied by means of exposing the transverse surface in contact with the water contained in the vat. The volumic water absorbed is then measured by weighing the sample using a 0.01g precision scale; the density of the absorbent is set equal to $1 g/cm^3$. Measurements are taken with a time step adapted to the kinetics of the phenomenon.

The volumic absorption rate per unit of area i (mm^3/mm^2) as a function of t is represented by:

$$i = \frac{M(t) - M(t_0)}{A.\rho_l}$$

with:

$M(t)$: mass of wet test specimen as a function of t
$M(t_0)$: dried mass of test specimen
A : section absorbante test specimen (4×4) cm^2
ρ_l : density of liquid water $(1 g/cm^3)$

Evolution in the volumic absorption rate per unit area was monitored until stabilization of the test specimen mass.

RESULTS AND DISCUSSION

Hygroscopic considerations

For the most unfavorable case of a 100% relative ambient moisture, the sorption kinetics have been depicted on Figures 3a and 3b.

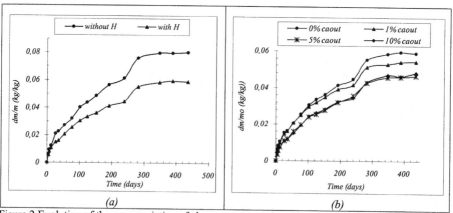

Figure 2. Evolution of the mass variation of clay-cement matrix with and without reduction (a) as well as clay-cement matrix with rubber content variation (b) according to time.

Figure 2a shows the influence of a reduction in water adsorption by the material; the maximum affixed water values are very low. This reduction slows the kinetics of affixing moisture as well as the maximum rate attained. The maximum adsorption rates are 0.08 kg/kg for an unreduced material and 0.06 kg/kg for a reduced material, respectively.

Sorption kinetics may be broken down into several phases: initial moisture absorption over time, followed by a leveling stage, and then another increase in water content until stabilization. The phenomena observed appear at the end of the same time period regardless of whether the material has been reduced or not. The porosity created by air entrainment does not therefore seem to be a factor.

This finding has been confirmed by the fact that the total adsorbed water mass is lower within the reduced material. Hence at equilibrium, the number of sites where water can become affixed is indeed fewer. It may then be assumed that those sites capable of affixing water molecules are the capillary pores of the matrix gel as well as the spaces between clay layers. Both parts of the moisture fixation curve would correspond to these two sites.

Figure 2b shows the evolution in the presence of water within the reduced material, which was used for inserting the rubber powder additives. The presence of rubber powder reduces adsorption even further and the shape of the curves remains identical. Stabilization is reached at the end of approximately 300 days for all compositions tested. The reduction observed is due to the fact that the presence of inclusions within the matrix influences the moisture-fixation mechanism during the gaseous phase and constitutes an obstacle that needs to be circumvented, thereby resulting in a deceleration of the sorption kinetics. The non-sorptive nature of the inclusions also serves to decrease the volumic fraction capable of affixing moisture.

Capillary Considerations

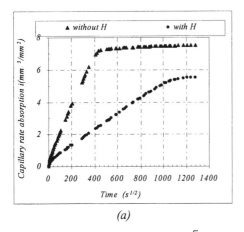
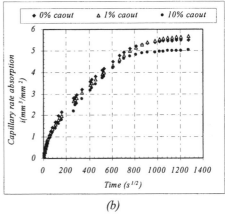

(a)   (b)

Figure 3. Capillary rate absorption vs. $\sqrt{t}$ (a) for the clayey material either with or without reduction, (b) for various rubber additive contents.

Figure 3a shows the rates of capillary absorption as a function of $\sqrt{t}$ for the clayey material either with or without reduction. It can be noted that the saturation stage is reached more quickly and the total quantity of absorbed water is higher in the case of the unreduced material. The curve corresponding to the reduced material always remains below that of the unreduced material, even over the first few minutes of imbibition.

The rate of absorption increases in a linear fashion up until $\sqrt{t} = 400$ and $\sqrt{t} = 1{,}000$ s$^{1/2}$ (the unit of time is the second) for the unreduced and reduced materials, thereby leading a stage to y-axis values of 7.31 and 5.53 mm^3/mm^2, respectively (see Figure 3a). The sorptivity measurements given during the first hour were 0.017 and 0.0056 mms$^{-1/2}$, respectively, for the reduced and unreduced materials, i.e. a ratio of 3 in favor of the reduced material.

Hydric transfer thus takes place more slowly in the reduced material. The difference in quantity of entrained air may be estimated at approximately 15%; this value is very close to the difference in the ordinates of the stages corresponding to water content at saturation for either the reduced or unreduced material. Porosity due to entrained air does not therefore seem to be influenced by the infiltration process. This behavior is compatible with that described by Bellini [4] in the case of pressure-sealed gas concretes.

The curves depicting the evolution in the rate of absorption vs. time are given in Figure 3b for various rubber additive contents. It should be pointed out that while during the first few minutes of absorption no systematic evolution in additive proportions is actually taking place, this influence is marked for more significant durations. Let's recall herein that absorption upon initiating test specimen contact with the sheet of water remains a surface phenomenon and thus is not extremely sensitive to the presence and nature of the inclusions when proportions are not very significant, as is the case here.

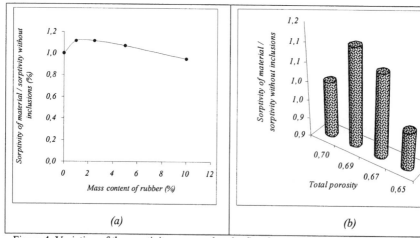

(a) (b)

Figure 4. Variation of the sorptivity measured at the first few minutes of material absorption, brought back to reduced material without addition of inclusion according to the mass contents (a) and according to total porosity (b).

Figure 4a displays the evolution in sorptivity versus inclusions content, while Figure 4b indicates the variation with respect to total material porosity. The total material porosity decreases as rubber content increases, whereas sorptivity shows an optimum value for a 1% rate of rubber inclusions; beyond this optimum, sorptivity decreases with porosity. This finding can be explained by the fact that macroporosity decreases as the proportion of rubber increases (see Figure 5). However as previously observed, these macropores constitute a barrier to hydraulic diffusion. For small percentages of rubber, sorptivity is thereby improved. When the percentage of rubber increases, the non-sorptive inclusions in the matrix once again tend to oppose hydric flow, which induces the curve to decrease.

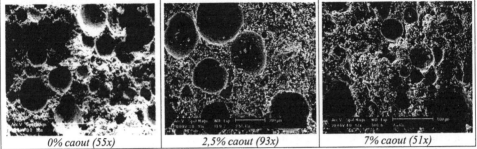

| 0% caout (55x) | 2,5% caout (93x) | 7% caout (51x) |

Figure 5. Variation of macroporosity as function of inclusions present in clay-ciment matrix

A comparison was conducted between the properties inherent in the material derived here and those of materials studied previously. The results have been listed in Table 1. It may be seen from these results that for the same clay-cement matrix, sorptivity is definitely weaker when the reduction is introduced by means of a proteinic foaming agent. This finding can be explained by the fact that during mixing, the protein acts as the cementing interface paste in order to form an impermeable film to effectively insulate the macroporosity. The porosity due to air entrainment thus remains unaffected by the hydrous invasion. Rubber additives in proportions of around 10%, i.e. proportions that are still low, improve sorptivity further. Let's note that the material remains competitive in comparison with plaster, even more so given the highly-competitive mechanical and thermal characteristics as well [4].

Table 1. Variation of sorptivity coefficient as function of density and porosity of different building material type

MATERIAL		DENSITY	SORPTIVITY $(mm/s^{1/2})$
Aerated clayey concrete (chimical reaction into the mass)		1,038	0,237
		0,962	0,235
		0,953	0,216
		0,903	0,214
		0,876	0,195
M.S Goual [5]		0,843	0,188
Plaster		1,390	0,210
H.Christopher et al [6]		1,430	0,195
Aerated clayey matrix with and without rubber powder inclusions	0% caout	0,97	0,024
	1%	0,99	0,0267
	5%	1,03	0,0257
	10%	1,04	0,0228

CONCLUSIONS

The study undertaken on this material makes it possible to conclude that the adsorption of moisture remains poor and the presence of a reducing agent allows diminishing even further the fixation of moisture. Reduction by means of proteinic foaming lowered by almost 3 times the coefficient of sorptivity. At equal density, the values are almost 10 times smaller in comparison with the reduction by chemical reaction within the mass. Once again, this finding demonstrates the protective role played by the protein. In both cases studied, the addition of rubber powder reduces the sensitivity to water, i.e. the affixed quantity and the kinetics of moisture fixation.

REFERENCES

1.   BENAZOUK A.: Contribution à la valorisation de déchets de caoutchouc : composites cimentaires à base de caoutchouc compact et cellulaire. Thèse de Doctorat de l'UPJV d'Amiens, 2002, 150p.

2.   RUZICKA M.: Optimisation d'un procédé de moussage protéinique de pâtes argile-ciment. Conséquences sur le comportement physicomécanique du matériau durci. Thèse de Doctorat, INSA de Lyon, 1998.

3.   Al-RIM K.: Etude de l'influence des différents facteurs d'allégement des matériaux argileux – Les bétons argileux légers, Généralisation à d'autres formes de roches, Thèse de Doctorat de l'Université de Rennes 1, 1995, 530p.

4.   BELLINI, J.A.: Transport d'humidité en matériaux poreux en présence d'un gradient de température. Caractérisation expérimentale d'un béton cellulaire. Thèse de Doctorat, Université Joseph Fourier-Grenoble. 1992, 194p.

5.   GOUAL M.S.: Contribution à l'élaboration d'un procédé de valorisation de co-produits argileux. Cas du béton argileux cellulaire obtenu par réaction avec l'aluminium pulvérulent : caractérisation et comportement thermohydrique. Thèse de Doctorat d'état de l'ENP d'Alger, 2001, 150p.

6.   CHRISTOPHER, H., HOFF W.D., MOIRA A.W.: Effect of non sorptive inclusions on capillary absorption by a porous material . Journal of Physics D : Appl.Phys, vol.26, 1993, pp31-34.

LEACHING OF PHENOL FROM TIRE SHREDS IN A NOISE BARRIER

R Aabøe

Norwegian Public Roads Authorities

Norway

A-O Håøya

Rambøll AS

Norway

T Edeskär

Luleå University of Technology

Sweden

ABSTRACT. As part of the Norwegian Roads Recycled Materials R&D Program (www.gjenbruksprosjektet.net), a large light fill noise barrier has been constructed along highway E6. The structure utilized 25% of all tyres that were collected in Norway in 2002. Four monitoring stations are used to sample leachate from drainage that enter local recipient.

The leaching of anti-oxidizing compounds from tyre shreds is of concern for Norwegian environmental authorities. In national pilot projects where tyre shreds are used as a light fill material special precaution is taken not to harm the surface water recipients.

A five-year monitoring program will document relative effect from different sources and the risk of environmental harm will be evaluated. Ongoing pilot projects indicate that leaching of nonyl-, octyl- or bisphenol from tyre shreds induces no environmental risk if applied under given design conditions. The way of application of recycled material will have an impact on long-term risk and the possibility of reuse or recycling of tyre shreds.

Keywords: Tyre shred, leaching, monitoring, legislation, phenol

Roald Aabøe is senior engineer at the Norwegian Public Roads Authorities, Geo- & Tunnel Technology .

Arnt-Olav Håøya is senior geologist working at Rambøll AS in Oslo, Norway.

Tommy Edeskär is MSc in Environmental Engineering and a PhD-student at Luleå University of Technology, Sweden.

INTRODUCTION

The Norwegian Government has identified undesirable properties of chemicals in two white papers from the Storting, (the Norwegian Parliament [13, 14]). The Norwegian Pollution Control Authority has further refined the list of undesirable properties and determined quantitative values (cut-off values) for the various properties [19]. Low biodegradability and a high bioaccumulation potential are considered to be particularly important. Other undesirable properties include toxicity to reproduction, mutagenicity, chronic toxicity, carcinogenic a nd s ensitising p roperties a nd o zone-depleting p otential. General l imit v alues are set for bioaccumulation, degradability, and acute and chronic toxicity.

Environmental risk characterisation is based on a hazard and an exposure assessment. Conclusions from the assessments vary depending on whether national-, regional- or site-specific considerations are applied. The reasons for this are the different types of scenarios applied for products, emissions and exposure. Emission of phenols from everyday use of tyres is not considered to be a particularly large environmental risk.

An "endocrine disruptor" is a naturally o ccurring c hemical or industrial chemical that c an bind to a receptor and prevent normal response, interfere with or act like hormones in animals or people. Such interference may have negative effects on fertility, be mutagenic or have other negative chronic effects on recipient life. As part of several chemicals that are suspected to have such effects Norwegian authorities have focused on nonyl-, octylphenol, their ethoxylates and bisphenol-A [18]. Car tyres (and shredded car tyres) contain phenols for anti-aging purpose.

BACKGROUND

Norwegian Roads Recycled Materials R&D Program [21] is set out to test different possible sustainable applications for shredded tyres. The program focuses on suitable technical application, efficient production line and long-term environmental effects. Shredded tyres have been used as a light fill material in a 450 m long noise barrier along highway E6 in the south Eastern part of Norway. Planning and building the barrier involved no major surprises compared to experiences from other projects [1, 5, 15]. The structure contains about 10 000 tons of tyre shreds and due to environmental concerns for a nearby lake the tyres are covered with a membrane. The long-term environmental effects are evaluated in the R&D program. The program also includes three other Norwegian pilot projects containing shredded tyres. This paper focuses on the ongoing monitoring program, environmental authorities' concern for phenol compounds and summarises facts about their eco-toxicological properties and about antioxidants in t yre rubber. Results from three years of monitoring natural leaching from t yre s hreds a re c ompared w ith analysis f rom w ater s ampled along h ighway E 6, i n a storm water basin along E6 and in its surface water recipient flowing from the nearby lake Vansjø.

LIGHT FILL NOISE BARRIER

"Huggenesvollen" noise barrier is situated along E6 highway in Rygge municipality South-Eastern Norway (Figure 1). The soil in the area mainly consists of marine clay and some fine sand. The ground under the 450 m long barrier consists of 2-3 m sand over a 10-15 m wide deposit of soft marine clay. The natural drainage is towards the sensitive recipient lake Vansjø. To protect this recipient, run-off from the tyre shreds was drained away form the lake.

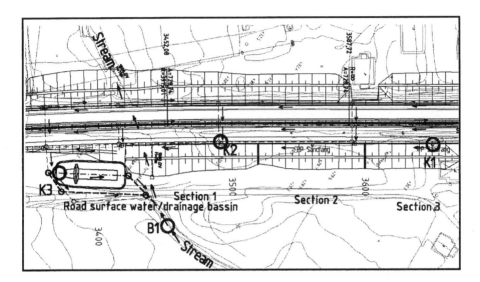

Figure 1. Samples are taken from the monitoring stations K1-3, K4 and B1 (each marked with a circle) over a five-year period starting 2003. The surface water samples are analysed for phenols, PAHs and metals. These stations document variations in runoff from shredded tyres, drainage and recipient not affected by surface water from the road. K4 has been used to sample runoff from the paved road. Arrows indicate the different directions of water flow. All of the water will mix with water from B1 in the end.

Run-off from surface water is gathered in the road drainage system, and is lead to a storm water basin that flows out into a small stream (B1, Figure 1). The core of the noise barrier is up to 5 m thick, and the barrier is built in several sections divided by 1-meter wide vertical layers of clay. The utilised fractions of shredded tyres are generally 5 – 30 cm, and the structure contains about 1 million tyres. In the construction process it was assumed that that shredded tyres can be compressed up to 15 %. The compression was performed by bulldozers and wheeled loaders.

Figure 2 shows a cross section at monitoring station K1 (section 3). In accordance with the demand from environmental authorities a needle punched bentonite membrane (Bentofix) was chosen to enclose the tyre shreds. This type of membrane was selected due to its physical properties (durability and self repairing properties) and easy installation. A 0.5 m thick layer of local soil was placed on top of the membrane (slope 1:1.5). Monitoring of surface water from four stations gives a five-year time line of chemical variations in water quality from shredded tyres (K1), from road water drain (K2), from mixing at storm water basin (K3) and in water coming from the lake Vansjø (B1). Water from road pavement is periodically monitored at station K4.

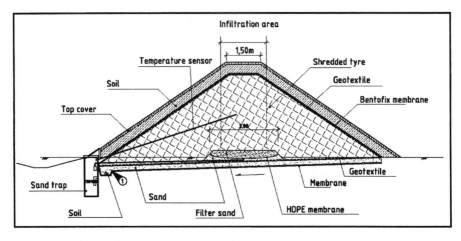

Figure 2. A cross section that shows light fill core of shredded tyres, collection of infiltrated water and
tubes for monitoring temperature and setting. Infiltrated water is collected in 5 litre glass bottles.
Bentofix is a membrane made of needle-punched layers of geotextile – bentonite – geotextile.

ENVIRONMENT AND ANTIOXIDICING PHENOLS FROM TYRES

Antiaging agents include antioxidants and other antidegrading agents. Antioxidants are added
to the rubber mixture in order to protect the rubber from degradation from oxygen, heat, UV-
radiation and chemical oxidation from other chemicals, for example metals. No single
antioxidant compound is effective against all of these degradation processes [9]. The primary
antioxidants within the tyre materials consist mainly of secondary amines and substituted
phenols. Most commonly used secondary amines is the p-phenylene diamines (PPD), because
they also have other functions in the rubber matrix. The phenoloic antioxidants are usually
used in non-black compounds where the amine oxidants cannot be used because of
discolourating reaction products. The most effective antioxidants are the hindered bisphenols
[4].

Antidegradants are used as additives in the car tyre production with a mass contribution of
respectively 1,5 % of the total car tyre. The most widely used antidegradant is *N-(1,3
dimethylbutyl)-N′-phenyl-p-phenylene diamine* (6-PPD) [2]. The antioxidant phenol is
included in the mentioned 1,5% of the tyre weight but the average proportion between PPD
and phenols has not been found.

Several authors have performed studies on phenols in tyre leachate [11, 16, 22]. Analyses
have been done from laboratory tests and from field tests part of monitoring programs. Håøya
2002 studied leaching of phenols according to CEN/TC 292 under neutral conditions. Table 1
shows leached amount at L/S 10 and the measured concentration in the eluate (tyre shred 5x5
cm).

Table 2 shows the predicted no effect concentrations (PNEC) for the selected phenols [3, 6-
8]. The values are collected from draft reports and are the best available knowledge for a safe
environmental acceptance criterion. Compounds of phenol combine in the natural

environment until the particles are decomposed (half-life <1 year). Increased concentrations of the examined phenols in surface water (recipient) are not detected.

Table 1. Phenols and total organic carbon (TOC) from leachate test at neutral pH at L/S 10 (CEN/TC292) from tyre shreds [10] (tyre shred 5x5 cm). Three parallel samples are tested

COMPOUND	RANGE [mg/kg TS]	L/S10 RANGE [µ/l]
4-tert-Octylphenol	0.002 – 0.05	2 – 5
Octylphenol ethoxylates (1-10)	0.01 – 0.03	1.5 – 2.4
4-n-Nonylphenol	1.001×10^{-5} – 0.003	0.01 – 0.03
Iso-nonylphenol (technical)	0.005 –0.007	0.5
Nonylphenol ethoxylates (1-10)	0.14 – 0.18	13.8 – 16.5
Bisphenol-F	0.007 - 0.03	2.2 - 2.5
Bisphenol-A	0.02 - 0.06	5.6 - 14.3
TOC	53 - 61	2900 – 6100

Table 2. Predicted no effect concentrations (PNEC) for fresh water, sediment and soil. Acceptable upper limit for 4 and 1 day average (once every 3 year on average) are listed for nonylphenol in freshwater and seawater.

CRITERIA/UNIT	NONYL-PHENOL	REF.	OCTYL-PHENOL	REF.	BISPHENOL A	REF.
$PNEC_{f.water}$ µg/l	0.33	[8]	0.122	[3]	1.6**	[7]
$PNEC_{sedimen}$ µg/kg wet weight	300	[8]	6.5	[3]	26	[7]
$PNEC_{soil}$ mg/kg	0.039	[8]	5.9	[3]	23	[7]
4 day average f.water µg/l	* <5.9	[6]				
1 hour average f.water µg/l	* <27.9	[6]				
4 day average saltwater µg/l	* <1.4	[6]				
1 hour average saltwater µg/l	* <6.7	[6]				

* Once every 3 year on average
** Based on effects on the population as reproduction and mortality

Bisphenol A is a solid at room temperature and will normally appear as flakes or powder. The substance is soluble in water with 300 mg/l at 20°C, and log K_{OW} = 3.4. This value indicates a low to moderate potential for bioaccumulation in aquatic species, and a moderate adsorption in soil. Bisphenol A has low biodegradability combined with high acute toxicity. Aquatic toxic data are reported for fresh water and salt-water fish, invertebrates and algae. These data cover conventional consequences as reproduction and mortality, but also endocrine disrupting effects [7]. Investigations indicate that Bisphenol A acts as the hormone estrogen on fish. Acute aquatic toxicity range from 1-10 mg/l, and algae is the most sensitive species.

The endocrine effects on aquatic invertebrates that are exposed for bisphenol A are for the time being not well understood [7]. It seems like endocrine-disrupting effects might be the most sensitive consequence. Still the PNEC values for bisphenol A are based on effects on the population, as for example reproduction and mortality. Recipients where sensitive species live should not have concentrations that exceed these PNEC values over longer periods of time.

Nonylphenol is a pale, very viscous liquid that has a weak phenolic smell and Log $K_{OW} = 3.8$ – 4.77. The substance is very dangerous for organisms that live in water, and can cause undesirable long-term effects in the water environment. Sediments or mud will easily adsorb it. Nonylphenol is bioaccumulated in organisms and can enter the aquatic environment directly as nonylphenol or as nonylphenol ethoxylates. In the natural environment nonylphenol ethoxylates rapidly break down to nonylphenol. Based on available data, nonylphenol is biodegradable and the speed of degradation is influenced by the adaptation of microorganisms. It has been demonstrated [6] that nonylphenol can be degraded by photochemical processes in 10 to 15 hrs (half-life) in bright summer sun when nonylphenol is near the water surface

Nonylphenol and its ethoxylates show estrogenic effect on fish. Most tests indicate that this effect will start at ca. 10 – 20 µg/l [8]. Nonylphenol is considered an endocrine disruptor chemical and induces production of vitellogenin in male rainbow trout. This is a process normally occurring in female fish in response to estrogenic hormones during the reproductive cycle. It also induces precocious development of ovaries and an intersex condition in some fish species [6].

Calculation of PNEC values has been based on both short term and long-term studies of nonylphenol and fish, aquatic invertebrates and algae. Nonylphenol is expected to adsorb easily by soil and sediments. Recipients where sensitive species live should not have concentrations that exceed these PNEC values over longer periods of time. The US EPA water quality criteria for nonylphenol (draft) [6] state an upper limit for concentration that should not have unacceptable effects on fresh- or seawater organisms. "1 and 4 day average more than once every three years on the average" values are listed in Table 2.

Octylphenol is a solid that is soluble in water with 19 mg/l at 22°C, and its log $K_{OW} = 4.12$. This log K_{OW} value indicates a moderate potential for bioaccumulation in aquatic flora and fauna. Available data indicate that octylphenol has a low solubility in water and will be absorbed by organic matter in soil, sediments and mud. Octylphenol seems to be degradable, even though the microorganisms might need some time to adapt. Both nonyl- and octylphenol are primarily found in sediments. Organisms that live in the sediments and organisms that live of these are vulnerable groups considering exposure to octylphenol.

Octylphenol is regarded acute toxic for aquatic organisms, and can cause long-term effects in the aquatic environment. It is also reported to have estrogenic effects. The safety factor that is used for octylphenol is 50 due to uncertainties concerning the sensitivity some invertebrates have shown. The safety factor for nonylphenol is 10. Recipients were sensitive species live should not have concentrations that over longer periods exceed these PNEC values.

ENVIRONMENTAL MONITORING – PHENOLS
Environmental monitoring of structures containing tyre shreds in Norway has been going on since 2001. The oldest structure that is part of this project is from 1991. Monitoring at

"Huggenesvollen" started before the construction in 2002 and is now part of a five-year monitoring program [11]. Figure 3 summarises the results from the first series of sampling. The suggested environmental acceptance criteria (PNEC from Table 2) are for comparison shown by the first bar from the right, for all except for "other nonylphenols". The first bar from the left shows concentration in water that infiltrated tyre shreds (K1, Figure 1 and Figure 2). Here 4-t-octylphenol slightly exceeds PNEC values. Along the highway, while snow was melting on icy ground and salty road, surface water was collected in the dyke at the side of the road (K4). Although there was only one water sample, these concentrations show the highest measured values for all monitored phenol compounds. Water quality in the storm water basin (K3) reflects the general runoff from the highway. Here no values exceed the PNEC values. Water coming from the lake Vansjo (B1) does not exceed PNEC, but both octhyl- and bisphenol A were detected. Surrounding land is used for agricultural purposes.

Three years of leaching from tyre shreds is documented at the Solgard project (Figure 4) [12]. The water at Solgard was collected directly under the tyre shreds. Figure 4 shows that 4-n-nonyl-, 4-t-octyl- and bisphenol-A are comparable and below PNEC values shown in Figure 3. Increased concentration of octyl- and nonylphenol may be due to decomposing etoxylates.

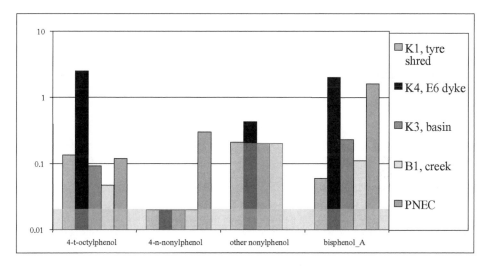

Figure 3. Phenol concentrations (log-scale) from monitoring stations (µg/l) at "Huggenesvollen" along highway E6. Values represent leaching the first 6-month period. Predicted no effect concentrations (PNEC) are here suggested as environmental acceptance criteria. Detection limits are overlaying in grey. "Other nonylphenols" may use PNEC for 4-n-nonylphenol. Collection system consists of HDPE-membrane, PE-tube and glass bottle.

DISCUSSION

Norwegian Roads Recycled Materials R&D Program is in a dialog with Norwegian Pollution Control Authority to find a sustainable solution for application of tyre shreds in light fill road structures. The R&D Program has adapted the European standard for characterisation of waste and the Norwegian guidelines for environmental risk assessment [20] to a method for evaluating long term environmental risks from recycled materials in a road structure [17].

Leaching tests have been performed by Zelibor 1991 [22], O'Shaughnessy 2000 [16] and Håøya 2002 [10] among others. Zelibor and O'Shaughnessy state that concentration of phenols in leachate ranges from <1-50µg/l. Results from Table 1 are in the same range, but field samples are generally <1 µg/l (Figure 3 and Figure 4).

Table 3 summarises temporary findings from laboratory and field measurements in the ongoing monitoring program. Field concentrations are by approximately 10 – 100 times smaller than laboratory concentrations. No change is found in the case of nonylphenols. Field concentrations are in a range that is acceptable when comparing to a conservative predicted no effect concentration.

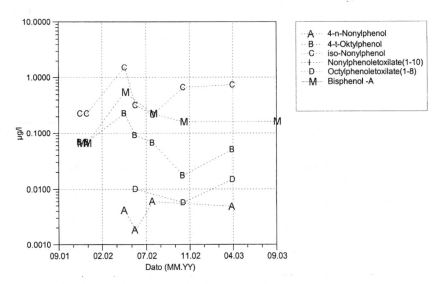

Figure 4. Monitoring station at Solgard production area Moss municipality. Concentration represents variations in the period 2001-03. Samples represent water that has infiltrated crushed rock (1m) and shredded tyre (1.5 meter). Water is collected in lysimeter 5x5 meter similar to Figure 2 [12]. Analyses below detection limit are left out (total of 7 samples). The collection system consists of PVC-membrane, PE-tube and glass bottle.

Table 3. Generalised phenol and etoxylate concentrations in laboratory L/S10 eluate and field leachate.

COMPOUND	L/S10 RANGE [µ/l]	FIELD LEACH. [µ/l]	PNEC -f.water [µg/l]
4-tert-Octylphenol	≈ 1	≈ 0.1	0.12
Octylphenoletoxylates (1-10)	≈ 1	≈ 0.01	-
4-n-Nonylphenol	≈ 0.01	< 0.01	0.33 - 6
iso-nonylphenol (other)	≈ 1	≈ 1	(0.33 – 6)
Nonylphenoletoxylates (1-10)	≈ 10	< 0.01	-
Bisphenol-A	≈ 10	≈ 0.1	1.6

CONCLUSIONS

The ongoing monitoring program and R&D on the application of shredded tyres indicate that leaching of mentioned phenols are at its max during the first year and are then reduced to levels that, when applied in a properly designed road structure, will be acceptable for sensitive recipients. Ongoing pilot projects indicate that leaching of nonyl, octyl- or bisphenol from tyre shreds induces no environmental risk if applied under given design conditions.

ACKNOWLEDGMENTS

We would like to thank individuals in The Norwegian Pollution Control Authority and U.K. National Centre for Ecotoxicology and Hazardous Substances who have been passing over ideas and important information regarding the environmental risk from nonyl, octyl- and bisphenol.

REFERENCES

1. ASTM, *Standard Practice for Use of Scrap Tires in Civil Engineering Applications. American Society for Testing and Materials.* 1998.

2. BLIC, *Life cycle assessment on an average European car tyre*, Bureau de Liaison des Industries du Caoutchouc (BLIC), Brussels, Editor. 2001.

3. Brooke, D., C Watts, R Mitchell & I Johnson, *ENVIRONMENTAL RISK ASSESSMENT REPORT: 4-TERT-OCTYLPHENOL (CAS NO: 140-66-9) DRAFT*, UK Environment Agency, Recipient. 2003, National Centre for Ecotoxicology and Hazardous Substances.

4. Ciullo, P.A., N. Hewitt, N., *The Rubber Formula. Noyes Publications, Norwich, New York.* 1999.

5. EPA, *Beneficial Use of Scrap Tires.* 2002, Division of Solid and Infectious Waste Management, Scrap Tire Unit.: State of Ohio.

6. EPA, *AMBIENT AQUATIC LIFE WATER QUALITY CRITERIA FOR NONYLPHENOL - DRAFT.* 2003, U.S. ENVIRONMENTAL PROTECTION AGENCY, Office of Water. http://www.epa.gov/waterscience/criteria/nonylphenol/draft-nonylphenol.pdf

7. European Union, *Risk Assessment Report on: 4,4'-isopropylidenediphenol (bisphenol-A). CAS No: 80-05-7. EINECS No: 201-245-8.* 2003, European Chemicals Bureau.

    http://ecb.jrc.it/existing-chemicals/

8. European Union, *Risk-Assessment Report on: 4-nonylphenol (branched) and nonylphenol.* 2002, European Chemicals Bureau. http://ecb.jrc.it/existing-chemicals/

9. Hofmann, W., *Rubber Technology Handbook.* 1989, New York: Hanser Publishers.

10. Håøya, A.O., *E6 Rygge Kommune - Miljørisikovurdering ved bruk av kvernet*, S. AS, Editor. 2002, Statens vegvesen, Vegdirektroratet.

11. Håøya, A.O., G.T. Unsgård, *Miljøovervåknig 2001-03 - Avrenning fra kvernet bildekk.* 2004, Scandiaconsult AS. www.gjenbruksprosjektet.net

12.   Håøya, A.O., R. Olsson, S. Torsøe, *Civil Engineering Rubber. Pilotprosjekt: Solgård - Moss. Arbeidsbeskrivelse med foreløpige resultater.* 2002, Scandiaconsult AS for Ragn Sells.

13.   Miljøverndepartementet, *Report no. 8 to the Storting (1999-2000) - Summary in English.* 2000. http://www.dep.no/md/engelsk/publ/stmeld/022051-040012/index-dok000-b-n-a.html

14.   Miljøverndepartementet, *Report to the Storting No. 58.* 1997. http://www.dep.no/md/engelsk/publ/stmeld/022001-040002/index-dok000-b-n-a.html

15.   Nauska, J., J. Forsman, *Noise barrier made of shredded tyres, experiences in Finland.*, project 110157A Ramboll Norway, Editor. 2002, SCC Viatek (Ramboll).

16.   O'Shaughnessy, V., V.K Garga, *Tire-reinforced earthfill. Part 3: Environmental assessment.* 2000(Canadien Geotechnical Journal, Vol. 37, pp. 117-131).

17.   Petkovic, G., C. Engelsen, A.O. Håøya, G. Breedveld, *Environmental impact from the use of recycled materials in road construction: Method for decision-making in Norway.* Resources, Conservation & Recycling, 2004 in press (RECYCL 1677). www.sciencedirect.com

18.   SFT, *Few chemicals with endocrine effects in consumer products in Norway,* www.sft.no, Editor. 1996. http://www.sft.no/publikasjoner/kjemikalier/1392/TA1392.html

19.   SFT, *Hazardous chemicals - Criteria for undesirable properties,* in *State of the Environment Norway (SOE),* www.sft.no, Editor. 2004, Norwegian Pollution Control Authority: Oslo. http://www.environment.no/templates/PageWithRightListing____3257.aspx

20.   SFT, *Risikovurdering av forurenset grunn.*, S. forurensningstilsyn, Editor. 1999. http://www.sft.no/publikasjoner/kjemikalier/1629/ta1629.pdf

21.   Statens vegvesen Vegdirektoratet, *National Roads Recycled Materials R&D Program.* 2004. www.gjenbruksprosjektet.net

22.   Zelibor, J.L. *Leachate from Tire Samples, The RMA TCLP Assessment Project: Radian Report. Education Seminar on Scrap Tire Management, Scrap Tire.* in *Management Council, Washington, D.C., September, pp. 381-391.* 1991.

Draft report [3] and previous drafts of [7,8] are distributed by:
Environment Agency's Project Manager Steve Dungey. U.K. National Centre for Ecotoxicology and Hazardous Substances. Environment Agency. Chemicals Assessment Section. Isis House, Howbery Park, Wallingford. OX10 8BD, UK. Fax: +44 (0)1491 828556. http://www.environment-agency.gov.uk/

PREPARATION OF CARBONACEOUS ABSORBENTS FROM RUBBER OF TYRE WASTES- ADSORPTION OF MERCURY FROM AQUEOUS SOLUTION

V Gómez Serrano

A Macías García

A Nadal Gisbert

C Fernández González

Extremadura University   Polytechnic University of Valencia

Spain

ABSTRACT. Rubber from tyre wastes has been used to prepare carbonaceous adsorbents and the products obtained have been tested as adsorbents for mercury in aqueous solution. The adsorbents have been prepared by applying thermal, chemical and combined (thermal and chemical or vice versa) treatments. Tyre rubber has been heated at 400 °C for 2 h in N_2. It has also been chemically treated with H_2SO_4, HNO_3 and H_2SO_4/HNO_3 solutions for 24 h. Finally, tyre rubber in two successive steps has been heated at 400 °C for 2 h in N_2 and treated with an H_2SO_4/HNO_3 solution for 24 h, or vice versa. All products have been characterised texturally by N_2 adsorption at -196 °C, mercury porosimetry, and helium and mercury density measurements. The adsorption of mercury has been studied from kinetic and equilibrium standpoints.The treatments effected to tyre rubber cause strong changes in its composition. The heat treatment results in a larger development of surface area, microporosity and mesoporosity than the chemical treatments. These treatments produce a great creation of macropores. The adsorption process is faster and the adsorption capacity is higher for the product prepared by heat treatment of tyre rubber.

Keywords: Tyre rubber, Carbonaceous adsorbents, Mercury adsorption.

Professor Dr V Gómez Serrano is Heat of the Inorganic Chemistry Department, Faculty of Science, at the Extremadura University. His research interests include study of the gas/solid and liquid/solid interfaces, and preparation and characterisation of activated carbon from biomass and industrial wastes.

Dr A Macías García is Associate Professor in the School of Industrial Engineerings at the Entremadura University. His research interests include the preparation and characterisation of activated carbon, composite materials and ceramics.

Dr A Nadal Gisbert is Titular Professor of Universitary School at the Polytechnic University of Valencia. His research interests include preparation and mechanical characterisation of polymeric materials from industrial residues.

Dr C Fernández González is Associate Professor in the Inorganic Chemistry Department, Faculty of Science, at the Extremadura University. Her research interests include adsorption from the liquid phase and preparation and characterisation of activated carbon and low-cost adsorbents.

INTRODUCTION

Carbonaceous m aterials, s uch as a ctivated carbon, h ave b een v ery extensively u sed i n t he adsorption of organic and inorganic solutes from aqueous solution [1]. The properties of such adsorbents that are important to adsorption processes depend on the starting material and the method u sed i n t heir p reparation. A ccordingly, the u se o f i nexpensive m aterials a s w astes with such an aim will certainly lower the production cost of the adsorbents. At present, in fact, low-cost adsorbents are being frequently tested for heavy metal removal from contaminated water [2].

More of 330 million waste tyres are discarded each year [3]. A recent EEC regulation, which has come into force on July 2003, establishes that the owner can not bury the tyres in a single piece, i.e., as such, but after their size reduction and only as a transitional measure for three years. On the other hand, there is a controversial about who must pay the recycling cost of the tyres used. As a result, tyres are frequently dumped in the open and have become a serious source of environmental pollution. From environmental and economical points of view, however, a good solution is likely to convert the tyre wastes to valuable products. The carbon content is high in tyres, i.e., 70-75 wt % for cars and 68-72 wt % for lorries [4]. Tyre wastes, owing to their abundance, acquisition price and carbon content, appear to be a suitable starting material to be used in the preparation of low-cost production carbonaceous adsorbents. An additional advantage is related to the fact that the starting material is produced on a world scale while other low-cost adsorbents are only locally available.

The use of waste tyre rubber for removing inorganic mercury from solution has been studied previously [5]. Then, research parameters included aqueous mercury concentration, rubber sorbent particle size, solution temperature, and hydrogen ion concentration. Sulphur-free rubbed was also evaluated. Recently, also using waste tyre rubber, carbonaceous materials have been prepared by applying thermal, chemical and combined methods and the resultant products were characterised texturally [6]. Here, some selected samples are tested as adsorbents of Hg^{2+} from aqueous solution. The adsorption process of this metallic ion is studied from both kinetic and equilibrium standpoints.

MATERIAL

The starting material used in this study was size-reduced residual rubber (RR, hereafter) obtained from tyre wastes. The material (average particle size between 1 and 3 mm) was supplied by the Escuela Politécnica Superior de Alcoy (Alicante, Spain).

PREPARATION OF ADSORBENTS

In the heat treatment, approximately 10 gm of RR was weighted and heated at 400 °C for 2hrs in N_2 (flow rate = 225 ml min^{-1}). The heating rate was 10 °C min^{-1}. In the chemical treatments, however, 25 g of the material, 125 ml of distilled water, and 125 ml of concentrated H_2SO_4 and HNO_3 solution were added to a glass flask and the system was allowed to react for 24 h. In the combined treatments, RR was first heated at 400 °C for 2 h in N_2 (flow rate = 225 ml min^{-1}) and then chemically treated with an H_2SO_4/HNO_3 solution, and also vice versa. The H_2SO_4/HNO_3 ratios used in the chemical treatments of RR and the notations of the samples can be seen in Table 1.

Table 1. Preparation of adsorbents

TREATMENT	TEMPERATURE(°C)/ACID SOLUTION	NOTATIONS
Heat	400	H-400
Chemical	$H_2SO_4/HNO_3(75\%/25\%)$	C-S/N(3:1)
Chemical	$H_2SO_4/HNO_3(25\%/75\%)$	C-S/N(1:3)
Heat/Chemical	$400-H_2SO_4/HNO_3(25\%/75\%)$	HC-400-S/N(1:3)
Chemical/Heat	$H_2SO_4/HNO_3(25\%/75\%)-400$	CH-S/N(1:3)-400

ELEMENTAL CHEMICAL ANALYSIS

The elemental analysis of RR and the carbonaceous adsorbents prepared from it was determined in the Instituto Nacional del Carbon y sus Derivados (C.S.I.C., Oviedo, Spain), using a LECO micro-analyser. This was made up of both VTF-900 and CHNS-932 determination units with suitable detectors. Data of the analysis are collected in Table 2.

Table 2. Data of the elemental analysis (wt.%) of RR and derived products

SAMPLE	C	H	N	S	O
RR	83.52	7.28	0.33	0.02	3.08
H-400	71.63	0.94	0.25		7.21
C-S/N(3:1)	68.24	3.84	2.93		13.85
C-S/N(1:3)	69.89	2.28	3.15		11.24
HC-400-S/N(1:3)	78.43	1.05	0.70	0.06	6.10
CH-S/N(1:3)-400	73.79	1.81	3.20		7.69

The treatments of RR cause a significant decrease in the carbon content and in the hydrogen content and a great increase in the oxygen content. The nitrogen content also increases for all samples, except for the heat-treated one. The hydrogen content and the oxygen content are higher for C-S/N(3:1) and C-S/N(1:3), which were not heated in their preparation. Sulphur is not detected in a large number of samples, which is worth noting.

TEXTURAL CHARACTERISATION

The textural characterisation of the samples was accomplished by gas adsorption (N_2, - 196 °C), mercury porosimetry, and density measurements, as reported before [6]. The values of textural parameters (i.e., specific surface area and pore volumes) are given in Table 3. As can be seen, RR is practically a nonporous material (V_T is equal to 0.08 cm^3 g^{-1} for this product). Furthermore, its extremely reduced porosity is made up almost exclusively mesopores and macropores. Because of W_0 is very low in RR, S_{BET} = 0.0 m^2 g^{-1}. All single treatments effected to RR, in particular the heat treatment at 400 °C, develop S_{BET} and W_0 in the resultant products. Nevertheless, the W_0 values indicate that the volume of micropores, in spite of its increase, is still very low in the samples. Thus, as a guide, for different activated carbons (i.e., these carbon materials are usually regarded as typical microporous solids) the volume of micropores lies between 0.15 and 0.50 cm^3 g^{-1} [7].

Table 3. Textural data for the samples[*]

SAMPLE	$S_{BET}/m^2\,g^{-1}$	$W_0/cm^3\,g^{-1}$	$V_{me}/cm^3\,g^{-1}$	$V_{ma}/cm^3\,g^{-1}$	$V_T/cm^3\,g^{-1}$
RR	0.0	0.001	0.04	0.03	0.08
H-400	18.1	0.043	0.40	0.21	0.77
C-S/N(3:1)	5.7	0.012	0.13	0.52	0.84
C-S/N(1:3)	7.5	0.041	0.07	0.69	1.02
HC-400-S/N(1:3)	14.0	0.050	0.24	0.24	0.94
CH-S/N(1:3)-400	5.0	0.010	0.07	0.61	0.92

[*] N_2 isotherms at -196 ºC: S_{BET} (specific s urface area, BET equation, p/p^0 = 0.05-0.35, a_m = 16.2 $\AA^2$), W_0 (micropore volume, Dubinin-Radushkevich equation). Mercury porosimetry: V_{me} (mesopore volume), V_{ma} (macropore volume). V_T (total pore volume) = $1/\rho_{Hg} - 1/\rho_{He}$, ρ_{He} = helium density and ρ_{Hg} = mercury density.

The mesoporosity is also much better developed in H-400 than in C-S/N(3:1) and C-S/N(1:3). V_{me} = 0.40 cm^3 g^{-1} for H-400. C onversely, t he macropore v olume greatly i ncreases in C-S/N(3:1) and C-S/N(1:3). For activated carbons, the volume of mesopores ranges usually between 0.02 and 0.10 cm^3 g^{-1} and the volume of macropores between 0.20 and 0.80 cm^3 g^{-1} [7]. Accordingly, the RR derived products are much more mesoporous solids than a widely used adsorbent as activated carbon.

The c omposition o f t he acid s olutions u sed i n t he c hemical t reatments of R R a lso m ainly affects the development of the macroporosity. Thus, V_{ma} is significantly higher for C-S/N(1:3) than for C-S/N(3:1). From these results it is clear that a higher content of nitric acid in such a solution favours the creation of macropores. In contrast, an increased concentration of sulphuric acid in the acid solution mitigates the development of the microporosity, as W_0 is lower for C-S/N(3:1) than for C-S/N(1:3).

As f ar a s t he c ombined treatments o f R R i s c oncerned, t he e ffect o f t he c hemical o r h eat treatment of the previously heated or chemically treated product depends on the porosity region (for comparison purposes one can use the couple of samples H-400 and C-S/N(1:3), respectively).The chemical treatment cause an increase in the micropore volume and a decrease in the volumes of mesopores and macropores. However, the heat treatment results in a decrease in the volumes of micropores and macropores, the mesopore volume remaining unchanged. For the carbonaceous adsorbents V_T ranges between 0.77 cm^3 g^{-1} for H-400 and 1.02 cm^3 g^{-1} for C-S/N(1:3). Therefore, C-S/N(1:3) possesses the best developed porosity.

The textural modifications produced in RR are associated with composition changes originated in the material as a result of the heat and chemical treatments. In this connection it should be noted that the heat treatment only causes mass loss by release of volatile matter, whereas the chemical treatments may produce not only mass loss by, e.g., solution of a RR component as zinc oxide in the acid solution, but also an increase in the mass of sample by formation of surface complexes in the carbonaceous material present in RR.

ADSORPTION KINETICS OF Hg^{2+}

Approximately 0.08 g of sample was first placed in a suit of test tubes provided with Bakelite screw-up caps. Then, 25 mL of a 4 x 10^{-3} M Hg^{2+} aqueous solution were added.

Next, the tubes were placed in a Selecta thermostatic shakerbath, containing water at 25 °C. The liquid and solid phases were maintained under continuous agitation of 50 oscillations min^{-1} a different time ranging between 5 min and 360 h. The supernatant liquid was filtered and analysed by UV-VIS spectrophotometry, using a Shimadzu equipment. The absorbance measurements were effected at 230 nm, at which the Cl_4Hg^{2-} complex ion formed between Hg^{2+} and HCl possesses its absorption maximum. The Hg^{2+} solution was prepared using $HgCl_2$ of reagent grade. Figure 1 shows the plots of the amount of Hg^{2+} adsorbed per unit mass of adsorbent (X/mg g^{-1}) against contact time (t, h) between the liquid and solid phases.

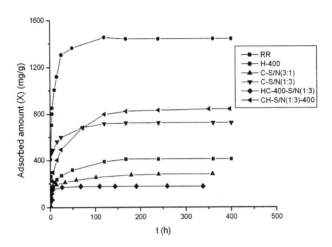

Figure 1. Variation of X with time.

From the X-t data the first-order adsorption rate constant (k) was estimated by applying expression (1), which was proposed by Lagergren [8]. It was derived in a kinetic model based on the assumption that chemisorption is the rate limiting step.

$$\log_{10}(X_e - X) = \log_{10} X_e - k\, t/2.303 \qquad (1)$$

where X_e is the amount of metallic ion adsorbed at equilibrium per adsorbent mass unit (mg g^{-1}). The values thus obtained of r (i.e., the linear correlation coefficient) and k are listed in Table 4. The high r values for all adsorption systems indicate that the X-t data fit quite well to equation (1). Good correlation coefficients indicate that Lagergrens's equation is applicable and the adsorption process is first-order [9].

For RR the adsorption of Hg^{2+} to a large extent occurs in a few hours, and therefore it is dealt with a fast process. This kinetic behavior is consistent with fact that RR is a nearly nonporous solids and hence the adsorption sites are fast accessible to the adsorptive ions. k is 2.1 x 10^{-2} h^{-1} for RR (Table 4). For the carbonaceous adsorbents, depending on the preparation method, k is either higher or lower than for RR The former holds for H-400 and C-S/N(1:3), and the latter for C-S/N(3:1), HC-400-S/N(1:3) and CH-S/N(1:3)-400. The slowing down of the adsorption process in particular for C-S/N(3:1) and CH-S/N(1:3)-400 is worth noting.

Table 4. Adsorption rate constants

SAMPLE	$k\ 10^2\ (h^{-1})$	r
RR	2.1×10^{-2}	0.9996
H-400	3.5×10^{-2}	0.9999
C-S/N(3:1)	2.6×10^{-3}	0.9971
C-S/N(1:3)	3.1×10^{-2}	0.9998
HC-400-S/N(1:3)	2.7×10^{-4}	0.9962
CH-S/N(1:3)-400	1.7×10^{-2}	0.9996

As is well known, in the case of the adsorption of solutes from aqueous solution by porous solids, the kinetics of the process not only is influenced by the functional groups present on the surface of the adsorbent but also by its pore size distribution, which is the factor that controls the facility of access of the adsorptive to the active sites. The mesoporosity, in particular, appears to play an important role in connection with adsorption kinetics from the liquid phase. As shown in Table 2, V_{me} is low for C-S/N(3:1) and CH-S/N(1:3)-400. However, V_{me} is also small for C-S/N(1:3) and the adsorption process is faster for this sample. In the case of C-S/N(1:3), as for CH-S/N(1:3)-400, the adsorption kinetics may be influenced by the macropore volume, as V_{ma} is higher for these samples than for the rest of the adsorbents.

ADSORPTION ISOTHERMS

The adsorption isotherms for Hg^{2+} were determined using between 0.01 and 0.25 g of sample. An aliquot of 25 mL of a 4×10^{-3} M Hg^{2+} solution was brought into contact with each adsorbent sample. The adsorption isotherms are shown in Figure 2.

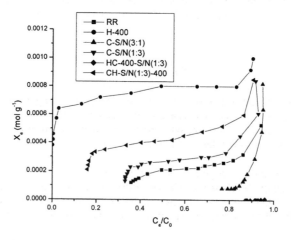

Figure 2. Adsorption isotherms of Hg^{2+} from aqueous solution.

The Freundlich equation (3) [10] was applied to such isotherms. The Freundlich isotherm is

$$X_e = K_f C_e^{\frac{1}{n}} \qquad (2)$$

where C_0 is the initial concentration of the adsorptive solution, C_e is the equilibrium concentration (mg l^{-1}), and X_e is the amount adsorbed (mg g^{-1}) at equilibrium. K_f and n are two constants which incorporate all factors affecting the adsorption process, such as adsorption capacity of the adsorbent (K_f) and the variation of the adsorption with concentration (1/n). The values of r, K_f and n are listed in Table 5.

Table 5. Parameters of the Freundlich equation

SAMPLE	K_f	n	r
RR	1.8	1.3	0.9987
H-400	89.1	9.8	0.9996
C-S/N(3:1)	2×10^{-32}	0.08	0.9977
C-S/N(1:3)	5.0	2.3	0.9997
HC-400-S/N(1:3)	2.3×10^{-92}	0.03	0.9982
CH-S/N(1:3)-400	17.0	3.3	0.9997

As inferred from the K_f values, the adsorption capacity is low for RR, which is in line with the poor development of surface area and porosity in this product. Moreover, the adsorption capacity is much higher for H-400 than for the rest of the samples, in particular C-S/N(3:1) and HC-400-S/N(1:3). For C-S/N(1:3) and CH-S/N(1:3)-400 the adsorption is still significantly higher than for RR. From these results it becomes clear that the adsorption of Hg^{2+} can be favoured by heat, chemical and combined treatments of RR. In the chemical and combined treatments, however, it is only so when the most concentrated HNO_3 solution is used and when in the combined treatment of RR the heat treatment is effected second. In brief, heating and a greater presence of HNO_3 in the acid solution have a favourable effect on the adsorption of Hg^{2+}.

CONCLUSIONS

- As a result of the treatments of tyre rubber, important changes occur in the chemical composition of the material. Usually, the carbon content and the hydrogen content suffer an important decrease, whereas the nitrogen content and the oxygen content increase. Sulphur is not detected in most samples.

- Tyre rubber may be regarded as a nonporous material. The heat treatment of the material mainly develops the microporosity and, in particular, the mesoporosity. The mesopore volume may become higher than even for a typical adsorbent as activated carbon. The chemical treatments, instead, favours the creation of macropores.

- The adsorption of Hg^{2+} is noticeably faster for the heat-treated product than for the starting rubber and also, though less, for the product prepared using the most concentrated HNO_3 solution. The rest of the treatments effected to the rubber have an unfavourable effect on kinetics, in particular when the most concentrated H_2SO_4 solution is used and when the product is successively heated and treated chemically.

- The adsorption capacity of tyre rubber is greatly enhanced by heat treatment of the material at 400 °C. The favourable effect on the extent of adsorption is weaker when the heat treatment is effected after the chemical treatment and even more when the concentrated HNO_3 solution is used. However, the other treatments result in a decrease in the adsorption of Hg^{2+} in comparison to the starting rubber. It is so in particular for the product prepared by heat and chemical combined treatments, in whose case the adsorption is almost negligible.

REFERENCES

1. RADOVIC, L. R., MORENO-CASTILLA, C. and RIVERA-UTRILLA, J.: Carbon materials as adsorbents in aqueous solution, In: Chemistry and Physics of Carbon (L. R. Radovic, editor), Marcel Dekker, New York, Vol. 27, 2000, 227-405

2. BABEL, S., KURNIAWAN, T. A.: Low-cost adsorbents for heavy metals uptake from contaminated water: a review, J. Haz. Mater., B97, 2003, 219-243.

3. CUNLIFFE, A. M.: Influence of process conditions on the rate of activation of chars derived from pyrolysis of used tyres, Energy & Fuels, 13(1), 1999, 166-175.

4. CASTELLS, X. E.: Reciclaje de Residuos Industriales, Díaz Santos, Madrid, 2000, 495.

5. KNOCKE, W. R. and HEMPHILL, L. H.: Mercury (II) sorption by waste rubber, Water Res., 15, 1981, 275-282.

6. MANCHÓN-VIZUETE, E., MACÍAS-GARCÍA, A., NADAL GISBERT, A., FERNÁNDEZ-GONZÁLEZ, C. and GÓMEZ-SERRANO, V.: Preparation of mesoporous and macroporous materials from rubber of tyre wastes, Microporous and Mesoporous Materials, 67, 2004, 35-41.

7. COOKSON, J. C.: Adsorption mechanisms: the chemistry of organic adsorption on activated carbon, In: Carbon Adsorption Handbook (P. N. Cheremisinoff and F. Ellerbusch, editors), Ann Arbor Sci., Ann Arbor, Michigan, 1978, 241-279.

8. LAGERGREN, S. and SVENSKA, K.: About of the theory of so-called adsorption of soluble substances, Vetenskapsakad Handl, 24 (2), 1898, 1-39.

9. JAIN, A. K., GUPTA, V. K., BHATNAGAR and SUHAS A.: Utilization of industrial waste products as adsorbents for the removal of dyes, J. Haz. Mater., B101, 2003, 31-42.

10. FREUNDLICH, H.: Adsorption in solution, Phys. Chem. Soc., 40, 1906, 1361-1368.

IMPROVING MARKETS FOR SECONDARY MATERIALS: CASE STUDY REPORT ON RUBBER

P van Beukering

S M Hess

Institute for Environmental Studies, Vrije Universiteit

The Netherlands

ABSTRACT: In addition to littering landscapes, the improper disposal of used tyres often results in health and environmental hazards, though used tyres are not considered as a hazardous waste. Because of all these potential environmental hazards, most OECD countries now regulate land-filling of used tyres, often banning them altogether, and strongly encourage their reuse, recycling and recovery. The objective of this study is to reassess recycling policy in light of an improved understanding of the functioning of the secondary rubber markets. The paper focuses particularly on the economic aspects of the tyre lifecycle and its market failures such as excessive market power, imperfect information, transaction costs, and technological externalities. In addition, there may be other important barriers to market development such as steep learning curves and price volatility that reduce the potential for secondary materials to compete with substitute primary materials. The paper also discusses the influence of policies on secondary rubber markets and provides policy recommendations concerning the most effective ways to solve market failures or re-define recycling policies. Throughout the paper specific examples of the secondary rubber markets in the Netherlands, the United Kingdom and the United States are provided.

Keywords: Used tyres, Environmental hazards, Economic aspects, Technological externalities, Secondary rubber markets

Dr. Pieter van Beukering is Economist at the Institute for Environmental Studies, Vrije Universiteit, The Netherlands.

INTRODUCTION

If markets operate in conditions of maximum efficiency and thus regulatory standards for different waste management options are such as to reflect their external environmental effects, recycling may become increasingly profitable in a number of cases. However, failures such as market power, imperfect information, transaction costs, and technological externalities are thought to be prevalent in many markets for recyclable materials. In addition, there may be important barriers to market development such as steep learning curves and price volatility that reduce the potential for secondary materials to compete with substitute primary materials.

Therefore, there is a need to complement existing work on environmental policy choice in the area of solid waste, by taking a step backward and looking first at the nature of markets for recyclable materials. It is felt that such an analysis is required since many policy discussions assume p erfect m arkets in a ll r espects e xcept w ith r espect t o t he p resence o f t he e nvironmental externality. However, in the presence of market failures or barriers, policy prescriptions may be very different. This paper provides a review and analysis of the markets and policies for recyclable rubber. Particular attention is paid to rubber tyres. Tyres account for approximately 50% of the total rubber market by weight and are responsible for a much larger share of the environmental problems caused by rubber materials.[1] The objective is to reassess recycling policy in light of an improved understanding of the functioning of the secondary rubber markets. These issues will be discussed in the light of at least three OECD member countries.

The paper is structured as follows. In Section 2 describes the life cycle of tyres. Section 3 focuses particularly on the economic aspects of the tyre life cycle and its market barriers and failures. Section 4 discusses the influence of policies on secondary rubber markets and provides policy recommendations concerning the most effective ways to solve market failures or redefine recycling policies. Throughout the paper specific examples of the secondary rubber markets in the Netherlands, the United Kingdom and the United States are provided in the boxes. The appendix provides several elaborations on specific aspects of the market for secondary rubber and its failures.

THE LIFE CYCLE OF TYRES

The increased number of vehicles has led to a tremendous growth in the volume of used tyres. Over a billion tyres reach their end of life in the world each year (Brown and Watson, 2002). This amount is expected to increase further by 1.4% for cars and 2.2% for commercial vehicles (UNCTAD, 1996; EEA, 1995). Although used tyres represent only a limited portion of the total waste stream, in terms of volume and chemical composition, they are very important. Yet, besides posing a pressure to the existing waste management sector, this enormous waste flow also creates opportunities for new recycling markets to evolve. The tyre lifecycle traditionally comprises five main stages. These include extraction, production, consumption, collection of used tyres and waste management. A simplified version of the tyre cycle for one region is depicted in Figure 1. The tyre life cycle is rather extensive and complex, both in vertical and horizontal directions, with numerous feedback loops and interdependencies between processes and stakeholders. Therefore, it is difficult to evaluate the post consumption stage of tyres, independent of the extraction, production and consumption stage. Moreover, it is difficult to distinguish between demand and supply, as most processes in the post-consumption stage require inputs and provide outputs.

---

[1] In 1997, the share of tyres in the overall consumption by weight was as follows: USA 64%; Germany 47%; Japan 59%; UK 47%; France 55% (Derived from IRSG 1998, p.39).

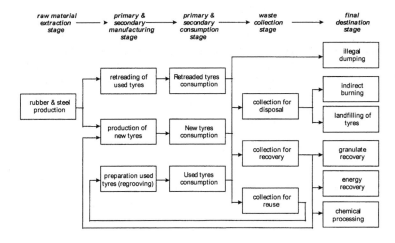

Figure 1   The lifecycle of a tyre

Extraction

In the extraction stage, the generation of the basic components of a tyre takes place. The components consist of synthetic and natural rubber, textile, steel and chemical additives. The proportions in which these components are used depend heavily on the specific characteristics of the tyre. This is clearly demonstrated if we look at the ratio between natural and synthetic rubber in tyres: generally, truck tyres have a larger natural rubber content than passenger car tyres. An alternative component for rubber is "reclaim" which is the material recovered from used rubber products. Because its physical properties (i.e. elasticity, flexion, and chemical resistance) are not as good as new rubbers, the proportion of reclaim in tyre applications is limited to 10 % (Guelorget et al. 1993).

Natural rubber comes from the sap collected from *Hevea brasiliansis* (rubber tree) plantations. Synthetic elastomers are obtained from petroleum and coal requiring several stages to produce. The most important chemical additive is zinc oxide, which is used as an activator. Carbon black is added to further improve the rubber properties, prevent oxidation and provide greater abrasion resistance. All the input materials are finally mixed and vulcanised using sulphur. Vulcanization is a thermochemical process that gives the tyres the characteristics to their performance—in the consumption phase of the product life cycle—important for their consumption but it makes further processing in post consumption stages more difficult.

Production

The tyre roughly consists of the casing or carcass that forms the skeleton of the tyre and the tread that consist mainly of rubber and therefore in most cases can be renewed (e.g. retreading). As shown in Figure 1, the tyre can be (re)manufactured in three ways: as a new tyre, as a retreaded tyre and as a re-used tyre. The manufacturing of a new tyre is a complicated process requiring a high level of technology. Therefore the scale of operation is also relatively large, exceeding 50,000 metric tons[2] per year. Labour account for 30 % of the total costs (U.S. EPA, 1995). The

---

[2]   One metric ton = one megagram = 1.102 short tons. Beyond this point the term "tons" refers to "metric tons".

second option for tyre manufacturing is through the retreading of a used tyre casing.[3] Retreading involves stripping the old tread from a worn tyre and reclothing the old casing with a tread made from new materials.[4] Retreading brings environmental benefits, as it extends the tyre life span. It saves 80 % of raw material and energy necessary for production of a new tyre and reduces the quantity of waste to be discarded. Although the price of retreaded tyres is between 30-50 % lower than the price of a new tyre, they deliver the same mileage as new tyres (Ferrer 1997; ETRA 1996).

Although this is not truly a manufacturing option, the third alternative for generating tyres is to prepare partly worn tyres for reuse. This may involve regrooving by which a new pattern is grooved into the tread base that remains after the pattern has been worn away by use. This technique is carried out primarily on truck tyres because these are designed with significant tread thickness. If the process is carried out correctly, about 30% extra mileage will be obtained for only 2.5% of the cost of a new tyre (World Tire Industry 1997). Retreaders oppose direct reuse and regrooving because it makes further retreading more difficult, more expensive and in most cases even infeasible. Depending on the remaining tread depth, discarded tyres are also reused directly. Drivers replace tyres before this minimum tread depth is reached. These tyres generally enter international trade for direct reuse. From an environmental perspective, direct reuse and regrooving prolongs life span of a tyre. The increased imports of reusable tyres, however, may also increase the waste burden due to the short life span of reusable tyres. Moreover, increased risks for accidents may result from driving on worn-out tyres.

It is expected that the most extensive increase in tyre production by year 2020 will occur in the Asian newly industrialised economies. Already today, China has the largest global market share. Supported by its close proximity to the major natural rubber suppliers, cheaper labour, it is expected that China's market share in the world market will increase even further.

Consumption

An important product characteristic of the demand for tyres is the type of application: i.e. passenger and truck tyres. This distinction is important as both types have rather different material properties, thereby influencing its retreadability and recyclability. Approximately, 70% of total weight of car tyres and 65% of truck tyres is rubber compound that is a combination of natural and synthetic rubber hydrocarbons. In general, truck tyres have larger natural rubber content compared to car tyres. Steel, textile and carbon black are the main reinforcement materials of tyres. The amount of steel wire used in tyres is larger for truck tyres compared to passenger car tyres. The tyre weight varies from 7 kg for a passenger car tyre to about 55 kg in average for a heavy truck tyre. In numbers of tyres, passenger car uses by far outweigh the commercial applications. Approximately 85% of the used tyres in the US and the UK are passenger car tyres. In weight, however, truck tyres (i.e. 60%) outweigh the passenger car tyres (i.e. 40%) in both the US and in the UK.

---

[3] Two technologies are used: hot and cold retreading. Combining heat and pressure, "hot retreading" takes place in a mold that creates a new tread design. In cold retreading, the tread is molded and cured in advance and then chemically bound to the prepared casing.

[4] Today retreading is more common for truck than for passenger car tyres. The retread rate of truck and passenger tyres is approximately 80 and 20 percent, respectively (U.K. Environment Agency, 1998). Car tyres can be retreaded only once, truck and bus tyres 3 to 4 times and an aircraft tyre 8 times. In practise, truck tyres are retreaded fewer times (average 1.5 times in the Netherlands, 2.5 times in Eastern Europe).

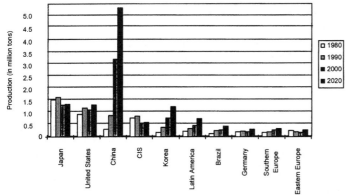

Figure 2. World tyre production in 1980-2020; Source: Smith, 1995

Driving behaviour and tyre maintenance are the main factors in the consumption stage. Improvements in the tyre manufacturing over the past 40 years have more than doubled the mileage of tyres, yet this technical limit is rarely met. Quick acceleration, not observing speed limits, abrupt braking and not taking into account the state of road surface are all forms of driver behaviour that cause the original tread to dwindle at a high rate. Currently, steel belted radial passenger tyres last about 65,000 kilometres (about 40,400 miles). If these tyres are properly inflated, rotated, and otherwise cared for, a lifetime of 95,000 to 128,000 kilometres lifetime may be achieved. A tyre loses up to 10% of its weight until it is disposed of. Most of the dissipated material comes from the tread, which is made of rubber only. If the casing is in a good state once the tread is finished, tyres can generally be retreaded. Although no scientific proof has been found, retreads historically have a poor public image. Yet, most retreaders claim that there is no quality difference between new tyres and retreads (U.K. Environment Agency, 1998). Another issue in the consumption stage is the introduction of energy-efficient tyres (often labelled as eco-tyres, or smart tyres). These can save up to six% of a vehicle's fuel. The retreadability of these tyres, however, is said to be limited.

Collection and Waste management

The final stage in the life cycle describes the ultimate destination where used tyres arrive. The term "used tyre" defines a tyre at the end of its first lifecycle. In this paper, the term "used tyre" defines a tyre at the end of its first lifecycle. Two sub-types of used tyres are distinguished. The "part worn tyre" is a used tyre that can either directly be reused or retreaded. The "worn out" or "scrap tyre" is a used tyre that cannot be reused for its original purpose but may have a further use as a material or for energy recovery.

Used tyres are accumulated after replacement or when scraping a vehicle. Various actors are involved. Generally, tyres are collected in tyre service centres. In some countries, consumers pay a limited fee to the service centre for proper disposal of the used tyre. For example, in Canada, consumers pay approximately € 2 per tyre for disposal. In turn, the service centre passes part of that fee (roughly 50%) on to the broker who separates out the reusable and retreadable tyres.

One of most common ways of dealing with worn-out tyres is material recycling. The options to recover the material in tyres include mechanical grinding, cryogenic grinding, and pyrolysis. In mechanical grinding, scrap tyres and tyre related rubber waste are reduced into various particle sizes. After grinding the material, steel and textile are removed. In the cryogenic grinding process the whole tyres are cooled down to below the glass transition temperature, using liquid nitrogen. The cooled rubber is reduced to a very fine powder. The process enables rapid separation of textile, steel and rubber. In view of its environmental performance, grinding is an energy intensive process and has relatively high dust emissions. The economic and environmental advantage of grinding is that it generates recyclable rubber and useful by-products such as steel and textile, which also can be recycled. The most common application of granulate is in rubberised asphalt. Although this seems to be a promising outlet for recycled rubber, because of its relatively high cost, this application is not widespread.

Chemical processing of size-reduced tyres, such as pyrolysis, produces monomers. The resulting material is submitted to a further thermo-mechanical or high-pressure steam process where additives are incorporated depending on the final product requirements. Although the end product is inferior to virgin rubber, it can still be used as a component in high value commercial applications requiring high performing rubber such as tyres, bicycle tyres, automotive moulded parts, soles and heels. Chemically recovered rubber is approximately half the price of virgin rubber. Using recovered rubber can be economically feasible for the tyre industry, especially when production waste is recycled and reused within the factory where it is generated. This might result in additional savings from the elimination of disposal fees and transportation costs.

The high-energy content of tyres has led to several applications of post-consumer tyres for energy recovery. For example, many worn out tyres are used as a supplemental fuel in cement kilns. Depending on the technology used, tyres can compose up to 25% of the total fuel of cement kilns. A major advantage of using worn out tyres in cement kilns is that it does not generate solid waste because the ash residues from the tyre combustion are bound to the final product. Furthermore, sulphur emissions are not of a major concern as the sulphur is transformed and bound into gypsum, which is added to the final product (Jones 1997). In Europe, the USA, Japan and Korea, cement kilns are among the most common end users of tyres for their energy content. In some countries, such as Austria, France, Germany and Sweden, up to 65% of the total quantity of used tyres is incinerated in cement kilns. In an alternative to cement kilns, totally dedicated tyres-to-energy power plants have been built in Europe and the US.

Traditionally, landfilling has been the most common method for disposal, mainly due to the low price of landfilling. Two forms of disposal can be identified: disposal in a landfill and disposal in a monofill. A scrap tyre monofill is a landfill that only stores tyres. When disposed of in landfills, scrap tyres occupy a large space and remain intact for decades posing increased environmental and public health risks related to possible leakage and the danger of uncontrolled burning. Furthermore, when whole tyres are buried in a landfill they trap air and have tendency to migrate to the top of a closed landfill breaking the landfill cap and causing costly damages to the landfill cover that increases the instability of sites. Also, used tyres easily trap rainwater and therefore create a favourable environment for insects such as mosquitoes, which increases the risk for malaria (U.S. EPA, 1995). In 1998, the European Commission accepted a directive that bans the disposal in landfills of whole tyres by 2003 and shredded tyres by 2006 (EC, 1997).

Monofills are more desirable than landfills as they facilitate material and energy recovery in the future. After the European ban on landfills is operational, monofills form a temporary solution in those European countries where capacities for processing used tyres are limited. The potential advantage of such monofills is that they can be reconsidered as future used tyre collection sites and distribution centres. However, examples around the world show that monofill sites frequently become abandoned without processing the stored tyres. Monofills also are a serious source of fire outbreaks.

International Trade

International markets are important throughout the life cycle of tyres. Natural rubber can be produced only in tropical areas and high-quality tyres are manufactured in just a limited number of industrialised countries. The waste management stage is also increasingly subject to international trade. Yet, knowledge on the commodity and regional patterns of international trade in used tyres and t yre-derived r ubber waste i s s cant (Hoffmann, 1 995). H owever, b ased on t he l imited d ata available, it can be concluded that trade in used tyres has become more important in the 1990s. Moreover, typical patterns in the trade of used tyres can be recognised. For example, Rosendorfová at al. (1998) show that the share of imports of used tyres by Eastern European countries in Europe expanded from 19% in 1992 to 47% in 1997. They conclude that trade of used tyres with neighbouring countries still dominates. Transport costs of the bulky tyres still seem to be a crucial factor vis-à-vis trading distance. This is confirmed by the trade situation for the UK, the US and the Netherlands, presented in Box 1.

Several arguments are put forward to explain the increasing flow of tyres from high- to lower-income countries. First, due to the low wage level and the relatively simple process of retreading and recycling, low-income countries may have a comparative advantage in the labour-intensive retreading a nd r ecycling of t yres. Second, m any t yres a re i mported f or r euse p urposes. S afety standards regarding minimum tread depth and the enforcement of these standards are less strict in low-income countries. Third, international differences in disposal fees promote the trade of used tyres that are not recyclable. Because disposal fees are much lower in low-income countries, it is a lucrative business to collect tyres in the North, collect the disposal fee paid for by consumers in the North, and export these tyres to low-income countries. For example, the disposal fee in the Netherlands is twice the fee in the Czech Republic (Rosendorfová et al., 1998).

THE MARKET FOR SECONDARY RUBBER

The configuration of the market for secondary rubber in each country depends on local economic and institutional conditions. Therefore, differences in recycling activities and waste management of used tyres occur naturally between countries. Moreover, market failures and distortions may be present in certain countries that reduce the efficiency with which markets for recyclable material operate, possibly leading to sub-optimal levels of recovery and recycling. This chapter describes the current configuration of the market for used tyres in various countries and presents evidence for the proposition that this configuration is not optimal from an economic point of view.

Current configuration of the used tyre market

The international comparison depicted in Table 11. shows how the configuration of options to process used tyres varies widely between countries. The Northern European countries have all achieved their objective to ban or significantly reduce tyres from the landfill. The Southern European countries, on the other hand, still landfill the majority of their used tyres. Another typical feature in Table 1 is that countries such as Denmark and Finland are fully dedicated to material recycling while the Netherlands, Belgium and Germany utilise the energy contents of tyres instead.

In a number of European countries, the configuration of recycling and waste management options has changed significantly over time (see Figure 4). The options that have become relatively less important include retreading, energy recovery and landfilling. Given the announced landfill ban in Europe for 2003 it is not surprising that landfilling has declined from 32% in 1996 to 28% in 2000. The retreading industry suffered seriously from the cheaper tyres coming from Russia and Asia and therefore reclined from 23% to 16%. One explanation of the relative decline in energy recovery is the growing supply of alternative energy sources such as biomass and waste plastics. Improvements in technologies and the implementation of a European landfill ban, provided a strong incentive for the material recycling industry from 11% in 1996 to 16% in 2000. Also, the net-export of used increased significantly during this period.

Optimal configuration of the used tyre market

The main question is whether the current configuration of processing options in the post-consumption stage of tyres is optimal from an economic point of view. Deviations from the optimal configurations can indicate the presence of market failures and distortions. At present, no studies have addressed the optimal configuration of the complete range of recycling and waste management options of used tyres. A limited number of studies, however, have made a comparison of the economic feasibility of specific processing options. These studies can provide some insight in the desired ranking of options.

Box 1. Trade patterns for used tyres

The majority of the traded used tyres moves between neighbouring countries. The bulkiness of tyres make it an expensive commodity to transport. This rule is confirmed if we consider the trade flows in 2001 for the US, the UK and the Netherlands (see Figure below). The Figure also shows that all three countries are net-importers of tyres.

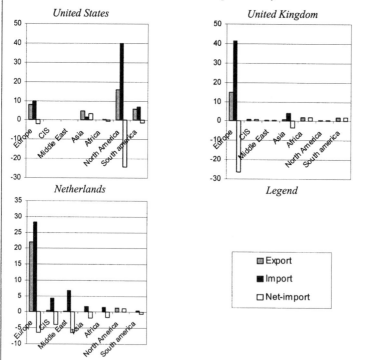

Figure 1. Trade volume of used tyres in 2001 in terms of sources and destinations for the United States, United Kingdom and the Netherlands (in 1000 tons)

Source: UNSD Comtrade Database 2002.

Table 1. Processing options of used tyres in Europe for 2000 or the most recent available estimate and ranked by descending level of landfilling (in%)

	ARISING (tons)	REUSE	RETREADING	RECYCLING	ENERGY	LANDFILL / incineration [1]	EXPORT	MISCELLAN EOUS[1]
Denmark	37,500	0	3	70	15	0	12	0
Finland	30,000	4	6	80	0	0	10	0
Luxembourg	2,750	0	5	0	0	0	95	0
Netherlands	67,000	0	2	30	50	0	18	0
Sweden	60,000	1	12	31	34	2	6	14 [2]
Belgium	70,000	1	15	14	55	4	12	0
Germany	650,000	0	18	12	43	5	17	5 [3]
USA	3,600,000 [7]	11	9	29	34	10	5	2
France	370,000	25	20	15	8	20	5	7 [4]
UK	428,000	5	15	27	16	29	2	6
Austria	50,000	0	9	1	40	40	10	0
Ireland	32,000	40	5	0	0	55	0	0
Portugal	52,000	0	3	11	13	60	1	12 [5]
Italy	350,000	0	8	10	14	66	2	0
Poland	150,000	0	12	8	10	69	0	1
Hungary	50,000	6	10	10	0	74	0	0
Greece	58,500	0	3	3	7	80	0	7 [6]
Spain	244,000	0	13	3	3	80	2	0

[1]*Incineration without energy recovery is included in column "landfill / incineration" and "miscellaneous". Stockpiling is part of "landfilling";* [2] *Sweden: misc. 4,800, unknown 3,600;* [3]*Germany: Unknown;* [4]*France: Unknown 25,900;* [5]*Greece: Unknown;* [6]*Portugal: Unknown;* [7]*UTWG 1999 figures. Source: ETRA (2001); Sunthonpagasit and Duffey (2000b); U.S. EPA (2003); and RMA (2002).*

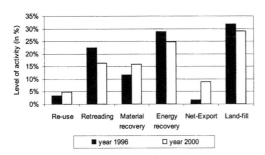

Figure 4   Change in processing activities in Belgium, Denmark, France, Germany, Italy, Netherlands, Spain, Sweden and the UK between 1996 and 2000.
Source: Rosendorfová et al. (1998) for 1996 estimate; ETRA 2002 for 2000 estimate.

Rosendorfová et al. (1998) study the options for post-consumed tyres and tyre related rubber waste in Europe in order to create a ranking on the basis of economic feasibility. Considering the average performance of the industry in Western Europe, they compared the economic feasibility of retreading, grinding, reclaiming, pyrolysis and incineration in cement kilns. The economic feasibility has been calculated by subtracting the total financial costs from revenues. The results of this analysis are presented in Figure 5. Retreading is clearly the most desirable option from economic point of view. A significant gap exists between the benefits of retreading and the other options. The financial performance of mechanical grinding, incineration in cement kilns and materials recycling do not vary widely. Although the revenues and costs differ among the processing options, their total gross profit varies only between €115-118 per ton of used tyres. Assuming the end products of pyrolysis to be utilised as fuels, leads to the conclusion that pyrolysis is not a financially viable process, unless the production costs will decline substantially over the years. Given the modest progress of pyrolysis applications for comparable waste materials such as plastics, this is unlikely to happen (US EPA, 1991).

In addition to the above study, several other works have been conducted that provide a better understanding of the optimal configuration of used tyres. Ferrer (1997) demonstrates the economic rational of maximisation of retreading before alternative processing options are considered. Ferrer shows that, when retreading is no longer technically feasible, heat generation is the only true recovery alternative because it is economically viable, the technology is satisfactory and the demand is constant. The other options have technological, economical or demand limitations that make them less feasible. It should be mentioned that techniques have progressed since Ferrer's study and that his conclusion are unlikely to longer for a number of alternatives, such as asphalt application.

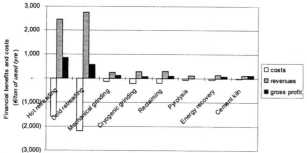

Figure 5.   Financial costs of various recycling and waste management options in Western Europe

Sunthonpagasit and Duffey (2003) examine the engineering economics of crumb rubber facilities in the US. Following a literature review and interviews with producers, a financial model of a nominal processing operation was created to aid the analysis of different market, crumb size, and production scenarios. The profitability of a crumb facility appears to be particularly sensitive to crumb rubber prices, operating costs, and raw material availability. Particularly the lack of standards leading to large variations in quality of rubber crumb is a handicap for the market of material recycling.

Using information on scrap tyre composition and the current markets using them, Amari et al. (1999) examine the technologies used in the US to recover their value either for energy or as rubber. They also conclude that retreading offers the best strategy for value recovery, requiring least new material and energy to achieve the highest value-added use in the economy. Amari et al. (1999) also recognise energy recovery as the second best option after retreading, but note that further expansion of TDF is particularly hampered by local regulations and lack of adequate infrastructure for collection and transport. The conclusion from this literature review is that the current configuration of processing options of used tyres is far from optimal. Generalising across countries, retreading seems to be practised below the economically optimal level. The findings for TDF are more divers but predominantly indicate the need for expansion of energy recovery. Material recycling is the most uncertain process, which leads to the conclusion that no immediate economic justification exists for expansion. Without exception, landfilling and stocking is considered to be both environmentally as well as economically unjustifiable.

Market failures: The conclusion about the sub-optimality of the composition of processing alternatives is an indication of the presence of market failures. This chapter provides an overview of the potential market failures in the used tyre sector. These market failures will be described subsequently for the main categories of recycling and waste management options: retreading, material recycling, energy recovery and landfilling/illegal dumping.

Retreading: When examining market failures for retreads, it is important to make a distinction between truck tyres and passenger car tyres. Although the technique of retreading tyres has been established for both new and retreaded tyres for decades, it has never broken through in the passenger car tyre market as a serious substitute for new tyres. Retreads are fully accepted for truck tyres, where about 50% of used tyres are retreaded. The limited share of retreads in the passenger car market is somewhat surprising. According to the above mentioned engineering studies, retreading is clearly indicated as the most environmentally and economically efficient method of recycling used tyres. Retreads are 30% to 50% cheaper than new tyres. The main question in this section is why the market for retreaded tyres is not more important than it is. In the following paragraphs, several possible explanations are provided for this issue.

Scientific and technical debate: It is not surprising that retreaders claim that there is no quality difference between new tyres and retreads (Environment Agency, 1998). However, all published engineering studies lead to similar conclusions. Also, a number of reputed government agencies confirm the fact that retreaded tyres are perfect substitutes, at least in terms of functional attributes, for new tyres. US EPA (2000) dispels the myth of retreads being less safe than new tyres. "Statistics compiled by the U.S. Department of Transportation show that nearly all tyres involved in any tyre-related accidents were under-inflated or bald. Properly maintained tyres, both new and retreaded, do not cause accidents." This is further explained in Box 2. US EPA (2000) also repudiates the notion that retreads have a higher failure rate than new tyres. "Rubber on the road comes from both new tyres and retreaded tyres, primarily from truck tyres that are overloaded, under-inflated, or otherwise abused." Studies of tyre debris in the UK have shown that it arises from a mixture of around 46% new tyres and 54% retreads (Transport Research Laboratory, 1992). This is representative of the use pattern of truck tyres. No evidence has been found in the literature or elsewhere of reports that claim a structural lower performance of retreads compared to new tyres. This leads to reject the hypothesis that the engineering studies are wrong about their conclusion of complete substitutability of retreaded and new tyres.

Quality and Risk aversion

Despite the lack of scientific evidence for the quality differences between new and retreads, the public image of retreaded tyres remains poor among passenger car owners. This can partly be explained by the fact that consumers are generally risk averse. The 'risk aversion' literature points out that even a slight inferiority in perceived quality can have significant repercussions on demand. This is certainly also true for car tyres that are crucial for the safety of a car. Many studies show that people are disproportionately averse to low-probability high-impact risks that may lead to morbidity and mortality. The incident of a blow-out, full speed on the highway is considered to be every car drivers' nightmare. Moreover, although retreads are up to 50% cheaper than new tyres, the price difference is still insignificant compared to the value of the car. Therefore, it seems crucial for the retread market to eliminate the perception of car users that retreads are inferior in quality to new tyres.

Signalling and consumption externalities: Both 'consumption externalities' and 'signalling' effects may contribute to passenger car owners to favour new tyres over retreaded tyres. 'Consumption externalities' refer to the effect of consumers take their 'cue' from other consumers (i.e. my consumption provides information to other consumers). This may, for example, result from public procurement policies that favour new tyres over retreads. Although US EPA (2000) strongly promotes the market for retreads by encouraging the government agencies to purchase retreads for their fleet, legislation has also been implemented in the US that is likely to strengthen the public in its mistrust towards retreads. This legislation prohibits the use of retreaded (and regrooved) tyres on the front wheels of buses. Although this legislation is relatively unknown to the general public, and therefore have only a small influence, it does show the government has mixed feelings about retreads that are not justified by its own research or that of others. 'Signalling' occurs in a situation where the perceived value of a car is affected by the use of retreads. Because the use of retreads sends a negative signal to the potential buyer of a car, the cost savings of assembling retreaded tyres are more than nullified by the reduction in the value of the car itself. This explains why car manufacturers sell cars with new tyres.

Box 2. The truth behind the gators.

In the United States several organisations, such as the Maintenance Council of the American Trucking Association and the American Retreader's Association and government agencies from Virginia and Arizona have researched the performance of retreaded or recapped tyres compared to new ones. This research was initiated because of public concerns about the quality of retreaded tyres. In the eye of the public many of the failed tyres routinely found lying on and alongside roadways – the so-called road gators – are believed to originate from retreaded tyres often associated with heavy-duty trucks and other large road equipment. Unlike for passenger car and light truck retreaded tyres there are no federal standards for retreaded heavy-duty truck tyres, nor are there any plans to establish them in the near future (Federal Motor Vehicle Standard Number 117 sets norms for retreaded passenger car tyres comparable to those for new tyres). From this research it was established that poor maintenance of tyres was the foremost cause of failure (especially underinflation). Even though retreaded tyres were over-represented in the recovered tyre parts, this was mainly due to their use on failure-sensitive vehicles like tractor pulled trailers (this was the conclusion in the Virginia study; the Arizona study did find other reasons for the over-representation of retreaded tyres).

Sources: Virginia Department of State Police, 2000; Carey, 1999; AAMVA, 2000.

Market segmentation: The tyre manufacturing industry can be characterised as an oligopolistic market with a limited number of large brands. In 1999, the major production of tyres in the global market was held by six companies: Michelin (France), Bridgestone (Japan), Goodyear (USA), Continental (Germany), Sumitomo (Japan) and Pirelli (Italy). Based on the global market sales, the top three controlled 57% of the world market (See Table 0). Given the individual market power in the tyre sector, tyre manufacturers are, in principle, to a certain extent, able to segment markets and apply price discrimination.

As opposed to the manufacturing industry, the majority of tyre retreading and recycling companies in Europe are small and medium enterprises. Recycling operators at the collection and sorting level are commonly thought to be price takers in their transactions with buying traders. Moreover, they have little influence over their costs in terms of the price they pay for waste (EC, 1998a). Their low market power is further influenced by competition with other ways of waste elimination as well as the fragmented characteristics of collection and sorting stages. The literature provides little evidence of price discrimination or market segmentation by the primary tyre manufacturers. Retreaders in the UK were said to face difficulties in reaching their customers due to the fact that the main retailers have strong ties with the primary manufacturers of tyres, and therefore only promote new tyres (Aardvark Associates, 2001). Random checks at tyre retailers in the Netherlands confirm this experience but this test cannot be considered representative for Europe as such. Another important segment in the market structure of the tyre supply chain is the collection and processing network of used tyres. Figure 6. shows the actors and the level of concentration in the Dutch tyre supply chain. As mention earlier, particularly the level of concentration at the stage of the producers and importers is particularly high. At the retail and car service centres, the dispersion of the market is large. Approximately 13,000 car service stations, 279 tyre replacement shops and 300 spare part c entres are involved in the replacement of old for new tyres. The large number of entrepreneurs makes it necessary to implement collective initiatives to improve efficiency in the post-consumption stage rather than pushing for individual initiatives.

Table 0. Production data of major tyre producers in 1999

RANK	COMPANY	OUTPUT/TONNES (*in US$ million*)	MARKET SHARE (%)
1	Bridgestone	13,750	20
2	Michelin	13,200	19
3	Goodyear-Dunlop	12,725	18
4	Continental	4,955	7
5	Sumitomo	2,783	4
6	Pirelli	2,600	4
7	Yokohama	2,514	3
8	Cooper	1,803	2
9	Toyo	1,323	2
10	Kumho	1,235	2

Source: BLIC, 2002.

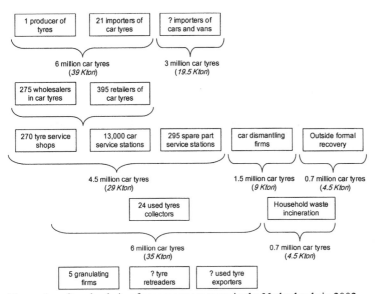

Figure 6.   Supply chain of passenger car tyres in the Netherlands in 2002
Source: VROM, 2002.

Competition from non-retreadable tyres: In the last decade, the import of new tyres from China and other Asian newly industrialised countries to Europe has increased significantly. These tyres are considerably cheaper than the high-quality tyre produced in Europe and the US. Due to the lower quality of the casing, these cheaper tyres are less suitable for retreading. The concern expressed by Rosendorfova et al. (1998) regarding the negative impact of this trend on the overall performance of the retreading sector has proved to be valid. The continuing decline in the passenger car retread market has forced the closure of a number of retread companies in the UK. Despite the improved quality of retreads, sales have dropped by over 50% in the past five years. Traditional key selling points for retreads were that they were significantly cheaper. However, the growth in the budget tyre market, where prices may be marginally higher than retreads, has significantly affected retread business. Moreover, retailers' margins on budget tyres are often higher. This too leads to a decline in sales promotion with potential customers (DTI, 2001).

Rubber recycling: Shredded tyres, also called crumb rubber, have various applications in the rubber recycling sector. Figure7.a. shows that in the US in 2001, of the total 0.45 million ton (996 million pounds) of crumb rubber produced, asphalt and moulded products were almost equal in market share, and combined had approximately 60% of the total market. The remaining 40% was used for the manufacturing of new products. Figure7.b shows that although consumption by all crumb rubber markets increased from 1997 to 2001, the crumb rubber market share of animal bedding, construction, plastic blends, and sport surfacing increased while the other crumb rubber markets shares decreased.

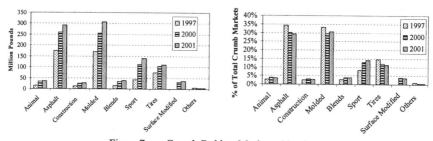

Figure7.   Crumb Rubber Markets: North America
Source: Sunthonpagasit and Duffey, 2000a.

The reported engineering studies provide limited support for further relative expansion of rubber recycling operations. Also, most governments are cautious in unambiguously promoting rubber recycling. The UK Government's Department of Trade and Industry reject the notion that recycling is underdeveloped due to the lack of capacity (DTI, 2003). DTI shows that there is capacity in place now capable of handling many more tyres than are being processed at present. The main reason for the limited share of rubber recycling is the low profit margin in the crumb rubber sector. This is mainly caused by technical constraints and the low quality of the end product. Whether this situation will change depends on price developments of primary natural and synthetic rubber and on the options available to reduce the cost of recycling or expand the market for products made of secondary rubber further.

World rubber prices are expected to fluctuate around the current level or drift lower in the short and mid-term. Low prices for primary rubber discourage the use of secondary rubber in various products. Further price improvements are unlikely because of the great potential for increased supply from more intensive tapping and from the increased production capacities in new producing countries (FAO, 2002). Given these exogenous developments in the primary market for rubber, the main issue with material recycling is whether or not the market for products of secondary rubber (i.e. rubber crumb) is 'immature' and thus whether or not it should be supported to get over learning curves, etc.

Whether strong market distortions are present remains unclear. High price volatility is often recognised as a symptom of the presence of market distortions. There are some claims in the United States of high month-to-month price instability and shifting demand, especially for lower quality crumb rubber, but this only seems to apply to a limited number of markets within the rubber-recycling sector (Sunthonpagasit and Duffey, 2000a). In the following paragraphs, several potential market failures will be discussed.

Information failure: Because of the large variety in crumb rubber size and quality, every rubber recycler in effect is said to produces a different product (Owen, 1998). Lack of uniform specifications in the crumb rubber market implies that between suppliers have to submit their products for approval and testing in each new locality where they were proposed. The resulting high search costs seriously hamper the maturation of the crumb rubber market. The use of standards could help to improve this situation. Another information failure is not directly related to used tyres, but to granulated rubber processing equipment. In the US, the reported maintenance costs of this equipment are reportedly 200-300% higher than the costs claimed by equipment manufacturers. One reason for this is the shorter than projected service lives of perishable items, such as shredder knives. Maintenance costs and the timing of maintenance seem to be important since one processor claimed his shredder machine worked twice as fast with new knifes. Such information failures make the planning of market entry and production volumes difficult. Sunthonpagasit and Duffey (2000b) consider this to be one of the reasons many companies fail within several years.

Technical failure: Tyres are designed – for safety and durability reasons – to make them withstand the wear and tear of their everyday use as well as possible. Tyre strength originates from the added steel and fibre but mostly from the vulcanisation of its rubber. The steel and fibre increase *recycling* costs because it blunts the knives or wears down the hammers that cut or ground the tyres into smaller pieces. After cutting and grounding the steel and fibre have to be separated from the rubber, which also adds to the costs. Of course, we – as drivers – want tyres to be strong, we want them to be safe and we want to get a good mileage. These are the basic requirements a tyre has to live up to. Still, one could ask if the current balance between strength and recyclability is the right one (Amari et al., 1999). A possible way to increase the likelihood of a correct or optimal balance would be to make the producers of tyres responsible for the cost of disposing or recycling them when they are worn down. This could be achieved through an Extended Producer Responsibility (EPR) approach, which will be discussed in the next section.

But, even if this recycling could be made easier, it would still not be true recycling as in the case of secondary metal or glass, which can be melted down and then reused as a perfect substitute for the virgin material. The reason for this is vulcanisation. In this process rubber, carbon and sulphur are mixed together using heat and pressure to form a strong and durable material. This chemical process has proved hard to reverse and has been likened to "unbaking a cake and then reusing the eggs". Recovery of useful, uncontaminated materials is even more complex for multi-material laminated products such as modern tyres (Brown and Watson, 2000). There are currently many recycling techniques but these either produce an end-product which is inferior to virgin rubber, such as the size reduction techniques mentioned above, and can only be used for its original purpose in small percentages, or are at present economically unfeasible due to high energy costs (e.g. pyrolysis and gasification). New techniques, such as chemical and biological devulcanisation, mechanochemical recycling, and de-wiring technologies need to be developed further to produce a satisfactory product (Brown and Watson, 2000).

Institutional failure: In the US, each state has its own laws and regulations with regard to waste management and recycling of tyres. Regulatory practices to stimulate recycling include landfill bans and disposal (tipping) fees. Ironically, however, many in the industry have perceived government grants and subsidies to some rubber recyclers as counter-productive. By allowing some facilities to access to subsidies for tipping fees and capital or operating costs, they have put downward pressure on secondary rubber prices, scrap tyre availability, and tipping fees. This affects the survival of existing un-subsidized plants. Numerous subsidized rubber recycling facilities in the US closed down because they could not sustain profitability or they failed to find markets for processed material. For example, tyre-recycling programs in Oregon and Wisconsin provided end-users a subsidy of US$20 per ton. The used tyres were collected and processed when the subsidy was in place, after which most of the new end users stopped processing.

Efforts to create a level playing field in the tyre-recycling sector have also been made at the Federal level in the US. Congress passed the Intermodal Surface Transportation Efficiency Act (ISTEA) in 1991, requiring the states to use scrap tyres for surfacing of federally funded highways. If this act had been implemented, proponents claim it would have increased the use up to 70 million used tyres in 1997. However, in 1995 ISTEA was repealed, presumably as a matter of lobbying efforts of the asphalt industry. As a result, the use of crumb-rubberised asphalt (CRA) now depends on the willingness of the state to initiate and sustain programs. After the repeal of the ISTEA most processors who came into this business in anticipation of this potential market left due to downward pressure on secondary rubber prices (Sunthonpagasit and Duffey, 2000a).

ENERGY RECOVERY

Engineering studies are generally positive about expanding the capacity of energy recovery. Still, as was shown in Figure, the relative importance of energy recovery declined in the past five years. This trend can partly be explained by the increasing popularity and promotion of material recycling (see Box 3). However, with the landfill ban in place in Europe and several States in the US, it seems likely for energy recovery to increase as well. Similar to material recycling, there is sufficient capacity available in the incineration and cement industry to use a higher proportion of used tyres than is presently the case. The British Cement Association estimates that in 1997 the UK cement industry could potentially recover up to 190,000 tons of used tyres (Environment Agency, 1998). This is much more than the 22,000 tons processed by the cement industry in that year. In some regions, local environmental regulations and the lack of adequate infrastructure of collection and transportation may hamper further market development for energy recovery (Amari et al., 1999). However, several additional potential market failures may be causing tyre-derived fuel (TDF) to remain underdeveloped.

Information and technology failure: As well as, in the granulated rubber market, different users of scrap tyres in the energy utilisation segment require different characteristics of the waste. Some cement kilns can process whole tyres, while others use shredded ones. Cement kilns typically burn at sufficient temperatures to oxidize the wire and benefit from both the energy release from oxidation and the resultant iron oxide that becomes a critical component in cement chemistry. At lower temperatures, however, the energy contribution from the wire is nonexistent and will account for a lower product energy value than that of either a wire free or relatively wire free TDF. In these facilities steel also leads to bigger ash disposal problems, so generally wire free TDF will be used. If the steel is not removed, TDF must be cleanly cut with minimal exposed wire protrusion from the chips to facilitate mechanical handling. The only tyre incinerator in the UK at Wolverhampton closed down mainly because the available technologies did not allow separation of good quality steel. Investments to upgrade the technology were considered to be economically infeasible (Green Consumer Guide, 2001).

An important reason for energy recovery to decline in a number of countries is the introduction of strict environmental laws. In Austria, for example, energy recovery declined from 70% in 1993 to 40% in 2000, partly due to special emission regulations for TDF in 1993 (MoA, 1993). The Austrian cement industry has been using the thermal input of tyres since 1979 successfully (Reiter and Stroh, 1995). According to the Regulation, the emission limits for particulates are 50 mg/m^3, for SO_2 200 mg/m^3 and 500 mg/m^3 for NO_2. The incineration of other waste is not regulated by the same regulation but individually by other competent authorities. As a result, it has become more attractive to use alternative waste materials (e.g. plastics) as fuel input for the cement industry.

Other important specifications for TDF are the fuel's combustion characteristics, the handling and feeding logistics and environmental concerns. The recent development of American Society for Testing and Materials (ASTM) standards for TDF must be recognized as another step toward making tyre-derived materials a more accepted fuel input. The main advantage in this effort is that end users and potential end users now have an industry-accepted standard against which to compare all tyre chips. The other benefit to the industry is the development of a single sampling and testing protocol (RMA, 2002).

High search and transport costs: For tyres several observations can be made in context of search and transport costs. Given the fact that spatially dispersed waste generators and a fragmented recycling industry can be an indication for high transport costs, one can assume that this problem is less severe in highly populated countries such as the Netherlands. Nevertheless, the bulkiness of tyres implies relatively high transport costs. The transport of shredded tyres is about 30% to 60% cheaper, simply because fewer trips are necessary (Jang et al. 1997). High costs limit trade in used tyres in Europe and requires recyclers to be near the raw material sources (Rosendorfová et al. 1998). In various studies it was estimated that transporting whole tyres for material recycling and energy recovery is not economically feasible over distances beyond approximately 150 to 250 kilometres (Sunthonpagasit and Duffey, 2000b). As a result, the area in which used tyre processors can retrieve their used tyres is relatively small. This limits the number of buyers and sellers thereby hindering the retrieval of a reliable flow of tyres, which is especially important for energy generators. This would also make an often-heralded solution to the problem of thin markets for secondary materials, the Internet, less suitable for used tyres, even though there are many sites that do offer the possibility to sell or buy tyres.

Incineration and Landfilling
Landfilling of tyres is categorically rejected by most engineering studies. These options are commonly considered a waste of valuable materials and causing unnecessary environmental problems. Still, despite the implementation of the landfill ban in Europe by 2006, these options are still heavily used in some countries.

Institutional failure: The cost for used tyre collectors of landfilling and incineration versus alternative management options is often the main driver of the configuration of the waste stage of used tyres. In the Netherlands, the disposal fee is completely set upon the commercial deals between the collectors and the processors. Because the disposal fee represents an important source of income for the tyre processing companies, it is difficult to obtain exact and reliable information on disposal fee for individual processing options. Some of the Dutch collectors claim that the disposal fee is the same for material and energy recovery options which represents €83 per ton of passenger car tyres and €68 per ton of truck tyres (Rosendorfova et al., 1998). Based on several interviews in the sector and taking into consideration a relatively high share of energy recovery options, it can be assumed that the disposal fee paid to cement kilns is lower than the disposal fee paid to grinding companies. Disposal fee for shredded tyres (TDF), in turn, is usually lower than the disposal charge for whole tyres. Figure 8. shows a comparison of incineration and disposal across Europe. Assuming the above mentioned recovery costs are representative for the rest of Europe, it becomes clear that in a number of countries it is cheaper to landfill or incinerate tyres, rather than to recover them.

International differences in rules and regulations can be a cause for the transboundary movement of used tyres. Typical examples of such differences are the existence of regionally variation of tipping and hauling fees. Besides state and local environmental regulations, regional conditions and local labour rates influence these costs. In 2001 US tipping fees for passenger car and truck tyres ranged from $34-300 per ton. For used tyre processors these tipping fees are essentially a "negative cost" for raw materials and impact the producer's ability to keep crumb-selling price competitive with other scrap processors and their virgin counterparts. Therefore the high variance of these fees seriously hamper the conditions needed for a level playing field. As was shown in Figure 8., the cost of different processing options varies widely within Europe.

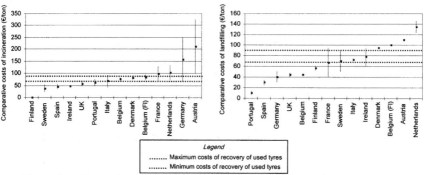

Figure 8. Comparison between incineration and landfill costs in Europe with (€/ton)
Source: based on Dominique Hogg (2001).

By comparing the levels and costs of recovered and landfilled used tyres reported in Table 1 and Figure 8., respectively, it is possible to see reveal correlations between the two variables. Figure 9. shows that landfill costs are a good indicator for the landfilling level of used tyres. Despite the correct sign, this is not true for the recycling rate of used tyres. In other words, high landfill costs are a pre-requisite to divert used tyres from the landfill but are not a guarantee that they will be used optimally.

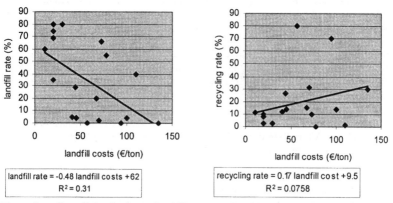

Figure 9. Correlation between landfill costs and the levels of landfilling and recycling of used tyres in Europe in 2000.

Illegal dumping: A growing problem in the waste management stage is the increasing incidents of illegal dumping of old tyres. Generally these tyres have already been sorted: only the tyres that are no longer retreadable or reusable are fly-tipped. Related to this problem is the abandoned of monofill sites without processing the stored tyres. Such examples have been recorded in Canada, USA, the Netherlands and the UK (Environment Agency 1998, EPA 1995). Unfortunately, there is limited information available on the extent of the problem, although it could be about five per cent of fly-tipped waste by incident (Greater Manchester Waste Regulation Authority, 1995). UK's Environment Agency responded to over 1,300 incidents involving tyres in 2002. The actual total is likely to be substantially higher since many incidents are reported directly to local authorities and do not feature in Environment Agency statistics (UK Parliament, 2003).

The introduction of landfill taxes and collection fees are closely linked to this trend. After the introduction of a landfill tax in the UK in 1996, the Agency's North East Region found a 25% increase in fly-tipping the year after (Environment Agency, 1998). Generally, collectors accumulate used tyres from car repair shops, receive the collection fee, sort out the useful tyres and dump the remaining. In response to this trend, many governments have increased monitoring efforts of fly-tipping and strengthened the enforcement of penalties for this illegal practice. The UK's Department of Trade and Industry is considering the introduction of statutory reporting requirements through both the new tyre supply and used tyre disposal chains with the aim of improving the information base, promoting responsible tyre recovery and disposal practices while at the same time making it increasingly difficult for those fly-tipping tyres (UK Parliament, 2003).

POLICY INFLUENCES ON THE MARKET FOR SECONDARY RUBBER

Public policies can have both a positive and a negative impact on the economic and environmental performance of recycling and waste management of used tyre sector. On the one hand, government strategies can be developed to correct the above market failures. On the other hand, if applied inappropriately, policies are sometimes counterproductive in making the waste stage of tyres more sustainable. This chapter aims to evaluate the existing tyre-related policies and suggest potential improvements in policy strategies.

Existing Tyre-related Policies

The different policy regimes in the tyre waste management sector are shown in Figure 10.0. The policy instruments that deal with waste and therefore encourage recycling, either directly or indirectly, can be divided into three broad categories: direct regulative, economic and communicative policy instruments (Opschoor and Turner, 1994). In the following overview these instruments are briefly explained, supplemented by examples from the used tyre sector.

Direct regulative instruments: Direct regulative instruments include the compulsory net legislation that prevents environmentally undesirable practices. The application of direct regulation in environmental policy has a long tradition. These instruments are designed to set fundamental levels of environmental protection, to implement wider international commitments and provide necessary rules and standards. The most commonly used direct regulative instruments are series of regulations, permits, technical standards, bans and restrictions, which provide regulatory framework for environmental policy. Additionally, setting targets defined in a legislation is becoming an important instrument (Rosendorfová et al. 1998).

A crucial regulative instrument for the used tyre sector is the ban on landfilling of whole and shredded tyres. Landfill bans stimulate the recycling of tyres by making dumping impossible and therefore other ways of dealing with the tyres have to be found. Currently several European countries, such as Belgium, Denmark, France and the Netherlands have already installed a landfill ban on (whole or shredded) tyres and the EU Directive 1999/31/EC on the landfill of waste will oblige all EU countries to ban the disposal of whole tyres to landfill from July 2003 and shredded tyres from July 2006. This will probably result in a significant increase of used tyres being put on the market after 2008.[5] In the US most municipalities also no longer permit the inclusion of tyres in regular landfills (Owen, 1999). The undesirable effects of tyres in landfills instigate landfill bans. Tyres tend to "float" to the surface, damaging the surface layers. Tyres in landfills also pose serious fire and health risks. Major fire episodes may last for a long time, affecting the quality of air by uncontrolled releases of air pollutants. Because of their shape, landfilled tyres can collect rainwater and windblown pollen, which creates an environment favourable for pests, rodents and mosquitoes representing health hazards, including mosquito-born diseases (Rosendorfová et al. 1998). A second problem is the loss of valuable materials disposal.

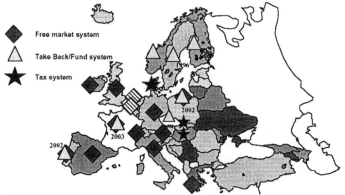

Figure 10. Policy regimes in the used-tyre sector of Europe in 2001.
Source: Pyanowski, 2002.

The EU has an attempt to tackle the problem of consumer's distrust of the safety of retreads by introducing a more uniform (safety/quality) standard. There were various national standards for retread tyres before, like the British BSAU 144 requirements, but in June 2001 the EU has acceded to the UNECE (United Nations Economic Commission for Europe) Regulations 108 and 109 for retread passenger car and truck tyres respectively. These Regulations require more or less the same quality controls as the widely applied UNECE Regulations 30 and 54 for new car and truck tyres. It is not yet mandatory for member states to adopt these Regulations as national standards but several countries, such as Belgium, Denmark, Portugal, Spain, the Netherlands and the UK have done or will do so in the next two years (2003-2005) (VCA, 1999). This might help to free retreads from their bad image.

Specific targets for recycling sometimes supplement these bans. The new Dutch legislation on passenger car tyres, which is scheduled to be implemented in July 2003 demands that material recycling will be employed for 20% of the collected used tyres. Because current processing capacity or other outlets for material recycling in the Netherlands are insufficient to achieve the target, this will stimulate the various options for material recycling. The Dutch government envisages producers to add a fee of on new tyres to raise the money needed for this development. The new law does not state a target for product reuse. One of the underlying reasons is the fact that tyres suitable for reuse – either directly or through retreading – have an economic value and are therefore not expected to end up in the take back systems that will be used for scrap tyres. Another

---

[5] Calculations show an increase of 3,500,000 tons per year.

reason is the lack of influence producers are thought to have on the many factors that affect the extent to which this reuse will be adopted (OBba, 2002).

Technical standards also fall into the category of direct regulative policy instruments. In an environmental context standards usually state a maximum allowable content of certain substances in products or emissions, but in the case of used tyres – and secondary materials in general – they serve a different purpose, namely to enhance uniformity and certify a minimum quality. In the previous chapter the new standards for retread tyres have already been discussed. First and foremost these are meant to increase the safety of these tyres, but because safety perceptions by the public have given retread tyres a bad name, they may also increase demand for this very desirable option of dealing with used tyres. Initiatives are also taken to develop standards for granulated rubber and recycled rubber products. European co-operation processes have started to produce standards for recycled tyre materials. The European Tyre Recycling Association (ETRA) has prepared a basis document (CWA) for a standard, in close co-operation with a large number of organisations and companies. The European standardization body (CEN) will formulate the final standard (CEN, 2000). Ultimately, standards for granulated rubber are aimed at creating a more transparent market for this rubber product by increasing its uniformity.

Economic instruments: Economic instruments are defined as instruments that affect the market conditions under which people and firms make their decisions, without directly reducing the decision space available to them. Instruments are labelled "economic" when they affect estimates of costs and benefits of alternative actions open to economic agents (OECD, 1998). Economic instrument can also be used to internalise the external costs of various activities. The most common examples of economic instruments are taxes and subsidies.

Box 4. The British approach: will voluntary prove Viable?
Extended Producers Responsibility (EPR) approach, the concept where producers and retailers accept responsibility for the waste stage of their products, is gaining popularity in the tyre sector. Within EPR there is a discussion about the way this responsibility should be implemented: through imposed regulations from governments or voluntary initiatives from the industry itself. In Britain the tyre sector has clearly expressed their preference for the voluntary approach. The government is willing to follow this route as long as the legal requirements are met. For the most part, these requirements stem from the national "Duty of Care" requirement, which is part of the Environmental Protection Act of 1990 and the EU Landfill Directive. Under the Duty of Care requirement anyone dealing with waste tyres is required to make sure tyres are not handled illegally and are only transferred to an authorised person together with a waste transfer note. The EU Directive will ban landfilling of whole tyres from July 2003 and tyre chips three years later. Because in Britain almost 30% of waste tyres are currently being landfilled the industry will have its work cut out for it.
To comply with both the national legislation and to fulfil the obligations emanating from the EU Directive the industry has set up several initiatives, the largest being the Responsible Recycler Scheme (RRS). This scheme was created in 1999 by the Tyre Industry Council. Its goals – besides preventing regulation – are to make sure used tyres are properly reused or recycled, to reduce illegal dumping, to create consumer awareness and to encourage best practice in the industry. Independent auditors monitor participants in the scheme annually and award a certificate, which can than be used as a marketing tool to reassure customers that tyres are being disposed of responsibly. A similar initiative, launched by Waste Tyre Solutions, the British market leader in the disposal and recycling of waste tyres, also aims to provide evidence that waste tyres have been reused and recycled in an environmentally friendly way. Both these schemes work with the Waste Transfer Note system, which records the movements of waste materials. If the combined efforts of the British tyre sector prove unsuccessful the government is, among other options, considering a statutory Producer Responsibility arrangement.
Sources: DTI, 2002; UTWG, 2001; TIC, 2001.

Besides landfill bans, governments also raise taxes or levy charges on the deposition of tyres going to landfill, as is currently the case in the UK and in some parts of the US (Sunthonpagasit and Duffey, 2000a). Like a ban, this also stimulates the use of other, more desirable, ways of dealing with tyres by making them comparatively cheaper.

Examples of a tax used to internalise the costs of handling used tyres are the Danish and Hungarian taxes levied on the producers of new tyres. These taxes are passed on to consumers through higher prices. The revenues of the tax are used to pay for the organisation and recycling of the tyres. A similar system is currently installed in the Netherlands will leads to an increase of the price of a new tyre of approximately €1.10. Secondary material industries can also be stimulated through the use of direct subsidies. This policy instrument has in general not proved to be very efficient. A telling example, as reported here, is the American use of grants and subsidies to some granulated rubber producers, which created unfair competition for the existing un-subsidized plants. Another problem related to the subsidies is the failure to find markets for the processed materials, resulting in stockpiling of shredded tyres (Sunthonpagasit and Duffey, 2000a). Some of these problems could be solved by better instrument design.

Communicative instrument: Communicative instruments are aimed at voluntary adaptations of individual and group behaviour in a more environmentally friendly (in this case reuse or recycling enhancing) direction. Information and education campaigns, product policies, eco-labels or voluntary sectoral agreements (covenants) and public procurement (by which governments set an example by purchasing for example recycled products and thereby may pave the way for advancement in products and technologies) are all examples of policy tools with a large potential in the waste management.

An example from Italy shows government support for retread tyres. The Financial Act of 2002 demands that 20% of replacement purchases of public motor vehicle fleets are retreads (AIRP, 2002). This stimulates the retread sector, already important in Italy, and helps convince the public of their safety. The US government is also active in promoting retreads through public procurement program. US EPA (2002) recommends t hat p rocuring agencies establish preference programs consisting of two components: (a) procurement of tire retreading services for the agencies' used tire casings; (b) procurement of tires through competition between vendors of new tires and vendors of retread tires. In the event that identical low bids are received in response to a solicitation, all other factors being equal, procuring agencies should provide a preference to the vendor offering to supply the greatest number of retread tires.

Government procurement can also be found in the use of granulated rubber in asphalt. In 1991, the US Congress passed the Intermodal Surface Transportation Efficiency Act (ISTEA), requiring the s tates t o use s crap tyres f or s urfacing o f federally funded h ighways. If it h ad b een implemented, proponents claim the act would have increased the use of scrap tyres up to 70 million in 1997. However, in 1995 ISTEA was repealed, presumably as a matter of lobbying efforts of the asphalt industry. ISTEA had initially shown promise of developing granulated rubber markets for asphalt but after repeal most processors who came into this business in anticipation of this market left due to downward pressure on granulated rubber prices (Sunthonpagasit and Duffey, 2000a).

Comparative assessment: None of the above-mentioned instruments is capable of addressing all of the identified market distortions and failures. Each policy type has its specific pros and cons. Although economic and communicative instruments seem to be most in line with the generally recognised principles of promoting the market economy, it is unlikely that these instruments eliminate the need for regulation. Regulatory instruments provide a greater degree of certainty of outcome than other types of instrument. The establishment of a ban on landfilling used tyres, for instance, is considered to have been the strongest incentive for tyre recycling activities in the last decade. Therefore, a pragmatic approach should be followed in designing policy schemes to reduce failures in the secondary rubber market.

Sets of measures should be tailored to suit the local circumstances, the problems addressed and product types for which they are applied. Ogilvie and Poll (1999) address the relationship between the instrument choice and the problem addressed. They suggest the implementation of a large variety of policy instruments for different purposes. Technical problems should ideally be addressed through research and subsidies, while the imbalance between the supply of, and the demand for recyclable materials requires awareness campaigns and waste charges to be introduced. Alternatively, waste exchanges could bridge this gap. What instruments are bested suited to address problems such as illegal disposal and consumer perception will be described in the following section.

Policy Recommendations

If recycling has significant environmental and economic benefits, then the expansion of the capacity of the recycling industry and the improvement of the secondary rubber market has to be promoted further. Most countries discussed in this study acknowledge this notion. The question remains how this aim should be accomplished. Several policy recommendations have been derived from the above analyses that are aimed specifically at reducing the market failures and barriers for rubber recycling markets. By combining these principles, a more effective market for secondary rubber can be achieved.

Create appropriate market conditions: The prime role of the government is to remove economic and technological obstacles for the rubber recycling industry, rather than directly intervene in the recycling sector. Certainly, governments would better avoid participating directly in recycling activities. Instead, economic measures, such as tax exemptions, could be introduced. This may give the rubber recycling industry a competitive advantage over the established primary rubber sector. Such measures, however, are particularly effective if the primary industry is receives all kinds of government support in the form of subsidies and preferential treatments. In the rubber industry, this does not seem to be the case. Therefore, it is doubtful whether tax exemptions would create fairer market conditions for the rubber recyclers. Similarly, subsidies may be helpful in the short term to support the recycling industry during its infancy stage but can cause inefficiencies in operations in the long term.

Set clear targets while maintaining flexibility: In Europe, the implementation of a European wide ban on landfilling has had an enormous impact. Although such uniform ban may not have necessarily led to the most effective outcome in economic terms, it certainly created large momentum in the tyre recycling business. Countries and organisations are forced to come up with creative solutions to meet with the European legislation. Earlier attempt on a purely voluntary basis, such as attempted in the Netherlands, failed miserably. An argument in favour of voluntary agreements is that the industry is faced with maximum flexibility in meeting the agreement. However, the earlier experiences with voluntary schemes show that such systems only function well if economic gains can be achieved. As shown in the US, voluntary programmes without these gains will only be set-up to avoid legislation. Another drawback of voluntary schemes is that they are particularly difficult to implement if there are many players, as seen in the Dutch experience. The advantage of mandatory policies is the creation of a clear set of rules for all players in the market. The European industry favours mandatory systems to minimize the problem of free-riders and reduce the uncertainty surrounding future legislation. Within mandatory schemes producers should have the flexibility to manoeuvre in a way they consider optimal.

Cautiousness in supporting R&D and compensating for low prices: At present, the rubber recycling sector suffers from a number of technological impediments. Governments could support R&D to overcome these problem areas in the recycling industry. First, the currently limited market of secondary material applications could be expanded. For example, products could be designed in such a way that they could contain a higher content of recycled materials. In addition to R&D support, government procurement policies of recycled products could support the adoption of these products. Secondly, improved product design can increase the recyclability of tyre related products. As mentioned earlier, government support in the form of subsidies in technological development has not proved to be very effective. Therefore, governments should be cautious in providing these, particularly at the longer term.

Actively fight illegal dumping with regulatory instruments: In the case of used tyres, the main market distortions to be addressed include illegal disposal, consumer perceptions, and exports. Illegal disposal is generally dealt with through the establishment of deposit refund schemes because these provide a strong incentive for the consumers to return their used products in a proper state. In the case of used tyres, however, illegal disposal does not occur at the consumer level, but at the collectors level. Therefore, illegal dumping of tyres is best addressed through the certification of tyre collectors and through increased monitoring if illegal dumping events. The UK Environment Agency is running a Tyre Watch campaign, which both makes businesses aware of their responsibilities and pushes for stiffer sentences for illegal dumping. The Agency actively seeks prosecution. The Environmental Protection Act makes provision for fines of up to £20,000 and possible imprisonment for EACH deposit of waste (Environment Agency, 2003).

Promote retreads to the public: Retreading should be seen as the first step in management of post consumed tyres. It saves 80% of raw materials and energy necessary for production of tyres and reduces the quantity of waste to be disposed. Retreading, therefore, should be promoted by all possible means including prolonging the life cycle by producing retreadable tyres and improving their image, thus create markets for retreaded tyres. Possible measures to achieve that are to implement quality standards for tyre manufacturers to produce retreadable casings, promote public procurement policy (use of retreads on governmental vehicles) and, most importantly, provide information to the public on the quality and existence of retreaded tyres. Retailers play an important role in this respect. If retailers promote retreads more often, and pronounce the economic advantages to their customers, the retreading industry would probably not be suffering such heavy losses.

Encourage Extended Producer Responsibility: OECD countries recognise that while they have implemented a variety of policies and programmes to reduce pollution, the generation of rubber waste continues to grow. Faced with the increase in rubber waste, and the need to reduce pollution and increase resource efficiency, governments are looking for new policies and instruments to help them address the environmental impact of rubber-based products at their post-consumer phase. There are a number of policy choices available to governments to address the environmental impacts from products at their post-consumption phase. Extended producer responsibility (EPR) is an approach being used more and more in Member countries.

EPR programs aim at shifting the financial and/or physical responsibility of a product at the post-consumer stage upstream at the producer. EPR is driven by clear and strong signals upstream to change inputs and product design in order to reduce materials and resource inputs, eliminate toxic chemicals in products and to increase recyclability. One of the main goals of an EPR program is, by making producers pay for the costs of recycling or disposal, to create incentives for easier and cheaper recycling and the prevention of waste. Producers are expected to take into account the effects in the waste stage of a product, when designing it. The costs of EPR programs are passed on to consumers, either through visible fees or through price increases, and therefore internalise the costs of waste management. The instruments used in EPR programs can come from all three discussed categories.

Current trends indicate an expansion in the application of EPR-based policy instruments (deposit-refund, take-back, advance disposal fees, material taxes, an upstream combination tax/subsidy, etc.) to new products and waste streams. The tyre manufacturing industry in Europe has formally accepted its responsibility in early 2002. Plans for setting up the EPR scheme are currently being developed by BLIC, the European Association of Tyre Manufacturers. It is unclear whether the scheme will be brand related or whether a collective scheme will emerge. In developing the scheme, promotion of retreads is an important aspect. The primary tyre manufacturers are a powerful player in the tyre supply chain and therefore are in a good position to stimulate the use of retreaded tyres. EPR can also form an incentive for the Asian manufacturers that produce the cheap non-retreadable tyres, to increase the retreadability of their product.

Implement harmonised (safety) standards for retreaded tyres: Safety should of course not be compromised just to reduce the problem of waste tyres, but studies have shown that retreads can now be just as safe as new tyres and the retread industry even claims they are of a higher quality than the budget tyres from Asia and Russia. The main problem then is to convince the public of this fact. One way to do this is the introduction of clearly communicated safety standards for retreaded tyres that should be very similar to standards for new tyres. The newly adopted UNECE standards by the EU, referred to earlier, are a good example but because it will not be mandatory for countries to adopt these standards, a lot of the benefits of having one uniform standard might be lost. It is therefore required that as many (future) Member States as possible adopt the standards. It should not however be expected to be a panacea for retreaded tyres. In the US where standards for retreaded passenger car tyres do exist, their use still falls short of potential. Other stimulants like public procurement are necessary.

Expand public procurement: Governments are in a strong position to boost the demand for recycled materials. Government procurement can benefit the recycling sector of secondary rubber tremendously. Setting minimum content rules for, for example rubber crump in road surfaces, a substantial volume of scrap tyres can be deviated from the landfill. Moreover, by prescribing government-owned vehicles to use retreaded tyres, government procurement schemes can have a direct (i.e. expanding the market for retreads) and an indirect (i.e. signalling function for citizens) impact on the market for retreaded tyres. As mentioned before, several stimulation measures have been taken in the US to promote the use of retreaded tyres. In 1998 President Clinton signed Executive Order 13101, which mandated the use of retreaded tyres on all government vehicles. Combined with strong endorsements from for example the EPA, most federal government fleet vehicles are now using retreaded tyres. The US Postal Service has, for instance, successfully utilised retreads on all their vehicles for several years and the US Army Tank-Automotive & Armaments Command won a recycling award in 1999 from the Clinton Administration for its program in retreading tactical tyres. In this program retreaders are tested and certified annually and lists of certified retreaders are made available to other government institutions.

Support development of standards for TDF and crumb rubber: Even though the TDF and crumb rubber industries are certainly not in their infancies anymore and have proven their market viability, it cannot be said that they have fully matured yet. TDF has not taken the place among other fuels it deserves on the basis of its characteristics. Though this can partly be explained by the fact that there are reliability issues in the supply of TDF, compared to conventional fuels, there are also institutional factors that limit its growth. The debate about TDF being a fuel or a form of solid waste was already addressed in Box 6 and another example is the extensive testing phase British cement kilns have to undergo before they are authorized to use TDF. With clear air emission standards for tyre using facilities it ought to be much easier to check if the requirements are met and then issue the permits. Of course there should be proper air emissions for TDF, but this should not needlessly hinder its adoption. Where air emission standards should clearly be a government issue, other standards for TDF relating to the wire content, size etc. can be developed by the industry itself. This has indeed happened in the US, where the American Society for Testing and Materials (ASTM) has developed such standards. Where such standards do not yet exist governments could stimulate their development or adoption of existing foreign standards. Governments might also have a role to play in harmonizing different existing standards. Both the ASTM and the European Committee for Standardisation (CEN) have already developed standards for crumb rubber, so the problems relating to uncertainty about quality and other matters should be substantially reduced in the near future. Again, in countries where these standards do not yet exist governments could promote their adoption.

ACKNOWLEDGEMENTS

This work is undertaken under the direction of the Working Group on Waste Prevention and Recycling, the National Policies Division of the OECD Environment Directorate as part of the programme "Improving Recycling Markets". The authors are grateful for the financial of the OECD and the excellent advice provided by Dr. Nick Johnstone and Dr. Soizick de Tilly.

REFERENCES

AAMVA (2000). *The Commercial Driver's Handbook.* American Association of Motor Vehicle Administrators, Washington DC.

Aardvark Associates (2001). *Post Consumer Tyres: Shifting Perceptions to Create Opportunities*, Working Paper prepared for the Retread Manufacturers Association, Dorset.

AIRP (2002). *Drop in energy consumption and environmental pollution: One million of oil barrels were saved in 2001 thanks to retreads*, Press Release 3 December 2002, Italian Association Tyres Retreaders, Bologna.

Brown, D.A. and W.F. Watson (2000). *Novel Concepts in environmentally friendly rubber recycling*, paper presented at the International Rubber Forum 2000 held in on 9 November 2000, Antwerp.

Burger, C.P.J. and H.P. Smit (2001). Economic growth and the future of natural rubber', presented at Yamoussoukro, Cote d'Ivore, 5-9 November.

Carey, Jason (1999) *Survey of Tire Debris on Metropolitan Phoenix Highways*, Arizona Department of Transportation, report no. ATRC-99-11, Phoenix.

CEC (1999) *Council Directive on the Landfill of Waste, 1999/31/EC*, Commission of the European Communities, Brussels.

CEC (2003). *Towards a Thematic Strategy on Waste Prevention and Recycling.* Commission of the European Communities. COM(2003)yyy final, Brussels.

CEN (2000). *CEN Workshop Business Plan N2", CEN Workshop on the preparation of standards for post-consumer tyre materials and applications*, European Committee for Standardisation 26 May 2000, Brussels.

Curlee, R.T. (1986) The Economic Feasibility of Recycling: A Case Study of Plastic Wastes (New York: Praeger).

DTI (2001) *Tyre Recycling,* Environment Directorate, Department of Trade and Industry, London.

DTI (2003) *Discussion Paper on a possible Producer Responsibility Model for Used Tyres.* Sustainable Development Directorate. Department of Trade and Industry (DTI), London. http://www.dti.gov.uk/sustainability/pub.htm

ECOTEC (2000) Policy instruments to correct market failure in the demand for secondary materials, Report prepared by Ecotec Research and Consulting Ltd., Birmingham.

Environment Agency (1998) Tyres in the environment. Government of the UK, London. http://www.environment-agency.gov.uk/commondata/105385/ea_tyres_report.pdf

Environment Agency (2003) Tyres Watch Programme. Government of the UK, London. http://www.environment-agency.gov.uk/business/444251/444707/288582/?lang=_e&region=

FAO (2001) Commodity notes: Rubber. Food and Agriculture Organisation of the United Nations. Economic and Social Department. Rome. http://www.fao.org/

Greater Manchester Waste Regulation Authority (1995). Fly-tipping in Greater Manchester. Greater Manchester Waste Regulation Authority, Manchester.

Green Consumer Guide (2001). Tyre group push recycle scheme. Newsletter #62. Greenmedia Publishing. 24 August 2001. http://www.greenconsumerguide.com/news62.html

Hogg, D. (2001) *Costs for Municipal Waste Management in the EU*. Final Report to Directorate General Environment, European Commission. Eunomia Research & Consulting.

Jang, Ji-Won, Taek-Soo Yoo, Jae-Hyun Oh and Iwao Iwasaki (1997) "Discarded Tire Recycling Practises in the United States, Japan and Korea", Resources, Conservation and Recycling 22, pp.1-14.

Massachusetts Operational Services Division (2000). "Retread Tires", Recycled Product Fact Sheet # 9, available on the internet at: www.state.ma.us/osd/enviro/products/tires.htm.

MoA (1993). Regulation of the Federal Ministry of Agriculture for Air Emission Limits in Cement Kilns (BGBI No. 63/1993), Vienna.

OECD (1998) Evaluating Economic Instruments for Environmental Policy, OECD, Paris.

OECD (2002) *Improving Recycling Markets*, Paper OECD/ENV/WGWPR(2001)1/REV1, OECD, Paris.

Opschoor, J.B. and R.K. Turner eds. (1994). *Economic Incentives and Environmental Policies Principles and Practice*, Kluwer Academic Publishers, Dordrecht

Owen, K.C. (1998). *Scrap Tires: A Pricing Strategy for a Recycling Industry*, Corporate Environmental Strategy, 5(2): 42-50.

Pyanowski, D. (2002) European End of Life Tyres (ELT), Presentation for the Rubber Manufacturers Association (RAC/RMA) Conference held on 23-25 October 2002, Montreal.

Reiter, B. and R. Stroh, R. (1995). Use of Waste in the Cement Industry. Federal Environmental Agency-Austria.

Rosendorfová, M., I. Výbochová and P.J.H. van Beukering (1998). *Waste Management and Recycling of Tyres in Europe*, R98/13, Institute for Environmental Studies, Amsterdam.

Sunthonpagasit, N. and M.R. Duffey (2002a). *Scrap Tires to Crumb Rubber: Market and Production Issues for Processing Facilities*, School of Engineering and Applied Science, George Washington University

Sunthonpagasit, N. and M.R. Duffey (2002b). *Scrap Tires to Crumb Rubber: Feasibility Analysis for Processing Facilities*, School of Engineering and Applied Science, George Washington University.

TIC (2001). *Responsible Recycler Scheme*, in TIC Report, Tyre Industry Council, July 2001.

TRL (1992). *The incidence of HGV tyre debris on the M4 motorway*. WP/VS/222. Transport Research Laboratory (TRL), Crowthorne, Berkshire.

United Kingdom Parliament (2003) Question on tyres by Norman Baker for the Secretary of State for Environment, Food and Rural Affairs [99271]. London.

UNSD (2002) COMTRADE United Nations, Geneva.

US EPA (1991). *Markets for scrap tires*. In Scrap Tires Technology and Markets, published by Noyes Data Corporation. Park Ridge.

US EPA (1993) "Developing markets for recyclable materials; policy and program options", Report prepared by Mt. Auburn Associates, Inc. and Northeast-Midwest Institute, for U.S. Environmental Protection Agency, Washington D.C.

US EPA (1999) State Scrap Tire Programs. A quick reference guide: 1999 Update. United States Environmental Protection Agency. Washington DC.IRSG (1998) Rubber Statistical Bulletin. 52(4), International Rubber Study Group, Wembley.

US EPA (2000). *2000 Buy-Recycled Seriles: Vehicular Products*. United States Environmental Protection Agency. Washington DC. www.epa.gov/cpg/pdf/vehi-00.pdf

US EPA (2002) Comprehensive Procurement Guidelines: Retread Tires. US Environmental Protection Agency (EPA), Washington DC. http://www.epa.gov/cpg/index.htm

UTWG (2000). *Fourth Annual Report*. Used Tyre Working Group, London.

UTWG (2001). *Fifth Annual Report*. Used Tyre Working Group, London.

Van Beukering, P.J.H. van and M.A. Janssen (2001). A dynamic integrated analysis of truck tires in Western Europe, *Journal of Industrial Ecology* 4(2): 93-115.

VCA (1999) "VCA Guide to the Type Approval of Retread Tyres", VCA 036, Vehicle Certification Agency, Bristol.

Virginia Department of State Police (2000) "Need for Standards for Recapped Tires", Commonwealth of Virginia, Richmond.

CONFERENCE CLOSING KEYNOTE PAPERS

RECYCLING POWER STATIONS BY-PRODUCTS-
A LONG HISTORY OF USE?

L K A Sear

United Kingdom Quality Ash Association

United Kingdom

ABSTRACT. The UK coal fired power industry has been recycling ash for over 50 years. Pulverised Fuel Ash (PFA) and Furnace Bottom Ash (FBA) have been used for a wide variety of applications with in excess of 50 million tonnes being utilised. As well as the environmental benefits of using PFA and FBA, there are often considerable technical benefits compared to naturally occurring materials. These markets have been successfully developed, but they are now under threat.

European Directives, which have existed for some time, are beginning to negatively impact on recycling industries. Recent European and National court rulings, whilst seeking to clarify the situation, have highlighted weaknesses in the legislation. These judgements have also been subject to misinterpretation. This has led to materials now being considered by the regulatory authorities as being waste. While being labelled a 'waste' in some applications is enough to put off many construction companies from using PFA and FBA, the bureaucracy and requirements of the Waste Management Licensing are such as to put the 'nail in the coffin' of ash recycling.

This paper will review the current situation, the problems with the Waste Management Licensing system and to try to predict the future for the PFA and FBA recycling industry.

Keywords: Pulverised Fuel Ash, PFA, Fly Ash, Environment, Recycling, Waste Management Licensing, European Legislation.

Lindon K A Sear is the Technical Officer of the United Kingdom Quality Ash Association representing the interests of the UK coal fired power station operators. He represents the members of the UKQAA on a number of British and European Standard Committees. He is involved in the steering committees of many research projects ranging from the environmental aspects of PFA/fly ash through to the thaumasite form of sulfate attack. In addition, Lindon has been closely involved with developments within the environmental field in recent years and has observed the increasing bureaucracy and regulation that is in fact harming the environment.

INTRODUCTION

Pulverised fuel ash (PFA) and Furnace Bottom Ash (FBA) have been produced in significant quantities since World War II, with the introduction of modern steam raising plant. Following research carried out in the late 1940's it was discovered that PFA could be used in cementitious applications as well as being used for fill applications. The first UK use in concrete was in the construction of the Breadblane Hydro electric scheme in 1954. Similarly, in 1952 PFA was first used as a fill material. FBA found its market was within the production of lightweight aggregate concrete blocks. The markets for the products developed gradually, culminating in the preparation of British Standards and incorporation within National specifications as being suitable for many applications.

Since the UK joined the European Community, various pieces of legislation have been enacted that affect industry. Environmental legislation has increasingly come to the fore as having the greatest effect on the construction industry, in particular. This legislation was introduced through directives and subsequent court cases that are legally binding on the UK regulators. It would appear in recent months that the interpretation of the directives and court cases has become an industry in its own right, though with a consequential threat to the by-products and recycling industries. The following is a review of the situation on power station by-products and the environmental legislation.

THE HISTORY OF PFA AND FBA

The first reference to the idea of utilising coal fly ash within modern day concrete was by McMillan & Powers[1] in 1934 and research in the United States of America [2] indicated that fly ash had a role in concrete in 1935. Later research also in the US [3] reported that fly ash was a possible artificial pozzolana. Trial applications and continuing research promoted the idea that introduction of a proportion of fly ash as replacement of cement would limit shrinkage cracking in mass concrete by reducing internal hydration temperatures.

The introduction of pulverised coal steam raising plant in the UK, particularly after the 1939-1945 war, resulted in the production of fly ash and it was the late 1940's that saw research into the use of the material. In particular the example of using fly ash in mass concrete dams was considered, and, following research at the University of Glasgow [4], the practice was adopted for construction of the Lednock[5], Clatworthy and Lubreoch Dams, see Figure 1. In 1954, construction commenced on Lednock dam, which was the first structure built with some 62,500 m^3 of concrete containing PFA being used, replacing some 3,000 tonnes of Portland cement. The dams formed part of the Scottish Hydro-Electric Board's Breadblane scheme and the subsequent durability of the structures has been found excellent.

There followed in the period 1954-58 numerous examples of the use of fly ash as cement replacement in structural concrete at the Fleet Telephone Exchange, Newman Spinney Power Station [6] and the High Marnham sub-station [7]. By the mid 1970's fly ash was regularly being used in concrete as an addition at the concrete plant within many power company structures and some notable public works [8] being constructed. Such usage was always on a basis of close monitoring by the site and within large construction projects. Within the UK, fly ash from coal combustion became known as Pulverised Fuel Ash (PFA) around this time to differentiate it from ashes derived from other processes.

Figure 1 – Placing concrete in Lednock Dam, ~1956

Although the use of PFA in concrete was accepted by British Standards it was not until 1965 when the first edition of BS3892 [9] was published that there was a standard for PFA for use in concrete. PFA was treated as a fine aggregate having three classes of fineness based on the specific surface area. During this period acceptance in the routine readymixed concrete supply market was not being achieved. During the 1970's readymixed concrete suppliers were producing ever more technically demanding concretes of higher strength and lower water cement ratios. It was perceived that the variability in quality and the supply problems of PFA when taken directly from the power station were unacceptable.

Within the UK one solution was found to the fineness variability problems when in 1975 Pozzolan Ltd. introduced the concept of supplying controlled fineness material. Controlling the PFA to a tightly controlled fineness involved either classifying the ash, to remove the coarse fractions, or selection of the finer material by continual monitoring of the ash production. In general, finer PFA enhances the pozzolanicity whilst reducing the water demand. An Agrément Board Certificate [10] was obtained for controlled fineness PFA in 1975. These changes were reflected within BS3892 [11] in 1982 with the various parts of the standard indicating the uses and quality of PFA. Controlled fineness PFA to BS3892: Part 1 was accepted as counting fully towards the cement content of a mix, whereas 'run of station' ashes were at the discretion of the site engineer. The latter were usually considered as inert fillers and are covered by BS3892: Part 2: 1984.

In 1985 two British Standards were published for cements containing pulverised fuel ash.
- BS6588 for Portland pulverised fuel ash cements permitted an ash level between 15 and 35% by mass of cement and;
- BS6610 for pozzolanic pulverised fuel ash cement permitted an ash level of 35 to 50% by mass of cement.

Before 1985, interground Portland PFA cement had been produced by Blue Circle in the North of England, under an Agrément Certificate. Classified PFA was increasingly accepted for use within concrete both on technical and economic grounds. Currently the use of classified PFA is widespread within the UK readymixed and precast concrete industries. Some 25% of the readymixed concrete produced in the UK contains a binder that consists of, typically, 30% PFA and 70% Portland cement. Currently some 500,000 tonnes per annum of classified PFA are used in readymixed and precast concrete. With European harmonisation, a new standard for fly ash, BS EN450 [12] 1995, was introduced. With the exception of the UK and Ireland, no other European countries routinely classify PFA for use in concrete. EN450 reflects this differing approach and allows a wider range of fineness for use in concrete than

BS3892 Part 1[13]. The enabling standard for EN450 fly ash, EN 206 [14], has taken a number of years to finalise and consequently the use of EN450 fly ash is somewhat restricted. However, the complementary standard to BS EN206, BS 8500 [15], reflects the better performance of finer PFA and selected/classified PFA to BS3892 Part 1 will remain permitted under BS8500 for the foreseeable future.

Figure 2 – PFA used as a fill material A45, Packington nr Coventry

As stated above, PFA's first recorded use as a fill material was in 1952. It has been extensively used in highway construction following considerable research during the 1950's and 1960's into its properties. It was incorporated into the Specification for Highway works and widely used as embankment fill during the period the motorway network was being built. It was found to be a very stable, lightweight material that settles very little with increasing strength with age, see Figure 2. It has also been used successfully on reinforced earth structures.

More recently PFA has been used in numerous other applications, e.g. grouting, sub-base layers in road construction, in brick manufacture, for soil stabilisation and remediation, etc. FBA has been used in block making for many years. Many still refer to 'breeze blocks', with breeze being the fore-runner to FBA. Because FBA is flushed from the furnace by high pressure water jets, it is a far superior product to 'breeze', which ceased to be available anyway as the older furnaces were replaced. Subsequently FBA became the preferred product by the block manufacturers as a lightweight aggregate. Currently 99% of UK FBA production is used in lightweight aggregate block manufacture.

Since its introduction well in excess of 50 million tonnes of power station ash products have been used in a wide variety of applications. To our knowledge there has been no recorded incident of significant environmental pollution due to use of these products, and yet they are under threat on environmental legislative grounds.

ENVIRONMENTAL LEGISLATION

The legislation that potentially affects PFA and numerous other by-product materials stems from the EU "The Waste Framework Directive (75/442/EEC as amended by 91/156/EEC)". This directive was enforced in England and Wales by the Environmental Protection Act of 1990. A series of exemptions were permitted under resulting legislation, The Waste Management License (WML) regulations, which were produced in 1994 and are interpreted using DOE Circular 11/94 [16].

In recent years the Environment Agency (EA) has stated that there is doubt as to the validity of DOE 11/94 resulting from various EU court cases. This resulted in the EA regarding the document as no longer valid and this being stated within parliament. However, even though this statement was made, the document was not withdrawn from the public domain. A revision of DOE 11/94 by the Department of the Environment, Food and Rural Affairs (DEFRA) has recently taken place. Additionally, the permitted exemptions have been revised and these should be published by the time of this conference. It is understood the main changes to the exemptions system are:

1. Applications for exemption are no longer automatic and a minimum of 21 days notice must be given.

2. The EA may object to an exemption being granted within the 21 day period.

3. A charge for the application for exemption will be made.

4. There will be no more significant exemptions permitted from the 1994 categories. There will be more restrictions to some exemptions, e.g. a maximum thickness limit on land restoration of 2m.

Having said all the above the legislation only relates to materials that are classified as 'wastes'. Obviously, domestic refuse being disposed of in a landfill operation is a waste and requires Waste Management Licensing (WML). What is less clear is when a material is a waste and when does it cease to be a waste, say after processing or use by another industry. So does a by-product, like PFA, legally become a waste? PFA is occasionally disposed in landfills that have WML's. However, the majority of the material is sold, therefore not discarded and sold for beneficial use to a construction company, i.e. it has a market, surely this is not waste? It is for this reason there are important questions such as;

- When is a material 'recovered'?

- When does it cease to be a waste – when it's recovered?

- What processing is considered necessary for 'recovery' to have occurred?

THE DEFINITIONS, UK and EU LAW AND COURT CASES

The overarching aims of the EU Waste Framework Directive are as follows:

- ***Waste Management Hierarchy.*** Waste management strategies must aim primarily to prevent the generation of waste and to reduce its harmfulness. Where this is not possible, waste materials should be reused, recycled or recovered, or used as a source of energy. As a final resort, waste should be disposed of safely (e.g. by incineration or in landfill sites).

- **Self-Sufficiency at Community and, if possible, at Member State level.** Member states need to establish, in co-operation with other Member States, an integrated and adequate network of waste disposal facilities.

- **Best Available Technique Not Entailing Excessive Cost (BATNEEC).** Emissions from installations to the environment should be reduced as much as possible and in the most economically efficient way.

- **Proximity.** Wastes should be disposed of as close to the source as possible.

- **Producer Responsibility.** Economic operators, and particularly manufacturers of products, have to be involved in the objective to close the life cycle of substances, components and products from their production throughout their useful life until they become a waste.

These aims of the directive are very laudable and fully supported by most. However, the same directive does seem to have created a situation that will in fact reduce '*re-use, recycling and recovery*' simply because these terms are ill defined both in the mind of the producers, end users and regulators. While various bodies have asked for clarification, to date little has happened that gives the producer or user any confidence the aims are achievable. In fact the directive is in danger of having the opposite effect – to reduce the use of by-products, recovery and recycling. The problem is outlined as follows.

The definition of waste used in the EU Waste Framework Directive is:

- 'Waste' means any substance or object which the holder disposes of or is required to dispose of.

- 'disposal' means :

  o The collection, sorting, transport and treatment of waste as well as its storage and tipping above or below ground.

  o The transformation operations necessary for its re-use, recovery or recycling.

DOE 11/94 gives guidance on the concept of waste. It states in paragraph 2.28 that if a substance can be used in its present form in the same way as any other raw material without being subjected to a specialised recovery operation this would provide reasonable indication that the substance or object has NOT been discarded and therefore is not a waste. In 2.32 there is a specific comment on by-products, stating that useful by-products that change hands for value and remain part of the normal commercial cycle should not be regarded as being discarded. As PFA and FBA are both products that are used as alternatives to other raw materials, such as sand for fill and grouting and cement in cementitious applications, this would suggest they are not wastes.

Subsequent European Case Law has confused the interpretations of DOE 11/94. The following cases asked some specific questions:

- **Euro Tombesi and Adino Tombesi etc**[17]**:** Is a material that has economic value ever a waste? Answer: Waste is not to be understood as excluding substances and objects that have economic value.

- **Inter-Environnement Wallonie ASBL and Region Wallonne** [18]: Can a material that forms part of an integrated industrial process be regarded as a waste? Answer: Yes

- **Mayer Parry Recycling Ltd v Environment Agency** [19]: Under what circumstance is scrap a waste? Answer: Recovered material is not a waste. Difficulty arises from the definition of a recovery process and the point at which recovery is regarded as complete. Clarity was not given on when "recovery/recycling" was regarded as complete.

- **ARCO Chemie Nederland Ltd and Minister van Volkshuisvesting, Ruimtelijke Ordening en Milieubeheer** [20]: Is a residue used as a fuel a waste? Answer: Unclear answer – depends on circumstances. The concept of waste cannot be interpreted restrictively.

- **Mayer Parry Recycling Ltd v The Environment Agency** [21]: When has waste been recycled and therefore ceased to be a waste? This relates to the previous Mayer Parry case and the Packaging Regulations. Answer: When recovery is complete. This has been referred to the European Court of Justice for further consideration.

- **Castle Cement v The Environment Agency** [22]: Is waste derived fuel a waste? Answer: Yes

- **Palin Granit Oy v Korkein hallinto-oikeus** [23]: Should left over stone that is no threat to the environment awaiting suitable markets for sale be classified as a waste? Answer: The holder of leftover stone resulting from stone quarrying, which is stored for an indefinite length of time to await possible use, discards or intends to discard that leftover stone, which is accordingly to be classified as waste.

- **AvestaPolarit Chrome v Korkein hallinto-oikeus (Supreme Administrative Court, Finland)** [24]; Is leftover rock resulting from the extraction of ore and/or ore-dressing sand resulting from the dressing of ore in mining operations to be regarded as waste? Answer: As in Palin Granit leftover rock resulting from the extraction of ore and/or ore-dressing sand resulting from the dressing of ore in mining operations which is stored for an indefinite length of time to await possible use are to be classified as waste

- **Tribunale di Gela (Italy) PET coke ruling.**[25] Does petroleum coke fall within the meaning of waste? Answer: Petroleum coke which is produced intentionally or in the course of producing other petroleum fuels in an oil refinery and is certain to be used as fuel to meet the energy needs of the refinery and those of other industries does not constitute waste.

The EA interpretation of these cases, in particular the Palin Granit and AvestPolarit cases, leads to them to use a three point test for whether a product is a waste:

1. Re-use is not a mere possibility, but a certainty;

2. There must be no further processing required prior to re-use, and

3. The re-use must be an integral part of the production process.

In respect of PFA and FBA produced for sale the Electricity Supply Industry (ESI) would comment of these requirements as follows:

Re-use is a certainty: The design of the coal milling plant and the boiler are optimised to produce PFA and FBA of saleable quality. In addition the PFA is stored in both dry and conditioned forms for sale to the various construction markets, e.g. concrete, fill, grouting, block making, etc. There are dedicated sales teams for these materials that are active within the construction markets. In addition, the ESI has invested in a considerable amount of research over many years to develop the various applications for the products. It has been so successful that 99% of FBA produced is used in block making and 55% of PFA produced is used in a variety of applications. While it is not the intention of the power station to discard any PFA, any material that cannot be sold is then consigned to lagoons or landfill sites, see Figure 3. Here this material is regulated as a waste and covered by Integrated Prevention of Pollution and Control (IPPC) licensing.

Figure 3 - An ash disposal site - Barlow mound at Drax power station

The ESI feels it can clearly demonstrate that PFA and FBA have a certainty of use through the markets it has developed.

There must be no further processing required prior to re-use: PFA and FBA for re-use does not undergo any significant processing. For concrete applications PFA is normally supplied dry in cement tankers. It may be processed to enhance its properties, but this does not preclude from use without any processing. For fill and grout applications, water will be added to PFA to prevent dust problems. Usually, it will then be delivered in normal sheeted tipping vehicles, allowing it to be used as an alternative material to naturally occurring sand. FBA may be screened and crushed to appropriate sizes for the use, otherwise there is no processing. Any processing that does take place is substantially no different than would be applicable to naturally occurring materials, e.g. sand and aggregates. Additionally, the markets for PFA and FBA are in direct substitution for those of either the cementitious, fine and coarse aggregate markets.

Considering the above the ESI feels it demonstrates that no processing or recovery is required before it can be used in production processes.

The re-use must be an integral part of the production process: This test is disputed by the ESI. It results from the Palin Granit (paragraph 36) court ruling as follows:

> *However, having regard to the obligation, recalled at paragraph 23 of this judgment, to interpret the concept of waste widely in order to limit its inherent risks and pollution, the reasoning applicable to by-products should be confined to situations in which the reuse of the goods, materials or raw materials is not a mere possibility but a certainty, without any further processing prior to reuse and <u>as an integral part of the production process</u>.*

This paragraph seems to be contradicted by other paragraphs in the ruling and by paragraph 37 that states:

> *It therefore appears that, in addition to the criterion of whether a substance constitutes a production residue, a second relevant criterion for determining whether or not that substance is waste for the purposes of Directive 75/442 is the degree of likelihood that that substance will be reused, without any further processing prior to its reuse. If, in addition to the mere possibility of reusing the substance, there is also a financial advantage to the holder in so doing, the likelihood of reuse is high. In such circumstances, the substance in question must no longer be regarded as a burden which its holder seeks to 'discard, but as a genuine product.*

The wording in paragraph 36 relating to 'part of the production process' has been taken to mean by the EA that the re-use must occur within the power station. However, it could be interpreted that the by-product is an integral part of the production process and it requires no further processing prior to re-use, e.g. it has markets and is a genuine product. To an extent this view is supported by the PET coke ruling.

The ESI takes the latter view and concludes that:

- PFA and FBA are NOT wastes;

- They have certainty of re-use;

- They require no further processing;

- They are marketed as genuine products for use in the cementitious, fine and coarse aggregate markets.

THE EFFECTS ON MARKETS

The EA is responsible for the enforcement of waste management controls. It states in its Internal Note 1 [26] that explains their Definition of Waste that "*It is the responsibility of the person who produces or holds a substance or object to determine whether what they are holding is waste. People who are unclear as to their obligations should consider taking their own legal advice as ultimately the interpretation of the law is a matter of the courts.*" However, this does not stop the EA from giving its opinion when asked. Rather than make the above statement to an enquirer, the EA advice at the time of writing this paper is that PFA is a waste and will, depending on the application, either require an exemption or a Waste Management License. Clearly the ESI view is contrary to that of the EA's, i.e. PFA is NOT a waste. Additionally, the EA should not be giving such advice, based on its own internal documents that states this decision shall be made by the producer.

This complex legal position has been subject to review by a top barrister, who concurs with the ESI view. In addition other producers of by-products of a similar nature to power station ash have also sort legal review and been advised similarly, their products are NOT wastes. As a result this has resulted in a legal impasse that may only be resolved by yet another court case. It would appear the EU Waste Framework Directive has a number of flaws:

1. The definition of 'waste' is clear. However;

2. There is a lack of clear definitions of terms such as 'recovery', 'by-product', 'product', etc to support the definition of waste.

3. It was created with disposal of waste into landfill and the illegal dumping of wastes in mind – it did not consider the industrial by-product and recycling markets that were already in existence and how the Directive would impinge on such operations.

These problems are compounded by the National regulators who are concerned about correctly interpreting the directives and various court cases. As any EU country who fails to enact an EU Directive can be subject to very large fines, coupled with the UK's passion for exactly following the letter of the law, this leads to regulators who are not prepared to interpret or who take the most pessimistic view of the situation. The EA view is that '*the interpretation of the law is a matter for the courts*', e.g. that all decisions about a product will be made by the courts and not the regulator.

The result of this less than satisfactory situation is the regulator, if asked, will advise the end user of a product that by-products like PFA are classified as wastes and require either waste management licenses or exemption certificates. Of course the end user, not wishing to get embroiled in the bureaucracy of such legislation, opts for the simpler and totally unregulated natural aggregate option. Conversely if the end user deliberately decides that the material is NOT a waste and not subject to waste management or is ignorant of the situation, he accepts a small risk that he may end up defending this decision in court. Obviously the ESI would support any end user in such a battle, but many are put off such a decision. The result of this situation is:

1. While ignorance of the law is no excuse, badly drafted laws and directives lead to situations that can put the end user at risk of not complying.

2. The onus is placed on the producer and end user to decide whether a material is a waste and yet the regulator is able to advise to the contrary - with the only recourse being through the courts.

3. The markets for by-product materials are gradually eroded in favour of using natural materials, natural materials having less bureaucracy and risk associated with them.

4. The actual environmental impacts of the by-product or the natural material used in such construction applications have no bearing on the situation, which is solely one of legal interpretations.

CONCLUSIONS

The bureaucratic burden on the producers and users of by-product and recycled materials and the level of uncertainty over EU Directives, the UK interpretation of the directives and the inability of the regulators to make rulings other than to refer back to the courts is detrimental to both the environment, industry and ultimately the government. Such regulation is actively discouraging the use of by-products and recycled materials.

The solution is for the government and its departments, the regulators and the EU Commission to listen to industry and to work with industry. In this manner sensible, workable solutions will be forthcoming, rather than ad hoc legislation being created that is just counter productive. If this approach is not adopted, less recycling and recovery will occur, to the overall detriment of the environment. Eventually, because of increasing costs, industry will transfer to the developing countries where the environmental and bureaucratic burdens are less.

REFERENCES

[1] McMillan F R and Powers T C, A method of evaluating admixtures, Proceedings American Concrete Institute, Vol. 30, pp. 325-344, March-April 1934.

[2] Davis R E, Kelly J W, Troxell G E and Davis H E, 1935, Proportions of Mortars and Concretes containing Portland-Pozzolan Cements, ACI, Vol. 32, 80-114

[3] Davis R E, Carlston R W, Kelly J W and Davis H E, 1937, Properties of Cements and Concretes containing Fly ash, A.C.I., Journal 33, 577-612

[4] Fulton, A A and Marshall W T, 1956, The use of fly ash and similar materials in concrete, Proc. Inst. Civ. Engrs., Part 1, Vol. 5, 714-730

[5] Allen AC, Features of Lednock Dam, including the use of fly ash. Paper No. 6326 Proceedings of the Institute of Civil Engineers 1958:13 August: 179-196

[6] Richardson, L and Bailey J C, 1965, Design, construction and testing of pulverised fuel ash concrete structures at Newman Spinney Power Station, Parts I, II, III, CEGB Research and Development Report

[7] Howell, L H, 1958, Report on pulverised fuel ash as a partial replacement for cement in normal works concrete, CEGB, East Midlands Division. (also Ashtech '84, London, 1984)

[8] Central Electricity Generating Board Technical Bulletins Nos. 1 to 48

[9] BS3892: Pulverised fuel ash for use in concrete, 1965.

[10] The Agrèment Board Certificate No. 75/283. Pozzolan - a selected fly ash for use in concrete.

[11] BS3892 Part 1, Pulverised fuel ash for use as a cementitious component in structural concrete, 1982, BSI.

[12] BS EN 450 Fly ash for concrete - Definitions, requirements and quality control, 1995, BSI, ISBN 0 580 24612 4.

[13] BS 3892: Part 1, Specification for pulverised-fuel ash for use with Portland cement, 1997, BSI, ISBN 0 580 26785 7.

14   BS EN206: 2001, Concrete – Part 1: Specification, performance, production and conformity, BSI, London.

15   BS8500 (Draft for public comment): Concrete – complementary British Standard to BS EN206-1, Feb., 2001.

16   DoE Circular 11/94 Environmental Protection Act 1990: Part II Waste Management Licensing.

17   uro Tombesi and Adino Tombesi etc Joined Cases C-304/94, C-330/94, C-342/94 and C-224/95 – European Court of Justice – Advocate General F G Jacobs. *25 June 1997*

18   Inter-Environnement Wallonie ASBL and Region Wallonne – Case C-129/96 – European Court of Justice – Advocate General F G Jacobs. *18 December 1997*

19   Mayer Parry Recycling Ltd v Environment Agency – Chancery Division – Carnworth J - *9 November 1998*

20   ARCO Chemie Nederland Ltd and Minister van Volkshuisvesting, Ruimtelijke Ordening en Milieubeheer – Joined Cases C-418/97 (ARCO) and C-419/97 (Epon) – European Court of Justice – Advocate General S Alber - 15 June 2000

21   Mayer Parry Recycling Ltd v The Environment Agency – CO/512/00 – High Court of Justice – Mr Justice Collins - *8 September 2000*

22   Castle Cement v The Environment Agency - High Court of Justice – Justice Stanley Burnton - 22 March 2001

23   In Case C-9/00, Palin Granit Oy and Vehmassalon kansanterveystyön kuntayhtymän hallitus, JUDGMENT OF THE COURT (Sixth Chamber), 18 April 2002

24   Case C-114/01 AvestaPolarit Chrome Oy vKorkein hallinto-oikeus (Supreme Administrative Court, Finland), 10 April 2003

25   Case C-235/02, 15 January 2004, Article 104(3) of the Rules of Procedure - Directives 75/442/EEC and 91/156/EEC - Waste management - Definition of waste - Petroleum coke, REFERENCE to the Court under Article 234 EC by the Giudice per le indagini preliminari of the Tribunale di Gela (Italy) for a preliminary ruling in the criminal proceedings before that court against Mario Antonio Saetti and Andrea Frediani.

26   Environment Agency, Definition of Waste - Internal Note 1, UNDERSTANDING THE DEFINITION OF WASTE, September 2003.

MAKING RECYCLING ECONOMIC – THE SUSTAINABILITY OF MATERIALS FOR THE BUILT ENVIRONMENT

A J W Harrison

TecEco Pty Ltd.

Australia

ABSTRACT. Our interaction with our planet earth is described as the techno-process which is the process of taking resources, manipulating them as required (modifying substances), making something with them, using what is made and then throwing what has been made that no longer has utility[i] away. The techno-process of take, manipulate, make, use and waste is discussed particularly in relation to reducing, reusing and recycling materials, earth systems, the web of life and materials in the built environment which, at over 70% of all materials flows, comprise the major component of the flow through the techno process. The most significant material flow is that of concrete as over two tonnes are produced per person on the planet per annum. The use of new calcium magnesium blended cements (TecEco cements) invented by the author that utilise wastes and sequester carbon dioxide is discussed as an example of the significant impact changes in materials could make.

Reducing, re-using and recycling materials would reduce the impact of the techno process on the planet, but is currently undertaken more for "feel good" political reasons than sound economic reasons in many instances. Some unique practical solutions are offered to resolve this dilemma including a unique electronic identification system for materials and the use of new generation TecEco cement composite materials as potential repositories of wastes including CO_2.

Keywords: Abatement, Sustainable, Sustainability, Sequestration, CO_2, Brucite ($Mg(OH)_2$), Durability, Reactive magnesium oxide, Magnesian, Magnesia, Reactive magnesia (MgO), magnesite ($MgCO_3$), Hydromagnesite ($Mg_5(CO_3)4(OH)_2{\cdot}4H_2O$), Fly ash, Pozzolan, Hydraulic cement, Portland cement, Concrete, Process energy, Embodied energy, Lifetime energy, Shrinkage, Cracking, Extract, Permeability, Rheology, Emissions, Flow, Matter, Materials, Substances, Wastes, Reduce, Reuse, Recycling, Manipulate, Use, waste, utility, digital, silicon chip.

A John W Harrison, *B.Sc. B.Ec. FCPA*. John Harrison is managing director and chairman of TecEco Pty. Ltd. and best known for the invention of tec, eco and enviro-cements known mainly for their impact on sustainability. John is an authority on sustainable materials for the built environment and was a founder of the Association for the Advancement of Sustainable Materials in Construction.

THE IMPACT OF POPULATION GROWTH, TECHNOLOGY AND CONSUMPTION

There is not the room in this paper to go into the detail of our legacy on this planet. Suffice to say we have taken over, we control the world and our impact has been very detrimental to virtually all earth systems. Our detrimental linkages with the environment have grown due to population increases and partly due to shifts in the technological basis of the techno – process whereby we take resources from the environment, manipulate the molecules, make something, use it and then when we have finished it waste it.

According to the American Association for the Advancement of Science Population and Environment Atlas[ii], "Consumption and technology impact on the environment by way of two major types of human activity. First, we use resources. We occupy or pre-empt the use of space, and so modify or remove entirely the habitats of many wild species. We extract or take resources -- growing food, catching fish, mining minerals, pumping groundwater or oil. This affects the stock of resources available for humans and for other species in the future.

Second, we dump wastes -- not just those that consumers throw away, but all the waste solids, liquids and gases that are generated from raw material to final product. These affect the state of land, groundwater, rivers, oceans, atmosphere and climate." If we want to survive the next millennia as a race we will need to take more responsibility for the environment.

THE TECHNO-PROCESS

Our interaction with the geosphere-biosphere[iiiiv] is described as the techno-process which is the process of extracting resources, manipulating them as required (modifying substances), making something with them, using what is made and then throwing what has been made that no longer has utility[v] away. The techno-function (Take→Manipulate→Make→Use→Waste) describes this techno – process.

The impact of the techno - function on the planet is significant. Resources are not unlimited and the planet does not have an infinite capacity to reabsorb wastes. To reduce linkages with the environment and for our own long term sustainable survival the take and waste need to be reduced and preferably eliminated to what is renewable and preferably biodegradable. To do this we must adopt the philosophy of Reducing, Re-using, Recycling and Recovering. Resources extracted from the geosphere-biosphere can be classified broadly into several non exclusive types. Resources are renewable or non renewable, short use or longer use materials.

- *Renewable Resources*
  A renewable resource is any natural resource (such as wood or solar energy) that can be replenished naturally[vi] with the passage of time. Can be either short use (renewable energy) or long use (wood). Depend on the health of the geosphere-biosphere for natural replenishment.

- *Non-Renewable Resources*
  The use of non-renewable resources as materials or energy sources leads to depletion of the Earth's reserves. Non renewable resources are characterised as non-renewable in human relevant periods.

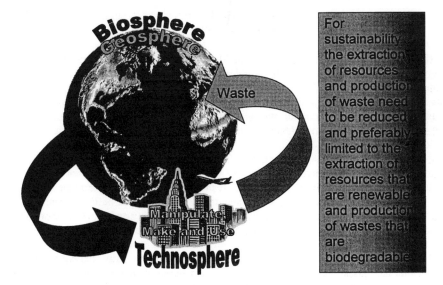

Figure 1 –The Techno - Process.

- ***Short Use Resources***
  Are renewable (food) or non renewable (fossil fuels). Have short use, are generally extracted modified and consumed, may (food, air, fuels) or may not (water) change chemically but are generally altered or contaminated on return back to the geosphere-biosphere (e.g. food consumed ends up as sewerage, water used is contaminated on return.)

- ***Long Term Use Resources or Materials***
  Materials are "the substance or substances out of which a thing is or can be made[vii]." Alternatively they could be viewed as "the substance of which a thing is made or composed, component or constituent matter.[viii]"
  Some materials are renewable (wood), however most are not renewable unless totally recycled (metals, most plastics etc.) Materials generally have a longer cycle from extraction to return, remaining in the techno-sphere[ix] whilst being used and before eventually being wasted. Materials may (plastics) or may not (wood) be chemically altered and are further divided into organic (e.g. wood & paper) and inorganic (e.g. metals minerals etc.)

Other classifications are possible such as surface or sub surface resources, etc. but not relevant to my arguments in this paper. The techno-process is very inefficient in that large quantities of renewable and non renewable resources are extracted to produce small quantities of materials which themselves are used to produce even smaller volumes of things actually used, many of which do not retain utility (value to us) very long before they are in turn discarded. "Studies show that between a half and three-fourths of the materials used in our industrial economy are generated and treated as waste before ever entering the economy. They are not seen or treated as commodities and aren't valued as such[x]". It is essential that we find more uses for these wastes for linkages to the biosphere-geosphere to be reduced. The inventive is that economically we would be better off.

EARTH SYSTEMS

The Earth has well-connected systems. Carbon dioxide emitted in one country is rapidly mixed throughout the atmosphere, and pollutants released into the ocean in one location are transported to distant parts of the planet. Local and regional emissions create global environmental problems. It is difficult to completely understand let alone put numbers to the complex flows and balances that go on around the planet. We do know however that pollution from wastes of various kinds has affected atmospheric composition, land cover, marine ecosystems, coastal zones, freshwater systems, global biological diversity and many other global systems.

Due to our pervading interference the constituent components of matter which are molecules are no longer produced or used in equilibrium. Of particular concern and therefore the most studied is the carbon cycle which is out of balance. Complex carbon based molecules put together by living matter over many millions of years are being used as if there was no tomorrow. The level of carbon dioxide waste from this process is rising too rapidly for conversion by photosynthesis or utilization by organisms for skeletons and shells. As a consequence the level of CO_2 in the air has risen from 280 parts per million in pre-industrial times to around 370 parts per million today. Methane concentrations have also risen by 145 percent over the same period. Before the industrial revolution gaseous chlorines did not exist in the atmosphere. By 1996 there were 2 731 parts per trillion, most of these produced in the 20th century[xi].

Rising atmospheric carbon dioxide concentration and its potential impact on future climate is an issue of global economic and political significance. Of possible even greater importance is the depletion of oxygen in the atmosphere. A study of all the other earth systems including for example the hydrosphere of which freshwater systems are a part and in relation to which water quality, salinity and supply are major issues or sea fisheries which are in major decline is beyond the scope of this paper. The Affect of the Techno-Process on the Web of Life

Figure 2 – Most Pollution Eventually Makes it to our Waterways Killing Fish and other Life[xii]

What distinguishes our planet from any other we have yet discovered is that there exists life, comprising carbon based molecules which have evolved in a delicate balance with the rest of the atoms and molecules that make up planet earth. Living matter is different from dead matter in that it contains genetic coding and has the ability to take atoms and molecules from the environment to build new replicates of itself for the future. This delicate balance is characterized by the flow of substances from the dead world to living matter and in reverse and has gone on for billions of years. Since the dawn of mankind and in particular the industrial revolution our ability and willingness to manipulate everything around us has however has wreaked havoc with living life forms.

For example, according to some estimates, seventy percent of Earth's coral reefs will cease to exist in the next forty years if the current trend continues. Every year, around one thousand (1,000) species are driven to extinction. The loss of tropical forests is especially alarming as they are the home habitat of over fifty percent of the world's species of plants and animals[xiii]. There is no doubt that we have seriously disturbing the "web of life" and evidence is mounting of worse future problems unless we can reduce our impact.

We take atoms and molecules from the dead and living matter around us in what is the techno-process and then when finished throw them "away". There is no such place as "away" Many of these transformed atoms and molecules enter the global commons and return as part of the flow negatively affecting our wellbeing and that of other living organisms on the planet. Persistent chemicals are not confined to the area in which they are created. Gases like Chloro fluoro hydrocarbons (CFC's) which is a waste enter what is the global commons. CFC's were developed during the 1930s and found widespread application after World War II. They are halogenated hydrocarbons, mostly trichlorofluoromethane and dichlorodifluoromethane and were used extensively as aerosol-spray propellants, refrigerants, solvents, and foam-blowing agents because they were non-toxic and non-flammable and readily converted from a liquid to a gas and vice versa.

CFCs were however found to pose a serious environmental threat because in the stratosphere they broke down under ultraviolet light releasing chlorine which destroyed ozone. A hole over Antarctica developed in the ozone layer which shields living organisms on earth from the harmful effects of the sun's ultraviolet radiation. "Because of a growing concern over stratospheric ozone depletion and its attendant dangers, a ban was imposed on the use of CFCs in aerosol-spray dispensers in the late 1970s by the United States, Canada, and the Scandinavian countries. In 1990, 93 nations agreed to end production of ozone-depleting chemicals by the end of the century, and in 1992 most of those same countries agreed to end their production of CFCs by 1996[xiv]."

Heavy metals have been of particular concern. The term "heavy metal" refers to metals that are relatively high in density and toxic or poisonous even at low concentrations. Examples include mercury (Hg), cadmium (Cd), arsenic (As), chromium (Cr), thallium (Tl), and lead (Pb). Heavy metals are natural components of the Earth's crust and cannot be degraded or destroyed. They are particularly dangerous when released as wastes because they tend to bio-accumulate up the food chain. For example, marine organisms can consume a particularly dangerous form of mercury called methylmercury. When fish eat these organisms, the methylmercury is not excreted, but retained in bodily tissues. The older the fish and the more organisms further down the food chain they have consumed, the greater the amount of methylmercury in their tissues. The accumulated methylmercury is concentrated as it is passed up the food chain and any organism at the top such as us faces a serious risk of mercury poisoning by eating such fish.

Heavy metals can enter a water supply from industrial and consumer waste, or even from acidic rain breaking down soils and releasing heavy metals into streams, lakes, rivers, and groundwater. We are constantly being alerted to the fact that living organisms in the far reaches of the globe contain significant traces of organic and metallic pollutants and that the deepest marine sediments, remotest glaciers and icecaps are contaminated. The list of contaminants is frightening and long. Pollution from waste is everybody's problem.

The Environmental Affects of Resource Extraction in the Techno – function

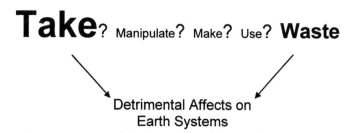

In the past the main cause of concern was that resources would not be sufficient to sustain the human race let alone the techno-process (even if it was not called that) "Frequent warnings were issued that we faced massive famines, or that we would "run out" of essential fuels and minerals.[xv]" Renewable resources such as water, fish stocks, even the air we breathe are today of much greater concern because they are now understood to be much more fragile and influenced strongly by overuse and pollution

According to the recent report "Global Change and the Earth System - A Planet under Pressure" IGBP SCIENCE No. 4[xvi], funded largely by the Swedish Government, our planet is changing quickly. In recent decades many environmental indicators have moved outside the range in which they have varied for the past half-million years. We are altering our life support system and potentially pushing the planet into a far less hospitable state. It is not population growth per say that is the problem; it is the increase in flows through the techno-process previously defined associated with increasing levels of the technology factor and associated consumption.

Exponential Growth

There is an explosion of substances through the techno-process many of which have damaging wastes associated with them. The worst are fossil fuels and cement production. The Industrial Revolution was the beginning of the transformation of societies into the energy-intensive economies of today. The consumption of fossil fuels has had a big impact on atmospheric composition. Another major source of emission is the production of cement. In 2003 the world produced 1.86 billion tons of cement[xvii] -- about a quarter of a ton for every man, woman and child on Earth. Production is now probably well over 2 billion tonnes. Over 13 billion tonnes of concrete are the result which is over two tonnes per person per annum on the planet.

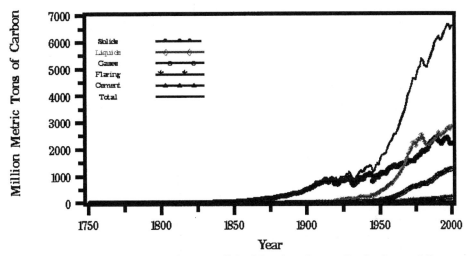

Figure 3 - Global CO_2 Emissions from Fossil Fuel Burning, Cement Production, and Gas Flaring for 1751-2000.[xviii]

The growth of energy consumption is closely correlated with the increases in gross national product which is a measure of economic development. The current consumption patterns of fossil fuels, as well as contributing to emissions, is not sustainable and neither is the production of cement (See Reducing the Impact of the Techno Process on page 316.) The emissions from the burning of fossil fuels and production of cement are shown in Figure 3.

The Environmental Affects of Wastes in the Techno-function

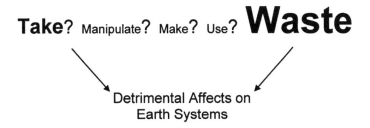

Of major concern is the problem of wastes which are the output of the techno function according to which wastes are created in producing and consuming resources. Huge volumes are produced. In the mid-1990s for example countries belonging to the OECD produced 1.5 billion tons of industrial waste and 579 million tons of municipal waste -- an annual total of almost 2 tons of waste for every person[ii]. The figures for building materials in waste streams vary around the globe and one of the problems is that the method in which audits are conducted also varies making it hard to obtain comparative statistics.

According to Maria Atkinson of the Green Building Council of Australia the figure nationally of waste going to landfill from construction and deconstruction activities (predominantly the churn of refurbishments) was around 40%[xix]. The flow of unwanted or waste materials is affecting our planet. The solid wastes that are not incinerated generally go to landfill and pollute water courses and the local area. Liquid and gaseous pollutants are more insidious and spread invisibly in the global commons.

Landfill is the technical term for filling large holes in the ground with waste. These holes may be specially excavated for the purpose, may be old quarries, mine shafts and even railway cuttings. More recently the mountains or islands made of waste are being created. Apart from wasting what are potentially resources landfill sites produce climate changing gases such as methane which is some 25 times more powerful than CO_2 as a greenhouse gas but only remains in the atmosphere for about ten years and so looses it's greenhouse effect quickly compared to CO_2 which remains in the atmosphere significantly longer.

The current atmospheric concentration of methane is 1.8 ppm or $25 \times 1.8 = 45$ ppm CO_2 equivalent. This is 12% of CO_2 concentration and its growing 2.5 times as fast[xx]. The current concentration of CO_2 on the other hand is around 370 ppm. Landfill can cause ill health in the area, lead to the contamination of land, underground water, streams and coastal waters and gives rise to various nuisances including increased traffic, noise, odours, smoke, dust, litter and pests.

According to the EPA "Resources that simply become waste are not available for future generations and extraction and harvesting of additional resources can have long term environmental impacts. Even as we implement protective waste management programs, toxic chemicals still can find their way into the environment throughout the life cycle of materials in extraction, production, transportation, use, and reuse. Persistent, bio accumulative and toxic chemicals released into the environment can present long term risks to human health and the environment, even when released in small quantities.[xxi]"

Reducing the Impact of the Techno Process

It is essential that the human race, with all the power it has over the environment moves rapidly towards reducing the linkages between the techno-sphere and the geosphere-biosphere before it is too late. To do this the inputs and outputs of the techno-function need to be reduced. We need to change the techno function to:

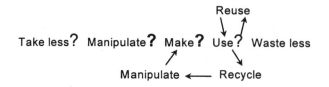

And more desirably to:

To make a material difference to the quantum of resources extracted and consequent and subsequent w aste w e n eed t o t ackle t he b ig p roblems f irst a nd t he b iggest p roblem i s t he weather. So far "everybody is talking about the weather but nobody does anything about it[xxii]" Now is the time for focussed action to modify the principal techno sub processes that pollute with carbon dioxide.

Fossil Fuels

Energy consumption results in the most gaseous releases because of our dependence on fossil fuels. There is a strong need to kick the fossil fuel habit however this is unlikely to happen unless alternative sources of energy become more economical. "This may be sooner than we think as "just under half of the world's total endowment of oil and gas has been extracted already, and that output will begin to decline within the next five years, pushing prices up sharply.[xxiii]" Most geologist however concur that thirty rather than five years is more likely. Even if we do kick the fossil fuel habit before it kicks us, it will take centuries to bring the carbon balance back down to levels in the 50's. Abatement and sequestration on a massive scale are essential. "Complementary to traditional areas of energy research, such as improving energy efficiency or shifting to renewable or nuclear energy sources, carbon sequestration will allow continued use of fossil energy, buying decades of time needed for transitioning into less carbon-intensive and more energy-efficient methods for generating energy in the future.[xxiv]" It is encouraging that there is a slow shift to renewable energy as Figure 4 shows.

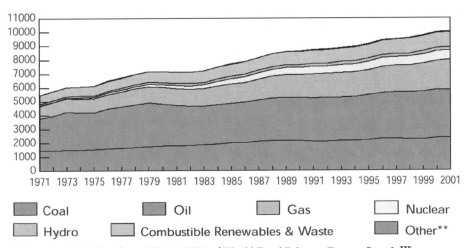

Figure 4 - Evolution from 1971 to 2001 of World Total Primary Energy Supply[xxv]

Cement and Concrete

The main material used for buildings and infrastructure is concrete. Concrete is made by utilising a cement such as Portland cement to bond stone and sand together. Ordinary Portland Cement (OPC) is the most common cement used and the concrete made with it is an ideal construction material, as it is generally economic, durable, easily handled and readily available. Contrary to lay understanding Portland cement concretes have low embodied energies compared to other building materials such as aluminium and steel, have relatively high thermal capacity and are therefore relatively environmentally friendly.

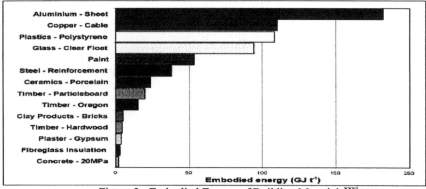

Figure 5 - Embodied Energy of Building Materials[xxvi]

However concrete, based mainly on Portland cement clinker, is the most widely used material on Earth. Production for the year ended 30 June 2003 was 1.86 billion tonnes[xvii], enough to produce o ver 7 c ubic k m o f c oncrete p er year or o ver t wo t onnes o r o ne c ubic m etre p er person on the planet resulting in significant global emissions.

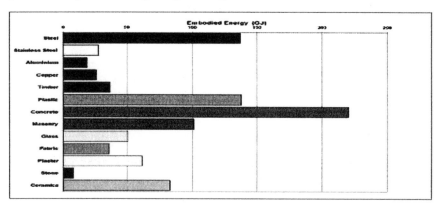

Figure 6 - Embodied Energy in Buildings[xxvi]

As a consequence of the huge volume of Portland cement manufactured, considerable energy is consumed (See Figure 6 - Embodied Energy in Buildingsxxvi on page 318) resulting in carbon dioxide emissions. Carbon dioxide is also released chemically from the calcination of limestone used in the manufacturing process. Various figures are given in the literature for the intensity of carbon emission with Portland cement production and these range from 0.74 tonnes coal/ tonne cement [xxvii] to as high as 1.24 tonne [xxviii] and 1.30 tonne.[xxix] The figure of one tonne of carbon dioxide for every tonne of Portland cement manufactured[xxx] given by New Scientist Magazine is generally accepted.

The production of cement has increased significantly since the end of World War II.

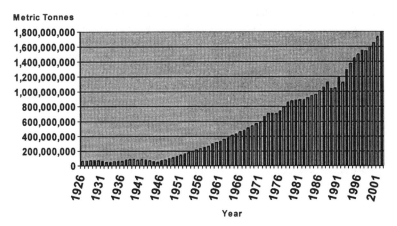

Table 1 - Cement Production = Carbon Dioxide Emissions from Cement Production 1926-2002[xxxi]

These releases are due to:

- The burning of fossil fuels in the kilns used;
- Emissions associated with electricity used during the manufacturing process, and;
- The chemical release of CO_2 from calcining limestone.

As of 2004 some 2.00 billion tonnes of Portland Cement (OPC) were produced globally[xxxii]. This accounts for more embodied energy than any other material in the construction sector[xxxiii]. The manufacture of OPC is one the biggest single contributors to the greenhouse effect, accounting for between 5%[xxxiv] and 10%[xxxv,xxxvi] of global anthropogenic[xxxvii] CO_2 emissions. Global production of cement is likely to increase significantly over the coming decades as:

- Global population grows;
- GDP grows;
- Urban development continues; and,
- Through increasing industrialisation.

A direct consequence of such huge usage and growing demand is the associated enormous potential for environmental benefits and improvements in sustainability.

Summary

The key to more rapid moves toward sustainability is to change the technology paradigm and this is discussed in more detail later in this paper (See Making Reducing, Re-using and Recycling Work in the Long Term without Subsidies or Taxes On page 324). If solar cells for example suddenly became very cheap to make a far higher proportion of electricity would be generated using them.

THE BUILT ENVIRONMENT - A FOCUS FOR SUSTAINABILITY EFFORTS

Our understanding of the flows and interactions in the global commons is very inadequate. The widely held view is that sustainable management strategies are complex to devise and politically difficult to introduce. What if they were economic? The obvious place that seems to have been missed by just about everybody to focus sustainability efforts is the built environment. It is our footprint on the globe. Given the size of the built environment there are huge opportunities for changing the techno function.

The d ominant p roportion o f w hat w e t ake, m anipulate a nd m ake t hat we d o n ot consume immediately goes into the materials with which we build the techno-sphere. Buildings and infrastructure are our footprint on the globe and probably account for around 70% of all materials flows and of this "Buildings account for 40 percent of the materials and about a third of the energy consumed by the world economy. Combined with eco-city design principles, green building technologies therefore have the potential to make an enormous contribution to a required 50% reduction in the energy and material intensity of consumption in the post-modern world.[xxxviii]"

"In 1999, construction activities contributed over 35% of total global CO_2 emissions - more than any other industrial activity. Mitigating and reducing the impacts contributed by these activities is a significant challenge for urban planners, designers, architects and the construction industry, especially in the context of population and urban growth, and the associated requirement for houses, offices, shops, factories and roads[xxxix]." According to the Human Settlements Theme Report, State of the Environment Australia 2001[xl], "Carbon dioxide (CO_2) emissions are highly correlated with the energy consumed in manufacturing building materials. "On average, 0.098 tonnes of CO_2 are produced per gigajoule of embodied energy of materials used in construction. The energy embodied in the existing building stock in Australia is equivalent to approximately 10 years of the total energy consumption for the entire nation. Choices of materials and design principles have a significant impact on the energy required to construct a building. However, this energy content of materials has been little considered in design until recently, despite such impacts being recognized for over 20 years."

To date the main practical emphasis has been on designing building with low lifetime energies. Little effort has been made to reduce the impact of materials on lifetime energies, embodied energies and emissions.

WHAT GOVERNMENTS ARE DOING TO ENCOURAGE SUSTAINABILITY

For sustainability the take and waste components of the techno-process need to be reduced and preferably eliminated to what is renewable and preferably biodegradable.
Governments generally view sustainability as a desirable goal and various policy options are being experimented with such as:

1. Research and Development Funding Priorities.

2. Procurement policies.
   Government in Australia is more than 1/3 of the economy and can strongly influence change through:

- Life cycle purchasing policy.
- Funding of public projects and housing linked to sustainability such as **recycling**.
3. Intervention Policies.
    - Building codes including mandatory adoption of performance specification.
    - Requiring the recognition and **accounting for externalities**
    - **Extended producer responsibility (EPR) legislation**
    - Mandatory use of minimum standard materials that are more sustainable
    - Mandatory eco-labelling
4. Taxation and Incentive Policies
    - Direct o r i ndirect t axes, b onuses o r r ebates t o d iscourage/encourage s ustainable construction etc.
    - A national system of carbon taxes.
    - An international system of carbon trading.
5. Sustainability Education

Consider building codes, research and development funding and policies of encouraging recycling and legislating for extended user responsibility as they are most relevant to the materials theme of this paper.

Building Codes

The emphasis has been on lifetime rather than embodied energies because potential lifetime energy reductions through good design are significant. Most OECD countries have set up energy efficiency standards for new dwellings and service sector buildings: this includes all European countries, Australia, Canada, the USA, Japan, Korea and New Zealand. Some non-OECD countries outside Europe have also established mandatory or voluntary standards for service buildings and Singapore and the Philippines were among the first. To date building codes have not encouraged the use of more energy efficient materials, in spite of the huge impact of materials not only on embodied energies but lifetime energies as well.

Research and Development Funding Priorities

The early North American and to some extent European approach was to "prime the pump" and research global warming. The early Australian approach to sustainability was much cruder and involved the outright purchase of abatement with little research. To date materials science, which the paper demonstrates a s fundamental has however r eceived little funding globally. As of early 2004 European priorities were genomics and biotechnology for health, information society technologies, nanotechnologies, intelligent materials and new production processes, aeronautics and space, food safety and health risks, sustainable development and global change, citizens and governance in the European knowledge-based society. In the USA Federal funding priorities include nanotechnology, defense, and aeronautics.

Geological sequestration has also been a priority in many countries as it is associated with the petroleum industry and doubts have been raised as to the transparency of funding[xli] To date Australian research priorities have not included materials science however the Australian research funding priorities for 2004 – 2005 may well lead the way globally as included under the heading "Frontier Technologies for Building and Transforming Australia" are advanced materials. "Advanced materials for applications in construction, communications, transport, agriculture and medicine (examples include ceramics, organics, biomaterials, smart material and fabrics, composites, polymers and light metals).[xlii]" The Killer Application – TecEco Cements on page 327 are material composites that include wastes and sequester CO_2.

Recycling

Recycling involves a series of activities by which wastes are collected, sorted, processed and converted into raw materials and used in the production of new products. Recycling is carried out by individuals, volunteers, businesses and governments. For high value waste recycling is profitable and undertaken by business, usually by buying back wastes, but not so as the value declines. Governments generally have recognized the importance of recycling but have gone about the introduction of recycling through councils and local authorities in completely the wrong way. As the hazards of discarded wastes do not correlate with their value, many wastes are recycled by the authority of legislation or power of producer organisations.

Instead of being forced upon us using good taxpayer dollars for "feel good" reasons, much more effort should have been put into the development of technologies to make the process economic. With market forces driving recycling much more would occur much more efficiently. The problem is to make the process of recycling less "feel good" and more economic so it is driven by market forces.

Accounting for Externalities - the True Cost of the Techno-process

"…the exponential growth curve of cost associated with negative impacts or "externalities" such as climate change, salinity, acid sulphate soils, river system degradation, or general pollution, has up until now, been a legacy for future generations to deal with. For decades the cash p rice o f g oods a nd s ervices h as b een a rtificially d eflated, w ith m uch o f t he r eal c ost being outsourced on to the environment. The costs, however, that are backing up on us - bush fires, dust storms, floods, soil erosion, salinity, changes in disease patterns, hurricanes and cyclones - can often be attributed, at least in part, to climate change. An integral part of the dilemma we have is the denial that anything truly threatening is happening"[xliii].

Accounting systems that recognise the value of natural capital[xliv] are required so that the true costs of sub techno-processes that extract and waste are born by those who gain the benefit of doing so.

Extended producer responsibility (EPR)

EPR incorporates negative externalities from product use and end-of-life in product prices Producers are made responsible for environmental effects over the entire product life cycle so that the cost of compliance cannot be shifted to a third party and must therefore be incorporated i nto p roduct p rices. E xamples o f E PR r egulations i nclude e missions a nd f uel economy standards (use stage) and product take back requirements (end of life) such as deposit legislation, and mandatory returns policies which tend to force design with disassembly in mind.

Producers are made responsible for collecting and recycling end-of-life products. Waste-management costs are shifted to those most capable of reducing disposal costs by changing designs for recyclability, longevity, reduced toxicity, and limited volume of waste generated. Disposal costs are reflected in product prices so consumers can make more informed decisions. The above solutions all involve a cost. What if benefits could be incorporated?

What Governments Should be Doing and Why

Much as been written about the role of governments and the need to bring about common good.

1. The first requirement is that the people in power realise their urgent responsibility to promote sustainability. The democratic system has a fatal flaw in that the outlook of politicians and therefore governments is usually not much beyond the next election. As a consequence policy is generally extremely short sighted and too directly connected to the needs of the here and now rather than mindful of the future. Change is occurring, sustainability issues are becoming recognised as important but all too slowly.

2. The second requirement is that governments all over the world co-operate to bring about sustainability

Problems on a global scale are not just the concern of one or two countries but all people on the planet. World federalists believe we need a system of democratic global governance on top of (not instead of) national governments. Such a system would provide enforceable legal mechanisms for resolving conflicts and safeguarding the environment. Perhaps they have a point.

In spite of the two UN 'Habitat' conferences on urban prospects,[xlv] and their huge impact, cities have not been given serious attention in the mainstream sustainability debate until very recently. For example the World Conservation Strategy of 1980, which first used the term "sustainable development," paid little attention to accelerating urbanization. The Brundtland report[xlvi] did discuss the issue, but the main emphasis was on the "urban crisis in developing countries." The role of the built environment, particularly in rich cities has been neglected; however this is difficult to reconcile with physical reality.

"The world population reached 6 billion in 1999.....At the current rate the world will have 7 billion people soon after the year 2010. The overwhelming share of world population growth is taking place in developing countries (...95.2% in 1990-2000; 97.6% in 2000-10; and 98.4% in 2010-20). The population of developing countries has more than doubled in 35 years, growing from 1.89 billion in 1955 to 4.13 billion in 1990. Significant proportions of population increases in the developing countries have been and will be absorbed by urban areas (...71.8% in 1990-2000; 83.4% in 2000-10; and 93.4 in 2010-20). Urban settlements in the developing countries are, at present, growing five times as fast as those in the developed countries. Cities in the developing countries are already faced by enormous backlogs in shelter, infrastructure and services and confronted with increasingly overcrowded transportation systems, insufficient water supply, deteriorating sanitation and environmental pollution.[xlvii]"

Since the wealthiest 25 percent of the human population consume 80 percent of the world's economic output[xlviii], approximately 64 % of the world's economic production/consumption and pollution is associated with cities in *rich* countries. Only 12 percent is tied to cities in the developing world[xlix]. In short, "half the people and three-quarters of the world's environmental problems reside in cities, and rich cities, mainly in the developed North, impose by far the greater load on the ecosphere and global commons[l]". It is time for governments to take an active role, to recognize their responsibility to seek sustainability as a cornerstone to all government expenditure and policy and facilitate economic systems that encourage sustainability such as carbon trading and EPR. The problem is to achieve "common good" without a disproportionate impact on taxation.

Making Reducing, Re-using and Recycling Work in the Long Term without Subsidies or Taxes

Even though governments through policy can introduce change it is important that technologies that seek sustainability are also fundamentally economic otherwise they are inefficient and not viable in the long run.

Economic viability attracts investment, and insufficient investment is finding its way into sustainability. Natural capital is undervalued.

Consider the techno-function: Take→Manipulate→Make→Use→Waste

The function has an input and output rate and volume dimension. If the impacts of the techno-function on the geosphere-biosphere are to be reduced then the rate and volume of flows through the function need to be reduced and they are therefore of vital interest. A large proportion of what passes through the techno-process that is not renewable or easily reassimilated ends up as the materials with which we build our techno-sphere. The rate and volume of these flows can be reduced by:
- Reducing the input to produce the same output
- Recycling so that fewer resources are required to be extracted.

By reducing, re-using and recycling the function becomes:

And more desirably:

Reducing the "Take" & "Waste"

The biggest factor in increasing economic growth and raising living standards over time has been the economy's ability to produce more out of less, i.e. to become more productive. Productivity is good economics and driven by positive market forces. Productive companies reduce inputs for the same output quality, volume and cost. An increase in productivity would put less demand on natural resources which is something we all would agree is desirable.

Arguably on a personal values scale in the future productivity will become the domain of robots and the challenge will be what we do rather than how efficiently we do it. This is especially true of knowledge workers who in western countries comprise probably three quarters of the work force[li].

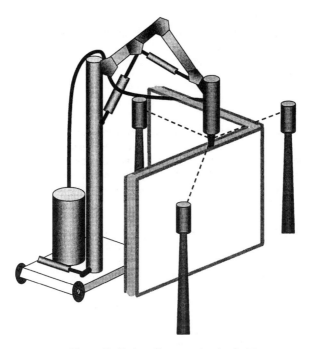

Figure 7 - Robot Construction in the Future

For robotics to be used in construction it will be necessary to squeeze self hardening materials out of a nozzle so they just sit without deformation until they gain full strength. Various materials from structural containing fibres for reinforcement to void filling and insulating will be required and like a colour inkjet printer will be selected as specified by the design. Accuracy will be far greater than currently possible, wonderful architectural shapes as yet unthought of will be used and fibres will provide reinforcing. Walls will most likely have a low strength foamed insulating cementitious material between the faces making services easy to add at a later time. Conduits could also be provided by design. The use of robots in construction will reduce the waste of new construction materials immensely. Just like an inkjet printer only uses the right amount of ink, only the exact amount of material will be used. The introduction of robots to construction will also mean more wastes can be utilised for building materials. More self hardening materials will be required, not less and mineral binders like TecEco's new cements have the obvious advantage of being able to utilise a large quantity of wastes (See The Killer Application – TecEco Cements on page 327).

There is no doubt that on a global scale, reducing the rate and volume of inputs required to satisfy the needs of the techno-sphere and output of waste materials that no longer satisfy needs will reduce our detrimental linkages on the environment. The use of Robots is but one practical idea as to how this could be done.

Re-using and Recycling

Before re-using and recycling can become economic the main economic hurdles to overcome are the laws of supply and demand and economies of scale. To do this we need to change the technical paradigm. Henry Ford leveraged his success selling cars to devise more efficient methods of production. As a consequence he was able to sell his cars more cheaply, increasing sales, providing more money for innovation, which reduced costs even further and so on. Ford was able to sell more at lower prices and yet make more money by achieving economies of scale. The laws of economics rely on positive feedback loops. Industrial economies of scale tend to increase value linearly, while the laws of supply and demand would dictate that exponentially more is sold or used the lower the price for the same quality. It can however take years before these laws kick in.

For example during the first 10 years, Microsoft's profits were negligible. They started to rise in 1985 and then exploded. The experience of Federal Express was similar. The same applies to fax machines and the internet which similarly festered for some time before becoming ubiquitous. The question is whether the world can wait for an explosion in the recycling business to take place. There is a desperate need to achieve sustainability quickly. What factor or factors are missing? What will make it happen as a matter of profitable economics rather than policy?

The trouble is that right now it just costs too much to reuse and recycle for these processes to be driven by economics alone. As a consequence government intervention in the form of regulation (Germany, some other countries and some states in some countries e.g. South Australia in Australia to some extent) and subsidies (most of the rest of the developed world) are required for what is no doubt a desirable social outcome. How can re-using and recycling move beyond the desirable subsidized by tax dollars to the preferred pushed and dragged by sound economics?

Currently it is more expensive to reuse and recycle than to use newly extracted resources. There would be a rapid turnaround in the sustainability industry if this hurdle could be overcome so that it was cheaper to reuse or recycle. There are two main costs involved in re-using and recycling. The costs of sorting waste streams and then transporting sorted recyclable materials back to a location in which they can be reused. The second law of thermodynamics (the l aw o f e ntropy) w as f ormulated i n t he m iddle o f the l ast c entury b y Clausius and Thomson. Like most natural processes, waste streams tend to follow this law in that wastes at the point of elimination from the techno-process tend to be all mixed up. Disorder is prevalent for two main reasons; things are made with mixed materials and the waste collection process tends to mix them up even more.

The current technical paradigm for the techno-process generally requires separate inputs. Costs are incurred and waste generated in separating what is required from the balance of material as nature itself rarely concentrates. As mentioned earlier, one study found that around 93 percent of materials used in production do not end up in saleable products but in waste. Re-using and recycling is even more uneconomic because the cost of un-mixing even more complex waste streams is prohibitive. After recycling is completed there is a cost of returning the materials back to manufacturers who can use them. Simultaneously dealing with the disassembly/sorting constraints, cost, material problems and transport issues during recycling are critical challenges. I once had the pleasure of a long discussion with Edward de Bono, the inventor of the words "lateral thinking" about a new technology I have invented that you will hear about later in this paper. He said that what was needed for market success was a "killer" application, an application that just could not help but succeed.

To get over the laws of increasing returns and economies of scale and to make the sorting of wastes economic so that wastes become low cost inputs for the techno-process new paradigms are required. The way forward involves at least:
- A new killer technology in the form of a method for sorting wastes
- A killer application for unsorted wastes

The "Killer" Technology - Silicon Identification of Materials

The means to very efficiently sort wastes may just lie in the silicon chip. The cost and size of intelligent silicon with embedded thought are both falling exponentially. Silicon chips already have a diverse range of uses For example they are being used in paint by car manufacturers for identification purposes and one was recently put in the ear of my dog for the same reason. Silicon chips will one day be as plentiful as what they could be embedded in. They will tell us the cost at the check-out, the manufacturer, warranty details who the owner is and what waste stream a robot should put them into when eventually wasted. Remember the impact bar-coding had in supermarkets? Silicon embedded in products will do the same thing for the cost of sorting waste streams. Robots will efficiently and productively be able to distinguish different types of plastic, glass, metals ceramics and so on.

The only economic hurdle that would remain would be the efficient transportation back to manufacturing points of these waste streams. This could be overcome with a ubiquitous killer application. We are progressing towards a silcon intelligence defined flow of materials from producer to consumer. Wal-Mart, one of the biggest US retailers has initiated the introduction of smart tagging of all goods that it will sell in the store. So too have the US defense department for all provisions. Everything will have a tag that indicates what order it was on, delivery details, price, disposal etc. The US packaging giant, Smurfit-Stone want to eliminate the smart label and implant chips directly into packaging. TecEco want to go a stage further and implant intelligent silicon that will do everything everybody wants it to do, directly into the materials out of which things are made.

The Killer Application – TecEco Cements

What if wastes could be utilized depending on their class of properties rather than specific properties? What if an application could be found that could utilize vast volumes of materials that offered useful broadly defined properties such as light weight, tensile strength, insulating capacity, strength or thermal capacity? After all, the best thing to do with wastes is to use them if at all possible.

There are many wastes that are just too costly to further sort into very specific wastes streams such as many plastics. There are also waste streams such as mine tailings, furnace sands, quarry dusts and the like for which no particular use could otherwise be found. Glasses tend to share in common a lot of properties as do plastics, wood, ceramics and so on. Glasses are brittle, tough and abrasion resistant. Plastics are generally light, insulating and have tensile strength. What if it did not matter if they were mixed up together?

The solution is to use these materials in composites for their properties rather than for their composition. The problem then becomes one of finding a potentially cheap, un-reactive but strong binder with the right rheology for use by for example robots of the futureReducing the "Take" & "Waste" on page 324. Eliminate plastics, epoxies and other inorganic binders that are just too expensive and the choice for durability and cost is a mineral binder. Ordinary Portland cement concretes are a good start; over two tonnes are produced per person on the planet per annum. Unfortunately they are too reactive to use with a wide range of fillers. The breakthrough has been the development of a wide range of blended calcium-magnesium binders with a low long term pH and that are internally much drier.

Sustainability by regulation subsidy or taxes is not itself economically sustainable. The new TecEco binder technologies are a breakthrough in that they change the technology paradigm. "...it is technology that defines what is a resource as well as what our effective supply of that resource is.[lii]" Wastes can be used and in large quantities, there is wealth in waste and significant overall improvements in sustainability are achievable with economic benefits. A major advantage of the TecEco technology over all other sequestration and abatement proposals it that the technology itself is viable even without a value being placed on abatement and sequestration. Another advantage of the magnesian tec, eco and enviro-cement technologies is that they define improvements in the material properties of concrete.

The TecEco technology is but one very important example of where materials can make a big difference to sustainability by providing composites that utilise wastes. There are other ways improvements in materials will make a big difference.

MATERIALS – THE KEY TO SUSTAINABILITY

Materials are the lasting substances that flow through the techno-process. They are the link between the biosphere-geosphere and techno-sphere. The use of more sustainable materials is fundamental to our survival on the planet. The choice of materials that we use to construct our techno-sphere ultimately controls emissions, lifetime and embodied energies, maintenance of utility, recyclability and the properties of wastes returned to the biosphere - geosphere.

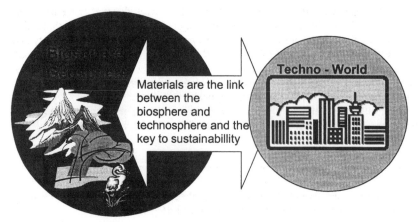

Materials are the link between the biosphere and technosphere and the key to sustainabillity

Figure 8 - Materials - The Link between the Biosphere - geosphere and Techno-sphere

Fundamental c hanges a re necessary to achieve real sustainability and if t hese are to occur without economic disruption, as the materials we use control the sustainability of the systems we proliferate, the materials paradigm we live in will also have to change.

- Materials science will become of great importance as the race to develop materials for the future gets underway

- The properties of many materials are too focussed. It should be possible in the future to develop new materials with more than one property currently considered as conflicting.

- For example materials that are good insulators do not generally have a high heat capacity. Combining insulating and heat capacity has huge potential for reducing the lifetime energies of buildings. Another example is that materials that are light in weight are not generally strong.

- The embodied energy of most materials is too high. In the future it may be possible to develop ways of making existing materials or new materials with the same functionality and properties but with lower embodied energies.

  The new TecEco kiln for example combines grinding which is only 1-2% efficient with heating to reduce overall energy inputs by some 30%

- Materials will be required that are either biodegradable or easily recycled within the techno-sphere techno – process are required.

  An example of a biodegradable replacement for a non biodegradable product includes rice paper takeaway eating containers and utensils instead of plastic. An example of easily recycled materials would be printer cartridges which are economic to return for refilling or polling booths in Australia which are all returned for recycling as paper under the watchful eye of the electorate commission.

- Materials that remain useful for longer are required.

  Things were once and still are to some extent built to break down after the period of their warranty. Henry Ford started this by reducing the quality of the items that lasted the longest in his cars. There is a way forward however. Imagine if functionality and service were purchased instead of energy and things. An example given in the book "natural Capitalism" was that instead of buying electricity one would purchase heating and lighting[liii]. I recently had the pleasure of entertaining in Tasmania the representative of a Brazilian company, Magnesita S.A. He told me that his company no longer just sold refractory bricks. They were paid on the basis of downtime experienced by their steel producing clients. With better quality bricks and less downtime they were paid more.

The Importance of Sustainable Materials for the Built Environment

Urbanization has serious negative implications for global sustainability yet the impact and the associated opportunities for improvement have been given little emphasis.
Given the enormous materials flows involved, the obvious place to improve sustainability is the built environment. The materials used determine net emissions, the impact of extraction,

how they can be reused and the effects on earth systems of wastage. To reduce the impact of the techno - function that describes the flow of these materials from take to waste it is fundamental that we think about the materials we use to construct our built environment and the molecules they are made of. With the right materials technology, because of its sheer size the built environment could reduce the take from the geosphere-biosphere and utilise many different wastes including carbon dioxide.

Materials used to construct the built environment should, as well as the required properties have low embodied energies, low lifetime energies, and low greenhouse gas emissions when considered on a whole of life cycle basis. They should also be preferably made from renewable resources and either easily recycled or reassimilated by the geosphere-biosphere

The Lesson for Governments

As Paul Zane Pilzer says "Technology is the major determinant of wealth as it determines the nature and supply of physical resources[lii]." Why is it then that so little government research funding is to change the technical paradigm for reducing, re-using and recycling materials? Materials are after all a major part of the flow of resources in the techno function and fundamental for sustainability. Instead of for example like the Australian Greenhouse Gas Abatement program which had little for science and financially supported projects with significant abatement including converting from coal to natural gas, governments need to focus on fundamental research that change the technology factor. As Pilzer's first law or alchemy states "By enabling us to make productive use of particular raw materials, technology determines what constitutes a physical resource[lii]." Pilzer goes on further to explain that definitional technologies are those that enable us to make use of particular resources. Wastes are potentially a huge resource. Improvements in recovery and utilisation technologies will one day make them of significant value.

Fortunately some governments such as the EU are starting to research how we could live more sustainably on the planet. As of today however I am not aware of any country or group of countries that prioritise the development research into materials as a way of reducing the take and waste in the techno - function, maximising utility and making re-use and recycling more profitable.

Concrete - The Material for the Future

As previously discussed under the heading THE BUILT ENVIRONMENT - A FOCUS FOR SUSTAINABILITY EFFORTS on page 320, concrete is the single biggest material flow on the planet by a big margin. There is tremendous scope to add strength and improve sustainability and other properties of concrete as a material through the addition of other substances including wastes, many of which would add tensile strength, insulating capacity or reduce weight. New composites made in this way will be the high performance materials of the future.

Materials such as the new magnesian tec, eco and enviro-cements will have a role in the development of these new materials as they not only absorb carbon dioxide in bricks, blocks, pavers, mortars and porous pavement, but also improve properties and allow the incorporation of a wider range of materials.

CONCLUSIONS

The way forward is clear, technology can help us change the techno process so that we take and waste less. By doing so the process becomes more economic and thus self propelled with less government intervention. Finding 3 under the heading Transport and Urban Design of the recent ISOS conference in Australia applies globally. It stated in part. "...The Federal Government should promote Australian building innovations (e.g. eco-cement) that contribute global solutions towards sustainability; provide more sustainable city innovation R&D funds; and re-direct some housing and transport funds towards sustainable cities demonstration projects[liv]."

Technology can make it possible to achieve a far greater measure of sustainability, to economically reduce, re-use and recycle. The potential multipliers from spending on research and development are huge.

With the development of definitional materials technologies as a result of appropriate research and development funding as Amory Lovins of the Rocky Mountain Institute puts it sustainability *"will happen, and happen rapidly – because it's profitable[lv]"*.

FOOTNOTES AND REFERENCES

[i] Utility is an economic term for value to the user.

[ii] The American Association for the Advancement of Science Population and Environment Atlas at http://atlas.aaas.org/index.php?part=1&sec=waste valid as at 24/04/04

[iii] For the purposes of this paper the geosphere is defined as the solid earth including the continental and oceanic crust as well as the various layers of the earth's interior

[iv] For the purposes of this paper the biosphere is defined as "living organisms and the part of the earth and its atmosphere in which living organisms exist or that is capable of supporting life"

[v] Utility is an economic term for value to the user.

[vi] Ed. Given a healthy environment

[vii] dictionary.com at http://dictionary.reference.com, valid as at 24/04/04

[viii] The Collins Dictionary and Thesaurus in One Volume, Harper Collins, 1992

[ix] The term techno-sphere refers to our footprint on the globe, our technical world of cars, buildings, infrastructure etc.

[x] David Schaller, Sustainable Development Coordinator, US EPA Region 8 - Denver, Beyond Sustainability: From Scarcity to Abundance, BioInspire Newsletter, 13 February 2004

[xi] WRI, World Resources 1998-99 Database Diskette, 1998.

[xii] Microsoft Office 2003 clipart.

[xiii] Powerof10 web site at http://www.powersof10.com/p10_day/planet.pdf

[xiv] http://www.c-f-c.com/supportdocs/cfcs.htm

[xv] The American Association for the Advancement of Science Population and Environment Atlas at http://atlas.aaas.org/index.php?part=1&sec=waste valid as at 24/04/04

[xvi] "*Global Change and the Earth System - A Planet under Pressure*" IGBP SCIENCE No. 4http://www.igbp.kva.se/cgi-bin/php/publications_books.show.php?section_id=48&article_id=105&onearticle=, download the summary from http://www.igbp.kva.se/cgi-bin/php/frameset.php)

[xvii] US Government Survey, Mineral Commodities Summary, Cement 2004 at http://minerals.usgs.gov/minerals/pubs/commodity/cement/cemenmcs04.pdf valid 27/04/04

[xviii] From Marland, G., T.A. Boden, and R. J. Andres. "*Global, Regional, and National CO2 Emissions. In Trends: A Compendium of Data on Global Change.*" 2003, Carbon Dioxide Information Analysis Center, Oak Ridge National Laboratory, U.S. Department of Energy, Oak Ridge, Tenn., U.S.A. at http://cdiac.esd.ornl.gov/trends/emis/glo.htm valid 27/04/04

[xix] Atkinson, Maria, Speech, Energy Efficiency Conference 14 November 2003, Green Building Council of Australia, at http://www.gbcaus.org/gbc.asp?sectionid=16&docid=116 as at 24/04/04

[xx] University of Oregon, Electronic Universe Educational Server http://zebu.uoregon.edu/1998/es202/l14.html valid 06/05/04

[xxi] Office of Solid Waste Strategic Planning Document, 2003 - 2008, 9/23/03

[xxii] Mark Twain

[xxiii] According to Dr. Colin Campbell, a petro-geologist in and article titled *How Long Can Oil the Last*, The Sunday Business Post 27th October 2002

[xxiv] National Energy Technology Laboratory (Numerous Authors) *Chemical And Geologic Sequestration Of Carbon Dioxide*, at http://www.netl.doe.gov/products/r&d/annual_reports/2001/cgscdfy01.pdf , page 7 valid 28/12/03.

[xxv] International Energy Agency, Key World Energy Statistics 2003 Edition downloaded from http://www.iea.org/bookshop/add.aspx?id=144, 27/04/04

[xxvi] URL: www.dbce.csiro.au/ind-serv/brochures/embodied/embodied.htm (last accessed 07 March 2000)

[xxvii] New Scientist, 19 July 1997, page 14.

[xxviii] According to the article *Cement and Concrete: Environmental Considerations* in Environmental Building News volume 2, No 2 – March/April 1993 researchers at the Oak Ridge National Laboratories (USA) put the figure at 1.24 tonnes of CO2 for every tonne of Portland cement.

[xxix] Pers comm. Dr Selwyn Tucker, CSIRO Department of Building Construction and Engineering, Melbourne

[xxx] Pearce, F., "The Concrete Jungle Overheats", New Scientist, 19 July, No 2097, 1997 (page 14).

[xxxi] Cement production = Carbon dioxide emissions at 1 tonne cement= 1 tonne CO_2 Source of data USGS cement XLS file. Data collected by Van Oss, Hendrik G. and Kelly, Thomas D. Last modification: April 15, 2004 Available at http://minerals.usgs.gov/minerals/pubs/of01-006/ as at 29/04/04

[xxxii] USGS figures extrapolated to 2004

[xxxiii] Dr Selwyn Tucker, CSIRO on line brochure at http://www.dbce.csiro.au/ind-serv/brochures/embodied/embodied.htm valid 05/08/2000

[xxxiv] Hendriks C.A., Worrell E, de Jager D., Blok K., and Riemer P. Emission Reductions of Greenhouse Gases from the Cement Industry. International Energy Agency Conference Paper at www.ieagreen.org.uk.

[xxxv] Davidovits, J A Practical Way to Reduce Global Warming The Geopolymer Institute info@geopolymer.org, http://www.geopolymer.org/

[xxxvi] Pearce, F., "The Concrete Jungle Overheats", New Scientist, 19 July, No 2097, 1997 (page 14).

[xxxvii] Anthropogenic – human produced

[xxxviii] *The Built Environment and the Ecosphere: A Global Perspective*, Rees, William E

Professor and Director, The University of British Columbia, School of Community and Regional Planning

[xxxix] *Energy and Cities: Sustainable Building and Construction Summary of Main Issues* IETC Side Event at UNEP Governing Council, 6 February, 2001 - Nairobi, Kenya

[xl] CSIRO (numerous authors), "Human Settlements Theme Report, State of the Environment Australia 2001", Australian Government Department of Environment and Heritage. See http://www.deh.gov.au/soe/2001/settlements/settlements02-5c.html, valid 29/04/04

[xli] Wilson, Nigel *"Call for public input to carbon plan"*, The Weekend Australian, May 1-2, 2004,'Resources',p 7.

[xlii] Descriptions of Designated National Research Priorities and associated Priority Goals, http://www.arc.gov.au/pdf/2004_designated_national_research_priorities_&_associate.pdf valid 06/05/04

[xliii] Fiona Wain, CEO, Environment Business Australia, Canberra Times, 5 February 2004

[xliv] Hawken Paul, Lovins Amory, Lovins L. Hunter, *Natural Capitalism: Creating the Next Industrial Revolution,* Earthscan Publications Pty. Ltd. *2000*

[xlv] Vancouver in 1976 and Istanbul in 1996.

[xlvi] In 1983 the United Nations appointed an international commission to propose strategies for "sustainable development" - ways to improve human well-being in the short term without threatening the local and global environment in the long term.The Commission was chaired by Norwegian Prime-Minister Gro Harlem Brundtland, and it's report "Our Common Future", published in 1987 was widely known as "The Brundtland Report."

[xlvii] http://www.unchs.org/habrdd/global.html, valid as at 22/02/04

[xlviii] WCED 1987

[xlix] Rees,W. E. (1999) *The Built Environment and the Ecosphere: A Global Perspective*, Building Research and Information 27: (4/5): 206-220

[l] Rees, W. E. (1997) Is "sustainable city" an oxymoron? *Local Environment* 2, 303-310.

[li] For an excellent discussion on the affects of knowledge on politics, business and society see Peter F Drucker, *Post Capitalist Society*, ButterworthHeinemann, 1993

[lii] Pilzer, Paul Zane, *Unlimited Wealth, The Theory and Practice of Economic Alchemy*, Crown Publishers Inc. New York.1990

[liii] Hawken Paul, Lovins Amory, Lovins L. Hunter, *Natural Capitalism: Creating the Next Industrial Revolution,* Earthscan Publications Pty. Ltd. *2000*

[liv] ISOS Conference, 14th November Canberra, ACT, Australia communique downloadable from http://www.isosconference.org.au/entry.html.

[lv] The Bulletin, April 25, 2000.

INDEX OF AUTHORS

SUBJECT INDEX

This index has been compiled from the keywords assigned to the papers, edited and extended as appropriate. Number refers to the first page of the relevant paper